A CENTRAL EUR
OF RADICAL AND MAGISTERIAL
REFORM

The Sacramental Theology
of Balthasar Hubmaier

Kirk R. MacGregor

University Press of America,® Inc.
Lanham · Boulder · New York · Toronto · Oxford

Copyright © 2006 by
University Press of America,® Inc.
4501 Forbes Boulevard
Suite 200
Lanham, Maryland 20706
UPA Acquisitions Department (301) 459-3366

PO Box 317
Oxford
OX2 9RU, UK

Library of Congress Control Number: 2006922975
ISBN-13: 978-0-7618-3460-1 (clothbound : alk. paper)
ISBN-10: 0-7618-3460-5 (clothbound : alk. paper)
ISBN-13: 978-0-7618-3461-8 (paperback : alk. paper)
ISBN-10: 0-7618-3461-3 (paperback : alk. paper)

⊖™ The paper used in this publication meets the minimum
requirements of American National Standard for Information
Sciences—Permanence of Paper for Printed Library Materials,
ANSI Z39.48—1984

Contents

Preface

Balthasar Hubmaier (1480-1528), an Ingolstadt *doctor theologiae* and one-time Catholic priest who turned away from Catholic sacramental theology and embraced the baptism of believers, is typically recognized by those of Anabaptist persuasion and like-minded groups as perhaps the greatest sixteenth-century opponent of infant baptism. While this description of Hubmaier is accurate in and of itself, it proves highly misleading due to its tacit yet erroneous implications (many of which are often taken for granted as factual in the Reformation historical academy), including the view that Hubmaier shared the same understanding of baptism, and consequently opposed pedobaptism for the same reasons, as his rebaptizing contemporaries. Recent studies of Hubmaier have done little to correct this and related misconceptions, due to their focus on particular aspects of the reformer's theology which, when examined by themselves apart from the full scope of his doctrinal formulation, are virtually incapable of revealing the profound divergence of his thought from all other sixteenth-century figures characterized as Anabaptists. Therefore, the present study aims to remedy the deficiencies in the currently incomplete portrait of Hubmaier by revealing for the first time the reformer's theological system in its entirety, consisting of an overarching three-tiered structure where each successive tier cumulatively builds upon the concepts developed in the previous tiers, and by furnishing an original analysis of the internal logic of each tier.

Since the spring of 2002 I have been studying the Hubmaier corpus *in toto*, consisting of the twenty-six German works in the *Hubmaier Schriften* as well as eight other writings (five Latin, three German) not included in this volume, seven of which date from before the reformer's 1525 rebaptism. Throughout my journey I have found that Hubmaier, as a theologian, was primarily concerned with constructing a novel sacramental theology which was rooted in a tripartite anthropology featuring *Freiheit des Willens*, or libertarian free will, as its distinguishing characteristic. Accordingly, Hubmaier's libertarian anthropology and sacramentology respectively make up the first and second tiers of his theological system. Concerning his libertarian anthropology, which is utterly dissimilar to anything known from other sixteenth-century reformers, its source has been sought in vain by scholars over the past three decades and, until the present study, has remained an unsolved mystery. Following in the footsteps of Franz Posset (*Pater Bernhardus*, 1999) and Dennis Tambrello (*Union with Christ*, 1994), who respectively exposed the profound impact of Bernard of Clairvaux on Luther and Calvin, I make the groundbreaking argument, based on careful linguistic analysis of the relevant German and Latin texts, that Hubmaier's anthropology was derived from the works of Bernard, thereby demonstrating that Bernard's early modern reception extended not only to the Magisterial branch of the Reformation but to the Radical branch as well. I proceed to explicate, moreover, why the intellectual history of Hubmaier from his student days at Ingolstadt to his 1528 martyrdom in Vienna cannot be fully understood apart from the influence of Bernard.

By integrating the ramifications of his anthropology with his notion of faith, Hubmaier formulated genuinely sacramental, or intrinsically grace-conveying, doctrines of baptism and the Lord's Supper characterized by a high degree of philosophical "realism," unlike his Anabaptist brethren who regarded the central Christian rituals as ordinances performed out of obedience to Christ but which did not serve as means or vehicles of grace. On the one hand, Hubmaier expanded the theory of baptismal regeneration to encompass dual theandric roles within the Trinitarian economy: the function of the Holy Spirit in remitting all sins of and imparting new spiritual life to all willing neophytes through his infusion of sanctifying grace into their souls; and the additional function of the Father in electing, or predestining to salvation, all those whom he discerned from the foundation of the world, through his foreknowledge of future contingents, would choose to receive the sacrament of baptism. Here we see that Hubmaier's opposition to infant baptism was due in large part to his Bernardian doctrine of human freedom, which conditioned the redemptive and predestinary effects of baptism upon the voluntary decision of the recipient. On the other hand, Hubmaier combined an Alexandrian (and Johannine) Christology with the Anselmian dichotomy between the definitive and repletive presence of God to develop a unique and radically anthropocentric doctrine of the Eucharist, in which the bearers of the real presence were not the bread and wine, but the individual believers who partook of these elements. Employing precise theological terms such as *Wesen* (essence) and *wesentlich* (essentially), Hubmaier insisted that the faithful, during the Supper, possess Christ's human nature while retaining their own human natures. This literal "consubstantiation" (*i.e.* the holding of two distinct natures simultaneously) of the church in general and each believer in particular was exegetically defended through Hubmaier's appeal to the Johannine and Pauline accounts of the Last Supper at the expense of the Synoptics.

Hubmaier erected a stairway bridging the sacramentological second tier with his ecclesiology, the third tier in his theological system, by identifying the two sacraments as the keys, described by Jesus in the famous "power of the keys" pericope (Mt. 16:16-19), to the entrance and exit doors of the kingdom of heaven, and then equating these doors with two distinct stages of church discipline. The first door represented the baptismal vow (*Tauff-glübde*), in which the believer promised to submit to the discipline of the community as articulated in Matthew 18:15-20. However, the second door alluded to Christian excommunication (*christliche Bann*), which Hubmaier defined as the exclusion of unrepentant sinners not from worship but from the separate weekly Lord's Supper services, the participants in which the reformer considered the precise composition of the true church at any given time. Only after miscreants ceased and made public reparations for the relevant sins would they be readmitted to Christ's ethical community. This disciplinary model was employed by Hubmaier to twice successfully implement the unique sixteenth-century historical modality of free churches administered by local governments in Waldshut, Germany and Nikolsburg, Austria, where initiation via baptism took place based on the voluntary decision of the individual while dissenters, such as Jews, Catholics, Lutherans, and Zwinglians, suffered no persecution as long as they refrained from undermining the public order. Through his planting of such "free state churches," Hubmaier instituted the first early modern attempt to forge a balance between the often encroaching realms of religious voluntarism and civil magistracy.

In sum, this monograph aims to constitute a watershed in Hubmaier research by making original contributions to four areas of knowledge: the study of Hubmaier as a constructive theologian, the sixteenth-century reception of Bernard of Clairvaux, the development of sacramental theology as correlated with philosophical anthropology, and church-state relations in the early modern period. It is my hope that the new discoveries presented in this text spark renewed interest in Hubmaier's life and thought as well as an increased recognition of his theological uniqueness and overall significance to the Christian tradition.

Kirk R. MacGregor
Cedar Falls, Iowa
November 2005

Acknowledgments

This monograph originated in a Ph.D. dissertation submitted to the University of Iowa in 2005. Sincerest appreciation is expressed to the co-supervisors of my doctoral study, Professor Ralph Keen and Professor Raymond A. Mentzer, who ensured that my time at Iowa was fruitful both academically and personally. My research would not have been possible without their contributions, which served only to strengthen this work. All weaknesses are entirely my responsibility.

Chapter 1

Reformation Taxonomies and Sacramental Theology

In contemporary Reformation historiography, one of the most uncontested and seemingly self-evident methodologies is the received classification system respectively rooted in the work of Ernst Troeltsch and George Huntston Williams in the first and second halves of the twentieth century. Heavily influenced by the Hegelian dialectic of the *religionsgeschichtliche Schule*, Troeltsch sought to prove that the history of Christianity is punctuated by a series of conflicts between the sociological realm, spanning family, economics, politics, and learning, and the theological realm, consisting of revealed religion in Scripture and dogma. His best-known work, *The Social Teaching of the Christian Churches* (1912), argues that the sociological and theological realms manifest themselves in two contradictory but complementary tendencies—compromise and the rejection of compromise. This rhythm of accommodation and protest was expressed in three forms of religious institution. First, the church compromises with society by devising strategies which enable as many people as possible to enter its ranks, seen historically in the sacramental practice of infant baptism which naturally initiated members without requiring a voluntary decision. Due to the temptations and influences of the surrounding culture, the church sets relaxed standards of belief and behavior and postulates that not all within its fold will be saved—this only God will decide at the Judgment Day. Second, the sect rejects all compromise with society by setting extremely high entrance standards for membership, an example of which is the sixteenth century practice of adult baptism among those disillusioned by the perceived secularism within the church, such as Conrad Grebel, Felix Manz, and Michael Sattler. Not surprisingly, the sect is a small and fiercely exclusivistic body of believers which stresses the necessity of internal discipline and regards anyone outside the group as condemned. Finally, Troeltsch located the Hegelian synthesis of the church (thesis) and sect (antithesis) in mysticism, which he defined as individual religious spontaneity unencumbered by collective organization of any sort.[1] As a social and philosophical generalist rather than a specialist of any particular era in church history, Troeltsch maintained that these three forms of religiosity permeated the twenty-century expanse of the Christian tradition.

Shortly after the close of the Second World War, Troeltsch's taxonomical lenses were focused sharply by Williams, indisputably the foremost twentieth-century historian of groups operating at the margins of the mainline Reformation, upon the early modern period (1450-1660). As Troeltsch had predicted, Williams' labors revealed the early modern emergence of three distinct types of reformers, each corresponding to a Troeltschian stage of religiosity. The Magisterials, analogous to Troeltsch's church-form, encompassed those who coexisted with the state and promoted a top-down model of reformation through the magistrates. For Williams, this type included sixteenth-century Lutheran, Zwinglian, Calvinist, Catholic, and Anglican reformers, as the defining theological element for all such figures was a doctrine of the church which rendered Christianity a natural religion through infant baptism and forbade judgment as to the identity of the elect and reprobate before the end of time. Representing Troeltsch's sect-form were the Radicals, whose practice of adult baptism rendered voluntary obedience to a life of Christian discipleship a prerequisite for admission to their conventicles. To ensure the perpetuity of such spiritual purity, rigid standards in belief and conduct were enforced through the Christian ban. Williams dubbed such rebaptizers as "Radicals," from the Latin *radix* (root), because they attempted to return to the root of New Testament Christianity. However, nowhere in his massive tome *The Radical Reformation* does Williams explicitly attempt to identify whether this root was primarily theological or social in character. Despite his withholding of judgment on this score, most Reformation specialists have read Williams, in light of his emphasis upon Magisterial coexistence with the state and his juxtaposition of Magisterials against Radicals, as implying that Radicals are to be defined socially as those who advocated the separation of church and state.

It seems to me, nevertheless, that the majority reading is here flawed for four reasons. First, this reading cannot account for the fact that several of the groups Williams classifies as "Radical" were not anti-statist, such as the Unity of the Czech Brethren, the Slavic Reformers in Poland and Lithuania,

---

1. Ernst Troeltsch, *The Social Teaching of the Christian Churches*, 2 vols. (London: Allen and Unwin, 1912), 2:993-94.

and the German university-based Unitarians from whom Williams traced his own spiritual lineage.[2] Second, it overlooks Williams' series of 1951 articles on the early church, in which he argues that the first century Christian position on church-state relations was the effect, not the cause, of the theological, and specifically Christological, nucleus of the New Testament: "For what the Christian is willing to render unto Caesar depends . . . on his understanding of Christ as God and of Jesus' commandments."[3] Third, even if, for the sake of argument, Williams had held the inverse position that first-century theology was the effect of a New Testament social nucleus, it is far from obvious that he interpreted the New Testament as advocating a separation of church and state rather than a division of powers between a complementary church and state. According to Williams' exegesis of the dominical trial before Pilate, "Jesus declared that the authority of Pilate was from God," which in turn led those second and third century theologians who suffered no imperial persecution to craft a doctrine of church-state cooperation rather than separation: "Christian theologians like Irenaeus and Origen soon placed the Roman Empire under the Eternal Logos."[4] Fourth, there was nothing intrinsically anti-statist about Troeltsch's sect, which form Williams correlated with the Radicals. Since the prevalent understanding of Williams' concept of religious radicalism lacks both the explanatory scope and power to account for this scholar's own delineation of various pro-statist groups as Radical Reformers and his research on the early church, it should be discarded as a hasty generalization. This fallacious inference was corrected in 1962 by Heinold Fast, who pointed out that the only coherent definition of "Radical Reformer" grounded in the Williams corpus was the theological definition as those who practiced the baptism of believers. For this, Fast noted, comprised the only trait common to all the disparate groups in *Radical Reformation*, from the Swiss Brethren to the Anti-Trinitarian Rationalists, whom Williams classed as Radicals. Thus, to claim that Williams de-

---

2. Williams, in *The Radical Reformation*, 3rd ed. (Kirksville, Mo.: Truman State University Press, 2000), reports that, far from being anti-statist, the Unity of the Czech Brethren "accepted civic offices and in other ways responded to the demands of state and town life" (322), the Polish Slavic Reformers were "destined to influence the prince palatine profoundly" (1024), the Lithuanian Slavic Reformers frequently "argued in the halls of nobiliary sponsors" (1026), and the university-based Unitarians arranged, at "the Diet of Speyer, 10 July 1570, to meet Chancellor Caspar Békés of Transylvania" (1234).

3. George Huntston Williams, "Christology and Church-State Relations," *Church History* XX (September 1951): 3; the second half of which was continued in *Church History* XX (December 1951): 3-34.

4. Ibid.

fined Radicalism in any other way, especially in the social sense of those who advocated the separation of church and government, would render him guilty of self-contradiction.[5]

Returning to his identification of the early modern exemplar for the Troeltschian mystic, Williams styled as "Spiritualists" the followers of Silesian nobleman Caspar Schwenckfeld, who held that they, through the "inner light" or vehicle of the Holy Spirit, could receive new and direct revelation from God which supplanted the old revelation indirectly mediated to the *literati* by Scripture.[6] For Williams, therefore, the Magisterial Reformers, Radical Reformers, and Spiritualists constituted the respective sixteenth-century analogues for Troeltsch's church, sect, and mystic types, a classification system which has won universal acceptance in the Reformation historical academy since the 1960s. Although, as previously noted, Williams recognized the possibility, however rare, of overlap between Magisterial and Radical Reform and even called attention to anomalous pro-statist groups which practiced believers' baptism, those who followed him tended to dismiss these minority factions and harden his delineation between Magisterial and Radical Reform into the following mutually exclusive social dichotomy. For Magisterial Reformers, the church and state were coterminous; for Radical Reformers, church and state, or the Kingdom of God and the Kingdom of Satan, must be separated to prevent the leavening yeast of the latter to despoil the purity of the former. As we will see throughout the course of this study, this anachronistic dichotomy utterly fails to explain the theological and social program of Hubmaier.

The Theological Essence of Anabaptism

One further issue left unanswered by Williams was his definition of Anabaptism. While it is clear that Williams operated with an implicit concept of Anabaptism which surpassed the trivial definition of those who rebaptize, as he constantly differentiated between Anabaptists and other Radicals who also, by definition, engaged in this practice, he neglected to spell out or even intimate the definition underlying such distinctions. For this reason, the quest to discover the irreducible essence of Anabaptism has constituted the major driving force behind Anabaptist scholarship since 1979, the advent of the so-called "third wave" of Radical Reformation historiography. Ushered in by the provocative collection of *Mennonite Quarterly Review*

---

5. Heinold Fast, *Der linke Flügel der Reformation* (Bremen: Carl Schünemann Verlag, 1962), xiii-xxii.

6. Williams, *Radical Reformation*, 385-87.

(*MQR*) essays published in that year's August edition featuring a variety of
(often deviating) perspectives on "History and Theology," contemporary
scholars have sought to find the core of Anabaptism by transcending the
divide between monogenesis and polygenesis, the two dominant theses regarding the origins of Anabaptism respectively proposed by the first two
"waves." The monogenesis theory of Anabaptist origins, introduced in 1943
by Harold Bender to the American Society of Church History through his
presidential address entitled "The Anabaptist Vision,"[7] postulated that a single *successio Anabaptistica*,[8] which spread throughout central and northern
Europe at the hands of prominent leaders like Pilgram Marpeck, Peter
Riedeman, and Menno Simons, was conceived at the Second Zurich Disputation in October 1523. At this time, Zwingli tempered his biblically purist
instincts by complying with the appeal of the city council to preserve Roman
ornamentation in the Mass, which provoked the opposition of his radical
disciples and set off a series of events culminating 21 January 1525 in the
"revolutionary rebaptisms" at the home of Felix Manz.[9] Refuting the notion
of a united dispersion of Anabaptism emanating from Zurich, in their semi-
nal 1975 *MQR* article James M. Stayer, Werner O. Packull, and Klaus Deppermann launched a paradigm shift to a polygenesis model by demonstrating
that a plethora of distinct strains of Anabaptism arose in South and Central
Germany, Austria, and the Netherlands which, in their judgment, could only
be disingenuously reduced to a radically Zwinglian lowest common denomi-
nator.[10] Nevertheless, recent scholarship, subtly critical of the inclination of
"polygenesis historians" to overemphasize the differences between the rebaptizing factions, nominates several candidates for the title of "central element of Anabaptism." Such suggestions range from more plausible suggestions by C. Arnold Snyder revolving around shared soteriological themes[11]

---

7. Harold Bender, *The Recovery of the Anabaptist Vision* (Scottdale, Pa.:
Mennonite Publishing House, 1957), 33.

8. I borrow the term from Stayer's article "Let a Hundred Flowers Bloom
and Let a Hundred Schools of Thought Contend," *MQR* 53 (July 1979): 212.

9. John H. Yoder, "The Turning Point in the Zwinglian Reformation," *MQR*
32 (1958): 140.

10. James M. Stayer, Werner O. Packull, and Klaus Deppermann, "From
Monogenesis to Polygenesis: The Historical Discussion of Anabaptist Origins,"
MQR 49 (April 1975): 87. They dub attempts to trace all varieties of Anabap-
tism back through Zurich as "unhistorical theological abstractions."

11. C. Arnold Snyder, *Anabaptist History and Theology* (Kitchener, Ont.:
Pandora Press, 1995), 47-48, 384. In their reviews of Snyder's book, both Stayer
and Wes Harrison praise Snyder for offering a broadly correct description of
salvific similarities which cut across Anabaptist lines; see James M. Stayer, re-

to less plausible ones by Kenneth Davis underlining resemblances in pneumatology which, in my judgment, fail to differentiate the Anabaptists from the Spiritualists.[12]

In the judgment of many historians, however, the issue of sacramental theology—or, more precisely, a denial of it in favor of the purely symbolic character of mere ordinances *sans* the power to mediate grace—constitutes the one common thread woven throughout the fabric of Anabaptism. Since there were many different definitions of the term "sacrament" in the sixteenth century, it would be helpful at this point to outline its primary meanings and explain how the word is commonly used in contemporary treatments of the Anabaptists. The traditional Catholic understanding of "sacrament" in the early modern period, stemming from such medieval scholastics as Bonaventure and Thomas Aquinas, maintained that a sacrament is both a sacred symbol and a container of grace instituted by Christ which actually gives the grace it symbolizes to its recipient *ex opere operato*, that is, from the performance of the act itself.[13] In the words of the Council of Trent, "a sacrament is something presented to the senses, which has the power, by divine institution, not only of signifying, but also of efficiently conveying grace."[14] While the Magisterial Reformers differed amongst themselves as to how such grace was mediated, they concurred in their predication of grace upon the recipient's faith against the Catholic conception of *ex opere operato*. For Luther, sacraments were the Word of God communicated visibly rather than simply orally. Just as with the Word, moreover, they possess an objective character, the good or evil effect of which depends on the belief or unbelief of the partaker. Hence sacraments taken with the proper attitude confer upon believers the promise of the gospel for remission of sins and eternal life; whereas if the sacraments are taken with disbelief, they not only fail to give grace but are positively harmful to

---

view essay of *Anabaptist History and Theology*, by C. Arnold Snyder, *MQR* 70 (October 1996): 474 and Wes Harrison, review of *Anabaptist History and Theology*, by C. Arnold Snyder, *Sixteenth Century Journal* XXVII (Summer 1996): 587.

12. Kenneth Davis, "Anabaptism as a Charismatic Movement," *MQR* 53 (July 1979): 219-34. My misgivings about Davis' proposals are shared by Hans-Jürgen Goertz; see Goertz, "Geist und Leben: Überlegungen zur pneumatologischen Grundlegung der Theologie," *Kerygma und Dogma* 28 (October-December 1982): 284-86.

13. Jaroslav Pelikan, *Reformation of Church and Dogma (1300-1700)* (Chicago: University of Chicago Press, 1984), 51-52.

14. J. Waterworth, trans. and ed., *The Canons and Decrees of the Sacred and Oecumenical Council of Trent* (London: C. Dolman, 1848), 235.

their recipients.[15] Owing to his *theologia pactum*, by contrast, Zwingli argued that sacraments were covenant signs which God has graciously provided to inform the church in general, not the individual believer, who belongs to the community of faith: "They have as their aim to certify your faith to the Church, rather than to give you certainty for yourself."[16] Nevertheless, the sacraments do provide their individual recipients with strengthening or actual grace, which empowers the faithful to perform good works and resist temptations to sin.[17] While agreeing with Zwingli that sacraments assist believers in living out the commands of Christ, Calvin repudiated the Zurich reformer's deemphasis of personal salvific certainty by insisting that the primary function of the sacraments was to confirm to the individual believer inwardly that he or she is one of the elect: "A sacrament is God's witness to us of his favor towards us, by means of an outward sign . . . by which the Lord assures us inwardly of his loving promises so that we can prove our calling in his sight."[18] One common thread running through all these Catholic and Magisterial definitions is the notion that sacraments, in and of themselves, constitute means of grace, regardless of whether that grace is dispensed *ex opere operato* (Catholic) or by virtue of the recipient's faith (Magisterial).

Among scholars of the Radical Reformation, in the past two decades there has emerged something of a consensus that a distinguishing mark of Anabaptism as a whole was the denial that either baptism or the Lord's Supper intrinsically conveyed grace in any form; rather, they were outward signs of inward spiritual realities that had already been accomplished. One could therefore characterize the Anabaptist position as a partial Zwinglianism: as in Zwingli's view, the central Christian signs furnished the community with evidence of the recipients' salvation; but unlike Zwingli's concept, these signs neither supplied actual grace to fortify their recipients spiritually nor bestowed a measure of grace upon the church. For these latter reasons, Anabaptists were said to avoid the term "sacrament" in their writings intentionally and to replace it with the seemingly more biblical "ordinance."[19] Such is certainly a correct assessment regarding almost all those normally regarded

---

15. Pelikan, *Reformation*, 179-80.

16. *Huldrych Zwingli: Writings*, trans. H. Wayne Pipkin (Allison Park, Pa.: Pickwick Publications, 1984), 3:261.

17. Huldrych Zwingli, *An Exposition of the Faith*, in *Zwingli and Bullinger*, trans. G. W. Bromiley (Philadelphia: Westminster, 1953), 263.

18. John Calvin, *Institutes of the Christian Religion*, trans. John T. McNeill and Ford L. Battles (Philadelphia: Westminster, 1960), 4.14.1.

19. Snyder, *History and Theology*, 128.

as sixteenth-century Anabaptists; to be sure, even a cursory reading of treatises authored by the Swiss Brethren, Marpeck, Riedeman, or Menno Simons
will illustrate how deliberately these notables distanced themselves from the
Catholic and Magisterial position that, in the famous dictum of Augustine,
rites such as baptism and the Lord's Supper comprised "visible signs of an
invisible grace."[20] Speaking for virtually the entire movement on the nonsac-
ramental nature of these two ceremonies, Michael Sattler declared:

> Baptism is an ordinance and not a sacrament. Although some highly
> boast here about an infused grace, there is no basis for that in Scripture.
> Baptism is nothing other than a public testimony of internal faith and
> commitment. . . . By the baptism of Christ the baptized testify to the
> forgiveness of their sins, which remission had already taken place in
> faith, before they had come to water baptism. . . . That the Supper of
> Christ is an ordinance and not a sacrament, we admit. From this it fol-
> lows that the Supper is nothing other than a memorial of the suffering
> of Christ who shed his crimson blood on the cross for the washing
> away of our sins.[21]

Due to its widespread success in accounting for the theological distinctive-
ness of those typically denominated as Anabaptists, it seems that Anabaptism should be formally defined as that set of Radicals, or rebaptizers, who
regarded baptism and the Lord's Supper as ordinances rather than sacraments.

Throughout this study, therefore, I shall be presupposing the following
eclectic taxonomy which merges the classification system of Williams, as
correctly interpreted by Fast, with the consensus view of Radical Reformation scholars on the nature of Anabaptism. The adjective "Magisterial" refers
to a top-down approach to religious reform through allegiance to magistrates. The adjective "Radical" alludes to individuals or communities administering the New Testament *radix*, or root, of adult baptism. The noun "Ana-

---

20. Augustine, *City of God*, trans. Henry Bettenson (New York: Penguin,
1984), X.5. Although interpreted in a variety of ways, as previously illustrated,
this definition, which stressed the intrinsic grace-conveying nature of sacraments, was endorsed by the Council of Trent (*Canons and Decrees*, 237), Luther
(*House Postil*, in *D. Martin Luthers Werke* [Weimar: Böhlau, 1888], 52:520),
Zwingli (*On Baptism*, in Bromiley, *Zwingli and Bullinger*, 131), and Calvin (*Institutes*, 4.14.1).

21. Michael Sattler, *Letter to Bürgermeister and Council at Horb*, trans.
Myron Augsburger, in "Michael Sattler, d. 1527, Theologian of the Swiss Brethren Movement" (Ph.D. dissertation, Union Theological Seminary, 1965), 89-91.

baptist" applies to practitioners of adult baptism who, denying the existence of sacraments (ceremonial mediators of grace), held that baptism and communion were ordained acts of obedience to Christ.

The Misclassification of Balthasar Hubmaier

Balthasar Hubmaier (1480-1528), an Ingolstadt *doctor theologiae* and one-time Catholic priest who turned away from Catholic sacramental theology and embraced the baptism of believers, is almost universally regarded by Reformation historians as an Anabaptist, and often as a leader of the Anabaptist movement and even the greatest sixteenth-century opponent of infant baptism. To appreciate this fact one need look no further than the title of his only English biography, *Balthasar Hübmaier: The Leader of the Anabaptists*, first published by Henry C. Vedder in 1905 and revised just before his death in 1935. Since that time the classification of Hubmaier by almost all early modern scholars has followed suit; for example, Williams touts Hubmaier as the most "sober and resourceful exponent of normative evangelical Anabaptism."[22] This judgment was recently echoed by the verdict of Baptist historian William R. Estep: "Undoubtedly, Dr. Balthasar Hubmaier was one of the most brilliant stars in the Anabaptist firmament . . . [and] the leading Anabaptist preacher."[23] However, two major problems plague the consensus view of Hubmaier: it was devised at a time when twenty-four of his thirty-eight works had never received careful attention, and it is yet to be tested against his works that have recently become accessible. Such lack of engagement with the primary sources alone opens up more than the possibility that a severely limited database may have given rise to a fallacious identification of this reformer.

Current Hubmaier research has only extensively analyzed a handful of his treatises, seeming to give excessive attention to his antipedobaptist polemics, which for obvious reasons became his most-utilized writings in the Swiss, South German, Austrian, and Dutch Anabaptist communities. Prior to 1962, moreover, no critical edition of Hubmaier's German works had been published, and past biographers such as Johann Loserth (1893), Henry Vedder (1905), Carl Sachsse (1914), and Torsten Bergsten (1961) only had ac-

---

22. Williams, *Radical Reformation*, 1253. "Evangelical Anabaptists" comprise those missionary-minded Anabaptists who sought converts to the movement by actively sharing their faith with non-Anabaptists, rather than isolating themselves completely from non-Anabaptists.
23. William R. Estep, *The Anabaptist Story*, 3rd rev. ed. (Grand Rapids, Mich.: Eerdmans, 1996), 77, 103.

cess to selected treatises defending believers' baptism along with a few other related texts. Anchored in the observation that these texts do not clearly affirm (or, let it be said with emphasis, clearly deny) the grace-conveying power of believers' baptism and make only passing references to the Lord's Supper, the presupposition that Hubmaier did not regard baptism and the Eucharist as sacraments but instead simply viewed them as ordinances became virtually ubiquitous among scholars of the Radical Reformation.[24] This assumption continues to persist among historians today despite the English translation in 1989 of Hubmaier's 1523-28 works, completed by H. Wayne Pipkin and John H. Yoder, several passages within which seem to call it into question.[25] The ordinance theory found its fullest elaboration in Eddie Mabry's 1994 monograph on the ecclesiology of the reformer: "Hubmaier rejects the view that a sacrament . . . actually communicated the grace of which it was the sign. Hubmaier also rejected the . . . term 'sacrament' . . . [and] did not believe that any grace was communicated by anything physical," and hence "baptism and Eucharist . . . he called ordinances (*die Ordnungen*) instead of sacraments."[26] Two years later, Estep maintained that "no one can successfully accuse Hubmaier of holding a sacramental view" of these rites, as he "was very careful to avoid any use of terms that might imply more than a purely symbolic meaning."[27] It is precisely at this juncture, nevertheless, that one must guard against the construction of hasty generalizations, especially when considering a thinker many of whose writings have not yet received sufficient examination. Even more decisive is this critical warning in view of the remarkable conclusions reached by the latest scholarship on the newly published Hubmaier corpus, which reveals him to be a theological maverick who dissented from his alleged coreligionists on a host

---

24. For verification of this point see Torsten Bergsten, *Balthasar Hubmaier, Seine Stellung zu Reformation und Täufertum* (Kassel, Germany: J. G. Oncken Press, 1961), 368-69; Henry C. Vedder, *Balthasar Hübmaier: The Leader of the Anabaptists* (New York: G. P. Putnam's Sons, 1905), 114; and Walter Klaassen, *Anabaptism: Neither Catholic Nor Protestant* (Waterloo: Conrad Press, 1973), 17-18.

25. Balthasar Hubmaier, *Theologian of Anabaptism*, trans. H. Wayne Pipkin and John H. Yoder (Scottdale, Pa.: Herald Press, 1989); I have carefully compared all my translations from Hubmaier's 1523-28 original German writings against the renderings in this volume for accuracy.

26. Eddie Mabry, *Balthasar Hubmaier's Doctrine of the Church* (Lanham, Md.: University Press of America, 1994), 165. Conspicuously absent, however, are any actual examples or citations from the reformer denominating baptism or the Supper as *die Ordnungen*.

27. Estep, *Anabaptist Story*, 209.

of fundamental principles, a fact not yet sufficiently appreciated in the Reformation historical academy. Five of the key areas hitherto disclosed where the Waldshut radical appears in stark contrast against all other "Anabaptists" portrayed by Williams are his relation between church and government, his concept of the psychic state between the believer's death and resurrection, the possibility of baptizing catechized children, his model of church discipline, and his acceptance of Catholic doctrines rejected by the Anabaptist movement as a whole.

One widespread bulwark of Anabaptist thought consists in the divorce between civil and ecclesiastical authority, most clearly articulated by Michael Sattler in the fourth article of the 1527 *Schleitheim Confession*. The fourth article of this doctrinal statement, which earned widespread acceptance by the Swiss, German, and Austrian Anabaptists, dubs the state "nothing but an abomination" and requires everyone to choose between the restored church (the kingdom of God) or the state (the kingdom of Satan), as "God's temple and idols, Christ and Belial . . . the world and those who are [come] out of the world . . . none will have part with the other."[28] In the perspective of the faithful, therefore, the most devastating tragedy in all of church history proved to be the recognition of Christianity as first legal and then official religion of the Roman Empire respectively under Constantine (313 C.E.) and Theodosius I (381). In contrast, Hubmaier insisted in his 1528 *Eine Rechenschaft des Glaubens* that the civil-ecclesiastical Christendom amalgam is a wonderful gift of God that should be appreciated. He dedicated twelve of his twenty-six works to nobles, some of whom even enter as characters into his dialogues.[29] Like Luther, Zwingli, and Calvin, moreover, Hubmaier propagated reform under the patronage of secular magistrates and successfully organized free state churches in both Waldshut (1523-25) and Nikolsburg (1526-28), a unique sixteenth-century historical modality in

---

28. Michael Sattler, *Schleitheim Confession*, in John H. Yoder, *The Legacy of Michael Sattler* (Scottdale, Pa.: Herald Press, 1973), 37-38. In modern times, the Anabaptist conviction regarding the oppressiveness of the state has been defended by Quentin Skinner, *The Foundations of Modern Political Thought*, 2 vols. (Cambridge: Cambridge University Press, 1978), 2:73-80 and Michael G. Baylor, ed., *The Radical Reformation* (Cambridge: Cambridge University Press, 1991), 175-76.

29. One remarkable instance occurs in his 1526-27 *Eine christliche Lehrtafel*, where "the noble and Christian Lords, Lord Leonhart and Lord Hans von Lichtenstein at Nikolsburg" catechize child and adult church initiates; in Gunnar Westin and Torsten Bergsten, *Balthasar Hubmaier Schriften* (Gütersloh: Gütersloher Verlagshaus Gerd Mohn, 1962), 306-26. See also Balthasar Hubmaier, *Eine Rechenschaft des Glaubens*, in Westin and Bergsten, *Schriften*, 488-91.

which baptism took place based on the free decision of the individual. Remarkably, dissenters, defined by Hubmaier as "heretics . . . who shamelessly resist the Holy Scripture"[30] and encompassing Jews, Catholics, Lutherans, Zwinglians, and those whom Williams classified as "revolutionary Anabaptists,"[31] suffered no persecution as long as they refrained from undermining the public order.[32] Consistent with such magisterial leanings, in his 1527 treatise *Von dem Schwert* Hubmaier repudiated the pacifism of the *Schleitheim Confession* as well as its prohibitions against serving in government and taking civil oaths in favor of the obligation of Christians to perform such duties of good citizenship as wielding the sword in defense of one's land, holding public office, pledging vows of allegiance, and paying taxes.[33] Although this consideration by itself does not dismiss him from the Anabaptist camp, Hubmaier must be reclassified as both a Magisterial and Radical Reformer, a strange hybrid that does not seem to be reflected by any figure or group in the Anabaptist movement.

Second, the doctrine of psychopannychism, or sleep of the soul in a sort of suspended animation between death and resurrection palpable in both the post-Worms Luther[34] and Swiss Brethren,[35] is completely unknown to Hub-

---

30. "Ketzer . . . die fräuenlich der hailigen gschrifft widerfechtend." Balthasar Hubmaier, *Von Ketzern und ihren Verbrennern*, in Westin and Bergsten, *Schriften*, 96.

31. "Revolutionary Anabaptists" refers to chiliastic groups, like the Apocalyptic Kingdom of Müntzer, which attempted to establish the Kingdom of God on earth through "holy violence"; Williams, *Radical Reformation*, 16.

32. The sole example of religious persecution in Hubmaier's congregations transpired in the spring of 1527 following the Nikolsburg Disputation, where Hans Hut insisted upon the chiliastic advent of the kingdom of God through holy violence on the part of the faithful. As such a program clearly threatened the commonwealth, Hubmaier experienced no qualms in soliciting the Lichtenstein lords to imprison Hut in the Nikolsburg Castle, an act met by bitter outcries from fellow anti-establishment Anabaptists throughout Moravia. For a complete report of the incident see Vedder, *Hübmaier*, 165-69.

33. Balthasar Hubmaier, *Von dem Schwert*, in Westin and Bergsten, *Schriften*, 435-57.

34. Representative instances of this belief appear as early as Luther's 1528 *Sermons on the Catechism*, in *Luther's Works, American Edition*, ed. Jaroslav Pelikan (St. Louis: Concordia Publishing House, 1955-86), 51:168-69.

35. This belief is nowhere more evident than in the 1528 trial of Michael Sattler in Württemberg, who explained to Archduke Ferdinand that the Virgin and the saints "could not be intercessors because, like the rest of the faithful,

maier. Rather, he taught that the mind, at the moment of death, enters a blissful yet disembodied and temporary state of apprehending the beatific presence of Christ and then is reinfused by God into the transformed spiritual body at the general resurrection heralded by Christ's second coming. Third, although some Anabaptists acknowledged solely adult baptism, Hubmaier firmly advocated literal believers' baptism for all—that is to say, while infants, who obviously cannot believe (at least with faith of their own), must be forbidden baptism, children should be baptized upon sufficient training in the faith. Fourth, the reformer's exercise of the disciplinary ban stood at variance to the typical Anabaptist practice of excommunicating miscreants failing to meet the sect's extremely high standard of orthopraxy and regarding them as if dead unless and until public repentance is freely accomplished. While parallels with Calvin's consistory at Geneva will be explored in chapter five, suffice it to say here that Hubmaier conceived of a "sacrament-powered model" for correction of the faithful. In this model, the repeated offender was excluded from the Eucharist but never (as for most Anabaptists) considered irredeemable,[36] resulting in the perpetual maintenance of contact between the person and the community. Finally, Hubmaier, against the later views of Menno Simons and those whom Fast denominates as "mainstream Anabaptists,"[37] taught the distinctly Catholic doctrines of the perpetual virginity of Mary, fasting, and the superiority of lifelong celibacy over the married state.[38] Although none of these matters decisively settle the issue at hand, Hubmaier's widespread disagreement with commonly held Anabaptist beliefs engenders reasonable doubt as to whether contemporary scholarship has correctly identified him as a *bona fide* Anabaptist.

Enquiry into this momentous question by a handful of historians challenging the majority position has yielded in my judgment both more and less fruitful responses, directly proportional to their level of engagement with the

---

they were sleeping (psychopannychism) and waiting Christ's judgment"; see Williams, *Radical Reformation*, 295.

36. That unrepentant sinners were irredeemable followed from the literalistic Anabaptist interpretation of Hebrews 6:4-6, which states that "it is impossible for those who were once enlightened, and have tasted the heavenly gift, and have become partakers of the Holy Spirit . . . if they fall away, to renew them again to repentance, since they crucify again for themselves the Son of God, and put him to an open shame." The typical Anabaptist exegesis of this pericope is fully explained by Menno Simons, *Admonition on Church Discipline*, in J. C. Wenger, *The Complete Writings of Menno Simons* (Scottdale, Pa.: Herald Press, 1956), 411-13.

37. Fast, *Der linke Flügel*, xiv-xvii.

38. Hubmaier, *Rechenschaft*, 470-71, 479-82.

primary sources. Through the analysis of a trio of brief yet pivotal treatises published by Hubmaier from 1526-27 explicating his startlingly philosophically sophisticated doctrine of the relationship between grace and free will, *Eine christliche Lehrtafel, Von der Freiheit des Willens,* and *Das andere Büchlein von der Freiwilligkeit des Menschen,*[39] David C. Steinmetz made a cluster of key initial findings in 1971 which served as a foundation for the watershed research of Walter L. Moore. Calling attention to Hubmaier's academic pilgrimage, which culminated in his doctorate of theology under the tutelage of Catholic polemicist *par excellence* and avowed nominalist John Eck first at Freiburg and then at Ingolstadt, Steinmetz successfully demonstrated the radical's appropriation of several Nominalist concepts. Most notably, Hubmaier subscribed to the belief that God will give salvation to those who do what is naturally in them (*facere quod in se est*) along with its corresponding system of merit. Accordingly, Hubmaier affirmed that God grants *meritum de congruo* when sinners do what is in them on their own behalf, *meritum digni* when sinners are worthy to be rewarded not only for themselves but also because just people prayed for their conversion, and *meritum condigni* when the newly redeemed perform good works.[40] Moreover, Hubmaier adopted the distinction between the absolute power of God, or God's power to do whatever he chooses, and the ordained power of God, or God's actions performed according to principles he has freely established.[41] Steinmetz also revealed that Hubmaier cloaked these concepts in the garb of scriptural exegesis to further wider acceptance among his biblicist constituency.[42] Building on such an extensive foundation, Moore disclosed that Hubmaier was, in his words, an "unremitting libertarian" concerning free will from the beginning of his career as a Catholic professor and priest at Ingolstadt to his 1528 martyrdom at Vienna under Austrian king

---

39. Working independently from the same presuppositions enunciated in these documents, the polished version of the reconciliation between grace and free will came to fruition in the thought of Catholic Reformer Luis de Molina (1535-1600), a Jesuit whose ingenious theory of *scientia media*, or middle knowledge, made room for creaturely freedom by exempting counterfactual knowledge from the divine decree to create the actual world; see Molina, *On Divine Foreknowledge*, trans. Alfred J. Freddoso (Ithaca, N.Y.: Cornell University Press, 1988), 46-62, 85-273. It remains for further investigation if Hubmaier and Molina received these presuppositions from a common source.

40. David C. Steinmetz, "Scholasticism and Radical Reform: Nominalist Motifs in the Theology of Balthasar Hubmaier," *MQR* 45 (April 1971): 134-35.

41. Ibid., 127-28.

42. Ibid., 137.

Ferdinand I as a seditionist.[43] Moreover, Moore showed that Hubmaier, while denying that anyone actually had lived a sinless life, went so far as to affirm (though not in Moore's precise terminology) the logical possibility that post-Fall humans could have continued as they were to salvation apart from any divine assistance other than their own intrinsic freedom to choose between opposites.[44] These discoveries flew in the face of two long-accepted hypotheses proposed by Armour, Seewald, Hall, Bergsten, and Williams: first, that Hubmaier advanced the late-Augustinian doctrines of the bound will and its corollary of predestination independent of divine foreknowledge from 1521-1525; and second, that Hubmaier's mind was changed at Augsburg in 1526 by personal contact with Hans Denck, who introduced the former to his own works, *Was Geredt sei* and *Vom Gesetz Gottes*, as well as Erasmus' 1524 *Diatribe de libero Arbitrio*.[45] In his 1991 *MQR* piece on Hubmaier, James William McClendon formulates several inferences from these additions to the database, the most controversial of which is his identification of the reformer as, in the end, a "Catholic baptist,"[46] in spite of Hubmaier's explicit endorsement during his final Nikolsburg period of "the joyful resurrection of [Christ's] living word in recent years . . . through Dr.

---

43. Walter L. Moore, "Catholic Teacher and Anabaptist Pupil: The Relationship between John Eck and Balthasar Hubmaier," *Archiv für Reformationsgeschichte* 72 (1981): 90. At this juncture a terminological distinction needs to be made. Since the late medieval period, scholastic theologians have differentiated between two competing views of free will: libertarian and compatibilist. Libertarian free will entails the freedom to choose between opposites in both the physical and spiritual realms, regardless of whether or not a person has been regenerated. Thus, a libertarian concerning free will would maintain that fallen humanity can freely choose whether or not to respond to God's saving grace. Compatibilist free will, by contrast, is the freedom to choose between the options compatible with one's nature. Thus, unregenerate humans, while possessing the freedom to choose between opposites in the physical realm, lack the ability to choose between spiritual good and evil due to original sin. Just as a bad tree can bear bad fruit or no fruit at all, unregenerate humanity can either perform spiritual wickedness by actively rebelling against God or do nothing spiritual at all by displaying passivity toward God.

44. Ibid., 91-94. For these reasons, Moore classifies Hubmaier as either a semi-Pelagian or a Pelagian.

45. Armour, *Anabaptist Baptism*, 24-27; Seewald, "Text dieser Hubmaier-Schrift"; Hall, "Possibilities of Erasmian Influence on Denck and Hubmaier," 149-70; Bergsten, *Hubmaier*, 441-48; Williams, *Radical Reformation*, 256.

46. James William McClendon, "Balthasar Hubmaier, Catholic Anabaptist," *MQR* 65 (January 1991): 32.

Martin Luther"[47] and Eck's memorandum to Pope Clement VII convicting his erstwhile student of "Lutheran heresy."[48] Immediately, our aforementioned question grows more provocative: Should Hubmaier not only be dismissed from the Anabaptist camp but also, apart from his divergent conceptions of creaturely freedom and sacramental theology, be regarded as a sympathizer of Luther and Zwingli? To this query I will return in chapter three.

As abundantly evidenced by Steinmetz and Moore, the aforementioned theological concord on the self-determining capacity of human will between Hubmaier and his mentor Eck elicits, in what appears to me a wholly unforeseen development in Anabaptist historiography, a plethora of new quandaries for which currently formulated monogenesis or polygenesis theories fail to suffice. Although Hubmaier clandestinely paraphrased from the works of Eck, especially the 1514 *Chrysopassus praedestinationis*, to both substantiate and formulate the logical implications of their shared libertarian dogma, this observation leaves as inexplicable the radical's unique metaphysical foundations, utterly dissimilar from those of his mentor, which gave birth to his synergism.[49] The presuppositional structure of the rebaptizer's thought, then, centered around a tripartite anthropology (as humans are created in the *imago Dei Trinitarii*) wherein each of the *Seel*, *Geist*, and *Leib* (*i.e.* soul, spirit, and body) possesses its own intrinsic freedom: the soul is endowed with freedom from necessity; the spirit with freedom from sin; and the body with freedom from misery.[50] While the Fall stripped humanity of its two latter liberties, respectively by virtue of the active rebellion and consequent suffering and physical death of the primal couple, only the soul "has retained its original righteousness in which it was first created. . . . [and] is happy, willing, and ready to do all good."[51] Contrary, furthermore, to all other proponents of free choice in the sixteenth century, including his predecessor

47. "Der freydenreychen vrsteend seins lebendigen worts newlicher Jaren . . . durch D. Martinum Luther." Balthasar Hubmaier, *Ein einfältiger Unterricht*, in Westin and Bergsten, *Schriften*, 289.

48. "der Lutherischen Ketzerei." Johann Eck, *Denkschrift zu Papst*, in *Dr. Johann Ecks Denkschriften zur deutschen Kirchenreformation*, 2 vols. (Gütersloh: C. Bertelsmann, 1895), 1:241.

49. Synergism is the doctrine of divine and human cooperation in conversion; monergism, by contrast, is the position that the grace of God constitutes the only efficient cause in beginning and effecting conversion.

50. Hubmaier, *Eine christliche Lehrtafel*, 311; Hubmaier, *Von der Freiheit*, 382-85.

51. "hatt sein erbgerechtigkeit, in der er erstlich erschaffen, erhalten. . . . [vnd] ist aber frölich, willig vnnd bereyt zů allem gůtten." Hubmaier, *Von der Freiheit*, 389-90.

ponents of free choice in the sixteenth century, including his predecessor Eck, contemporary Erasmus, and successor Denck, Hubmaier maintained that the unregenerate individual produces the *initium fidei* without the special assistance of grace by "hungering and thirsting for righteousness,"[52] in response to which God is obligated to send a preacher of the gospel. If not original to Hubmaier, any prior inspiration of the reformer's anthropology remains admittedly an unsolved mystery, as noted by Moore:

> In [contemporaneous works] there seems to be no trace of one of Hubmaier's most distinctive features, namely his tripartite anthropology. . . . Obviously, this view is integral to his discussion of free will; the fact that there is not a trace of it to be found . . . points toward other possible sources of influence on Hubmaier.[53]

Even advocates of the opinion that Hubmaier was "obviously influenced by Erasmus' definition of free will," such as Eddie Mabry, find themselves driven to admit that

> in their basic understanding of grace and free will, Hubmaier and Erasmus do not agree. . . . there are still enough differences between their views to indicate that Hubmaier may be operating from . . . different presuppositions. . . . his own definition reflects other possible influences that don't seem to be present in Erasmus' view.[54]

If research is not to reach a standstill on Hubmaier's "theology of grace," as Robert Friedmann predicts,[55] where are scholars to look for potential sources given the exhaustion of early modern options?

---

52. Hubmaier, *Von der Freiheit*, 388.

53. Moore, "Catholic Teacher and Anabaptist Pupil," 80.

54. Mabry, *Doctrine of the Church*, 26, 30. Williams makes precisely the same point in *Radical Reformation*, 334.

55. Astonishingly, Friedmann blames Hubmaier himself for modern academic frustration on this score, somewhat disingenuously alleging that we lack the ability to trace this doctrine since the sophisticated theologian "does not develop these ideas concerning grace"; *The Theology of Anabaptism* (Scottdale, Pa.: Herald Press, 1973), 93.

Sixteenth-Century Reception of Bernard of Clairvaux: Magisterial Reform Encounters Monastic Reform

During the second half of the twentieth century, Reformation historians have gained a new appreciation of the influence of Cistercian abbot Bernard of Clairvaux (1090-1153) on the theology of Luther and Calvin. Summarizing the scholarly consensus which has emerged from comparison of the Magisterial corpus with the abbot's *Opera*, Bernard McGinn declares, "It is common knowledge that among medieval authors Bernard stood second to none in the admiration of the Reformers."[56] It would be no exaggeration to affirm that Bernard stood as one of Luther's favorite authors, second only to the late Augustine; in the words of Luther,

> I regard [Bernard] as the most pious of all monks, and prefer him to all others. . . . He is the only one worthy of the name "Father Bernard" and of being studied diligently. . . . St. Bernard was a man so lofty in spirit that I almost venture to set him above all other celebrated teachers both ancient and modern.[57]

Moreover, Calvin's use of Bernard, on the whole, is remarkably positive, with forty-three ringing endorsements regarding the latter's perceived doctrinal faithfulness to Scripture out of forty-seven total citations.[58] There is only one major point where these foremost exemplars of the Magisterial Reformation impugn the Cistercian's authority—his synergistic concord of grace and free will.[59] The reason for such exasperation is not hard to find, as the foundational axiom of the theologies of both Luther and Calvin consisted in an extremist version of original sin, namely, that in the Fall our primal

---

56. Bernard McGinn, introduction to Bernard of Clairvaux, *On Grace and Free Choice*, trans. Daniel O'Donovan (Kalamazoo, Mich.: Cistercian Publications, 1988), 45.

57. Martin Luther, *Sermons on the Gospel of John*, 33, in *Luther's Works*, 22:388; Luther, *To the Councilmen of Germany*, in *Luther's Works*, 45:363.

58. Jill Raitt, "Calvin's Use of Bernard of Clairvaux," *Archiv für Reformationsgeschichte* 72 (1981): 98, 103-11, 119-20.

59. The respective objections of Luther and Calvin to Bernard's concord of grace and free will are outlined in Franz Posset, *Pater Bernhardus: Martin Luther and Bernard of Clairvaux* (Kalamazoo, Mich.: Cistercian Publications, 1999), 53-61 and Dennis Tambrello, *Union with Christ: John Calvin and the Mysticism of St. Bernard* (Louisville: Westminster John Knox Press, 1994), 23-35.

ancestors, originally created positively holy (*i.e.* not merely morally neutral) and as federal heads (*i.e.* chief representatives) over the human race, in an act of self-violation, paradoxically employed their freedom to destroy that very faculty whereby humanity could freely choose to respond to God by irrevocably breaking the initial covenant with their Creator. Thus, humanity is totally depraved, insofar as corruption extends to every facet of our being, including free choice. This judgment is rendered apparent by Luther's reflection that "this bombshell knocks 'free-will' flat, and utterly shatters it,"[60] which is subsequently mirrored by Calvin: "Man has been deprived of free will, and is miserably enslaved."[61] Not surprisingly, then, Luther's admiration of Bernard as biblical theologian carried no distributive force into Bernard as philosophical theologian: "Bernard was superior to all the Doctors in the Church when he preached, but he became quite a different man in his disputations, for then he attributed too much to . . . free will. . . . [while claiming that] nothing is worthwhile but Jesus, in his debates . . . about free will, Jesus is nowhere to be found."[62] While tolerating, remarkably, Bernard's assessment of merit, Calvin, surpassing the fiery Luther in judiciousness, supplies not only a detailed refutation of the Cistercian's purportedly erroneous libertarianism but reveals the same trichotomous anthropological basis as found in Hubmaier, unexpectedly yielding a potential watershed for Hubmaier research:

> Three kinds of freedom are distinguished: first from necessity, second from sin, third from misery. The first of these so inheres in humanity by nature that it cannot possibly be taken away, but the two others have been lost through sin. . . . The thing that displeases me about this division is that . . . man by his very own nature somehow seeks after the good.[63]

Preempting any misconception that his anthropology may be commonplace to the medieval period, Jill Raitt writes, "But here it should be noted that this threefold freedom is generally accepted by scholars to be original to Ber-

---

60. Martin Luther, *The Bondage of the Will*, in *Luther's Works*, 18:614.

61. Calvin, *Institutes*, 2.2.1.

62. Martin Luther, *Table Talk no. 584*, in *Luther's Works*, 54:105; Luther, *Table Talk no. 5439a*, quoted by Bernard McGinn, introduction to Bernard of Clairvaux, in *Grace and Free Choice*, 46.

63. Calvin, *Institutes*, 2.2.6.

nard."[64] With such an estimation both Artur Michael Landgraf and Jean Châtillon concur.[65]

It is well known from Hubmaier's personal letters spanning back to his Catholic days and his treatises as an evangelical reformer that he received an exceptional education in patristic and medieval theology.[66] Under the sponsorship of Eck at Freiburg, Hubmaier studied the writings of virtually all the church fathers, the *Sententiae* of Peter Lombard, as well as the entire *corpus juris canonici*. After the devoted student followed Eck to Ingolstadt, the illustrious teacher introduced Hubmaier to the major currents in medieval philosophical theology, including scholasticism, late medieval Augustinianism, and humanism.[67] Hubmaier himself confessed, after his rebaptism, that he was far better trained in the sources of church history than Scripture:

> I state without pretense, and God knows I do not lie, that I became a doctor in the Holy Scriptures . . . and at that time I had never read a Gospel or Pauline epistle from beginning to end. What type of a Holy Word could I then teach or preach to others? To be sure: Thomas, Scotus, Gabriel, Occam, decree, decretals, legends of the saints.[68]

In light of this broad and deep understanding in the history of Christian thought, two novel questions suddenly manifest: Was Hubmaier acquainted

---

64. Raitt, "Calvin's Use of Bernard," 104.

65. Artur Michael Landgraf, *Dogmengeschichte der Frühscholastik I, i: Die Gnadenlehre* (Regensburg: Friedrich Pustet, 1952), 103; Jean Châtillon, "L'influence de S. Bernard sur la pensée scholastique au XIIe siècle," *Analecta sacri ordinis cisterciensis* IX, 304 (1953): 280-81.

66. Christof Windhorst, *Täuferisches Taufverständnis, Balthasar Hubmaier Lehre zwischen traditioneller und reformatorischer Theologie* (Leiden: E. J. Brill, 1976), 1-18; Mabry, *Doctrine of the Church*, 5.

67. Carl Sachsse, *D. Balthasar Hubmaier als Theologe* (Berlin: Trowitsch und Sohn, 1914), 126-29; Reinhold Seeberg, *Text-book of the History of Doctrine*, Vol. KK trans. Charles E. Kay (Grand Rapids, Mich.: Baker, 1956), 185-90.

68. "Sag ich vnuerholen, vnd Got waiß das ich nit leüg, das ich also zů einem Doctor in der heiligenn schrift. . . . auch dantzmal nye kainen Euangelisten, noch Epistelen Pauli vom anfang biß an das end gelesen. Was möcht ich denn für ein heilig wort ander geleert oder jnen gepredigt haben. Ja, Thoman, Scotum, Gabrielem, Ocam, Decret, Decretalen, Lügenden von den heiligen." Hubmaier, *Eine christliche Lehrtafel*, 309. Here Hubmaier, displaying his dissatisfaction with his perceived deficiency of biblical knowledge, devised a pun by using *Lügenden* (lying) for *Legenden* (legends).

with Bernard's works?[69] If so, what degree of influence did the monastic reformer's writings exert upon those of the Magisterial Radical Reformer? The first question is, in my judgment, easily answered. While one could reasonably assume, given the circumstantial evidence alone, that a theologian of such erudition as Hubmaier would have familiarized himself with the favorite medieval author of the Magisterial Reformation, there exists one explicit piece of evidence, previously undiscovered, which definitively proves that Hubmaier read the Cistercian. In the 1526 *Ein einfältiger Unterricht*, Hubmaier supplies his one and only direct citation of Bernard anywhere in his corpus: a highly provocative allusion to Bernard's 1141 sermon entitled "On the Second Baptism," which describes religious profession as a second baptism. Devising a play on words between the name Bernard and the sixteenth-century German term for "bear," Hubmaier commends to Lord Leonard von Lichtenstein the spiritual mastery displayed by the twelfth-century monk:

> Bernard, because he strangled a lion and bear (*Bern*) . . . was inflamed in a Christian manner and especially blessed not only with the outward name of light, but also inwardly in the soul. May this God also protect Your Grace and all lovers of the light, of his living Word, from this time forth, so that we are never overtaken by darkness.[70]

In the passage to which Hubmaier referred, Bernard explains to the Benedictines at Saint-Père-en-Vallée why monastic life merited the rebaptismal appellation:

> Our first parents, most dearly beloved, were not overcome by the lion or the bear; no, they were seduced by the serpent. . . . Accordingly, dearest brethren, it behooves us to be baptized anew. Just as in baptism we are rescued from the powers of darkness and transferred to the

---

69. The works of Bernard in print during the sixteenth century are listed in Posset, *Pater Bernhardus*, 61-67.

70. "Bernhart, da er einen Lewen vnd Bern erwürgt hat . . . nit allain mit dem außwendigen namen des liechts, sunder auch inwendig an der seel so Christenlich entzündt vnd sunderlich begnadt hat. Dieser Gott beware E. G. auch furan vnnd all liebhaber des liechts, sunder auch lebenndigen worts, darmit wir von den fünsternussen nymmer mer ergryffen warden." Hubmaier, *Ein einfältiger Unterricht*, 287-88.

kingdom of light, so in this second regeneration of the monastic vows we are refashioned in the light.[71]

When one considers the fact that Hubmaier, who exhibits tremendous antipathy toward medieval theologians, never explicitly cites any other sources from the period, despite the fact that Steinmetz, Moore, John D. Rempel, and Mabry[72] have amply demonstrated his reliance upon realists Anselm and Aquinas, the Old Franciscans Alexander of Hales and Bonaventure, and nominalists Occam, Gregory of Rimini, and Gabriel Biel, a direct endorsement of Bernard (at least concerning his spirituality) from the radical's pen acquires decisive significance and becomes a necessary starting-point for the present study.

Requiring far greater comparison of the Hubmaier corpus with Bernard, however, is the second question, which constitutes the nucleus of the second chapter. Here several background observations are in order. Of all the Cistercian's treatises, Châtillon points out that *De gratia et libero arbitrio*, with which Luther and Calvin specifically took exception, "always remained the work most frequently cited and most constantly used."[73] Taking into account, furthermore, the strikingly similar trichotomous anthropologies of Bernard and Hubmaier, one wonders if the latter may have been influenced by the former. The plausibility of this hypothesis increases after reflecting on the inference by Rempel as to the origin of the radical's theological *sine qua non*, which departed from anything common to the Magisterial Reformers:

> Hubmaier built his theology on medieval anthropological motifs different from those held by the magisterial reformers. His beliefs about human nature stand in especially sharp contrast to those of Luther and Calvin. From the vantage point of his older anthropology, Hubmaier was convinced that belief in both the bondage of the will and predesti-

71. Bernard of Clairvaux, "On the Second Baptism," in *Sermons for the Seasons and Principal Festivals of the Year*, trans. by a priest of Mount Melleray (Westminster, Md.: Carroll Press, 1950), 422-24.

72. David C. Steinmetz, *Reformers in the Wings* (Grand Rapids, Mich.: Baker, 1971), 199-200; Moore, "Catholic Teacher and Anabaptist Pupil," 70-71, 87-93; John D. Rempel, *The Lord's Supper in Anabaptism* (Scottdale, Pa.: Herald Press, 1993), 43-47; Mabry, *Doctrine of the Church*, 5-8.

73. "Le *De gratia et libero arbitrio* . . . reste toujours l'ouvrage le plus fréquemment cite et le plus constamment utilisé." Châtillon, "L'influence de S. Bernard," 280-81.

nation violates the biblical picture of the human will and undermines human responsibility before God.[74]

In spite of this historical trajectory, Rempel not only pleads ignorance as to a particular medieval theologian who formulated the salient anthropology in general and dogmatic motifs in particular, but even goes so far as to both insinuate that such an originator cannot be identified, and to disparage any attempts at recovering this figure: "Nothing of Hubmaier's tripartite views can be found . . . [this] should be accepted as a caution against trying to identify Hubmaier completely with any one theology or trying to locate all his notions in the writings of known theologians."[75] The reason for what otherwise appears to be special pleading on Rempel's part, especially given his narrowing down the time period of theological origin, is suggested by Moore: "Whatever the source of this anthropology, it certainly did not come from Eck, whose analysis of human nature is within the mainstream of the medieval theological tradition."[76] Since Eck represents the most common medieval perspective on humanity, namely, that due to the effect of original sin, women and men cannot reach God on the basis of their unaided natural powers (hence God must provide them with prevenient but only extrinsically efficacious grace with which their free wills may choose to either cooperate or thwart), the tripartite anthropology is apparently as anomalous in the medieval era as in the early modern period.[77] Taken together, the aforementioned data point to Bernard as the prime candidate for the source of Hubmaier's doctrinal model of humanity. This possibility, coupled with the previously undisclosed yet almost exact resemblance of many statements in *Eine christliche Lehrtafel, Von der Freiheit des Willens,* and *Das andere Büchlein von der Freiwilligkeit des Menschen* with those of *De gratia,* to the point where one may well be able to account for the former's German as a translation of the latter's Latin, advances the hypothesis, I will contend in chapter two, to quite plausible.

In view of the fact, moreover, that Hubmaier overtly appropriated ideas from "On the Second Baptism," a number of even more fundamental and intriguing questions arise. Might Hubmaier at one time have believed, on the basis of Bernard, that his ordination served as the vehicle which remitted the

74. Rempel, *Lord's Supper,* 45.
75. Ibid., 43.
76. Moore, "Catholic Teacher and Anabaptist Pupil," 93.
77. The prevalence of the former view (and variations within its framework) is noted by Heiko Oberman, *The Harvest of Medieval Theology* (Cambridge, Mass.: Harvard University Press, 1963), 57-67, while the latter does not appear in Oberman's survey.

actual sins committed after his infant baptism? As Bernard informs the Abbot of Coulombs in *On Precept and Dispensation*, composed contemporaneously with and quoting verbatim from his sermon,

> [Religious profession] restores the divine image in the soul and makes us Christlike, much as baptism does. It is also like another baptism in that we mortify the earthly side of our nature and again put on the Lord Jesus Christ. . . . being now delivered, not from the darkness of original sin, but from the denser darkness of many actual sins.[78]

Further, this quotation points to the unique salvific role of holy orders in Bernard's *ordo salutis*.[79] Is it possible, then, that Hubmaier, following his rebaptism, substituted Bernard's figuratively rebaptismal sacrament of ordination, in which the initiate leaves a natural Christian community to enter a voluntary one, with a newly conceived and literally rebaptismal sacrament of believers' baptism, in which a similar transition occurs?[80] If so, precisely what role does believers' baptism play in the salvific process? Does salvation, for Hubmaier, depend upon freely choosing to enter an intentional Christian community?[81] Although these and similar issues will be addressed

---

78. Bernard of Clairvaux, *On Precept and Dispensation*, trans. Conrad Greenia, in *The Works of Bernard of Clairvaux*, Vol. 1, Treatises 1 (Spencer, Mass.: Cistercian Publications, 1970), 144; Bernard, "Second Baptism," 424.

79. Gillian Rosemary Evans, *Bernard of Clairvaux* (Oxford: Oxford University Press, 2000), 99-100; Peter Dinzelbacher, *Bernhard von Clairvaux* (Darmstadt: Primus Verlag, 1998), 60-61.

80. Although it may not be the case that believers' baptism literally replaces ordination on a theological level, since the former implies the invalidity of infant baptism while the latter complements it, it seems to me that for Hubmaier, believers' baptism serves as a functional equivalent for ordination, just as his newly instituted ceremony of child dedication (to be discussed in chapter three) serves as a functional equivalent for infant baptism. On the level of *praxis*, then, believers' baptism complemented child dedication at Hubmaier's Waldshut and Nikolsburg communities in a similar way that ordination complemented infant baptism at the medieval monastery.

81. The notion that salvation (or its analogue) is linked with joining a voluntary religious community, in the way that I am suggesting for Hubmaier, has been given considerable sociological analysis by James Luther Adams; see his *Voluntary Associations: Socio-Cultural Analyses and Theological Interpretation* (Chicago: Exploration Press, 1986), 171-200 and *An Examined Faith: Social Context and Religious Commitment* (Boston: Beacon Press, 1991), 104-06, 308-10.

in chapters three and four, one provocative quotation from the 1526 Hubmaier will whet the reader's appetite.

> Christian water baptism . . . is the right baptismal vow, above which none can be higher; and if we had followed it until now and had employed it in the churches, then the vows and duties of all monks, priests, and nuns would have been unnecessary. But since the right Christian baptismal duty has been pushed out of the middle, Satan has imposed himself with his cloister duties.[82]

One immediately wonders if this denigration of the sacrament of ordination may be rooted in what the rebaptizer perceived as a false confidence placed, perhaps on the authority of Bernard, in his own orders to wash away his personal sins. Such evidence furnishes us with a glimpse of the answer to our initial question: did Hubmaier formulate a genuine sacramental theology; that is to say, were baptism and the Eucharist envisaged by him as grace-conveying sacraments? In the fourth and fifth chapters we will see that he indeed conceived of baptism and the Eucharist in this way, thereby warranting his dismissal from the Anabaptist camp.

Hubmaier's Sacramental Theology: The Keys to the Kingdom of Heaven

Already famous throughout South Germany as a spellbinding preacher, in January 1516 Hubmaier accepted the invitation to become *Domprediger* (Chief Preacher) at the Cathedral in Regensburg. In contradistinction to his later philo-Semitism, the prestigious pastor led the battle of the Catholic citizens against the Jews in the city. After Hubmaier stirred up the City Council, the Jews were driven out of town entirely, and their synagogue was transformed into a Christian chapel dedicated *zur Schönen Maria* (to the beautiful Mary), where countless miracles allegedly transpired.[83] When great revenue

---

82. "Christenlichen Wassertauff . . . ist die recht Tauffglübd, vber wölhe kain höhere sein mag, vnnd wo wir der weren bißher nachgangen vnnd hettends recht gebraucht inn der kirchen, so werent für war all München, pfaffen vnnd Nonnen glübdenn vnnd pflichten schon vnnderwegen bliben. Da aber die recht Christenlich Tauffpflicht auß dem mittel gestossen ward, da selbs hat sich der Satan mit seinen kloster pflichten eingetrungen." Balthasar Hubmaier, *Ein Gespräch auf Zwinglis Taufbüchlein*, in Westin and Bergsten, *Schriften*, 187-88.

83. Before the City Council on 16 September 1519, Hubmaier testified to fifty-four miracles performed at the shrine, and portrayed great favor toward the

generated by hundreds and thousands of religious pilgrims visiting the new shrine roused the jealousy of the Dominicans, who had for three centuries been accustomed to receiving the lion's share of surplus wealth from the faithful, Hubmaier departed from Regensburg in an effort to forestall conflict. Amidst great fanfare from the populace and city council, the latter of which gave him a parting gift of forty gulden, Hubmaier left Regensburg and relocated at picturesque Waldshut on the Rhine.[84] At this time, however, a tremendous change started to blossom in the theological views of the new Bishop of Waldshut,[85] as he read Luther's 1519 sermons on the sacraments. Indeed, Mabry has suggested that among the "Anabaptists, perhaps no one was more influenced by the writings of Luther than Hubmaier,"[86] who embraced the Wittenberger's notion (at that moment in time) on the necessity of personal faith for valid reception of the sacraments. Hubmaier grew fond of quoting the following similes from article seventeen of Luther's homily on the Mass: "Baptism and the Supper mean nothing without previous faith—they are like a sheath without a knife, a case without a gem, a hoop before an inn without wine."[87] In the same year Luther also taught that infant baptism should, therefore, be disallowed, as the sacraments must not be received apart from faith; to do so would not only make a mockery of baptism itself, but would also result in the greater harm of the recipient.[88] It can be

---

pilgrimages. It should be noted that the radical, while questioned about these events in 1525 and 1528, neither denied the veridicality of the miracles nor disapproved of the pilgrimages.

84. Vedder, *Hübmaier*, 50.

85. Hubmaier was appointed Bishop of Waldshut in 1519. It should be emphasized that he did not disclaim this Catholic position upon embracing the Reformation. Moreover, in 1526, after being tortured by Zwingli in the Zurich *Wasserturm*, Hubmaier succeeded his retiring confidant Martin Göschl (both of whom, notwithstanding Catholic regulations of the bishopric, were married) as Bishop of Nikolsburg.

86. Mabry, *Doctrine of the Church*, 32.

87. "Tauff und das Nachtmal nichts sollent on vorgeenden glauben: Sy seyend wie ain schaid on ein messer, wie ain futteral on ein klaynott, wie ainn rayff vor dem wirtshauß on wein." Martin Luther, "Ein Sermon von dem neuen Testament, das ist von der heiligen Messe," in *Luthers Werke*, 6:363. Quoted verbatim repeatedly in the *Hubmaier Schriften*: for an example from the reformer's Waldshut period see Balthasar Hubmaier, *Eine Summe eines ganzen christlichen Lebens*, in Westin and Bergsten, *Schriften*, 114; and for another from his Nikolsburg period see Balthasar Hubmaier, *Der uralten und gar neuen Lehrer Urteil, Ausgabe* II, in Westin and Bergsten, *Schriften*, 233.

88. Martin Luther, *Werke*, 7:693.

ascertained, moreover, from a careful examination of three extant letters to his humanist friends of Regensburg days, Wolfgang Rychard, Beatus Rhenanus, and Johann Adelphi, that by 1521 Hubmaier was quite fascinated by Luther's hermeneutical principle of *sola scriptura* plus faithful reason,[89] which sparked his own systematic study of Erasmus' recently published *Greek New Testament*, particularly the Pauline epistles.[90] Hubmaier's adoption of such a theory of religious knowledge, which enabled Luther to recognize the classic creeds of Christendom as authoritative, elicits the question of whether the Waldshut reformer also embraced the authority of the Nicene Creed and Chalcedonian Definition, and if so, why he accepted these statements stemming from the Church Fathers while rejecting the medieval doctors. In other words, did Hubmaier, trying to strip away at least medieval accretions, perceive the goal of reformation as a return to the fifth-century church or the first-century church? Moreover, it is acknowledged that Hubmaier, while still formally styling himself a Lutheran as a sign of gratitude, broke with Luther in 1523.[91] Why did Hubmaier part company from Luther? I propose to address these matters in chapter three, where I will provide a new historical reconstruction of Hubmaier's theological pilgrimage based on the primary sources.

Concerning the first sixteenth-century believers' baptism, placed by the current scholarly chronology in Zurich on 21 January 1525, it can be shown, as I will argue in the third chapter, that Hubmaier both deemed infant baptism as unscriptural and practiced the baptism of those who professed faith long before Zwingli's radical followers. Since these changes apparently took

---

89. Expressed fully, Luther held that the sole source of truth is the Word of God as revealed in Scripture alone plus clear reason or rationality; this latter hermeneutical principle was necessary to defend the consistency of Scripture as well as the doctrine of the Trinity (Luther argued that by sound reason, the conclusions of the Nicene Creed can be derived from the biblical premises that there is only one God, the Father is God, the Son is God, the Holy Spirit is God, and that the three persons are distinct). See Luther, *Bondage of the Will*, 18:616 and Brian Albert Gerrish, *Grace and Reason* (Oxford: Clarendon Press, 1962), 168-71.

90. Balthasar Hubmaier, *Letter to Wolfgang Rychard*, in Johann Georg Schelhorn, Sr., *Acta Historico-Ecclesiastica Saeculi* XV & XVI (Ulm, 1738), 118-20; Balthasar Hubmaier, *Letter to Beatus Rhenanus*, in A. Horawitz and K. Hartfelder, *Briefwechsel des Beatus Rhenanus* (Leipzig, 1886), 263; Balthasar Hubmaier, *Letter to Johannes Adelphi*, in Geary Vessenmeyer, *Über Balthasar Hubmör, einen der berühmstesten Wiedertäufer zur Zeit der Reformation—Kirchenhist. Archiv 4* (Halle, 1826), 232-34.

91. Bergsten, *Hubmaier*, 103.

place as a result of reading the early Luther, a further enigma surrounds whether and to what extent Hubmaier's baptismal theology was influenced by the Wittenberg reformer's pivotal 1520 tracts, especially *The Babylonian Captivity of the Church*. Suffice it to reassert here that, contrary to widespread belief, Hubmaier certainly regarded baptism and the Eucharist as sacraments. In particular, the Waldshut reformer maintained that the sacraments formally consist in the sacred promises rather than the signs accompanying them: "Not the water, bread, or wine, but the baptismal vow or the pledge of love [in the Supper] is really and truly a sacrament."[92] Such a distinction is strikingly reminiscent of that made by Luther in the *Babylonian Captivity*:

> The mass or sacrament is Christ's testament, [which] is a promise made by a man in view of his death . . . the death of the Son of God. . . . In the mass, the greatest promise of all, Christ adds a sign as a memorial of this great promise, his own body and blood in the bread and wine, when he says: "This do in remembrance of me." So, at baptism, he adds the sign of immersion in the water to the words of the promise. From these instances we learn that . . . God presents two things to us, a word and a sign . . . [where] the merely outward sign is incomparably less important than the thing symbolized.[93]

Lest it be objected that he may have understood the pivotal term in a non-salvific way, thus sharing the belief of the Swiss Brethren, Hubmaier proceeded at the October 1523 Second Zurich Disputation, in direct opposition to Grebel and Manz, to define "sacrament" as "an outward, visible sign and seal through which we are completely assured of the forgiveness of our sins."[94] Although Luther and Hubmaier, then, agreed on what the controversial "power of the keys" pericope in Matthew 16:16-19 could not signify, they disagreed on exactly what it did signify. In order to avert the looming threat of particularly papal and generally Roman authority, both employed the standard argument juxtaposing the masculine singular Πέτρος (Peter)

92. "Nit das Wasser, brot oder wein, sonder die Tauffglübd oder Liebepflicht aigentlich vnd recht ist ein Sacrament." Balthasar Hubmaier, *Eine Form zu taufen*, in Westin and Bergsten, *Schriften*, 352.

93. Martin Luther, *The Babylonian Captivity of the Church*, in *Luther's Works*, 36:36, 49, 55.

94. "Ein Sacrament ist . . . ein ußwendig, sichtbarlich warzeychen und sigill, durch das wir gentzlich vergwüßt werden den verzyhung unserer sünde." The transcript of the Second Zurich Disputation is preserved in Emil Egli and Georg Finsler, *Huldreich Zwingli Sämtliche Werke* (Leipzig: M. Heinius Nachfolger, 1908), 2:786.

with the feminine singular πέτρα (rock) to insist that Peter's confession of faith that Jesus was the Christ, not Peter himself, constituted the antecedent of "rock." Luther would concur with the radical's following exegesis of the 1516 *Greek New Testament*: "Christ says, 'You are Peter, and on this rock (in other words, that which you confess) I will build my church'. . . . the Christian church [is] built . . . on the oral confession of faith that Jesus is the Christ, the Son of the living God."[95] However, both articulated quite dissimilar positions on the identity of the keys. For Luther, the keys denote the respective powers of the entire Christian community (not simply the clergy, in accordance with his doctrine of the priesthood of all believers) to pronounce the forgiveness and retention of sin.[96] Among Hubmaier's most creative reformulations of sacramental theology, by contrast, was his equation of the two sacraments, in my assessment, as the two keys[97] to the entrance and exit doors to the kingdom of heaven, where each door represents a distinct stage of ecclesiastical discipline. While such an idea will be fully developed in the fourth and fifth chapters treating the sacrament of believers' baptism, the doors of discipline, and "the sacrament of the altar" (das Sacrament des Alltars),[98] the reader may be fascinated by one of many telling passages analyzed therein: "In water baptism the church employs the key of admitting and loosing, but in the Supper the key of excluding, binding, and locking up, as Christ promises and gives to it the power of the forgiveness of sins."[99] From this it follows that the sacraments, for Hubmaier, effect forgiveness and therefore serve in some way as means of grace.

---

95. "Sagt Christus: Du bist Petrus, ein falser, vnd auff den felsen, (verstee, den du bekennest) wird ich bauen mein Kirchen. . . . die Christenlich Kirch gebaut . . . auff die mündlichen bekantnuß des Glaubens, das Jesus seye Christus, ein Son des lebendigen Gottes." Hubmaier, *Eine christliche Lehrtafel*, 315-16; Luther makes the Πέτρος-πέτρα argument in his *Sermon on Matthew 16*, in *Luther's Works*, 7:281-82.

96. Luther, *Babylonian Captivity*, 36:92.

97. The fixing of the number of keys at two hearkens back to the Scholastics, with whom Hubmaier was intimately acquainted; see Thomas Aquinas, *Summa Theologica*, 5 vols. (Westminster, Md.: Christian Classics, 1981), 5:2614-20.

98. Hubmaier, *Ein einfältiger Unterricht*, 290.

99. "In disem Wassertauff braucht die Kirch den schlüssel der einlassung vnnd auff lösung, jn dem Nachtmal aber den schlüssel der außschliessung, bindung vnnd versperrung, wie jr denn Christus den gwalt der verzeyhung der sinden verhayssen vnd geben." Hubmaier, *Gespräch auf Zwinglis Taufbüchlein*, 171-72.

Not only did Hubmaier regard the Eucharist as the sacred container of an invisible grace, but he also devised, as I illustrate in the fifth chapter, an original and radically incarnationist doctrine of the real presence of Christ. Contra the hypothesis of Rempel that the reformer propounded the belief, based on an Antiochene Christology, that "with the departure of the incarnate Christ from the world, the second person of the Trinity is . . . absent from the Lord's Supper. . . . Jesus instituted the Lord's Supper not as the promise of his presence when his disciples broke bread in his name but as a commemoration of his absence,"[100] Hubmaier explicitly rejected this Christology along with all its logical corollaries. As a matter of fact, and flying in the face of his "dear brethren," Hubmaier castigated any tropistic exegesis of the words of institution and explicitly denounced the sacramentarianism of Zwingli, with which all other rebaptizers agreed:

> The others employ the little word *est* for *significat*, that is, *is* for *signifies*, so that: "The bread signifies my body." Such an opinion can never be forced with clear and proper Scriptures. . . . [it] is too outlandish, strange, and circumlocutory. It fails to satisfy the human conscience; it gives more cause for erring and confusing the whole Bible than to satisfying or overcoming the opponents. For if this is the practice, then no one would be sure where *est* (is) stands in the Scripture for *significat* (signifies) or for itself. . . . So I would maintain just with identical authority and identical arguments that this bread must be the body of Christ, and therefore *is* is taken in the Old Testament for *is*, Genesis 1:3, "God said: Let there be light, and there was light." Similarly in the New Testament: "And the Word became flesh," John 1. Hence in this passage, "This is my body," the *is* must also be used in this way.[101]

---

100. Rempel, *Lord's Supper*, 66.
101. "Die andern brauchent das wörtlin Est für significat, das ist (Jst) für bedeütet, also: dz brot bedeüt den leib mein. Wölche Opinion nymmer mer mit klaren vnnd ordenlichen Schriften mag erzwungen. . . . ist zů außlendisch, frembd vnnd zu weytschwayffig, thut nit gnůg der gwyssen des menschens, gibt mer vrsach zů jrren vnnd zů verwirren die gantzen Bibel, denn zů befriden oder zů überwinden die widersprecher. Denn wo es also zůgienge, were doch niemant sicher, wo (Est, ist) für (Significat, bedeütt) steende in der schrifft oder für sich selber. . . . So wolt ich auch eben auß gleichem gwalt vnd Argumenten erhalten, das diß Brot der Leib Christi sein můst, vnd also (Jst) wirt genommen im alten Testament für Jst, Gen. 1. Got hat gesagt, Es werde ein liecht, vnd es ist ein leicht worden. Deßgleich im Newen Testament: Vnd das wort ist: fleysch worden, Joa. C. 1. Darumb můß in diser red, Das ist der leib mein, das (Jst) auch also gebraucht werden." Hubmaier, *Ein einfältiger Unterricht*, 291-92.

Despite Hubmaier's adherence, following his realist forebears, to an Alexandrian Christology, this theological maverick, by the same token, repudiated both the Roman and the Lutheran doctrinal inferences from it. In order to prevent his flock from "falling into the ditch with the blind leaders,"[102] Hubmaier first denies transubstantiation and then consubstantiation: "One must not toy with the Scriptures so arrogantly . . . that the bread is essentially transformed into the flesh through the words and the wine essentially into the blood. . . . [or] that the flesh and blood are hidden under the forms of bread and wine."[103] Several intriguing questions, to which I will return in chapter five, spring in Hubmaier's treatises from this discussion. How, in light of the *communicatio idiomatum*, does the ubiquity of the ascended Christ's divine nature transfer over to his human nature? Does Hubmaier draw the early Scholastic (pre-1215) distinction between the definitive presence of the Logos' humanity outside space and time and the repletive presence of that same humanity completely filling the universe? If so, how do Christians partake of, or even more radically, possibly become the physical body of Jesus in a literal sense and manifest within themselves a historical continuation of the Incarnation? On the condition that Hubmaier fashioned such a model, the church in general and the ethical conduct of its members in particular assume a paramount importance, which must be supervised in the administration of the sacraments, such administration serving as a vehicle to effective church discipline.

Ecclesiology and the Power of the Sacramental Keys

The importance of the power of the keys in Hubmaier's ecclesiology discloses itself in his elucidation of the statement in the Apostles' Creed regarding the church: "I believe and confess publicly . . . that whomever the Christian church so looses on earth, the same is also assuredly loosed and freed from his sins in the heavens. On the contrary, whomever the church . . . excludes from her fellowship on earth, the same is also bound before God in the heavens."[104] This notion is consistent with the late medie-

---

102. "also blinde mitt sambt dem Blinnden fierer in die grûben falle." Ibid., 291.

103. "Aber es gilt nit also mit der schrifft gaylen . . . das Brot werde wesentlich verwandelt in das fleysch durch die wort, vnd der wein wesenlich in das blût. . . . sunder vnder den gstalten des Brots vnd weins sey fleysch vnd blût verborgen." Ibid., 290, 292.

104. "Glaub vnd bekhenne ich offenntlich . . . das wôhlen die Christenlich Kirch also aufflôse auff erden, das derselb gwißlich auffgelôset, vnd von seinen

val Augustinianism of the Franciscan school, which formed, as recently demonstrated by Mabry, the brand of theology taught to Hubmaier in his baccalaureate and masters training at the University of Freiburg.[105] Its systematic categories, developed from the late thought of Augustine from the syncretism of Thomas Aquinas, modified to some extent by the *Via Moderna*, and finally reinterpreted through the more traditional lenses of the *Via Antiqua*, were assimilated into a coherent schema revolving around the axis of the catholic church as the visible society of baptized subjects under the oversight of the ecclesial hierarchy.[106] Several vestiges of this methodology persisted in Hubmaier's ecclesiological development, as intimated by his appropriation of both similar terms and the similar meanings assigned to them. Just as, for example, the medieval church equaled the tangible *ecclesia Romana*, Hubmaier too pronounces the church to be "a visible assembly" (eine eüsserliche versamlung) constituted of the "physical" (leyblich) body of believers who "had assembled" (versamlet) in one place and "had united" (verainigt) themselves in one common faith.[107] Whereas the church is made up of several local congregations, they coagulate, as affirmed by the Niceno-Constantinopolitan Creed, "in one God, in one Lord, in one faith, and in one baptism" (in einem gott, in aynem herren, in ainem glauben vnd in ainem tauff).[108] Employing the medieval ecclesiological "mother-daughter" analogy, Hubmaier deems the separate parishes as but "the daughters" (die töchter) of "the universal church, their mother" (die allgmain Kirch ir mûter); remarkably, moreover, while the former may err, the latter was in Hubmaier's estimation infallible and distributes her power to her daughters insofar as they act according to the new law of Christ.[109] Accordingly, Hubmaier allocates to the church a "shepherding" function as the pillar of truth where the faithful gather, quoting (but refusing to credit) Aquinas, "for teaching, for baptism, and for the Lord's Supper" (in der leer, im Tauff und

---

sünden entbunden sey, auch in den himelen. Herwiderumb wöhlen die Kirch . . . auß irer gmainschafft auß schliesse auff erden, das derselb auch gebunden sey vor Got in den himeln." Balthasar Hubmaier, *Die zwölf Artikel des christlichen Glaubens*, in Westin and Bergsten, *Schriften*, 219.

105. Mabry, *Doctrine of the Church*, 6-12.

106. Henry Marrou, *St. Augustine and His Influence Through the Ages*, trans. Patrich Hepburne-Scott (New York: Harper Torchbooks, 1957), 83-95; Seeberg, *History of Doctrine*, 185; Sachsse, *Hubmaier als Theologe*, 120-30; Windhorst, *Täuferisches Taufverständnis*, 16-18.

107. Hubmaier, *Eine christliche Lehrtafel*, 315.

108. Ibid.

109. Ibid.

Nachtmal),[110] since it is by obedience to the commands of Christ and participation in the sacraments that believers are strengthened.[111] Appropriating language quite similar to medieval theologians, Hubmaier perceived the church as "the communion of saints" (die gemainschafft der heiligen)[112] and supplemented this concept by attaching to it a powerfully ethical dimension which bears resemblances to the medieval penitential system. Like the medieval conception of the *communio sanctorum*, which partook of the sanctifying and actual grace of the sacraments, Hubmaier insisted upon a moral transformation into a communion of regenerated believers progressing toward sainthood. For Hubmaier, then, not only did the oft-quoted dictum of Cyprian, "outside the church there is no salvation" (extra ecclesiam nulla salus),[113] imply that one outside the church lacked access to the sacramental means of salvation, but it also entailed that one's sanctification could not be sustained apart from the church, for the saints need discipline from their "mother" (mûtter) in order to maintain holy lives.[114] Upon the evaluation of the sacramental enforcement of discipline in chapter five, we must investigate what disciplinary procedures and structures were instituted in Hubmaier's Waldshut and Nikolsburg and how they compare to the strategies employed by those typically classed as sixteenth-century Anabaptists.

Foreshadowing Calvin's famous warning that "discipline is the sinews of the church" (disciplina nervus ecclesiae) necessary for preventing its downfall,[115] Hubmaier exclaimed that where fraternal admonition fails to be administered, "there is definitely also no church, even if water baptism and the Supper of Christ are kept."[116] Hubmaier differentiated between public sin "committed shamelessly before all people" and secret sin "committed in

---

110. Ibid; Aquinas, *Summa Theologica*, 5:2439.

111. Hubmaier, *Gespräch auf Zwinglis Taufbüchlein*, 176.

112. Hubmaier, *Eine christliche Lehrtafel*, 315.

113. Hubmaier, *Bann*, 339; Cyprian, *The Letters of St. Cyprian of Carthage* (New York: Newman Press, 1984), 72:21.

114. The reformer asserts, "Where [church discipline] is not instituted and used according to the orderly and earnest command of Christ, there nothing reigns but sin, scandal, and vice" (Wo der selb nit auffgericht vnd gebraucht wirdt nach dem ordenlichen vnd ernstlichen beuelh Christi, da selbs regiert nichts denn sünd, schand vnd laster). Hubmaier, *Bann*, 367.

115. Calvin, *Institutes*, 4.12.1.

116. "Da ist gewißlich auch khain Kirch, ob schon der Wassertauff vnd das Nachtmal Christj daselbs gehaltenn werdent." Hubmaier, *Strafe*, 338.

stillness and hiddenness,"[117] where instances of the former must be publicly reprimanded, lest the church be scandalized, while the latter should be reproved privately according to Matthew 18:15-20. After repeated attempts had been made without success to convince a backsliding sheep to return to the fold, the miscreant suffered the ban; however, contrary to mainstream Anabaptism, the banned member was not excommunicated from the sect but excluded from the Eucharist. Unlike the usual Anabaptist practice of shunning the banned member as one who was totally given over to the devil, and on the other end of the spectrum from the Dutch Mennonite policies forbidding marital relations between a banned and faithful spouse and demanding the split of their families through divorce, Hubmaier insisted that the banned person be treated humanely and not denied physical needs.[118] Hence a hallmark of Calvin as well as Hubmaier is the antithetical relationship of the Lord's Supper and the excluding stage of church discipline; Calvin in my judgment clearly implies[119] and Hubmaier explicitly asserts, that participation in the intimate meal of the Eucharist, which denotes a moral community, comprises for the former the best approximation, and for the latter the exact representation, of the visible church. The Waldshut reformer, unlike other rebaptizers who in the opinion of many scholars are more than a little suspect (at least implicitly) of teaching Christian perfectionism,[120] pointed out that one was not banned from the community as a result of sinning but due to perseverance in sin and refusal to turn away from wickedness and back to the congregation. If a lost sheep returns to the fold, the assembly "unlocks for him the heavens and allows him to return to the communion of Christ's Supper."[121] It follows for Hubmaier, therefore, that the church,

---

117. "Offentlich, als die beschehen on alle scham vor den menschen. . . . haimlich, die da in der stille vnd verborgenhait verbracht werdent." Hubmaier, *Strafe*, 341-42.

118. Hubmaier, *Bann*, 373-74.

119. Quite telling is Calvin's exegetical remark on the Pauline account of the Lord's Supper that participation in the sacred meal "contains promises by which consciences may be roused up to an assurance of salvation;" John Calvin, *Commentary on the Epistles of Paul the Apostle to the Corinthians*, trans. John Pringle (Grand Rapids, Mich.: Baker, 1996), 1.11.25.

120. Claus-Peter Clasen, *Anabaptism: A Social History, 1525-1618* (Ithaca, N.Y.: Cornell University Press, 1972), 95, 106-09; Lewis W. Spitz, *The Protestant Reformation, 1517-1559* (St. Louis: Concordia Publishing House, 1985), 155.

121. "schleüsset im auff den himel, vnd last in widerumb khummen zů der Gmainschafft des Nachtmals Christi." Hubmaier, *Eine christliche Lehrtafel*, 317.

which is (perhaps infallibly) guided by the Holy Spirit, truly and intrinsically possesses the power and authority to forgive sins.[122] These glimpses into the organization of the Waldshut and Ingolstadt congregations beckon for a complete elucidation of the ecclesial system devised by Hubmaier as well as an account of its inner workings, both of which will be furnished in chapter six.

The Libertarian Foundation and Its Theological Corollaries

In the sixteenth century, Hubmaier's rejection of infant baptism and practice of believers' baptism provided sufficient grounds for classifying him as an Anabaptist, coupled with its typical negative implications. His enemies, nonetheless, were quickly forced to recognize that they were not debating with an unlearned Anabaptist reactionary, but with an academically trained thinker armed with a sacramental theology grounded upon the doctrine of *Freiheit des Willens* and supplemented by a multiplicity of patristic and medieval constructs. Throughout this study, one underlying subtext will continually resurface: all of Hubmaier's doctrinal and liturgical innovations, such as his Christology, believers' baptism, the Eucharist, and church discipline, comprise corollaries of his tripartite and, as I will argue, Bernardian anthropology. Moreover, a detailed analysis of the reformer's life shows him to be, in terms of his relationship between church and society,[123] closer to Luther, Zwingli, and Calvin than to any Schleitheim-adhering Anabaptists. It is little wonder, then, that both Hubmaier and Eck viewed Hubmaier as a Lutheran rather than an Anabaptist; toward the end of his career the former encouraged his Nikolsburg parish that "we all want to be Christians and good Lutherans" (wir all wöllen Christen vnd gůtt Euangelisch),[124] and the most recently discovered inscription by the latter inside the front cover of a book given by his erstwhile protégé bemoans that Hubmaier "became a Lutheran."[125] The fact that perceived error was being expounded from Catholic

---

122. Hubmaier, *Bann*, 370. If the local church is not infallibly supervised by the Spirit, at least on this point, then it seems to me that the assembly faces the haunting prospect of mistakenly excluding saints as well as sinners.

123. But obviously not in his anthropology, to which Luther and Zwingli were (and Calvin would have) vehemently opposed.

124. Hubmaier, *Strafe*, 340.

125. The book was a 1505 Latin edition of Platina's *Hystoria de vitis pontificum pericundae diligeter recognita* presented to Eck on 18 July 1516 during a rendezvous with Hubmaier at Regensburg *en route* by boat down the Danube to

pulpits first at Waldshut and then in Nikolsburg, both of which lay in Austrian territory, sparked no little disquiet from Ferdinand I[126] and the Imperial Diet, which demanded the extradition of Hubmaier, evocatively, for joining the "Lutheran Sect."[127] Given the pivotal importance of sacramental theology, no less one based on libertarian human freedom, in the early modern period, as well as this reformer's remarkably understudied life, one cannot but agree with Robert Friedmann's verdict concerning the importance and fruitfulness of Hubmaier research grounded in a careful analysis of his primary texts: "And we know that quite a number of valuable [works] are waiting for publication while more are in the working, based on thorough research in original, still so little known sources."[128] The present study aims, therefore, to make a contribution to Hubmaier studies by offering a historical reconstruction of the radical's intellectual journey as well as a critical reassessment of both the anthropological presuppositions and the distinctive conclusions marking out his theological system, which defies standard categorization.

Vienna. See Werner O. Packull, "Balthasar Hubmaier's Gift to John Eck, July 18, 1516," *MQR* 63 (October 1989): 428-32.

126. Ferdinand I, who would claim succession to the Austrian throne in 1526, was at this time Archduke in the Austrian imperial government; see Pelikan, *Reformation*, 318-19.

127. Bergsten, *Hubmaier*, 91.

128. Robert Friedmann, "Recent Literature in the Field of Anabaptism," *Church History* 32 (September 1963): 359. Although Friedmann so commented in 1963, his statement still holds true, as little detailed investigation has been undertaken on the majority of Hubmaier's treatises.

Chapter 2

The Literary Dependence[1] of Balthasar Hubmaier upon Bernard of Clairvaux

From the outset of his ecclesiastical career in 1512 as priest and professor at Ingolstadt to his execution as a seditionist at Vienna in 1528, Hubmaier regarded a correct anthropology as the indispensable doctrinal foundation of all Christian thought.[2] Such a ground, as we shall see, furnished the root from which his Christology and sacramental theology sprang. Rejecting the monergistic late-Augustinian anthropology in favor of a tempered brand of the synergistic *facere quod in se est*, wherein God must, by virtue of the divine-human reciprocal relationship, respond to the person who sufficiently prepares for grace,[3] Hubmaier asserts: "Whoever denies the free will of humans and says it is an empty and vain title in name only and is nothing in itself . . . indeed overturns more than half of the Holy Bible."[4] The first

---

1. "Literary dependence" is a source critical term which means that an author drew upon earlier literature but does not speculate as to precisely how such transmission occurred. Thus, literary dependence does not restrict dependence to the author's having the literature immediately before him or her when composing his or her material—the author may well have read or heard the material at a previous time and then drawn upon notes or recollections of it at a later time.

2. Such has been substantiated through the detailed analyses by Steinmetz and Moore of treatises from the radical's Catholic, Waldshut, and Nikolsburg periods; see Steinmetz, "Scholasticism and Radical Reform," 129-44 and Moore, "Catholic Teacher and Anabaptist Pupil," 79-96.

3. A detailed explication of such an anthropology, which would be embraced by Luther, Zwingli, and Calvin, is provided by Oberman, *Harvest of Medieval Theology*, 57-67.

4. "Welcher vernaynd den freyen willenn des menschens vnnd sagt, wie der selb ein lerer vnd eitler tittl sey von Namen vnd an ן‎m selbß nichts . . . ja er

chapter demonstrated that Hubmaier, as part of his patristic and medieval theological training, read at least one sermon of the twelfth-century monastic reformer Bernard of Clairvaux, provocatively titled "On the Second Baptism," which Hubmaier explicitly cited in his 1526 *Ein einfältiger Unterricht*. Further, I suggested that Hubmaier, well-acquainted with Bernard's available writings, may have derived the broad contours of both his trichotomous anthropology, the source of which has in vain been sought by scholars over the past twenty years, and his doctrine of libertarian free will from Bernard's best known (and most attacked) writing by the sixteenth-century Magisterial Reformers, *De gratia et libero arbitrio.*[5] It is the goal of this chapter, accordingly, to verify the hypothesis of a Hubmaier-Bernard literary connection as probable through a careful comparison of the *corpora* of the latter *vis-à-vis* the former. This is revealed, among other ways, by the twin observations that the logic of Hubmaier's 1527 discourses on human freedom, *Von der Freiheit des Willens* and *Das andere Büchlein von der Freiwilligkeit des Menschen*, follows a Bernardian structure at several points, and that many Hubmaier passages can plausibly be explained as translations or paraphrases of Bernard's Latin into German.

The Parallels between *De gratia* and *Von der Freiheit des Willens*

While Hubmaier composed *Von der Freiheit* toward the close of his ministry, Moore has revealed that the viewpoint defended in this tract constitutes the same position held by Hubmaier throughout the entire course of his theological pilgrimage.[6] Contributing additional evidence in support of this

---

stosst auch zeboden mer denn den halben tail der heyligen Biblen." Hubmaier, *Rechenschaft*, 468.

5. Note that I am not arguing that Hubmaier received these ideas exclusively from Bernard. Whether or not (1) there was a third source (or sources) common to both Bernard and Hubmaier, (2) there existed a figure (or figures) between the twelfth and sixteenth century who mediated Bernardian concepts to Hubmaier, or (3) Hubmaier knew of and relied on those who influenced Bernard (for example, key aspects of Bernard's tripartite anthropology have deep roots in the patristic period; see Jaroslav Pelikan, *The Emergence of the Catholic Tradition (100-600)* [Chicago: University of Chicago Press, 1971], 287-91) remains for further investigation. Rather, I am simply arguing that Hubmaier probably read and drew upon Bernard with regard to the shape of the former's anthropology.

6. Moore, "Catholic Teacher and Anabaptist Pupil," 95.

premise from sources neglected by Moore, the reformer's 1521 letter to the humanist John Sapidus, which Bergsten lauds as singularly affording "a most informative insight into Hubmaier's inner life during his early days in Waldshut,"[7] includes what amounts to a summary or skeletal outline of the stance which was fully enunciated in the 1527 polemics:

> God has created humans with body, soul, and spirit. Before the Fall of Adam, the three substances were free to choose and to do good or evil. After the Fall, the body lost its freedom and its health; and through Adam's disobedience, the spirit was imprisoned. . . . but the soul is sound.[8]

Such a quotation answers in the affirmative the question regarding the constancy of Hubmaier's anthropology as well as refuting the notion that he changed his previously Lutheran-Zwinglian views upon reading Erasmus' *De libero arbitrio* or Denck's *Was Geredt sei* and *Vom Gesetz Gottes*.[9] This is because the epistle to Sapidus antedates by three years Erasmus' 1524 *Diatribe* and was composed five years prior to the 1526 writings of Denck. Moreover, a corroborating piece of evidence indicating Hubmaier's doctrinal independence from Erasmus and Denck appears in *Eine christliche Lehrtafel*. This catechism was published in Nikolsburg two years after the emergence of Erasmus' discourse. Nevertheless, by Hubmaier's own admission it had already (with the exception of the dedication to Martin Göschl and the substitution, in an attempt to favorably predispose the city magistrates to his reformation, of the names Leonard and Hans, the Lords von Lichtenstein, for the standard *Frage und Antwort*), been drawn up and sent to Sebastian Hof-

---

7. "Der Brief an Sapidus gewährt einen aufschlußreichen Einblick in Hubmaiers inneres Leben während seiner ersten Zeit in Waldshut." Bergsten, *Hubmaier*, 99.

8. "Gott ist menschen mit Leib, Seel, vnd Geist gemachet. Vor fal Adams die drei Substanzen frei, gutes oder schlechtes zů wählen waren vnd zů tun. Nach dem fall, der Leib hat seine freyhait vnd seine gesundheit verloren; vnd durch mißachtung Adam, wurde der Geist eingesperrt verwundt vnnd tödlich kranckh worden vnd des tuns gut äußerst unfähiges. Jedoch der Geist dagegen ist auch in vnd nach dem fal aufrichtig. . . . die Seele ist gesund." Balthasar Hubmaier, *Brief an Johannes Sapidus*, in *Täuferakten Elsass* 1 (Gütersloh: Gütersloher Verlagshaus Gerd Mohn, 1955), 40-41.

9. This notion is advocated by Bergsten, *Hubmaier*, 444, Armour, *Anabaptist Baptism*, 24-27, Steinmetz, "Scholasticism and Radical Reform," 137-144, Williams, *Radical Reformation*, 156, and Mabry, *Doctrine of the Church*, 26-30.

meister and John Oecolampadius in August 1524,[10] one month prior to the publication of Erasmus' work.[11] In the *primum exemplum* Hubmaier again gives a synopsis of his doctrine of humanity, at this juncture exegetically painting an introspective Pauline portrait which in turn lends credence to his tripartite configuration of humankind as image of the Trinitarian deity:

---

10. Hubmaier, *Eine ernstliche christliche Erbietung*, in Westin and Bergsten, *Schriften*, 75; Hubmaier, *Letter to Johann Oecolampadius*, in Ernst Staehelin, *Briefe und Akten zum Leben Oekolampads*, 2 vols. (New York: Johnson, 1971), 1:341-43.

11. E. Gordon Rupp, "Introduction: The Erasmian Enigma," in E. Gordon Rupp and A. N. Marlow, eds., *Luther and Erasmus: Free Will and Salvation* (Philadelphia: Westminster, 1969), 11-12. As a matter of fact, the evidence seems in my judgment to suggest that any dependence between Hubmaier and Erasmus points in precisely the opposite direction from that which has heretofore been assumed. For instance, one could make a strong case that Erasmus borrowed characteristic phrases of Hubmaier from two tracts disclosed by Bergsten as enjoying wide circulation (and probably published, as implied by a letter from Zwingli to Oecolampadius) in Erasmus' Basel prior to *De libero arbitrio*. On the title page of Hubmaier's *Axiomata—Schlußreden gegen Eck*, which had incited quite a stir in Basel no later than 13 August 1524, Hubmaier alludes to a metaphor from Lucian: "Theses which the fly Balthasar Pacimontanus, a brother in Christ of Huldrych Zwingli, has proposed to the elephant John Eck at Ingolstadt, to inspect them masterfully" (Axiomata qvae Baldazar Pacimontanvs, Mvsca, Huldrychi Zuinglij in Christo frater, Ioanni Eckio Ingoldstadiensi Elephanto, magistraliter examinanda proposuit), in Westin and Bergsten, *Schriften*, 87. Quite evocatively, Eck opens his subsequent treatise with this query: "Dare Erasmus attack Luther, like the fly the elephant?" (*De libero arbitrio*, 36). Moreover, another Hubmaier slogan, "If I have taught falsely and incorrectly, I call and scream to all Christian believers that they bear witness of the evil and lead me again to the right path . . . for I may be wrong, I am human, but I cannot be a heretic, since I am begging for instruction" (Hab ich vnrecht gelert vnd geirret, so rủff vnd schrye ich zů allen christgleủbigen, dz sy von dem übel zeủgknủß geben, vnd widerumb vff die rechten ban wysen . . . dan irren mag ich, ich bin ein mensch, aber ein ketzer sein mag ich nit, dieweil ich vmb vnderricht anrủffe), popularized in his June 1524 tract *Eine ernstliche christliche Erbietung*, 83, seems to be paraphrased by Erasmus in qualifying any potential error in his arguments: "For even though I believe myself to have mastered Luther's argument, yet I might well be mistaken, and for that reason I play the debater, not the judge; the inquirer, not the dogmatist: ready to learn from anyone if anything truer or more scholarly can be brought" (*De libero arbitrio*, 38).

If one says there is nothing good in humanity, that is stating too much. As Paul also stated too much when he said, I know that nothing good dwells within me. But he hurries to explain this by adding to this assertion: I know that nothing good dwells within me, that is, in my flesh, Rom. 7:18. Similarly all the other Scriptures should be understood which indicate that there is nothing good in humanity, that is, in our flesh, for God's image has never yet been totally obliterated in us. How can it be evil, for (like the law) it shows and teaches us the good. Far be it from us that we would call it evil. For we know that it is holy, makes us righteous, and is totally good. Note the Trinity in those three words. . . . God originally made us good and free in soul, body, and spirit. This goodness and freedom were through Adam's disobedience taken prisoner in our spirit . . . and even corrupted in our flesh . . . [yet] our souls are just as free in themselves to will good or evil as was Adam's soul in Paradise.[12]

Although it is clear from even a cursory comparison of *Das andere Büchlein* and *Diatribe* that the former drew heavily upon the latter, the internal evidence from *Eine christliche Lehrtafel* as well as *Von der Freiheit* reveals absolutely no trace that Hubmaier had yet read Erasmus' tract.[13] In light of the apparent anthropological continuity during the radical's career, therefore, the procedure of demonstrating Hubmaier's literary dependence on Bernard through a comparison of the 1527 work with *De gratia* is justified.

Concerned with the moral laxity exhibited among those whom he considered the antinomian pseudo-followers of Luther, who claimed to adhere faithfully to the gospel, Hubmaier opens *Von der Freiheit* with the following

---

12. "So man sagt, es ist nichts gůts im menschenn, ist es ze vil geredt. Wie auch Paulus ze vil geredt hett, da er sagt: Jch wayß, das nichts gůts in mir wonet. Aber eylents erklert er sich selbs, vnd setzt hin zů disen verstand: Jch waiß, das nichts gůts in mir, das ist, in meinem fleisch, wonet. Ro. 7 [V. 18]. Also sollen auch all ander schrifften, sich drauff ziehende, es sey nichts gůts im menschen, das ist, in seinem fleysch, verstanden werden, denn die Bildung Gottes ist ye noch nit gar in vns auß gwischt, wie kan aber die selb böß sein, die weyl sy vnns (wie das gesatz) gůts weyset vnnd leeret. Haissen wir sy nun böß, das sey ia ferr von vns. Denn wir wissenn, das sy heylig, grechtmachend vnd gantz gůt ist. Nim war der Dreyfaltigkayt in disenn dreyen wortenn. . . . Erstlich hat vnns ye Gott gůtt vnnd frey gemacht an seel, leyb vnnd geyst. Dise gůthayt vnd freyhayt ist vns durch die vngehorsame Adams am Geyst gefangen . . . vnd an dem fleysch gar verderbet worden . . . [noch] vnsere Seelen sind auff heütigen tag . . . gůts vnd böß ze wölln als frey in inen selbs, als die seel Adams im Paradeiß was." Hubmaier, *Eine christliche Lehrtafel*, 322-23.

13. Moore, "Catholic Teacher and Anabaptist Pupil," 72.

lament to the influential royal "protector of the Reformation in Hungary, Bohemia, and Moravia,"[14] Count George of Brandenburg-Ansbach: "Unfortunately I find many people who thus far have learned and understood no more than two points from all the preaching. First, one says: 'We believe; faith saves us.' Then: 'We can do nothing good. God works in us the willing and the performance. We have no free will.'"[15] While this undeniably reflected the doctrinal views of several lay followers of Luther, as criticized in a plethora of Anabaptist works,[16] both Hubmaier's presentation of the conundrum as well as its placement at the beginning of his treatise parallel the similar development by Bernard. He commences his discussion by relating a meeting with a former monk, who embraced (as did those whom Hubmaier criticized) a quasi-late-Augustinian interpretation of several Pauline texts, most notably Romans 9.[17] Such an interpretation, which was based on Augustine's beliefs in both the intrinsic efficacy of God's grace (*i.e.* that it, by reason of logical necessity, accomplishes the divine purpose for which it was bestowed) and the contribution of grace to all good works, held that all good works of humans, as sinful before and after regeneration, are determined by God. Bernard apperceives a central task of his treatise as providing the solution to the following questions:

When I was once speaking, I alluded to God's grace in me, insofar as I recognized myself as being impelled to good by its prevenient action . . . and helped to find perfection. "What role do you play," asked one standing by, "or what reward or honor do you hope for, if God does

14. Bergsten, *Hubmaier*, 459.
15. "Yedoch find ich fast vil volcks, das laider nit mer bißher denn zway stuckh auß allen predigen erlernet hat vnd gefasset. Ains, das man sagt: Wir glauben. Der glaub mach vnns selig. Das ander: Wir mügen nichts güts thon. Got würck in vns das wöllen vnd volbringen. Wir haben kainen freyen willen." Hubmaier, *Von der Freiheit*, 381.
16. For a handful of examples see Sattler, *Schleitheim Confession*, 38; Menno Simons, *Foundation of Christian Doctrine*, in *Complete Writings*, 207-08; Peter Riedeman, *Account of Our Religion, Doctrine and Faith* (London: Hodder and Stoughton, 1950), 91-95; and Dirk Philips, *A Loving Admonition*, in *Enchiridion*, trans. A. B. Kolb and Walter Klaassen (Aylmer, Ont.: Pathway Publishing, 1966), 425-26.
17. I call this interpretation "quasi-late-Augustinian" because, while it is based on premises found in the late Augustine's exegetical work, conclusions are drawn from those premises that Augustine (along with Luther, Zwingli, and Calvin) would not have accepted. For an excellent survey of this development see Marrou, *Augustine and His Influence*, 83-101.

all the work . . . [if] 'he saved us, not because of works done by us in righteousness. . . . [if] without me you can do nothing,' and [if] 'it depends not upon our running or desiring' . . . what role, then, does free will play?"[18]

Hence Hubmaier and Bernard, at the outset of their respective works, acknowledge their concern to refute certain opponents who affirm the all-determining nature of intrinsically efficacious grace. In addition to the analogous content from the two quotes, highly suggestive for the supposition that Hubmaier here paraphrased Bernard are the latter's Latin phrase "sine me nihil potestis facere" (without me you can do nothing) and term "volentis" (desiring), which translated into German respectively become "getrennt von mir könnt ihr nichts Vollbringen" and "Wollen," of which three words (nichts, Vollbringen, and Wollen) reappear in Hubmaier's early modern spelling.[19]

Hubmaier claims, on the basis of an allegorical exegesis of the creation narrative, that "the human being is a corporal and rational creature, created by God as body, spirit, and soul, Gen. 2:7 . . . these three unique and essential components—soul, spirit, and body—are fashioned and united in every human being after the image of the Holy Trinity."[20] He then proceeds to quote the linguistic handles for this trichotomy from a Latin source and then

---

18. "Loquente me coram aliquando, et Dei in me gratiam commendante, quod scilicet ab ipsa me in bono et praeventum agnoscerem . . . et sperarem perficiendum. 'Quid tu ergo,' ait unus ex circumstantibus, 'operaris, aut quid mercedis speras vel praemii, si totum facit Deus . . . salvos nos fecit, non ex operibus iustitiae quae fecimus nos. . . . sine me nihil potestis facere et neque currentis, neque volentis . . . quid igitur agit liberum arbitrium?'" Bernard de Clairvaux, *De gratia et libero arbitrio*, in *Sämtliche Werke lateinisch/deutsch* I (Innsbruck: Tyrolia-Verlag, 1990), 172-74. For accuracy I have carefully compared all my translations from *De gratia et libero arbitrio* with Bernard of Clairvaux, *On Grace and Free Choice*, trans. Daniel O' Donovan (Kalamazoo, Mich.: Cistercian Publications, 1988).

19. Christian Josef Kremer, ed., *Reallexikon für Antike und Christentum*, 15 vols. (Stuttgart: Anton Hiersemann, 2000), 6:1192-94, 7:621, 10:287-89; Benita von Behr, Jutta Bernard, and Kirsten Holzapfel, eds., *Metzler Lexikon Religion*, 4 vols. (Stuttgart: Verlag J. B. Metzler, 2002), 3:663-65.

20. "Der mensch ist ein leibliche vnd vernünfftige Creatur, also an leib, geyst vnd seel von Gott gemachet . . . dise drey sonderlich vnd wesenlich Substantzien Seel, Geist vnnd leib in einem yedlichenn menschen nach der bildung der heiligen dreyainikait gemacht vnd verainigt." Hubmaier, *Von der Freiheit*, 382-83.

translates the terms into German: "These three essential components [are] in Latin: *spiritus, anima, corpus*; in German: *Geist, Seel, Leib.*"[21] Reasoning from Christ's pathos in the Garden of Gethsemane, the radical alleges that each component possesses its own will:

> Christ also made this distinction more than obvious when he said . . . "My soul is distressed beyond measure, unto death. The spirit indeed is willing, but the flesh is weak." That is why the saddened soul of Christ screamed according to the will of the flesh: "My Father, if it is possible, then take this cup from me," but according to the will of the spirit the soul adds, "Nevertheless, not what I want, but as you want."[22]

Employing the same Latin terms quoted by Hubmaier, Bernard argues that between the body, "corpus," and spirit, "spiritus," stands "free choice, or, in other words, human will,"[23] thereafter denominated as "soul": "A perishable body weighs down the soul (lexical form anima)."[24] Moreover, both Bernard and Hubmaier assert that the libertarian power of each will is determined by its own distinct intrinsic freedom. In *De gratia* Bernard lists the respective freedoms of the body, spirit, and soul in an ascending scale, which Hubmaier appears to redraft in his enumeration:

Bernard	Hubmaier
Therefore, there are these three forms . . . freedom from misery, from sin, and from necessity. . . . There is a freedom from misery, about which the Apostle writes: "The creation itself will be liberated from its bondage to	I teach with clear writing the differing divisions of these three wills . . . the will of the flesh, which does not want to suffer; the will of the spirit . . . born in original sin and wrath; and the will of the soul . . . from the beginning is

---

21. "Dise dreÿ wesenlich Substantzien [sind] zů Latein Spiritus, Anima, Corpus. Ze teütsch Geist, Seel, Leib." Hubmaier, *Von der Freiheit*, 382.

22. "Christus hat auch mer denn augenscheinlich disen vnderschid auß getrukt . . . Vber die maß ist betrůbt mein seel, biß in den tod. Der geyst warlich ist berait, aber das fleisch ist schwach. Derhalb schreyet die traurig Seel Christi nach dem willen des fleischs: Mein vater, ist es můglich, so gehe diser kelh von mir. Aber dem Geyst nach setzt die Seel hin zů: Doch nit wie ich will, sonder wie du wilt." Ibid., 383.

23. "corpus . . . spiritus. . . . liberum arbitrium, id est humana voluntas." Bernard, *De gratia*, 232.

24. "Corpus quod corrumpitur, aggravat animam." Ibid., 234.

corruption in the glorious liberty of the children of God," [that no one] in this mortal state would dare arrogate to himself . . . [nor] claim to be free from sin. I maintain that this last form belongs to our natural condition.[25]

totally a divine creation and requires no rebirth.[26]

Following the precise sequence of chapters seven through ten in *De gratia*, Hubmaier proceeds to analyze the state of humanity as it was created, the human condition after the Fall, the importance of conversion, and how the likeness which properly belongs to the threefold divine image is restored through Christ.

In the first of Hubmaier's four divisions entitled "How the Human Being Was before the Fall of Adam" (Wie der mensch gewesen sey vor dem fall Adams), strikingly reminiscent of Bernard's seventh chapter dubbed "Whether Adam in Paradise Had this Threefold Freedom" (Utrum Adam in paradiso trinam hanc libertatem habuerit),[27] Hubmaier maintains, in a manner closely mirroring Bernard, that in the Garden of Eden God created each of the three human faculties with perfect operation of their elemental liberties:

Bernard

It is time to examine what we postponed doing earlier: whether the first human beings in paradise possessed all three of the freedoms, namely, freedom of choice (or from necessity), of counsel (or from sin) and of pleasure (or from sorrow). . . . Humanity re-

Hubmaier

The three substances—flesh, soul, and spirit—were good. The three substances were also totally free to choose good or evil, life or death, heaven or hell. Therefore they were originally made good and free also in the recognition, in the willing, and in the ac-

---

25. "Igitur, triplex sit proposita . . . libertas, a miseria, a peccato, a necessitate. . . . Est libertas a miseria, de qua itidem Apostolus: Et ipsa, inquit, creatura liberabitur a servitute corruptionis in libertatem gloriae filiorum Dei, [nemo] in hac mortalitate praesumit quispiam . . . [nec] vindicat libertatem a peccato. Hanc ultimo loco positam contulit nobis in conditione natura." Ibid., 182-84.

26. "Ich beybringe diser dreyen willen vnderschidliche zertailung mitt heller schrifft . . . den willen des fleischs (das da nit leiden will); den willen des geysts . . . in der erbsünd vnd im zorn geborn; vnd den willen der seelen . . . vor hin von götlicher erschaffung her gantz ist vnd bedarff kainer widergeburt." Hubmaier, *Von der Freiheit des Willens*, in Westin and Bergsten, *Schriften*, 383-84.

27. Ibid., 384; Bernard, *De gratia*, 204.

ceived in its very nature, along with full freedom of choice . . . its freedom of counsel and freedom of pleasure.[28]

complishing of good and evil by God. . . . Scripture clearly and plainly illustrates that the human being originally, in body, soul, and spirit, was given a free will to will and to accomplish good or evil.[29]

While the juxtaposition of choice and necessity along with pleasure and sorrow as opposites runs deep into the soil of patristic anthropology,[30] at this point the contrast between counsel and sin requires further explanation. Bernard defines spirit as the faculty which, prior to the Fall, generated good thoughts and suggested them to the soul; hence humans freely enjoyed the counsel of the honorable spirit. Since this spirit suffered corruption, however, it is now impotent to create virtuous possibilities and to subsequently advise the soul to act upon those possibilities.[31] Therefore, both theologians embraced, while offering similar modifications to, the foundational Christian doctrine that the great spiritual divorce from God occurred in the Fall, as original sin became humanity's anthropological condition and the problem that the race needed to overcome.

In virtually complete concurrence on the soteriological outcome of the Fall for humanity, Bernard and Hubmaier each profess that creaturely disobedience robbed body and spirit of their discrete liberties. Following the lead of the eighth chapter of *De gratia*, where Bernard explains the penalty suffered by the primal couple as a result of original sin, Hubmaier paints in bleakest strokes a dire portrait of the hereditary pain and mortality extending to their posterity:

---

28. "Locus est pervidendi quod supra distulimus, utrum scilicet totas tres illas quas diximus libertates, id est, arbitrii, consilii, complacti. . . . Simul cum plena libertate arbitrii homo in sui conditione accepit . . . consilii libertate et complaciti libertate." Bernard, *De gratia*, 182.

29. "Die drey Substantzien, fleisch, seel vnnd geist gût gewesen. Es waren auch die drey Substanzien ganntz frey, gûts oder böses, leben oder tod, himel oder hellen zû erwölen. Also gût vnd frey seind sy auch in der erkantnuß, im wöllen vnd volbringen des güttens vnd bösens, anfengklich von Got gmacht worden. . . . Die Schrifft zaigt augenscheinlich vnd sichtbarlich an, das der mensch vrsprüngklich an leib, seel vnnd geist eins freyen willens gûts oder böses ze wöllen vnd volbringen gewest." Hubmaier, *Von der Freiheit*, 384-85.

30. These dichotomies were enunciated, among others, by Origen, the early Augustine, and Boethius, as noted by Pelikan, *Emergence of Tradition*, 42-44, 313-14, 337-38.

31. Bernard, *De gratia*, 188-90.

Bernard

Likewise, from being able not to be agitated, he fell to not being able not to be agitated, with the *total loss of its freedom of pleasure.* . . . *Through his sin he became a debtor to death,* so how could he be capable of retaining his freedom of pleasure?[32]

Hubmaier

The flesh has *irrevocably lost its goodness and freedom through the Fall of Adam and has become entirely and wholly worthless and hopeless unto death* . . . starting from the hour that one receives life one begins to die and return to earth. . . . This is why Job curses the day of his birth and so does Jeremiah. For the same reason King David bitterly mourns the day of his conception and birth.[33]

If we translate Bernard's sayings "amissa ex toto complaciti libertate" (total loss of its freedom of pleasure) and "[p]orro per peccatum factus debitor mortis" (through his sin he became a debtor to death) into sixteenth-century German, the procedure yields "hat die Freiheit des Wohlgefallens vollständig verloren" and "er war durch die Sünde zum Schuldner des Todes geworden." These translations are highly analogous to the relevant phrases in Hubmaier, "sein . . . freyhait verloren vnwiderbringlich" (irrevocably lost its goodness) and "durch den fal Adams . . . vnd ist gantz vnnd gar biß in den tod zenichtig vnd hailoß worden" (through the Fall of Adam and has become entirely and wholly worthless and hopeless unto death).[34] Such a striking resemblance renders the thesis of the latter's literary reliance on the former as highly probable.

Proceeding to an equally grim depiction of pneumatic depravity, Bernard remarks that when fellowship with God was broken, humanity lost its natural liberty of spirit, thereby being reduced from the beatific absorption

---

32. "Itemque de posse non turbari in non posse non turbari, *amissa ex toto complaciti libertate.* . . . *Porro per peccatum factus debitor mortis,* quomodo iam retinere valebat libertatem complaciti?" Bernard, *De gratia,* 206.

33. "Das fleisch hat *durch den fal Adams sein gûthait vnnd freyhait verloren vnwiderbringlich, vnd ist gantz vnnd gar biß in den tod zenichtig vnd hailoß worden* . . . fahet an von stund an als bald er das leben vberkummen, wider sterben vnd zû erden werden. . . . Daher verflûcht Hiob den tag seiner geburt vnd Hieremias. Deßgleich bewainet hitzigklich der Khûnig Dauid den tag seiner enntpfengknuß vnd geburt." Hubmaier, *Von der Freiheit,* 385-86.

34. Kremer, *Reallexikon,* 2:542-45, 8:269-80; Behr, Bernard, and Holzapfel, *Lexikon Religion,* 2:336-39, 3:506-09.

of *unio mystica* to *homo diligit se propter se,* the lowest grade of self-love.[35] Hubmaier postulates a similar fate for the human spirit:

Bernard

In totally losing his freedom of counsel, he fell from being able not to sin to *not being able not to sin* [and was] enslaved by his own will to sin, [with] the affection languishing in carnal desires. . . . It is not as easy to climb out of a pit as it is to fall into one. By his will alone, man fell into the pit of sin; but he cannot climb out of his will alone, as now, *even if he wishes he cannot not sin.*[36]

Hubmaier

[The spirit] has through this disobedience of Adam been wounded in the will in such a way and become sick unto death so that it can by itself choose nothing good. Nor can it reject evil since it has lost the knowledge of good and evil. . . . It is *not able or capable of anything other than sin,* striving against God and being the enemy of his commandments.[37]

One is again immediately struck by the similarity of Bernard's (reinterpreted) late-Augustinian phrases "non posse non peccare" (not being able not to sin) and "si velit, non possit non peccare" (even if he wishes he cannot not sin), correspondingly rendered in German "nicht vermögen nicht zu sündigen" and "selbst wenn er wollte, kann est nicht mehr nicht sündigen," and their ostensible conflation into "kan noch vermag nichts denn sünden" (not able or capable of anything other than sin) by the radical.[38] However, in contradistinction to the all-embracing pessimism of the late-Augustinian compatibilist anthropology, revived less than two centuries earlier among

---

35. Bernard, *De gratia,* 204.

36. "Corruit autem de posse non peccare in *non posse non peccare,* amissa ex toto consilii libertate [et fuit] per propriam quippe voluntatem servus factus peccati [cum] affectio circa carnis desideria languens. . . . Non enim tam facile quis valet exire de fovea, quam facile in eam labi. Cecidit sola voluntate homo in foveam peccati; sed non ex voluntate sufficit et posse resurgere, cum iam et *si velit, non possit non peccare.*" Bernard, *De gratia,* 206-08.

37. "ist durch dise vngehorsame des Adams in dem willen dermassen verwundt vnnd tödlich kranckh worden, das sy auch auß ir selbs nichts gûts erwölen kan, noch das böß auß schlagen, wann sy hat die wissenhait böses vnnd gûtes verloren. . . . *kan noch vermag nichts denn sünden,* wider Got streben, vnd seinen gebotten feind sein." Hubmaier, *Von der Freiheit,* 385-86.

38. Heinz Brunotte and Otto Weber, eds., *Evangelisches Kirchenlexikon,* 4 vols. (Göttingen: Vandenhoeck and Ruprecht, 1961), 2:54, 170, 3:1217, 1454-58; Kremer, *Reallexikon,* 9:144-46; Behr, Bernard, and Holzapfel, *Lexikon Religion,* 3:407-08.

scholastic theologians as the keystone of an explanatorily sufficient post-Black Death theodicy,[39] both Bernard and Hubmaier championed a refreshingly uncharacteristic optimism concerning the inherent goodness and inalienable libertarian freedom of the human soul.

Of the three essential attributes of human nature, Bernard and Hubmaier pronounce that the will of the soul is the only faculty emerging intrinsically unscathed from the Fall, although the soul is extrinsically imprisoned in a sorrowful body. In addition, Bernard insists that sinful humans, amazingly to the same degree as God and the angels, enjoy full possession of free choice, a perspective which is echoed by Hubmaier:

Bernard	**Hubmaier**
Neither by sin nor by misery is it lost or decreased; nor is it greater in the just person than in the sinner, nor fuller in the angel than in humanity. . . . Freedom from necessity belongs equally to God and to every rational creature, good or bad.[40]	[The soul] has before, during, and after the Fall remained upright, whole, and good. . . . [and] is happy, willing, and ready to do all good. . . . [as] everything that God wills and does is orderly and good.[41]

At this point, both the twelfth-century and sixteenth-century treatises furnish a precise philosophical definition of this immutable psychological freedom from necessity, in which Hubmaier seems to reiterate in his own words precisely the same sentiments as Bernard:

Bernard	**Hubmaier**
Voluntary consent is a self-regulating habit of the soul [and] a spontaneous inclination of the will. Its action is	Since free will in the human being is nothing other than a power, force, energy, or dexterity of the soul to will or

---

39. Jaroslav Pelikan, *Spirit of Medieval Theology* (Toronto: Pontifical Institute of Mediaeval Studies, 1985), 15-16; F. Donald Logan, *A History of the Church in the Middle Ages* (New York: Routledge, 2002), 288-92.

40. "Nec peccato, nec miseria amittitur vel minuitur; nec maior in iusto est quam in peccatore, nec plenior in angelo quam in homine. . . . Verum libertas a necessitate aeque et indifferenter Deo universaeque, tam malae quam bonae, rationali convenit creaturae." Bernard, *De gratia*, 186.

41. "ist auch vor, in vnnd nach dem fal auffrichtig, gantz vnnd gůt belibenn. . . . [vnd] ist aber frölich, willig vnnd bereyt zů allem gůtten. . . . [als] alles was Gott will vnd thůt, ist ordenlich vnd gůt." Hubmaier, *Von der Freiheit*, 386, 390.

neither coerced nor extorted. It springs from the will and not from necessity, denying or giving itself on no occasion except by means of the will. . . . For the consent of the human will, which is turned by grace toward the good, makes man freely good, and, in the good, free, by the fact that it is voluntarily given and not unwillingly dragged out. Likewise, when it inclines willingly toward the bad, it makes man nonetheless free and spontaneous in the bad. He is not forced to be evil by some other cause, but simply chooses to be so at the request of his own will.[42]

not will something, to choose or flee, to accept or reject good or evil, according to the will of God, or according to the will of the flesh. . . . now no one may scream against Adam or Eve nor excuse or gloss over his sins with Adam's Fall.[43]

For both Bernard and Hubmaier, then, the soul possesses free will. Contra the late-Augustinian view on the bondage of the will adopted by Luther, Zwingli, and Calvin (which held that although the unregenerate soul, just like a bad tree that can only bear bad fruit or bear no fruit at all, lacks the ability to choose between good and evil and instead may only choose to act wickedly or not act at all), freedom for the monastic and Radical reformers was meaningless lest it entailed the ability to choose between opposite moral states. Commenting elsewhere upon Deuteronomy 30:19, wherein Moses, setting before the Israelites "life and death, blessings and curses," exhorted his people to "choose life," Hubmaier encapsulates the aforementioned

---

42. "Est enim habitus animi, liber sui. Siquidem non cogitur, non extorquetur. Est quippe voluntatis, non necessitates, nec negat se, nec praebet cuiquam, nisi ex voluntate. . . . Quomodo namque ad bonum conversus per gratiam humanae voluntatis consensus, eo libere bonum et, in bono, liberum hominem facit, quo voluntarius efficitur, non invitus pertrahitur, sic sponte devolutus in malum, in malo nihilominus tam liberum quam spontaneum constituit, sua utique voluntate ductum, non aliunde coactum ut malus sit." Bernard, *De gratia*, 176, 186.

43. "Seydmal der Frey will nichts anders ist im menschen denn ein macht, gwalt, krafft, geschicklichait der Seelen, etwas ze wöllen oder nit wöllen, ze erwelen oder fliehen, anzenehmen oder zeuerwerffen das gůt oder böß, nach dem willen gottes, oder nach dem willen des fleischs. . . . nun furan nyemant vber den Adam oder Heuam schreyen mag noch seine sünde mit Adams fal entschuldigen vnd bschönen." Hubmaier, *Von der Freiheit*, 393, 396.

point, drawing the corollary that the eternal destiny of all people lies in their own hands:

> See here, Christian reader, how bright and clear this Scripture illustrates that God has freely bestowed upon the human being . . . after the Fall the choice of evil and good, blessing and curse, life and death. Thus even if the whole world said otherwise, heaven and earth would . . . testify openly on the last day before the judgment seat of Christ . . . that not God, but we ourselves, out of free will (auß freyem mûtwillen), are responsible for our sins and eternal damnation.[44]

If such similarity is not telling enough to render likely the dependence of Hubmaier upon Bernard, then let the reader consider that the former, in his elaboration of the Fall, practically quotes the latter's allegorical commentary of Genesis 3. Here Hubmaier sees, according to a *lectio divina*, God as symbolic of the spirit, Eve as symbolic of the flesh, and the soul Adam suspended between the two:

Bernard

Free will stands between flesh and spirit. Between these two, the divine spirit and the fleshly desire, what is termed the free choice of humanity, also known as human will, occupies, so to speak, a middle position. Able to move in either direction, it is, so to speak, on the sloping side of a rather steep mountain.[45]

Hubmaier

The soul stands between the spirit and the flesh, as Adam stood between God, who told him not to eat from the tree of the knowledge of good and evil, and his Eve, who told him to eat from the tree. The soul is now free and is able to follow either the spirit or the flesh.[46]

---

44. "Sihe hie zû, Christenlicher leser, wie haytter vnd klar vns dise Schrifft anzaigt, das Gott dem menschen die waal des bösens vnd gûttens, segens vnd flûchs, des lebens vnd todes . . . nach dem fal frey haimgsetzt hab. Also das ob schon die gantz welt anders sagte, so wûrde doch himel vnd erden wider sy steen vnd am Jûngsten tag vor dem gericht stûl Christi . . . offentliche zeûckhnus geben, das nit Gott, sonder wir selber auß freyem mûtwillen an vnseren sünden vnnd ewiger verdamnûs schuldig seyen." Hubmaier, *Das andere Büchlein*, 406.

45. "*Inter carnem et spiritum medium fore liberum arbitrium.* Inter quem divinum spiritum et carnis appetitum, tenet medium quemdam locum id quod dicitur in homine liberum arbitrium, id est humana voluntas, et tamquam in devexo montis latere admodum ardui inter utrumque pendens." Bernard, *De gratia*, 232.

It should be emphasized that this passage and the trichotomous anthropological division, which the textual evidence also suggests stems from Bernard, constitute the only *loci* in the entire Hubmaier corpus where he breaks from a literal interpretation of Scripture. Such deviation from the radical's exegetical norm is even more remarkable when one considers his public declaration of the following axiom as necessary for all valid hermeneutics: "Whoever wishes to [make an argument], let him . . . do it with German, plain, clear, and unambiguous Scriptures."[47] The discovery of such a parallel dramatically heightens the probability, therefore, that Hubmaier copiously borrowed the terms and concepts from *De gratia* in writing *Von der Freiheit*.

Advancing along Bernardian lines, as developed in chapter nine of *De gratia*, Hubmaier expounds a fourfold *ordo salutis* through which humans respond to God and acquire everlasting life. The first step involves the activity of unregenerate persons prior to hearing the gospel. On the one hand, Hubmaier alleges that humans *post peccatum* cannot will the good, not because their souls are enslaved to concupiscence, as maintained by the radical Augustinians of the medieval period, but because their spirits are debarred from creating good thoughts, rendering their souls unable to discern between right and wrong. Fully consistent with the literary dependence thesis, Bernard depicts this same concept in his analysis of the frustration experienced by unsaved humanity:

Bernard

When someone complains by saying: "I wish I could have a good will, but I am unable" . . . this is because he feels freedom is lacking to him, namely freedom from sin, by which it grieves him that his will is oppressed, but not suppressed. . . . If he finds himself unable simply to will the good, this is

Hubmaier

With our soul after the transgression of Adam, as soon as he ate from the tree of the knowledge of good and evil, from that hour on he lost the taste of the knowledge of good and evil so that he could neither identify nor determine what is right, good, or evil in God's sight, what righteousness is ac-

---

46. "*Die Seel steet zwischen dem Geist vnd dem fleisch,* wie Adam zwischen Gott, der im sagt, er solt von dem holtze der erkantnuß des güttens vnd bösens nit essen, vnd zwischen seiner Heua, die im sagt, er soll von dem holtz essen. Yetz ist die Seel frey vnd mag dem Geyst oder fleisch volgen." Hubmaier, *Von der Freiheit,* 391.

47. "*Was da wölle* [ein argument machen], *das man . . . thüe mit teütschen, hällen, claren, eynfeltigen schrifften.*" Balthasar Hubmaier, *Öffentliche Erbietung,* in Westin and Bergsten, *Schriften,* 106.

an indication that he lacks free counsel, not free choice.[48]

cepted before God, or what works are pleasing to God; all this despite the fact that he would happily do right.[49]

Another pointer to literary dependence resides in the fact that Bernard's equation of the unregenerate human condition with disordered affections, including "*inordinate* love. . . . [and] desire,"[50] is reproduced (precisely as to the conceptual term) by Hubmaier: "His healthy nature and righteous constitution *have been disordered* by sickness."[51] On the other hand, Hubmaier argues that such people can make the *initium fidei* by doing what is in them *ex puris naturalibus*; although they cannot will the good, their souls still possess, by virtue of *Freiheit des Willens*, the ability to "hunger and thirst after righteousness" (hungert vnnd dürstet nach der frombkait).[52] Substantiating the dependence thesis, this quote is a verbatim translation of Bernard's "esuriunt et sitiunt iustitiam" (hunger and thirst after righteousness);[53] elsewhere Bernard identifies such a craving as *homo diligit Deum propter se*, in which humans love God for their own sake, namely, for the good things he gives us.[54] For neither the radical nor monastic reformer, then, does there

---

48. "Quod autem solent homines conqueri, et dicere: 'Volo habere bonam voluntatem, et non possum' . . . plane illa libertate, quae dicitur a peccato, se carere testantur. . . . sentit quidem sibi deesse libertatem, sed profecto libertatem a peccato, quo utique dolet premi, non perimi voluntatem. . . . Quod si velle bonum tantum non poterit, signum est quod ei desit liberum, non arbitrium, sed consilium." Bernard, *De gratia*, 188.

49. "Mit vnserer Seel nach der vbertrettung Ade, das als bald er von dem holtz der erkantnuß des guttens vnd bösens geessen, von stund an hat er verloren den gschmacken der erkantnuß gůttens vnnd bösens, also das er nitt mer waiß oder khan vrtailen, was doch vor Got recht gůt oder böß sey, wöhle frombkait vor Got gelte, oder was werckh gott gefellig seyent, ob er schon gern recht thon wolt." Hubmaier, *Von der Freiheit*, 387.

50. "amore *inordinato*. . . . [et] voluntate." Bernard, *De gratia*, 198.

51. "Das im sein gesunde natur vnnd rechtfertige Complexion durch die kranckhait *verruckt ist*." Hubmaier, *Von der Freiheit*, 387. As shown by Brunotte and Weber (*Kirchenlexikon*, 1:1175-76), *verruckt ist* (have been disordered) is the sixteenth-century German verbal equivalent of the Latin adjective *inordinatus* (inordinate).

52. Hubmaier, *Von der Freiheit*, 388.

53. Bernard, *De gratia*, 202; Brunotte and Weber, *Kirchenlexikon*, 1:1398-99.

54. Bernard de Clairvaux, *De diligendo Deo*, in *Sämtliche Werke lateinisch/deutsch* I (Innsbruck: Tyrolia-Verlag, 1990), 116.

appear to be much soteriological room for the *gratia gratis data*;[55] the power to will the good cannot be extinguished from humanity by virtue of our creation in the *imago Dei*.

Bernard	Hubmaier
The reason why free choice alone suffers no failing or decrease, is that in it, more than in the others, there seems to be imprinted some substantial *image* of the eternal and immutable deity.[56]	Now such a power for willing what is right and good is in us . . . for it is originally from God and his *image*, in which he created us originally.[57]

By virtue of Jesus' new and everlasting covenant with the church, according to Hubmaier, God is obligated to give his grace to those who will fully exercise their own natural powers in turning from sin and toward God. Clearly, then, Hubmaier agrees wholeheartedly with the *facere* doctrine formulated by the fourteenth-century nominalist William of Occam—"facientibus quod in se est deus non denegat gratiam" (to those who do what is in them, God will not deny his grace).[58]

---

55. John R. Sommerfeldt, who wants to guard against the idea that "Bernard is [a] Pelagian or Semi-Pelagian," admits that for Bernard, "the re-formation of humans must begin with the will," and that Bernard delimits any pre-conversion grace to "the gift of God in Jesus [as] the model human being to whom other human beings can conform and be conformed" and the perfect sacrifice for sin (*The Spiritual Teachings of Bernard of Clairvaux* [Kalamazoo, Mich.: Cistercian Publications, 1991], 28); such an assessment is also shared by Wilhelm Hiss, *Die Anthropologie Bernhards von Clairvaux* (Berlin: Walter De Gruyter, 1964), 66-70. Concerning Hubmaier, Steinmetz asserts that "there is no place" in his anthropology "for the *gratia gratis data*" ("Scholasticism and Radical Reform," 143-44), which is echoed by Moore, "Catholic Teacher and Anabaptist Pupil," 91-92.

56. "Hinc est fortassis, quod solum liberum arbitrium sui omnino defectum seu diminutionem non patitur, quod in ipso potissimum aeternae et incommutabilis divinitatis substantiva quaedam *imago* impressa videatur." Bernard, *De gratia*, 212.

57. "Nun yetz ein solhe krafft ze wöllenn was recht vnd gût in vns ist . . . dann sy ist vrspründlich her von Gott, vnd von seiner *Bildung*, in der er vns erstlich erschaffen." Hubmaier, *Von der Freiheit*, 389. Kremer (*Reallexikon*, 1:883) affirms that *Bildung* (image) is the German counterpart to the Latin *imago* (image).

58. William of Occam, *Quaestiones et decisions in IV libros Sententiarum cum Centilogio theologico* (Lugduni, 1495), 2:1.3. In his interpretation of the

Whereas the means of administering God's grace may differ for Bernard and Hubmaier, the resultant state of affairs is precisely the same. Both reformers agree that God must respond to spiritual seekers by supplying them with the opportunity to freely consent to the gospel. For Bernard, the Holy Spirit implants the saving message of Christ within the creaturely spirit, unable in and of itself to generate good thoughts at all, much less recognize the *summum bonum* of the gospel, and graciously confirms its validity by his *testimonium internum.*[59] Influenced by the Lutheran emphasis on the intrinsic power of the spoken Word of God to reawaken the spirit, the radical claims that God unfailingly sends to the sinner a preacher who will proclaim the good news.[60] Either directly through the Spirit or indirectly through the preacher, then, God places all persons longing for his kingdom in a position to make a genuinely free choice between the opposing eternal destinies of salvation through accepting Christ or damnation by rejecting Christ. If the first option is selected, the third step of both *ordines salutis* necessitates God to reciprocate with the grace of regeneration. Bernard summarizes eloquently this synergism of *gratia operans* and *liberum arbitrium*, with which Hubmaier concurs:

Bernard

Perhaps you are asking then: "What role does *free* choice play?" I will respond briefly: it is saved. Take away free choice and there is nothing to be *saved*. Take away grace and there is no means of saving. Without the two combined, this work cannot be done: the one as operative principle, the other as object toward which, or in which, it is accomplished. God is the author of salvation, the free willing faculty

Hubmaier

Here let whoever has ears take notice and hear, that we are made *free* again through the sent Word. . . . Here this old maxim is substantiated: "Person, help yourself; then I will also help you." Indeed God speaks first and *gives* power through his Word. Now the human being can also assist himself through the power of the Word or he can willfully disregard it; that is up to him. That is why one says: God

---

history of the *facere* doctrine, Oberman (*Harvest of Medieval Theology*, 129-45) highlights that although sinners may be certain of God's mercy in granting his grace to those who do what is in them, they possess no certainty that they have in fact done what is in them; apparently, however, this element of doubt was absent from Hubmaier. See Steinmetz, "Scholasticism and Radical Reform," 134-35; Moore, "Catholic Teacher and Anabaptist Pupil," 85-89; Mabry, *Doctrine of the Church*, 21; and McClendon, "Balthasar Hubmaier, Catholic Anabaptist," 31.

59. Bernard, *De gratia*, 240.
60. Hubmaier, *Von der Freiheit*, 388-89.

merely capable of receiving it. No one but God can *give* it, nothing but free choice can receive it. What, therefore, is given by God alone and to free choice alone, can happen no more without the consent of the recipient than without the grace of the bestower. . . . No one is saved unwillingly. God *judges* no one worthy of salvation unless he finds him *wanting* it. . . . Accordingly, free choice is said to cooperate with operating grace in its act of consent, or, in other words, in its order of salvation—since to consent is to be saved.[61]

made you without your help, but he will not *save* you without your help. Because God first created the light, whoever *wants* to accept it will do so based on the commandment of God, but whoever spurns it will fall into darkness due to the just *judgment* of God.[62]

---

61. "'Quid igitur agit ais, *'liberum* arbitrium?' Breviter respondeo: Salvatur. Tolle liberum arbitrium: non erit quod salvetur; tolle gratiam: non erit unde *salvetur.* Opus hoc sine duobus effici non potest: uno a quo fit, altero cui vel in quo fit. Deus auctor salutis est, liberum arbitrium tantum capax: nec *dare* illam nisi Deus, nec capere valet nisi liberum arbitrium. Quod ergo a solo Deo et soli datur libero arbitrio, tam absque consensu esse non potest accipientis, quam absque gratia dantis. . . . Nemo quippe salvatur invitus. Quod Deus neminem *iudicat* salute dignum, nisi quem invenerit *voluntarium.* . . . Et ita gratiae operanti salutem cooperari dicitur liberum arbitrium, dum consenit, hoc est dum salvatur. Consentire enim salvari est." Bernard, *De gratia,* 174-76, 224; my translation borrows several turns of phrase from Bernard, *On Grace and Free Choice,* 54-55.

62. "Hie merckhe vnnd höre wer da orenn hat, das wir durch das gesenndet wort . . . widerumb seind *frey* worden. . . . Hie hat auch statt das gmain sprichwort der allten: Mennsch hilff dir selb, so will ich dir auch helffen. Ja Got redt vor, vnd durch sein wort *gibt* er krafft. Yetz mag im der mennsch durch die krafft des worts auch selbs helffen oder müttwilligklich vnder lassen, das ist im haim gestelt. Daher sagt man: Gott hat dich erschaffen on dich, aber on dich wirdt er dich nit *selig machen.* Wann Gott erschafft ye erstlich das liecht, wer es annemen *will* der mags thon auß der haissung Gottes, wölher das veracht, der felt auß dem *gerechten* vrtail gottes in die finsternuß." Hubmaier, *Von der Freiheit,* 390-91. Note that *frey* is the German equivalent of the Latin *liberum* (Kremer, *Reallexikon,* 2:932); *gibt* is the German counterpart to the Latin *dare* (Kremer, *Reallexikon,* 5:1134); *selig machen* is the sixteenth-century German counterpart to the Latin *salveo* (Brunotte and Weber, *Kirchenlexikon,* 3:928-30); *will* is the German counterpart to the Latin *velle* (Kremer, *Reallexikon,* 11:141); and *gerecht* is the German adjective correlate of the Latin verb *iudicare* (Kremer, *Reallexikon,* 5:76-78).

In the soteriologies of both thinkers, then, the late-Augustinian notion of irresistible grace (*i.e.* intrinsically efficacious grace, which is logically impossible to resist) is meaningless, for human salvation can never be coerced.[63] This, as one would expect, exerts a profound impact on both thinkers' relationship between predestination and divine foreknowledge, with which the second of Hubmaier's treatises on free will is occupied. Before turning there, however, we must analyze the common final step in both salvific progressions—the ontological transformation of humanity achieved, in the words of Hubmaier, "after the revocation of the Fall through Christ."[64]

Bernard and Hubmaier respectively, in chapter ten of *De gratia* entitled "Through Christ the Likeness which Suitably Belongs to the Divine Image Is Restored in Us,"[65] paralleled by the fourth division of *Von der Freiheit* revealing how "there must be right health and freedom in humanity again after the restoration,"[66] contend that the Holy Spirit, through the work of regeneration, restores to the spirit the freedom of consent. This liberty empowers neophytes to derive good thoughts in and of themselves and thereby earn

---

63. Whether one regards this as truly a form of synergism depends on (1) whether one analyzes the problem *in sensu diviso* (in the divided sense) or *in sensu composito* (in the composite sense), (2) and if the latter, whether one regards composite states of affairs encompassing divine foreknowledge as causally necessary. *In sensu diviso*, a synergism exists in which both God and the human being must freely play their parts; *in sensu composito*, since God already foreknows whether the person would respond to his proferred grace if he so granted, the question of synergism hinges upon whether the logically prior existence of this foreknowledge compels the person to act as God foreknows. Since both Bernard and Hubmaier are here considering the problem *in sensu diviso* and, in any case, do not regard composite states of affairs encompassing divine foreknowledge as causally necessary, we may safely classify the interaction of *gratia operans* and *liberum arbitrium* as synergism when discussing these thinkers. For two fine elaborations on the aforementioned debate see William Hasker, "Foreknowledge and Necessity," *Faith and Philosophy* 2 (1985): 121-57 and John Fischer, "Freedom and Foreknowledge," *Philosophical Review* 95 (1986): 591-99.

64. "nach dem widerbrachten fall durch Christum." Hubmaier, *Von der Freiheit*, 391.

65. "Per Christum Similitudo qui Apte Erat Divinae Imagini Restitutum Est Nobis"; Bernard, *De gratia*, 218.

66. "So müß ein rechte gsundhayt vnd freyhayt widerumb in menschen sein nach dem widerbrachten fal (here I translate *dem widerbrachten fal* together, since it amounts to one concept, as "the restoration")." Hubmaier, *Von der Freiheit*, 390.

merits (*meritum de condigno*) from God for their righteous deeds. Bernard writes that three elements are present in a work of merit: free will, the grace of Christ's atoning death which facilitated the reformation of the spirit, and divine acceptance (*acceptatio*). Of these, the last is the most important—as it is the formal principle of merit—while free will and grace comprise the accessory or material principle.[67] By virtue of this distinction, Bernard hopes to forestall any suggestion that the accumulation of merit might serve as a font of pride, for no works are meritorious *per se*, but only insofar as God freely accepts them as such. The language of merit is justified, however, since God has bound himself to a covenant wherein each righteous deed reliably brings forth a reward (*praemium*).[68] Bernard goes so far, in his gloss on Paul's crown of righteousness, as to assert that God is forced by this bond to pay the apostle the promised wage: "Since he believed the promiser . . . the promise must be kept out of justice. . . . It is only just that the promiser should deliver what he owes; and he owes what he promised."[69] Hubmaier agrees with such a *theologia pactis* precisely; when the sinner responds to the offer of the gospel, God must restore one's spiritual freedom, not because of the quality of one's response but because Christ has literally enslaved himself by his promise to set those free who remain disciples of his Word. Thus God is a captive of his own covenant, which remarkably (impressing a weighty influence upon Hubmaier's doctrine of *praesentia realis*, to be discussed in chapter five) constitutes the radical's reconceptualization of God's presence: "Hence God is captured, bound, and overcome with his own Word by the believers. That is called in the Scriptures 'God being in our midst.'"[70] Moreover, while Hubmaier displays reluctance to use Bernard's term "merit,"[71] as there is no exact equality between our works and God's response to them (which, ironically, is precisely the same qualification of merit made by Bernard), he appears to directly translate Bernard's

---

67. Bernard, *De gratia*, 234-36.

68. Ibid., 234.

69. "Quia credidit promittenti . . . promissum . . . ex iustitia persolvendum. . . . Iustum quippe est ut reddat quod debet; debet autem quod pollicitus est." Ibid., 248.

70. "Derhalb wirdt Gott mit seinem aygnen wort von den Glaubigen gefangen, gebunden, vnd vberwûnden. Das haysset in der schrifft, Gott mitten vnder vns sein." Balthasar Hubmaier, *Das andere Büchlein von der Freiwilligkeit*, in Westin and Bergsten, *Schriften*, 418.

71. While the term "merit" (meritum) is not primarily associated with Bernard of Clairvaux, as he rarely employs it in his "spiritual" writings, it figures prominently in his only "scholastic" treatise, *De gratia*, 234-42.

"praemium" into the German "ein Lohn"[72] and thereafter to appropriate *in toto* (even duplicating the Pauline citation) the monk's theological reconciliation of grace and virtuous deeds:

> How is it possible for God in many passages of Scripture to promise a reward (einen lon) for our works?. . . . This is because of his gracious kindness. He attributes these to us as if we had done him a large favor by ourselves and by our own strength, although he obviously has no need whatsoever of us and does not desire our service except for our own good. So let God call it a reward (einen lon), but woe to you if you should regard it as a payment. Regard all God's dealing with you as sheer grace. There is nothing that God's grace can tolerate or esteem less than our own presumptuous merits, as Paul declares in Romans 3 and 4.[73]

Accordingly, despite Moore's conjecture that Hubmaier levies "objection to the term reward" and that his "conversion to a Biblical theological vocabulary is ample explanation for his refusal to use the technical language of meritum de congruo,"[74] it seems transparent that a vastly more probable solution is the hypothesis of Hubmaier's dependence on Bernard.

Among the good works performed by the faithful is *homo diligit Deum propter ipsum*, loving God for his own sake,[75] after frequently tasting the divine sweetness through keeping the commandments. "The heart grows purer in the obedience of love,"[76] remarks Bernard in *De diligendo Deo*; Hubmaier echoes his model of spiritual development: "Have fervent love . . .

---

72. Kremer, *Reallexikon*, 6:693.

73. "Wie kumbt es dann, das Got in der gschrifft an vil orten einen lon zůsagt vnseren wercken. . . . Es ist seiner gnadenreychen giette schuld, das er diß vnns zůschreybt also, gleich als hetten wir im etwas groß gethonn, auß vnns selber, vnd von dem vnsern, so er doch des vnsern gar nit bdarff vnnd er vnsers diensts nit anders begert, denn vnns ze gůttem. Also laß du es Gott einen lon hayssenn, aber trutz das du es wöllest für einen lon schetzen, sonder laß es alles gnad sein, was gott mit dir handelt. Die gnad gottes mag nicht minders gedulden oder zůsehen denn vermessen aygens verdiensts, wie vns Paulus leert zůn Rö. 3. 4. c." Hubmaier, *Eine christliche Lehrtafel*, 323.

74. Moore, "Catholic Teacher and Anabaptist Pupil," 92.

75. Bernard specifically calls such love for God a good (*i.e.* meritorious) work in *De gratia*, 234, 236.

76. "Castificans magis cor suum . . . in oboedientia caritatis." Bernard, *De diligendo Deo*, 118.

out of a pure heart, as those who are reborn."[77] The twelfth-century reformer affirmed, at this point, that believers experience a state of shock when they learn that God loves them in spite of their sinfulness, which enables them to regain temporally (not eternally) the freedom of pleasure, as the glimpse of the beatific vision causes the soul and spirit, in harmony, to infuse full joy into the body:

> Yet what about those who, being sometimes caught up in the Spirit . . . become capable of savoring a morsel of the sweetness of heavenly bliss? Do these experience freedom from sorrow as often as this occurs? Indeed they do. Even in this present life, those who with Mary have chosen the better part, which shall not be taken away from them, enjoy freedom of pleasure; rarely, however, and briefly.[78]

Amidst the believer's elusive rapture in the divine love, "the wine poured on it by the Samaritan Christ,"[79] the sixteenth-century rebaptizer insists, "this Fall [is] innocuous to us in the flesh," thereby overturning the effects of original sin: "Here one seizes with both hands how Christ made the Fall of Adam completely harmless for us and impotent to condemn, and how he crushed the head of the old serpent . . . and made its poison no longer deadly for us."[80] While the pneumatic liberty is forever restored in the present age,

---

77. "habt euch . . . inbrünstigklich lieb, auß rainem hertzen, als die widergeborenn seind." Hubmaier, *Von der Freiheit*, 384.

78. "An tamen fatendum est eos, qui . . . rapti quandoque in Spiritu, quantulumcumque de supernae felicitas dulcedine degustare sufficiunt, toties esse liberos a miseria, quoties sic excedunt? Hi plane, quod negandum non est, etiam it hac carne, raro licet raptimque, complaciti libertate fruuntur, qui cum Maria optimam partem elegerunt, quae non auferetur ab eis." Bernard, *De gratia*, 196.

79. "den eingegoßnen wein von dem Samaritan Christo." Hubmaier, *Von der Freiheit*, 395. Such a description of divine love, it should be pointed out, is quite evocative of Bernard's high poetic style in *De diligendo Deo*: "When will [flesh and blood] experience this kind of love, so that the mind, drunk with divine love and forgetting itself, making itself like a broken vessel, throw itself wholly on God and, clinging to God, become one with him in spirit" (Quando [caro et sanguis] experitur affectum, ut divino debriatus amore animus, oblitus sui, factusque sibi ipsi tamquam vas perditum, totus pergat in Deum et, adhaerens Deo, unus cum eo spiritus fiat), 120.

80. "vns diser fal am fleisch vnnschedlich sey. . . . Hie greifft man mit bayden henden, wie vns Christus den fal Adams gar vnschedlich vnd vnuerdamblich gemacht habe, vnd wie er der alten Schlangen . . . zerknischt . . . vnd ir gifft vnns vnntödtlich widerbracht." Hubmaier, *Von der Freiheit*, 395-96.

the somatic liberty will only be fully and eternally enjoyed in what seems to be the complete exaltation of physicality in the general resurrection at the end of the world.[81] With this perfect goal in mind, both Bernard and Hubmaier exhort their respective flocks to freely progress along the path of sanctification by heeding the good thoughts springing from the reborn spirit. "Here below," urges Bernard, "we must learn from our freedom of counsel not to abuse free choice, in order that one day we may be able fully to enjoy freedom of pleasure."[82] Hubmaier concurs in his explication of article twelve in the Apostles' Creed: "I believe and confess the resurrection of the body—indeed, of this very body now clothing me . . . I will . . . receive the right honor which is accepted before God, indestructible possessions, an impassable, transfigured, immortal body, and everlasting life on the day of the joyous resurrection of my flesh."[83] Rounding out Hubmaier's first volume on free will, we have seen powerful evidence that his trichotomous anthropology as well as his analysis of the human condition before and after both the Fall and conversion is borrowed directly from Bernard's *De gratia*, especially imitating the structure of and paraphrasing heavily from the monastic reformer's seventh through tenth chapters treating an identical fourfold *ordo salutis*. Although successfully harmonizing the Scriptural tenets that salvation and good works are simultaneously gifts of God and fruits of human freedom, it still remains for Hubmaier to provide a philosophical foundation which supplies the logical and theoretical underpinnings to reconcile such a practical solution with the issues of divine predestination and foreknowledge.

Harmony of Bernard and Hubmaier on *Praedestinatio* and *Praescientia*

In his second volume on human freedom, *Das andere Büchlein von der Freiwilligkeit des Menschen*, Hubmaier introduces a sophisticated discussion

---

81. Bernard, *De gratia*, 210, 212; Hubmaier, *Von der Freiheit*, 440.

82. "Discendum sane hic interim nobis est ex libertate consilii iam libertate arbitrii non abuti, ut plene quandoque frui possimus libertate complaciti." Bernard, *De gratia*, 212.

83. "Jch Glaub auch vnnd bekhenn ein vrsteennd des leibs. Ja ebenn des leibs, mit dem ich yetz vmbgeben bin . . . wirdt ich . . . die rechten eer, die vor Gott gilt, ein vnnzergengklichs gůt, einen vnnleydennlichen, clarificierten, vnnsterblichen leib, vnnd ein ewigs lebenn, auff den tag der freüdennreichen vrsteend meins fleischs erst recht vber khummen." Hubmaier, *Die zwölf Artikel*, 219.

of the perennial quandary between predestination and foreknowledge, one surprising for an alleged Anabaptist. A comparison of Hubmaier's work with forebear Bernard suggests that the former used the latter's delineation of divine omniscience as a springboard for his own theological system, which appears pregnant with doctrinal potentialities. Therefore, an explication of Bernard's teaching on *praescentia* and the divine decrees is in order. In chapters eleven through fourteen of *De gratia*, principally devoted to the divine basis of human salvation, Bernard draws a distinction between *potentia absoluta* and *potentia ordinata*;[84] the absolute power of God comprises his power to do whatever he chooses, unconstrained by any law above himself, while God has mercifully chosen, however, to act according to precepts he has freely instituted, and his acts according to these precepts amount to God's ordained power. Logically entailing a divine-command theory of ethics, Bernard declares that neither is God necessarily good, nor the devil necessarily bad, as both possess freedom of choice, but they retain their characters *via* their freedom:

> Even God himself remains freely good, that is, by his own will, not from any extrinsic necessity; so the devil freely both selected evil and persists in it, not by outside compulsion, but of his own free choice. . . . the fact that the former cannot be evil is not due to weak necessity but to a firm willingness in good and a willing firmness.[85]

Bernard employs the dialectics of the two powers of God to address the question *de ratione praedestinationis*; its key application is to explain that although God elects a few to salvation apart from any foreknown response on their part, he elects the vast majority on the ground of that foreknown

---

84. Explaining how the two powers can be known, Bernard writes: "The *potentia absoluta* of God extends itself to all things that do not imply a contradiction. However, the *potentia ordinata* is conformed to the ordained law which is known to us through scripture or revelation" (Potentia dei absoluta extendit se ad omnia illa quae non implicant contradictionem fieri. Potentia vero ordinate est conformis legi ordinate quod nobis constat per scripturam vel revelationem); *De gratia*, 188.

85. "Etiam ipse Deus, permanet libere bonus, propria videlicet voluntate, non aliqua extrinseca necessitate, sic profecto diabolus aeque libere in malum et corruit, et persistit, suo utique voluntario nutu, non alieno impulsu. . . . quod ille esse non potest malus, non infirma facit necessitas, sed firma in bono voluntas, et voluntaria firmitas." Ibid., 186, 222.

response.[86] For Bernard, therefore, the former set comprises those whom God predestines according to his *potentia absoluta*, while the latter set encompasses those predestined according to his *potentia ordinata*. Seemingly in a late-Augustinian fashion[87] regarding the smaller category, "converting their will from bad to good, he does not take away their freedom, but transfers its loyalty,"[88] but in a semi-Pelagian vein, the special treatment of the few does not stand in the way of "his judging worthy of salvation [the many] only such as [they] have previously proved to will it."[89] Significant in Bernard's use of the two powers, he refuses to speculate concerning the *potentia absoluta*; while there are a number of allusions to God's absolute power, they are brief and tangential to his arguments. In spite of his ensuing preoccupation with the *potentia ordinata* and the principles according to which God agreed to typically act, it appears that for Bernard the *potentia absoluta* is not merely the domain of unactualized possibility.[90] The context for such an element of unpredictability in salvation history is a gloss on Romans 9:18, "God has mercy on whom he wills, and whom he wills he hardens." The divine will alluded to in this verse, Bernard claims, is the absolute will of God, who "accomplishes the salvation of those whose names are in the book of life sometimes through the creature yet without it" and even "sometimes through the creature but against it."[91] Taken together, however, the monastic reformer tends to circumscribe such anomalous occurrences within narrow limits, such that the *operationes Dei externae* are, in the overwhelming majority of cases, knowable. In the redemptive realm, for example, the sinner may rest assured that it is impossible for God, given the order of eternal rules freely instituted by his will, not to predestine someone whom he

---

86. Jean Leclerq, *Bernard of Clairvaux and the Cistercian Spirit*, trans. Claire Lavoie (Kalamazoo, Mich.: Cistercian Publications, 1976), 102-03; Hiss, *Die Anthropologie*, 97; Dinzelbacher, *Bernhard von Clairvaux*, 79-80.

87. As identified by Sommerfeldt, *Spiritual Teachings*, 18, 39-40.

88. "quatenus dum de malo in bonum mutat voluntatem, transferat, non auferat libertatem." Bernard, *De gratia*, 224.

89. "iudicat salute dignum, quem ante . . . probaverit voluntarium." Ibid.

90. Sommerfeldt, *Spiritual Teachings*, 125-26. This notion is also common to many Church Fathers, such as Origen, Augustine, and Boethius, who often employ different terms than *potentia absoluta* and *potentia ordinata*; see Pelikan, *Emergence of Tradition*, 42-50, 294-97.

91. "Operatur . . . illorum salutem, quorum nomina sunt in libro vitae, aliquando per creaturam sine ipsa, aliquando per creaturam contra ipsam." Bernard, *De gratia*, 236.

foresees will respond to his grace.[92] Furthermore, where Bernard does appeal to the absolute power of God to explain actual events, he does so not to introduce but to avert disorder, not to preclude but to furnish rational explanation. This is evident in his treatment of a select number of people, such as Balaam and Cyrus, who (in his exegesis of Numbers 23:7-10 and Isaiah 45:4-5) are known to have been saved without reference to their foreseen response to grace and thus constitute the referent of Luke 14:23, "Compel them to come in."[93] The function of such an appeal, therefore, is to formulate a coherent justification for a limited set of clearly (in his mind) substantiated peculiarities inexplicable from the standard order, which special pleading serves to heighten not God's capriciousness but his mercy. Every exercise of *potentia dei absoluta* proposed by Bernard, it should be noted, yields salvation and not damnation.[94]

Embracing to all appearances the Bernardian theological categories, Hubmaier opens his 1528 sequel with an explanation of the Scriptures by which "my opponents (presumably Luther and Zwingli) hope to completely obliterate human free will."[95] Providing further evidence for the dependence hypothesis, the first passage analyzed by Hubmaier is Romans 9:18, which he recognizes as "a statement about the omnipotent and hidden will of God [which] is called absolute power [whereby] he can be merciful to whomever he wants without any injustice."[96] Not only does the radical allude to Bernard's *potentia absoluta*, but he actually quotes the Latin phrase in the margin.[97] Moreover, in what is almost certainly another direct quote from Bernard, Hubmaier juxtaposes God's absolute will with his ordained principles: "One also discovers a revealed will of God according to which he wants all people to be saved (*er will alle mennschen selig werden*)" termed as "an ordained power."[98] Immediately this passage, coupled with Hubmaier's cita-

---

92. Gillian Rosemary Evans, *The Mind of St. Bernard of Clairvaux* (Oxford: Clarendon Press, 1983), 147.

93. Bernard, *De gratia*, 224.

94. Evans, *Mind of St. Bernard*, 161.

95. "Mein widersprecher . . . verhoffen die Freywilligkhayt des menschen auß zůtilgen gentzlich." Hubmaier, *Das andere Büchlein*, 415-16.

96. "ain rede des allmechtigen vnd verborgnenn willen Gottes. . . . niemant . . . vollmechtigenn gwalt. . . . darumb mag er on alle ongerechtigkayt welhes er will sich erbarmen." Ibid., 416. Brunotte and Weber reveal that *vollmechtigenn gwalt* is the sixteenth-century German translation of the Latin *potentia absoluta*; *Kirchenlexikon*, 3:114.

97. "Potentia absoluta." Hubmaier, *Das andere Büchlein*, 416.

98. "findt man . . . auch ainen offenbartten willen Gottes, nach dem er will alle mennschen selig werden. . . . ainen ordenlichen gwalt." Ibid., 416-17.

tion of the second Latin expression in the margin, calls to mind Bernard's pastoral exhortation for his monastic brothers to find peace with "the kindly Father, who wants all people to be saved (*qui omnes vult salvos fieri*, the Latin equivalent of Hubmaier's parenthesized German)."[99] Not only does Hubmaier, like Bernard, insist in *Das andere Büchlein* that God "is not subject to any rule, [and] his will is itself a rule of all things,"[100] the former's supremely rational mind elsewhere draws, despite the reticence of the latter, the logical deduction that moral values are divinely commanded and hence could have been otherwise: "Now what God calls good is good. If he commanded you to butcher your son, then it would be a good work."[101] Nevertheless, Hubmaier, seemingly ethically appalled by his own conclusion, duplicates the monk's logic in forestalling any hint of divine arbitrariness: "Not that the first will is unordered, for all that God wills and does is orderly and good."[102] Hubmaier illustrates the two powers as follows: according to his *potentia absoluta*, God might consign Judas or Caiaphas to heaven; but no injustice would be involved in this display of gratuitous mercy so long as he is forbidden by his *potentia ordinata* from driving away Jacob, who wrestled for his blessing, or refusing to grant forgiveness to the repentant David.[103] Comparing Hubmaier's treatment of the *duplex potentia dei vis-à-vis* that of Bernard, we discover both a shared theological groundwork along with differing applications springing from such a foundation.[104] Both devote more attention to the ordained power than the absolute, appealing to the latter only to emphasize God's liberty from external constraints. Even when acting according to his absolute power, the divine will is not without order, and God lovingly revealed his ordained will in Scripture so that humans may comprehend and repose confidently in their salvation. The underlying subtext, ac-

---

Brunotte and Weber point out that *ordenlichen gwalt* is the sixteenth-century German translation of the Latin *potentia ordinata*; *Kirchenlexikon*, 2:1707.

99. "benignus Pater, qui omnes vult salvos fieri." Bernard, *De gratia*, 224; Brunotte and Weber, *Kirchenlexikon*, 2:59, 3:928.

100. "Er ist khainer Reglen vnderworffen. Sein will ist selbs ain Regel aller ding." Hubmaier, *Das andere Büchlein*, 417.

101. "Was nun Gott gůtt haißt, das ist gůt, vnd hieß er dich schon deinen Son metzgen, so wer es ein gůt werckh." Hubmaier, *Von dem Schwert*, 448.

102. "Nit das der erst will vnordenlich sey, denn alles was Gott will vnd thůt, ist ordenlich vnd gůt." Hubmaier, *Das andere Büchlein*, 417.

103. Moore, "Catholic Teacher and Anabaptist Pupil," 84.

104. This groundwork was also shared by several figures within fourteenth and fifteenth-century theology, including Johannes Tauler, Jean Gerson, and Gabriel Biel; see Oberman, *Harvest of Medieval Theology*, 30-37 and Steinmetz, "Nominalism and Radical Reform," 132-34.

cordingly, of both discussions is the conviction that God's *de facto* activity regarding humanity tends toward grace more than toward wrath.[105]

When it comes to the relationship between *praedestinatio* and *praescientia*, however, a subtle yet profound theological difference emerges between the twelfth-century and sixteenth-century reformer. Bernard, on the one hand, maintains that God typically predestines those whom he foresees will assent to the inner movement of the Holy Spirit. Behind such a claim lies a perceptualist model of foreknowledge, which is predicated upon the assumption that God, as the creator of the space-time universe, exists outside of time and thus lives in an "eternal now."[106] Construing prescience on the analogy of sense perception, Bernard asserts that the divine vantage point is like looking from a mountaintop, for God views all events as if they were taking place in the present. Definitively residing beyond the four-dimensional space-time manifold, "all time is subject to [God], not he to time. He does not look to the future or back at the past, or live in the present."[107] Such a model of *praescientia* entails that God lacks counterfactual knowledge, that is to say, cognizance of the truth-value of conditional propositions in the subjunctive mood (*i.e.* statements of the following form: if something *were* the case [when in fact it may or may not be the case], then something else *would be* the case).[108] Therefore, whereas God knows what every creature *will* freely do in the actual world, since the creature's actions supply the basis of divine foreknowledge, he is ignorant of what every crea-

---

105. Sommerfeldt, *Spiritual Teaching*, 30-36; Hiss, *Die Anthropologie*, 132; Steinmetz, "Scholasticism and Radical Reform," 141; Moore, "Catholic Teacher and Anabaptist Pupil," 83-84.

106. Alan Padgett, *God, Eternity, and the Nature of Time* (New York: St. Martin's Press, 1990), 75-76.

107. "Tempora sub ea transeunt, non ei. Futura non exspectat, praeterita non recogitat, praesentia non experitur." Bernard de Clairvaux, *Sermo LXXX super Cantica Canticorum*, in *Sämtliche Werke lateinisch/deutsch* VI (Innsbruck: Tyrolia-Verlag, 1995), 576.

108. Despite its counterintuitive appearance, since 1973 philosophers of religion have followed David Lewis (*Counterfactuals* [Cambridge, Mass.: Harvard University Press, 1973], 3, 26-30) in broadly defining the term "counterfactual" to encompass not only statements which are contrary to fact, but also true conditionals in the subjunctive mood. For instance, in his book *The Existence and Nature of God* (Notre Dame, Ind.: University of Notre Dame Press, 1983), 112, Alfred J. Freddoso explains, "We shall follow David Lewis' practice of not presupposing that the term 'counterfactual' is to be applied only to conditionals with false antecedents." The same point is enunciated by Thomas P. Flint, *Divine Providence* (Ithaca, N.Y.: Cornell University Press, 1998), 6.

ture *would* freely do in all other possible sets of circumstances not transpiring in the actual world. Hubmaier detects that this conception of simple foreknowledge trivializes the doctrine of foreordination, for once God sees that an event will take place in the future, there is nothing left for him to do, whereby we "make the eternal providence and unchangeable truth of God into a lie."[109] In summary, every person, on Bernard's view, innately possesses the ability to accept or reject God's proffered grace, and the foreknown response itself, rather than God's foreknowledge of the response, constitutes the *ratio praedestinationis*. On the other hand, Hubmaier alleges that God predestines before the creation of the world those whom he foreknows would appropriately respond to the gospel if he ordained to actualize this world (the content of such an appropriate response will be determined in chapter four). Hubmaier hence posits a conceptualist model of divine foreknowledge, wherein God, contrary to Bernard, does not acquire his knowledge of the world by anything like perception; his prescience is not based on an anthropomorphic "looking" into the space-time block from without and "seeing" what lies, from a human vantage point, in the future.[110] Scriptural language depicting God in human terms must be understood figuratively,[111] as "he does not therefore have eyes . . . like the anthropomorphites propose";[112] however, the text "accommodates itself to speak according to our human ignorance."[113] Properly understood, declares Hubmaier, God's

---

109. "die ewigen vorsehung vnd vnwandelbaren warhait Gottes . . . zû ainer lûgnerin machen." Hubmaier, *Das andere Büchlein*, 412.

110. Padgett, *God, Eternity, and the Nature of Time*, 72-74; Pelikan, *Reformation*, 379-80; Linda T. Zagzebski, *The Dilemma of Freedom and Foreknowledge* (Oxford: Oxford University Press, 1991), 125-28; James K. Beilby and Paul R. Eddy, *Divine Foreknowledge* (Carlisle, U.K.: Paternoster, 2002), 132-33, 208, 211.

111. It should be pointed out that the metaphorical interpretation of anthropomorphic language in Scripture constitutes a serious issue in the history of exegesis which hearkens back to the Alexandrian Fathers, such as Clement of Alexandria and Origen, and received further reflection by the Post-Nicene Fathers, including Chrysostom, Ambrose, and Augustine. For two fine discussions of this development see Bertrand de Margerie, *Introduction à l'histoire de l'exégèse*, 3 vols. (Paris: Les Éditions du Cerf, 1980), 1:118, 219-24 and Joseph W. Trigg, *Biblical Interpretation* (Wilmington, Del.: Michael Glazier, 1983), 23-38.

112. "Er hat aber darumb nit augen . . . wie die Antropomorphiten anzaigen." Hubmaier, *Das andere Büchlein*, 419.

113. "schickt sich nach vnserm menschlichen vnuerstandt zûreden." Ibid., 417.

knowledge is self-contained, analogous to the human soul's understanding of innate ideas. As an omniscient being, God essentially possesses the property of knowing all truths; since truths about potential states of affairs exist, it follows deductively that God knows all truths about potential states of affairs.[114]

At this point Hubmaier, granting the inscrutability and consequent futility of examining the *potentia absoluta*, turns to God's *potentia ordinata*, which is fully revealed in Scripture, and subdivides it into two aspects, namely, "the conversive will concerning the one to be converted (*voluntas conversiva a convertendo*) [and] the aversive will concerning the one to be turned away from (*voluntas aversiva ab avertendo*)."[115] The reformer defines the *voluntas conversiva* as God's desire, independent of libertarian freedom, for all persons to be saved: "That is why he turns himself toward all human beings with the offer of his grace and mercy, not sparing even his only begotten Son, but giving him up to death for us all so that we might not be lost but receive eternal life."[116] However, Hubmaier insists that the *voluntas conversiva* in no way restricts human freedom, which enjoys the option of accepting or rejecting salvation: "The choice lies with [humanity], for God wants them, unforced, sober, and without compulsion."[117] The *voluntas aversiva*, consequently, is defined as God's will, having already factored creaturely freedom into the equation, to reprobate persons who, outside of those specially saved by the *potentia absoluta*, would freely choose to reject the redemptive plan in the actual world; whoever would "not accept, hear, or follow after him, he turns himself away from them, withdraws from them, and allows them to stay as they themselves would want to be."[118] Hence the

---

114. Ibid., 418.

115. "Der erst will mag genennt werdenn . . . Voluntas conuersiua a conuertendo. Der ander Voluntas auersiua ab auertendo." Ibid., 419. According to H. Wayne Pipkin and John H. Yoder, these categories appear to be original with Hubmaier; see Pipkin and Yoder, *Hubmaier*, 475; Pipkin, "The Baptismal Theology of Balthasar Hubmaier," *MQR* 65 (January 1991): 40; and Yoder, "Enthusiastisches christentum," *Ecumenical Review* 23 (January 1971): 75.

116. "Darumb khert er sich zů allen mennschen mit anbiettung seiner gnaden vnnd barmhertzigkait, verschonet auch nit seins aingebornen Sons, sonnder gibt jn für vnns all in den tod, darmit wir nit verloren werden, sonder vberkhummen das ewig leben." Hubmaier, *Das andere Büchlein*, 418.

117. "steet bey jnen yetz die waal, wann Gott will sy vnzwungen, vntrungen vnd vngenöttigt haben." Ibid.

118. "nit auffnemen, hören, noch jm nachfolgen, von den selben khert vnd wendt sich Gott auch ab vnd lasset sy bleyben, wie sy selbs sein wöllen." Ibid., 418-19.

Scriptural passages, according to Hubmaier, which affirm God's universal salvific will, such as 1 Timothy 2:4, refer to the *voluntas conversiva*, while those teaching "that God wants to harden the godless and damn them"[119] allude to the *voluntas aversiva*. Given his *potentia absoluta et ordinata*, along with the latter's differentiation into the *voluntas conversiva et aversiva*, God completes the act of predestination by creating the actual world, thereby making it logically necessary that, although both the elect and the reprobate are free *in sensu diviso* to choose either salvation or damnation, the elect will be saved and the reprobate damned *in sensu composito*.[120] Each person does not predestinate oneself, since it is God who chose to create a world in which he foreknew that the predestined person by one's own freedom would choose eternal life rather than one in which the same person would freely choose damnation. Thus, on Hubmaier's analysis, it is up to God whether people find themselves in a world in which they are predestined, but it is up to the people whether they are predestined in the world in which they find themselves. In this rapprochement, Hubmaier asserts that divine grace is ultimately responsible for the salvation of the elect, while the reprobate bear full accountability for their condemnation and thus have only themselves to blame: "Whoever is not persuaded by this answer, namely, that the mercy of God is the cause of our salvation and our malice to blame for our damnation, must ask God himself."[121] Hubmaier summarizes the professed harmony and coherence of such an answer to the perennial theological quandary between predestination and human freedom:

> The [absolute] will of God yet remains upright and omnipotent, according to which he can do whatever he desires and no one should question, "Why are you doing that?" His conversive will is a will of mercy. His aversive will is a will of his justice and retribution, of which we are guilty with our immoralities, and not God.[122]

---

119. "Von dem andern sagt der ander tail der schrifften, das Got die gotlosen verhörten vnd verdammen wölle." Ibid., 419.

120. Although creation itself does not make a soteriological program necessary, Hubmaier finds himself driven to define predestination in terms of creation in order to make sense of the term "predestination" (προαιρέομαι) in the New Testament. Ibid., 420.

121. "Wer mit diser antwürt nit ersettigt ist, namlich, das die barmhertzigkayt Gottes ain vrsach ist vnser seligmachung, vnd vnser boßhayt ain schuld ist vnserer verdammnung, der frage Gott selber." Ibid., 414.

122. "Noch bleibt auffrecht vnd allmechtig Gottes . . . will, nach wölhem er mag thon, was er wil, vnnd bedarffe doch niemant fragen: Warumb thůstus? Sein zůkherender will ist ain will seiner barmhertzigkait. Sein abkherender will

Two provocative corollaries follow from this solution. First, Hubmaier furnishes an explication of how God hardened the hearts of various evildoers, such as Pharaoh (Ex. 7:13; Rom. 9:17), without turning the deity into the author of evil. For the reformer, God predetermined Pharaoh's iniquity in a manner consistent ₊with his goodness by choosing, in light of his *voluntas aversiva*, to actualize a world in which he foreknew that, were he to create that world, Pharaoh would freely contravene God's *voluntas conversiva* by oppressing the Israelites: "Consequently, it was never possible for Pharaoh . . . to will and work anything but evil, just as if falling by necessity from one trap into another, although it does not stem from God but his own guilt"; regarding Pharaoh and all others who would forsake him, "it is fair and right that they were all abandoned by God."[123] Second, it should be obvious (although I have not yet made it explicit) that Hubmaier's formulation of a conceptualist model of *praescientia* allows for God's possession of counterfactual knowledge. Clearly articulated by Hubmaier is a primitive version of what would fifty years later be developed, in my judgment without knowledge of Hubmaier, by Jesuit philosophical theologian Luis de Molina into the doctrine of *scientia media*, or middle knowledge. In a remarkable statement, Hubmaier delineates from his concept of omniscience, in order, an underdeveloped sequence of steps which would later constitute the essence of the three logical moments in Molinism, namely, God's necessary knowledge of every event which could happen, his counterfactual knowledge of whether each event would or would not happen, and finally his free knowledge of everything that will happen in the actual world: "Indeed, it is so, that God knows all things truly, necessarily, and unchangeably from eternity, but which one of two opposites he knows is still unknown to us. Therefore, which one of two possibilities will come true, we do not know because we are incapable of knowing the future, but God does."[124] It seems apparent, then, that the sixteenth-century reformer, upon the foundation laid by his twelfth-century predecessor, constructed a rather philosophically discriminating doctrinal edifice which, as we shall discover, would serve as the

---

ist ain will seiner gerechtigkhait vnd der straffen, an denen wir mit vnsern lastern, vnd nit Gott, schuldig seind." Ibid.

123. "Demnach war es nimmer möglich dem Pharaoni . . . denn böses wöllen vnd wirckhen, auch gleych als auß ainer nott (die doch nit von Gott sonder auß irer schuld her fleüsset) von einem laster in das ander fallen. Denn billich vnnd rechtlich werdent alle die von Gott verlassen." Ibid., 419.

124. "Ja, jm ist also, das Gott alle ding waarlich, nöttlich vnd vnwandelbarlich ways von ewigkait, welhes aber auß zwayen gegentaylen er wisse, das ist vns noch onbewist. Darumb kommt welhes aber auß zwayen zutreffend, wir wissen nicht, weil wir nicht die zukunft kennen können, aber Gott." Ibid., 413.

sine qua non of his theological views throughout his career in spite of his confessional movement.

Comparing the styles of argumentation in defense of predestination based on what free creatures respectively will or would do in the actual world throughout *De gratia* and *Das andere Büchlein*, one is immediately struck by similarities. Unlike the late medieval nominalists and early modern Catholic controversialists, who normally make their cases by citing scholastic and patristic authorities, the authorities in the treatises of both Bernard and Hubmaier are contained within the covers of the Bible, particularly the Pauline corpus. Highlighting the monk's reliance upon the Apostle, Bernard McGinn indicates, "While making use of a wide range of Paul's other writings, especially the Epistles to the Corinthians and the Galatians, it is certainly the Epistle to the Romans which is the major Scriptural basis for the *Grace and Free Choice*," even going so far to suggest that "the treatise might be said to be Bernard's commentary on Romans."[125] In a similar vein, Moore, notwithstanding his attempt to attribute Hubmaier's anthropological libertarianism to the influence of John Eck,[126] is forced to concede that although "the partners in [Eck's] conversation are the medieval doctores . . . Hubmaier's discussion appears in an exposition of Scripture, and his partner in dialogue is the Apostle Paul," thereafter candidly admitting that in the tract under consideration "one seeks in vain for evidence that Hubmaier was drawing specifically upon Eck."[127] In light of the high biblical densities in both works, therefore, one wonders whether the Hubmaier-Bernard dependence theory possesses the explanatory power to account for the phenomenon. To provide a sufficient answer to this question, we must analyze the pericopes common to both works and see whether the exegetical deductions drawn therefrom by Bernard are mirrored in Hubmaier. The first and fourth chapters of *De gratia*, along with the opening section of *Das andere Büchlein*, use Romans 7:18 ("I can will what is right, but I cannot do it"), a proof-text for compatibilist free will endlessly quoted by the late Augustine and his theological progeny, in a new way to demonstrate the inherent goodness of humanity:

---

125. McGinn, introduction to Bernard of Clairvaux, 5.

126. Moore is undoubtedly correct that Eck exerted a tremendous amount of suasion on his erstwhile disciple throughout the course of his theological pilgrimage, but would have been better served to make the more modest claim I suggested, which he substantiates with powerful evidence, rather than inadequately corroborating a more extravagant one.

127. Moore, "Catholic Teacher and Anabaptist Pupil," 85.

Bernard	Hubmaier
Whoever wants to have a *good will* proves by this that he has a will, since his desire could not be aimed at good except through his will. . . . For this reason it is highly likely that, since he *wants* to have a good will, he does, in fact, to some degree, have it. What he wants is good, and he could not want good except through a good will.[128]	Here one sees clearly the *desire* to do good in a human being, which is a good work. . . . Just as glory is glory and peace is peace, so also a *good will* is a good will for humankind.[129]

The next Pauline text quoted by Bernard and Hubmaier alike is Philippians 2:13 ("God works in you to will and to work according to his good pleasure"); notably, the former explicates this passage, contrary to its *prima facie* meaning, through the lens of his second soteriological step. Bernard, accordingly, interprets God's working as the *testimonium internum Spiritus Sancti*, infusing and confirming the gospel in the unregenerate human spirit: "The beginning of our salvation hence undoubtedly lies in God. . . . because the good thought (*i.e.* the gospel) is from God . . . by suggesting the good thought, he comes one step before us."[130] Highly indicative of Bernardian influence, Hubmaier deciphers the passage to mean that concerning "the salvation of the soul. . . . God works in us the willing and the doing,"[131] apparently failing to realize that such an exegesis contradicted his own notion that the ordinary human act of preaching the Word of God, not any special divine pneumatic motion, afforded the sinner the opportunity to appropriate

---

128. "Qui vult habere *bonam voluntatem*, probat se habere voluntatem: non enim vult habere bonam, nisi per voluntatem. . . . Quamquam iam procul dubio utcumque bonam habet, ubi habere *vult*. Bonum quippe est quod vult, nec posset bonum velle, nisi bona voluntate." Bernard, *De gratia*, 188.

129. "Hie sicht mann klarlich das gůt *wellenn* im menschen, welhes ye ain gůtt werckh ist. . . . Wie Glori glori vnnd frid frid ist, also ainn *gůter will* ist ye ainn gůtter will denn mennschenn." Hubmaier, *Das andere Büchlein*, 409. Brunotte and Weber point out that *wellenn* is the sixteenth-century German counterpart to the Latin *velle*, the lexical form of which is *vult* (*Kirchenlexikon*, 3:1702), and that *gůter will* is the German translation of *bonam voluntatem* (*Kirchenlexikon*, 3:477).

130. "A Deo ergo sine dubio nostrae fit salutis exordium. . . . quod bona cogitatio a Deo sit . . . siquidem immitendo bonam cogitationem, nos praevenit." Bernard, *De gratia*, 240.

131. "so der Seelen seligkhait anntreffent. . . . God wirckhe in vnns das wöllen vnd thon." Hubmaier, *Das andere Büchlein*, 425-26.

Christ's atoning death. In addition, Hubmaier then brings to virtual certainty the dependence thesis by quoting a Latin passage, which he attributes to the Apostle Paul, but which is actually a slight alteration of Bernard's exegesis where the former substitutes his characteristic *animi proposito* (purpose of the spirit) for the latter's interchangeable *voluntas* (will):

Bernard	**Hubmaier**
He who has given me to will, shall also enable me to perform by virtue of my good will (*perficere pro bona voluntate*).[132]	But then we perform a work according to good will if we will something according to the will of God, and also do the same with deeds, against the will of our own flesh. . . . Paul calls that *perficere pro bono animi proposito*.[133]

Such apparent consistency in Pauline authentication of the functions assigned to divine grace and human freedom up to the moment of conversion leads both thinkers into a Scriptural defense of a conception of divine conservation and concurrence which provides a basis for the spiritually liberated believer to earn *meritum de condigno*.

At the heart of the sanctification process proposed by the twelfth-century and sixteenth-century reformers lies a strongly indeterministic two-fold model of the divine-human relationship which allows for genuine discourse about meritorious creaturely actions. Both thinkers contend that the infinite grace imparted by the atonement, necessary to restore freedom of counsel in the believer's spirit, comprises God's *concursus generalis* which enables the performance of all good works. To illuminate this point, Bernard appeals to the causal influence of the sun on terrestrial events, whereby providing heat and light the sun contributes to animal reproduction on earth; hence a calf, for example, is conceived *from* solar energy.[134] But such a causal influence is general, since it must be channeled toward the production of a calf by secondary agents, *i.e.* a cow and a bull. Likewise, the sanctifying grace of Christ serves as a prerequisite for the spirit to derive good thoughts

---

132. "Qui dedit velle, det et perficere pro bona voluntate." Bernard, *De gratia*, 174.

133. "Denn aber thûnd wir ein werckh nach dem gûtten willen, so wir etwas wöllen nach dem willen Gottes, vnd thûnd das selb auch mit der that, wider den willen vnsers aignen fleyschs. . . . Das haist Paulus Perficere pro bono animi proposito." Hubmaier, *Das andere Büchlein*, 425.

134. Evans, *Mind of St. Bernard*, 146.

upon which the soul can freely act, thus rendering every righteous deed as empowered *from* grace but, at the same time, accomplished *in* free choice:

> What was begun by grace alone, is completed by grace and free choice together, in such a way that they contribute to each new achievement not singly but unitedly; not one at a time, but simultaneously. . . . Grace does the whole work, and so does free choice—with this one stipulation: that while the whole is done in free choice, so is the whole done from grace.[135]

Bernard substantiates this point through a gloss on 1 Corinthians 15:10, the significance of which Hubmaier also expounds, according to Bernardian logic, by modifying the analogy of the sun.

Bernard

Hence Paul, in recounting the many good deeds God had accomplished through him, qualifies, "though it was not I, but the grace of God which is with me." He might have said "through me," but, since that would have been too little, he preferred to say "with me," presuming himself to be not merely the minister of the deed through its performance, but in a way the worker . . . through his consent.[136]

Hubmaier

As you believe that not I but the grace of God is working, so I believe: with me and not without me. I see with the sun, not without the sun, nor the sun without me. Hence the Scripture does not say, "I without the grace" nor "the grace without me." Rather it says: "The grace of God with me."[137]

---

135. "Ita tamen quod a sola gratia coeptum est, pariter ab utroque perficitur, ut mixtim, non singillatim, simul, non vicissim. . . . totum quidem hoc, et totum illa, sed ut totum in illo, sic totum ex illa." Bernard, *De gratia*, 242.

136. "Unde Paulus, cum bona plurima, quae Deus per ipsum fecerat, enarrasset: Non autem ego, ait, sed gratia Dei mecum. Potuit dicere "per me", sed quia minus erat, maluit dicere mecum, praesumens se non solum operis esse ministrum per effectum, sed et operantis quodammodo . . . per consensum." Ibid., 238. Although working from the *Vulgate*, Bernard's distinction of "with" and "through" accurately reflects the difference between the respective Greek prepositions σύν, which is here employed by Paul, and δία.

137. "Wie du da findest, das nit ich sonder die gnad Gottes wirckhe, also finde ich: Mit mir, vnd nit on mich. Jch gesihe mit der sunnen, nit on die sunnen, noch die sunn on mich. Wann die Schrifft sagt nit: Jch on die gnad, oder die gnad on mich. Sonder sy sagt: Die gnad Gottes mit mir." Hubmaier, *Das andere Büchlein*, 427-28.

For Bernard and Hubmaier, therefore, the sanctifying grace of Christ coupled with *liberum arbitrium* constitutes the material principle for the creation of reward. However, the formal principle converting such an effort (which both thinkers, seeking to prevent *hubris*, insist lacks any intrinsic compensatory value) into heavenly merit is God's acceptance of the act as if it were creditable. This gracious overestimation of our achievements, to which God has bound himself through the terms of the new covenant, furnishes the *concursus particularis* for the production of merit, since the divine causal contribution by itself determines the specific nature of the effect. To support this dual conservation and concurrence, wherein humanity and God can each be said to fully perform meritorious works in the distinct and independent realms of decision and reception, Bernard first proof-texts the introductory clause of 1 Corinthians 12:6 to verify the existence of "different kinds of working" and then interprets the remainder of this passage ("God works all things in all people") accordingly: "It is not that grace does one part of the work and free choice the other; but each performs the whole work, by virtue of its own unique contribution."[138] Holding true to Bernard's dichotomy, Hubmaier, in his exegesis of the same Pauline text, expands this formulation of the mutually exclusive yet complementary roles of divine ascription and human completion:

> It should be emphasized that the Holy Scripture plays two kinds of role. Sometimes it plays the role of God when it takes the accomplishment of all things from the human being and assigns it alone to God. . . . Sometimes it plays the role of humanity and credits everything to the human being as if God did nothing at all. . . . And all this happens out of the rich grace and goodness of God, who ascribes to us what he does.[139]

Concerning the doctrines of divine conservation and concurrence, as well as their origin in the predication of *praedestinatio* upon *praescientia* (whether counterfactual or future knowledge), therefore, the textual evidence clearly

---

138. "Non partim gratia, partim liberum arbitrium, sed totum singula opere individuo peragunt . . . per singulos profectus operentur." Bernard, *De gratia*, 242.

139. "So ist zemercken, das die heilig Schrifft zwayerlay Person anthût. Etwann zeûhet sy an die Person Gotes, als da sy die wirckung aller ding vom menschen nimbt vnd aignets allain Got zû. . . . Etwann legt sy an die Person der menschen vnd gibts alles dem menschen zû, als thet Gott gar nichts. . . . Vnd solchs alles bschicht auß der reychlichen gnad vnd güettigkait Gottes, der vnns zûschreibt, das er thût." Hubmaier, *Das andere Büchlein*, 429.

affirms that Hubmaier was not merely libertarian in his perspective,[140] but faithfully represented the perspective of Bernard.

Further Cistercian Traces in the *Hubmaier Schriften*

At this juncture we shall examine several pieces of corroborating evidence which, while not directly indicative of Hubmaier's usage of Bernard, help support the literary dependence hypothesis. (One additional parallel where this hypothesis can in my judgment be proven beyond a reasonable doubt, namely, Hubmaier's pre-1525 reliance upon ordination as a second baptism and subsequent sacramental theological transposition from ordination to literal rebaptism, will be addressed in chapters three and four.) A prevailing characteristic of all Bernard's writings is threeness, since, exalting nature over grace, he found the reflection of the triune God stamped throughout both the ultimately real realm of ideas and the tangibly real realm of material beings. Endeavoring to kindle affective piety, in his treatise *De diligendo Deo* Bernard recapitulates his soteriology, wherein humans owe God two times themselves, as a succession of three acts including creation, atonement, and redemption: "Therefore what should I repay the Lord for all that he has bestowed upon me? In the first act he gave me myself; in the second he gave himself; and when he did that, he gave me back myself. Given and given again, I owe myself in return for myself, two times over."[141] While not employing the same terms, Hubmaier patterns the arrangement of biblical material in *Das andere Büchlein* according to precisely this tripartite logic. The first division of proof-texts, suitably, treats the creation of "the human being, how he was originally made by God and how he was before the Fall, namely, totally free to do good and so surrounded by grace so that in this very grace of God he could have kept his commandments, lived forever, and been saved."[142] This description of the

---

140. Recognizing (and possibly overstating) this point, Armour asserts that Hubmaier's "position departed from the Catholic view, [and] to that extent he also drew a step closer to Pelagianism"; *Anabaptist Baptism*, 34.

141. "Quid ergo retribuam Domino pro omnibus quae retribuit mihi? In primo opere me mihi dedit, in secundo se; et ubi se dedit, me mihi reddidit. Datus ergo, et redditus, me pro me debeo, et bis debeo." Bernard, *De diligendo Deo*, 100.

142. "dem menschen, wie er erstlich von Gott gemacht vnd vor dem fal gewest sey. Namlich gantz frey zů dem gůtten vnd also begnadet, das er in der selben gnad Gottes hat mögen halten seine gebott, ewigklich leben vnd selig werden." Hubmaier, *Das andere Büchlein*, 402.

Adamic nature, moreover, immediately conjures up the monk's prehistoric anthropological plotline in *De gratia*:

> Among all sentient beings, to man alone was given the ability to sin, as part of his prerogative of free choice. But he was given it, not that he might sin, but rather that he would appear the more glorious if he did not sin with the ability to do so. For what, in fact, could provide him greater glory than that these words of Scripture be applied to him, saying: "Who is he, and we will praise him?" From what does this praise arise? "For he has done remarkable things in his life." What things? "He had the power to transgress," it says, "and he did not transgress, and to do evil and did not do it." This honor, therefore, he retained as long as he was sinless.[143]

Extending hope toward fallen humanity, which has degenerated into the progeny "of sin, wrath, and death," Hubmaier cites passages in his second division revealing how, through "a unique and new grace of God" in the sacrifice of the second divine person, the race can "be saved."[144] After the restoration by Christ, Hubmaier exposits the Scriptures disclosing that the spirit of each believer "received again his freedom and a new grace to will and to be able to do good."[145] Two further examples of triplicity in the Hubmaier corpus evoke a Bernardian influence. In the only catechism composed by a sixteenth-century rebaptizer, the suspected Lutheran distinguishes three kinds of baptism, "a baptism of the Spirit, a baptism of water, and a baptism of blood."[146] The first naturally denotes the "inward illumination of our hearts that is sent by the Holy Spirit, through the living Word of

---

143. "Soli inter animantia datum est homini potuisse peccare, ob praerogativam liberi arbitrii. Datum est autem, non ut perinde peccaret, sed ut gloriosior appareret si non peccaret, cum peccare posset. Quid namque gloriosius ei esse poterat, quam si de ipso diceretur quod Scriptura perhibet, dicens: Quid est hic, et laudabimus eum? Unde ita laudandus? Fecit enim mirabilia in vita sua. Quae? Qui potuit transgredi, inquit, et non est transgressus, facere mala, et non fecit. Hunc ergo honorem quamdiu absque peccato fuit, servavit." Bernard, *De gratia*, 206-08.

144. "vnd wie er sey ain khind der sünden, des zorns vnd des tods worden. . . . on ain sondere vnd neue gnad Gottes . . . selig werdenn." Hubmaier, *Das andere Büchlein*, 403.

145. "sein freyhait vnnd ain neue gnad, das gůt zů wellen vnnd thon mogen." Ibid., 405.

146. "Ein Tauff des geysts, Ein tauff des Wassers, Ein tauff des blůts." Hubmaier, *Eine christliche Lehrtafel*, 313.

God."[147] However, the third, in contradistinction to the Swiss Brethren and later Mennonites, alludes not to martyrdom, notwithstanding the vast numbers of Anabaptist executions having already occurred and still taking place, but was merely metaphorical for the sanctification process of "a daily mortification of the flesh until death."[148] While the idea of a threefold baptism, to be sure, was common among the Scholastics, equally standard was the equation of the baptism of blood with martyrdom, a theme stretching back to the early Church Fathers.[149] Hubmaier's remarkable departure from the established view is inexplicable apart from literary dependence upon a thinker who also deviated from the norm. Such a mind we locate in Bernard; in his homily for the feast of St. Clement, the monk, in admonishing his brothers to discipline, remarks that the forms of baptism are three, "the Spirit, the water, and the blood," the last of which one attains when "you chastise your body by penitential toil and restrain the motions of carnal concupiscence. . . . Whoever would experience, therefore, the delight of this crowning grace must already have died to the world."[150] Developing an allegory based on the story of Absalom, who was stabbed to death while hanging between heaven and earth, Hubmaier avers that unregenerate humanity has been stabbed "with three wounds: of consent, word, and deed,"[151] insofar as all sinful acts entail at least one of these aspects. Such a delineation is strikingly reminiscent of Bernard's triple description of the twelfth step of pride, *i.e.* habitual sin, in *De gradibus humilitatis et superbiae*: "Nothing restrains [the sinner] . . . from evil thoughts, plans, or actions. Whatever is in his heart arrives at his mouth and at his hand: he conceives an idea, talks about it, and does it."[152] Clearly the exact synonymity between conceiving an idea and consent, talking and word, and doing and deed points implicitly if not ex-

---

147. "Er ist ein jnwendige erleúchtung vnnserer hertzen, die da beschicht von dem heiligen geyst, durch das lebendig wort Gottes." Ibid.

148. "Er ist ein tegliche tödtung des fleyschs biß in den todt." Ibid., 314.

149. Prominent exponents of this theme include such ante-Nicene theologians as Tertullian, Irenaeus, and Cyprian; Pelikan, *Emergence of Tradition*, 163-64, 291-92; Armour, *Anabaptist Baptism*, 52.

150. Bernard of Clairvaux, "Sermon for the Feast of St. Clement," in *Sermons for the Seasons and Principal Festivals*, 30-32.

151. "mit dreyen wunnden, der bewilligung, worts vnd der thaten erstochen werde." Hubmaier, *Von der Freiheit*, 391.

152. "Iam ab illicitis cogitandis, patrandis, investigandis . . . non prohibentur; sed quidquid in cor, in buccam, ad manum venerit, machinatur, garrit, et operatur." Bernard de Clairvaux, *De gradibus humilitatis et superbiae*, in *Sämtliche Werke lateinisch/deutsch* II (Innsbruck: Tyrolia-Verlag, 1990), 120.

plicitly to the sixteenth-century radical's usage of the twelfth-century reformer.

Among the most memorable of Bernard's sermons concerned the Virgin
Mary, the focal point of which revolved around Mary's being *theotokos*, the
Mother of God. While such a belief was consonant with Chalcedonian or-
thodoxy and thus found defenders in many scholastic writers, the polemics
in which Hubmaier safeguards the Blessed Mother may specifically echo
Bernard. In his 1528 *Eine Rechenschaft des Glaubens*, an apologia from
prison to Ferdinand intended to save his life, Hubmaier elucidates in theological detail how every believer must esteem Mary: "A Christian professes
that Mary is not only the mother of Christ but also truly the mother of God.
It is an error of the Nestorians to maintain that Mary was *Christotokos*, the
mother of Christ, but not *theotokos*, the mother of God, against which error I
have constantly fought."[153] With respect to this latter assertion, there has
been a common tendency, perhaps unconsciously motivated by the ecclesiastical bias of confessional historians, to regard Hubmaier's allegation of a
continual high Mariology as a cowardly fabrication in his futile attempt to
avoid the stake.[154] The consensus view of Baptist and Mennonite scholars is
expressed by Estep: "The broken man affirmed Roman Catholic dogmas
which he had forsaken at Waldshut five years before . . . [for example, that]
Mary is the mother of God . . . which he sent to Ferdinand in the vain hope
that his life might be spared."[155] Conspicuous by its absence is any evidence
for the claim that Hubmaier renounced at Waldshut his devotion to the Virgin in 1523 (or at any other time, for that matter). Even worse, however, the
confessional stance is demonstrably false, based upon Hubmaier's prior treatises. Two years before the trial, Hubmaier lauded Mary in *Eine kurze Entschuldigung*: "So I profess the pure Virgin Mary . . . to be the true mother of
God"; notably, in the next sentence he praised the saints, "The dear saints I
honor in God as his vehicles through whom he performed several mira-

---

153. "Ein Crist bekennt, das Maria nit alain sey ain muetter Cristi, sonnder
auch warlich ain muetter gots. Es ist ain Jrsal der Nestorianer gewest, das sy
gesagt, Maria sey Cristotocus, ein muetter Cristi, aber nit theotocus, ein mutter
gots, wider welchen Jrsal jch ye vnnd albeg gestritten." Hubmaier, *Rechenschaft*, 471.

154. Exponents of this view include Vedder (*Hübmaier*, 235-38), Bergsten
(*Hubmaier*, 477-48), Armour (*Anabaptist Baptism*, 54), Eberhard Arnold (*Early
Anabaptists*, rev. ed. [Rifton, N.Y.: Plough, 1984], 51-52), Walter Klaassen
("Baptism of Adult Believers," *Mennonitische Geschichtsblätter* 46 [1989]: 87),
and Pipkin ("Baptismal Theology," 53).

155. Estep, *Anabaptist Story*, 102.

cles."[156] Also in 1526, Hubmaier, in *Eine christliche Lehrtafel*, instructs young catachumens in the state believers' church at Nikolsburg: "What do you believe regarding Our Lady?. . . . I believe that she [was] . . . the mother of God, and blessed, because she believed those things that were told her by God. I cannot possibly (*Kainen . . . nit*, a double negative expressing impossibility) give her any greater title, name, or praise."[157] Not only did Hubmaier always regard Mary as *theotokos*, but he maintained faith in the perpetual virginity of Mary throughout his career. In 1526, while imprisoned by Zwingli in the Zurich *Wasserturm*, Hubmaier prayed, "I also believe and profess, my Lord Jesus Christ, that you were conceived of the Holy Spirit, without any manly seed, born of Mary, the pure and eternally chaste virgin."[158] Hubmaier, likewise, wrote a few months later in his Nikolsburg apologetic that Mary was "a chaste maiden before and after the birth,"[159] and he perspicuously affirmed this sentiment in his catechism: "She was a pure, chaste, and spotless Virgin before, during, and after the birth."[160] Finally Hubmaier, in his *Rechenschaft*, faithfully summarizes his changeless Mariology in an entire article devoted to a biblical defense of the Blessed Mother's lifelong chastity:

> The Holy Scripture communicates clearly and plainly the virginity of Mary, and we never read anywhere that any man knew her. Therefore it is incumbent upon us to believe that she was an eternally chaste virgin before, during, and after the birth. This article is hence substantiated: God said to Eve that her seed would crush the head of the serpent. Now

---

156. "So bekhenn ich die rainen Junckfrawen Mariam . . . sy zesein ein ware mûter gottes. . . . Die lieben Heiligen eere ich in Got als seinen werckzeüg, in wölchen er vil wunderzaichen gewürckt." Balthasar Hubmaier, *Eine kurze Entschuldigung*, in Westin and Bergsten, *Schriften*, 273.

157. "Was glaubstu von vnnser frawen. . . . Jch glaub das sy . . . ein [ware] mûter Gottes, vnd selig, die weil sy gelaubt hat denen dingen, so ir von Got gesagt worden. Kainen grössern Titel, namen vnnd lob khann ich ir nit geben." Hubmaier, *Eine christliche Lehrtafel*, 319.

158. "Jch glaub auch vnd bekhenn mein herr Jesu Christe, das du entpfangen seyest von dem heiligen Geyst, on allen mänlichen samen, geboren auß Maria der rainen vnd ewig keüschen Junnckfrauen." Hubmaier, *Die zwölf Artikel*, 216. While this language is probably formulaic, it does show Hubmaier's similarity of belief with Bernard.

159. "Mariam ain keüsche magt vor vnd nach der geburt." Hubmaier, *Entschuldigung*, 273.

160. "Sy ein rayne, keüsche vnnd vnbefleckte Junckfraw sey vor, jn vnd nach der geburt." Hubmaier, *Eine christliche Lehrtafel*, 319.

Eve was betrothed to Adam but was, nevertheless, a pure virgin, as the text clearly affirms that Adam knew her only after their expulsion from Paradise, Genesis 3 and 4. Therefore it is inescapable that Mary, the bearer of our Savior Jesus Christ, who has crushed the head of the hellish serpent, must have been a chaste virgin even after the birth, although she was married to a man.[161]

Returning to the comparison of the original quote from the *Rechenschaft* with Bernard, one wonders why Hubmaier feels inclined to defend Mary as God-bearer as opposed to Christ-bearer. Such cannot supply a refutation of the views of his alleged coreligionists, since no Anabaptist advocated monophysitism during Hubmaier's lifetime. It is well-documented by Williams that this ancient "heresy" first reemerged in the sixteenth century from the ubiquitous heterodoxical woodwork underlying the Christian tradition in the obscure 1530 essays of Melchior Hofmann and only became prominent in the notorious "heavenly flesh" doctrine of Menno Simons, which would be rejected by the later Mennonite movement.[162] Moreover, there seems to be no known historical antecedent in Catholicism, Lutheranism, or Zwinglianism to prompt a polemic against an apparently nonexistent deviation. This problem is intractable, in my judgment, unless we turn to Bernard's discussion of Mary in *De consideratione ad Eugenium papam*; here Bernard repu-

---

161. "Die heylig schrifft druckht häll vnd klärlich auß die Junckhfrauschafft Marie vnnd wierdt niendert gelesen, das sy von einem man erkennt worden. Demnach solle sy pillich fur ein eewig keusche Junckhfrauen vor, in vnd nach der geburt von vnns gelaubt werden. Diser Artigkl wirt also bewisen: Gott sagt zu Heue, das jr samen der Schlanngen das haubt zerkhnischen werd. Nun was Heua dann zmal dem Adam vermechlet vnd doch darbey ein raine Junckhfraw, wie der text haytter außweiset, das sy erst nach dem Ausstoß auß dem paradeys von Adam sey erkennt worden. Gen. 3. 4. c. Demnach mag sich nymermer felen, Marie, ein gepererin vnnsers haylannds Jhesu Cristi, der diser hellischen schlanngen jren Kopf zerknischt hat, mueß vnnd ist auch ain raine Junckhfraw gewest, auch nach der geburdt, ob sy wol einem Man vermechlet war." Hubmaier, *Rechenschaft*, 470-71.

162. Menno's docetism affirmed that the Logos did not assume his own anhypostatic human nature from Mary, as pronounced by Chalcedon, but that Mary simply constituted the incubator for the already enfleshed Son, who was granted a heavenly, non-Adamic body prior to the Incarnation: "For Christ Jesus, as to his origin, is no earthly man, that is, a fruit of the flesh and blood of Adam. He is a heavenly fruit or man, for his beginning or origin is of the Father"; Simons, *Brief and Clear Confession*, in *Complete Writings*, 437. See also Williams, *Radical Reformation*, 596-98.

diates the Nestorianism championed by Abelard, *i.e.* "that the flesh of Christ is something new created in the Virgin, and not taken from the flesh of the Virgin."[163] Inveighing against Abelard and his followers, Bernard provides a typological argument in defense of the true humanity of Christ:

> Let those who attempt to alienate us from the flesh of Christ be alienated from us, for viciously insisting that the flesh of Christ was created newly in the Virgin and not taken from her. Long before that prophetic spirit referred beautifully to this notion, or rather, blasphemy, of the impious, with these words, "A shoot shall come forth from the root of Jesse, and a flower shall spring up from his root" (Is. 11:1). He could have said, "and a flower from the shoot," but he preferred "from the root" in order to demonstrate that the shoot and the flower had the same origin. Hence flesh was assumed from the origin from which the Virgin sprang and was not created new in the Virgin; for it was produced by the same root.[164]

The notion that Hubmaier paraphrased from Bernard, therefore, carries tremendous explanatory power to account for the former's unnecessary rehashing of a doctrine condemned by all sides in 1528; with this in mind, we may inquire further as to whether the sixteenth-century reformer may have derived his devotion to the perpetual virgin from the twelfth-century monk. Although this question cannot be definitively answered, as Mary's lifelong chastity was a widespread belief in the period (held even by Luther),[165] all that can be legitimately argued here is the plausibility of Hubmaier's acceptance of Bernard's entire Mariology given the former's probable reception of a significant portion of it. To be sure, Bernard publicly championed the perpetual virginity of the Holy Mother in no less than a dozen homilies; strik-

---

163. "carnem Christi novam in Virgine creatam et non de Virginis carne sumptam." Bernard de Clairvaux, *De consideratione ad Eugenium papam*, in *Sämtliche Werke lateinisch/deutsch* I, 810.

164. "Alieni sint a nobis qui Christi a nobis carnem alienare conantur, novam creatam in Virgine, et non de Virgine sumptam, impie asserentes. Pulchre propheticus spiritus longe ante occurrit huic sententiae, immo blasphemiae impiorum: Egredietur, inquiens, virga de radice Iesse, et flos de radice eius ascendet. Dixesse poterat: "et flos de virga", sed maluit: de radice, ut unde virgam, inde florem duxisse originem demonstraret. Inde igitur sumpta caro, unde orta Virgo, nec nova in Virgine, quae prodiit ex radice." Bernard, *De consideratione*, 812.

165. Pelikan, *Reformation*, 354-55.

ingly evocative of the later synopsis from the *Rechenschaft* is the monk's encouragement during the Feast of the Assumption for her *hyperdulia*:

> What tongue, I ask, whether angelic or human, can worthily eulogize the Virgin Mother, the Mother not of a mere man but of true God?. . . . You see, my brethren, so firm was her purpose to live always as a virgin that it could not be shaken even by the words of the heavenly envoy promising her a son . . . [for] neither the desire of a son nor the hope of posterity shall ever induce her to abandon her resolution of remaining always a virgin.[166]

Echoed by Hubmaier as well was Bernard's hallmark conception of, in the vivid phrase of Peter Berger, "a permanently enchanted universe,"[167] wherein the sum total of human communication with miracle-working saints comprises a vast intercessory network between heaven and earth.[168] Astonishingly, the monk proclaims amid the feast commemorating the beatified departed that we should maintain more confidence in their approachability and power because of a common human nature, than in angels who cannot experientially sympathize with humans:

> Although persuaded that I may presume much on the love of . . . the holy angels . . . I ought to be more confident in those who, as I know, participate with me in the same human nature, and therefore ought to feel a more affectionate and tender compassion for one that is bone of their bone and flesh of their flesh.[169]

Taken together, the parallels between the Mariology of Bernard and Hubmaier tend, at minimum, to strengthen the thesis that the latter relied upon the writings of the former.

Two additional Cistercian echoes in Hubmaier consist in his exaltation of lifelong continence over the married life, despite the fact that he anticipated the nuptials of Luther and Zwingli by marrying Elizabeth Hügline, the daughter of a burgher, in 1524,[170] and in his uniquely anti-Anabaptist stance

---

166. Bernard of Clairvaux, "Fourth Sermon for the Feast of the Assumption," in *Sermons for the Seasons and Principal Festivals*, 253-54.

167. Peter Berger, *The Sacred Canopy* (New York: Anchor Books, 1967), 112.

168. Luddy, *Life and Teaching*, 745-46.

169. Bernard of Clairvaux, "Fifth Sermon for the Feast of All Saints," in *Sermons for the Seasons and Principal Festivals*, 395.

170. Vedder, *Hübmaier*, 72-73.

on the legitimacy of just war and Christians wielding the sword. Surprisingly, Hubmaier explicates Matthew 19:12, which intimates that those who can embrace continence should do so, to demonstrate

> that those who for the sake of God retain their virginity do well, for virginity is far better and more beneficial to the kingdom of God than marriage and widowhood. . . . That human state is higher which is closer to its original source. Now, humanity existed first in a virginal state, then entered the married state, and third, after this followed the widowed state; hence the state of virginity stands closest to God.[171]

Such a devaluation of conditions based on their distance from a state of nature recalls the Bernardian exaltation of nature over grace and the role of grace as the vehicle through which humanity is restored to its created perfection and innocence.[172] From Bernard's veneration of the Virgin during the feast celebrating her nativity came quite possibly the original source of Hubmaier's logic: "In Mary human nature is found entirely pure, not alone pure from all defilement (*i.e.* sexual immorality), but pure also from composition with another nature (*i.e.* any sexual intercourse)."[173] For Bernard as well as Hubmaier, therefore, the immaculate human essence necessarily subsists in its primeval chastity.

In his apologia for the Knights Templars, then a completely new modality of the religious life, the preacher of the Second Crusade praised this militia who, by taking the Benedictine vows of poverty, chastity, and obedience, endeavored to sanctify the idea of knighthood. At the outset, let it be noted, Bernard qualified his espousal of "holy violence" by degrading secular chivalry: "What, therefore, is the result or fruit of this worldly knighthood, or rather malice, as I should classify it? What if not the mortal sin of the victor

---

171. "das die, so vmb gottes willenn jr Junckhfrauschafften behalltenn, wol thient, wann vil pesser vnnd furderlicher ist die Junckfrauschafft zum Reich gottes denn die Ee vnd wittschaft. . . . Der stannd des menschens ist höcher, welcher seinem erssten vrsprung nächner ist. Nun ist der Mensch erstlich in junckhfreulichem stannd gewest, darnach in den eerlichen khumen, zum dritten ist auch hernach geuolgt der witwen stannd, darumb wiert auch der junckhfreulich stannd der negchst bey gott seinn." Hubmaier, *Rechenschaft*, 479.

172. Evans, *Mind of St. Bernard*, 120-25.

173. Bernard of Clairvaux, "Sermon for the Feast of the Nativity of the Blessed Virgin Mary," in *Sermons for the Seasons and Principal Festivals*, 288.

and the eternal death of the defeated?"[174] Likewise, in his refutation of Article Six of the *Schleitheim Confession*, Hubmaier writes in reassurance to Lord Arkleb of the Moravian Margraviate and in denunciation of his so-called misguided brethren that he enjoys no company with Anabaptists who, contrary to the Pauline principle in Romans 13, deny that Christians should sit in authority or wield the sword. While denying that the common Anabaptist proof-text, "Whoever takes up the sword shall perish by the sword" (Mt. 26:52), prohibits violence as such, Hubmaier mirrors the perspective of Bernard in his exposition that the verse does, however, forbid carnal violence not sanctioned by the duly established government: "They take up the sword who wield it without calling, unorderly, and on their own authority. But no one should take up the sword himself, except where one is chosen and ordered for that task. Then he does not take it up of himself; rather, it is put before him and given to him."[175] By contrast, both Bernard and Hubmaier champion the proper use of the sword, employing, once allowance is made for translation, precisely the same vocabulary. The twelfth-century reformer points out that there are "two swords,"[176] one spiritual and one carnal, discussed in the New Testament; likewise, the Nikolsburg bishop makes the same distinction four centuries later: "These two swords . . . of which one belongs to the soul and the other to the body, so you must, dear brothers, leave both of them in their dignity."[177] In what seems a highly telling parallel, Hubmaier, despite the extinction of manorial ideas of chivalry, enlightens his audience that 2 Corinthians 10:4 describes "the weapons of our knighthood (*ritterschaft*)."[178] This very term, along with the identical Scripture reference, previously appeared in Bernard: "On the new knighthood (*militia*, Latin equivalent of *ritterschaft*). . . . Let both swords of the faithful disconnect the necks of the enemy, in order to destroy every high thing ex-

---

174. "Quis igitur finis fructusve saecularis huius, non dico, militiae, sed malitiae, si et occisor letaliter peccat, et occisus aeternaliter perit?" Bernard de Clairvaux, *Ad milites Templi: De laude novae militae*, in *Sämtliche Werke lateinisch/deutsch* I, 274.

175. "Das schwert nemendt die, so es on erwölunng, vnordenlich vnnd auß aygnem gewallt brauchen. Aber nyemandt soll das schwert selbs nemen, sonder wo ainer erwölet vnd darzů eruordert wirdt, denn so nimbt erß nit auß jm selbs, sonnder man tregt jms dar vnnd gibt jmß." Hubmaier, *Von dem Schwert*, 436-37.

176. Bernard, *Ad milites Templi*, 270, 278.

177. "Dise zway Schwerter . . . dero ains gehört zů der Seel, das ander zům Leib, so müessent irß baide, lieben Brüeder, in iren wirdikayten pleiben lassen." Hubmaier, *Von dem Schwert*, 446-47.

178. "Die waffen vnserer ritterschaft"; Ibid., 445.

tolling itself against the knowledge of God (2 Cor. 10:4-5)."[179] Both thinkers additionally employed the same line of reasoning, namely, that prominent biblical figures never barred the sword when having perfect opportunities to do so, to defend the rightful exercise of the physical sword. Commenting on John the Baptist's encounter with the soldiers, Bernard queries, "If a Christian is not permitted to strike with the sword, why did the Savior's forerunner tell the soldiers to be content with their pay, and not rather forbid them to serve in the military?"[180] Advancing to the Baptist's successor, Hubmaier seemingly tries to upgrade this argument: "Moreover, you hear that Christ said to Peter, 'Put your sword back into the sheath.' He does not say, 'Untie it and throw it away.' For Christ rebukes him because he drew it and not because he had it hanging at his side. Otherwise he would have rebuked Peter long before if that were wrong."[181] On the issues of just war and violence, then, Bernard the monk and Hubmaier the radical stand very close together.

Synopsis of Evidence for the Literary Dependence Hypothesis

In his 1993 study of Hubmaier's theological underpinnings, Rempel, acknowledging the failure of past historians to explain the reformer's trichotomous anthropology or libertarian free will, offers the following suggestion: "One has the sense that it was mediated to him by another thinker or spiritual tradition."[182] Even more provocatively, the latest edition (1992) of Williams' authoritative tome *The Radical Reformation*, while never considering the prospect that Hubmaier relied upon Bernard, reveals that two major strands of medieval mysticism inspired the German Anabaptists, one of

---

179. "De nova militia. . . . Exseratur gladius uterque fidelium in cervices inimicorum, ad destruendam omnem altitudinem extollentem se adversus scientiam Dei (2 Cor 10, 4-5)." Bernard, *Ad milites Templi*, 276-78; Brunotte and Weber, *Kirchenlexikon*, 2:966.

180. "Si percutere in gladio omnino fas non est christiano, cur ergo praeco Salvatoris contendos fore suis stipendiis militibus indixit, et non potius omnem eis militiam interdixit?" Bernard, *Ad milites Templi*, 276-78.

181. "Dar zů hörstu hie, das Christus sagt zů Petro: Steck das schwert ein in die schaiden. Er spricht nit: Thůs ab, wirffs von dir. Denn darumb, das erß zuckht, strafft jn Christus, vnd nit darumb, das erß hett an der seytten hangen, er hett in sonnst vorlangst gestraffet, so es wer vnrecht gewesen." Hubmaier, *Von dem Schwert*, 437.

182. Rempel, *Lord's Supper*, 84.

which was "devotional, affective, penitential, and Christocentric, developed by Cistercians or Franciscans and represented initially by Bernard of Clairvaux."[183] The present chapter demonstrates that such speculations indeed pointed in the right, but perhaps unexpected, direction. Drawing together the threads exposed through detailed comparison of Bernard's *De gratia et libero arbitrio* with the radical's two central treatises on free choice, *Von der Freiheit des Willens* and *Das andere Büchlein von der Freiwilligkeit der Menschen*, the foregoing discussion reveals powerful evidence that the latter relied heavily upon the former's treatise in both his argumentation and support thereof. Hubmaier's tripartite model of humanity, for example, mirrors precisely that proposed by Bernard, and notable turns of phrase from the former amount minimally to paraphrases or even verbatim translations from the latter. In every detail, down to the level of the specific freedoms assigned to each component of the human being and the intricate consequences the Fall imposed on each one, the sixteenth-century reformer palpably reflects the theology of his twelfth-century predecessor. As optimists with regard to the human condition,[184] both thinkers were stalwart defenders of a libertarian view of creaturely freedom over and against the prevailing compatibilist Augustinianism, such that even the *initium fidei*, concurrently defined as hungering and thirsting after righteousness, may be produced by the unregenerate wholly apart from grace. This is of utmost importance, for all other orthodox defenders[185] of libertarian free will from the early church (*e.g.* Chrysostom) until the 1648 Peace of Westphalia (*e.g.* Molina) strenuously insisted that prevenient, yet resistible, grace comprised the necessary soteriological first step. Coupled with the similar fourfold *ordo salutis* in both thinkers, such evidence renders it all but certain that Hubmaier was depend-

---

183. Williams, *Radical Reformation*, 81.

184. Bernard specialist R. J. Zwi Werblowsky underscores the fact that the virtuous monk too often projected his lifestyle upon those less deserving: "An impulsive and generous nature, St. Bernard often entertained higher hopes of human nature than it deserved, and he consequently came to grief"; Introduction to Bernard, in *The Works of Bernard of Clairvaux*, Vol. 7 (Kalamazoo, Mich.: Cistercian Publications, 1977), 119. By the same token, Henry Vedder, the author of the only twentieth-century English biography of Hubmaier, reproves the radical's view of freedom as "an impracticable ideal"; *Hübmaier*, 103.

185. Of course, Pelagius infamously held to human generation of the *initium fidei*, but upon this and many other grounds was condemned for heresy by the Third Ecumenical Council of Ephesus in 431. See Pelagius, *Commentary on St. Paul's Epistle to the Romans*, trans. Theodore de Bruyn (Oxford: Oxford University Press, 1995), 107-12.

ent on Bernard with regard to both his theological anthropology and his libertarian concept of freedom.

Turning to the interrelated doctrines of divine predestination and foreknowledge, it seems clear that Hubmaier embraces the metaphysical foundation of Bernard, which predicated election upon prescience, and refines it to accommodate a meaningful, rather than redundant, providence by including counterfactual knowledge within the scope of God's omniscience. At several points Hubmaier echoes both the outline and the content of Bernard's conversation with Paul, citing the identical proof-texts from the Pauline epistles and duplicating the monk's exegetical formulation therefrom concerning divine conservation and concurrence. Using more than a few untranslated Latin phrases found in *De gratia*, Hubmaier harmonizes in Cistercian fashion human ability to fully earn heavenly merit on the level of psychic freedom with divine grace mercifully giving the same merit on the levels of potentiality and acceptance. These observations are further bolstered by the characteristically threefold salvific, baptismal, and hamartiological enumerations peculiar to both thinkers, especially poignant by virtue of Hubmaier's espousal of novel definitions given by Bernard to standard terms based on his experience in the cloister. Manifesting the functional equivalent of physical execution, the "white martyrdom" of monastic self-mortification found its way at the most unlikely of times (simultaneous with the hunting of *Täuferjäger* for their prey[186] and mere months before the radical's own martyrdom) as the definition of the "baptism of blood" in contradistinction to its *prima facie* understanding as the preeminent earthly sacrifice. In addition, the otherwise idiosyncratic juxtaposition of Hubmaier's high Mariology as *theotokos* paired with its defense against a defunct Nestorianism can only be accounted for if the reformer followed the corresponding line of argumentation in Bernard's dialogue with Eugenius III on consideration. The last touches are placed on the literary dependence hypothesis by the radical's anti-Anabaptist attitudes toward marriage and pacifism coupled with matching depreciations in the Bernardian *Opera*. Taken together, these copious independent lines of verification constitute a highly probable cumulative case that Hubmaier was not only intimately acquainted with several treatises and homilies of Bernard, but directly and purposely quoted, paraphrased, and imitated the twelfth-century monastic reformer at many points. One significant point, however, which functions as the nucleus for a thoroughgoing revision of Hubmaier's theological pilgrimage as well as, most importantly, his entire sacramental theology remains yet to be explored. To this water-

---

186. Williams, *Radical Reformation*, 316.

shed in the historiography of the Waldshut and Nikolsburg shepherd of souls we shall set our sights in the next chapter.

Chapter 3

Framing a New Theological Pilgrimage of Balthasar Hubmaier

Well-versed in patristic and medieval theology (including, as we have demonstrated, many of the available writings of Bernard of Clairvaux) under the famous polemicist John Eck at the universities of Freiburg and Ingolstadt, in 1512 new *doctor theologiae* Balthasar Hubmaier commenced his theological and pastoral career in the latter institution as professor and university chaplain at the Church of our Beloved Lady (*Kirche unserer geliebten Dame*). Concerning his own salvation, the young priest was firmly committed to the intrinsic efficacy and necessity of the sacramental system, holding an unusually high view of the three sacraments conferring a *character indelibilis* upon the soul.[1] The external evidence reveals that such an emphasis persisted until his rebaptism; indeed, Johann Fabri, later to serve as prosecutor at Hubmaier's sedition trial, remarked after his 1521 trip to Waldshut that he had never before seen a bishop carry out baptism, confirmation, or holy orders with "such elaborate or impressive ritual."[2] Nevertheless, Hubmaier had become fascinated with the Wittenberg Reformation two years earlier, paying special attention to Luther's sermons and treatises on faith and the sacraments. At this early stage, Luther emphasized the necessity of personal faith for the sacraments; in his 1519 *Disputatio de lege et fide* he wrote, "If indeed we are justified by faith, it follows that the sacra-

---

1. Bergsten, *Hubmaier*, 96.
2. As recalled by Fabri in his pamphlet *Reason Why Dr. Balthasar Hubmayr, Head and Founder of the Anabaptists, Was at Vienna*, trans. William R. Estep, *Anabaptist Beginnings* (Nieuwkoop: de Graaf, 1976), 139.

ments are not efficacious except by faith in Christ."[3] Reading Luther via the lenses of his tripartite anthropology and libertarian concept of free will, Hubmaier interpreted the former's *fides* as something arising out of innate human ability. Shortly thereafter, Hubmaier seems to have instituted the practice of believers' baptism, as revealed by three previously neglected sources, two of which flowed from the radical's pen and one from the Swiss reformer and historian Füsslin. This chapter, accordingly, offers a new historical reconstruction of Hubmaier's theological development, explicating the influence of Bernard, Luther, and other theologians upon Hubmaier's view of the three aforementioned sacraments, tracing each step of Hubmaier's pilgrimage relevant to his post-rebaptismal sacramental theology, and analyzing the relationship between the atypical Magisterial Radical and other Magisterial Reformers, including the former's initial attraction and 1523 distancing (but not complete break) from Luther. What impact, we may ask, did Luther's *Babylonian Captivity of the Church* exert on Hubmaier's view of confirmation and ordination, especially in light of the emphasis given to these rites between 1520 and 1525? Moreover, how, in the incisive remark of Rempel, did "the great passion" and "preoccupation" of Hubmaier's work "to correctly set forth the relationship between the divine initiative and the human response in salvation,"[4] mediated through the *sine qua non* of *Freiheit des Willens* (Hubmaier's term for libertarian free will), comprise the ubiquitous driving force that shaped and directed the course of an all-encompassing journey spanning the polarities of Catholicism and religious radicalism? Upon such an excursion we shall now embark.

Bernard and Hubmaier: The Salvific Import of the First and Second Baptisms

As discussed in chapter one, the solitary mention of Bernard's name by Hubmaier occurs in a provocative allusion to the former's 1141 homily, "On the Second Baptism," wherein ordination is identified as a rebaptism necessary for the remission of all actual sins committed after baptism. Hence, Bernard exhorted his novices to commit to the religious life: "[I]t behooves us to be baptized again. Just as in baptism we are rescued from the powers of darkness and transferred to the kingdom of light, so in this second regenera-

---

3. "Si quidem Fide justificamur, consectaneum est, et Sacramenta non nisi per Fidem in Christum efficacia esse." Martin Luther, *Disputatio de lege et fide*, in *D. Martin Luthers Werke*, 6:24.

4. Rempel, *Lord's Supper*, 40, 44.

tion of the monastic vows we are refashioned in the light."[5] When questioned by the Abbot of Coulombs that same year as to why holy orders should be considered as a second baptism, in his *On Precept and Dispensation* Bernard provides the following suggestive response:

> Why has our program of life rather than other penitential disciplines merited the prerogative of this designation? I think it is because of the perfect renouncement of the world and the singular excellence of spiritual life, which makes those who live it preeminent to all other kinds of men. . . . Just as in baptism we are drawn out of the power of darkness and transferred into the kingdom of light, so likewise in the second regeneration of this holy profession we are recreated in sanctity, being now redeemed, not from the darkness of original sin, but from the denser darkness of many actual sins. This is announced to us by the Apostle: "The night is far spent, and the day is near" (Rom. 13:12).[6]

By his own admission in several treatises, it is clear that Hubmaier, before his rebaptism, also espoused the view that consecration to the priesthood was not only analogous to baptism, but also remitted his actual sins. While debating with Zwingli in December 1525, Hubmaier explains what belief he formerly held concerning holy orders: "Water baptism is an initiatory sign, ceremony, or *Teleta* (in Greek), just as when young people are thrust into the orders."[7] After being subsequently tortured by Zwingli for his refusal to cease rebaptizing, Hubmaier insisted, in a telling conditional statement, that if the sacrament of believers' baptism had not been forsaken by the patristic church, then the allegedly false sacrament of ordination would have never arisen:

---

5. Bernard, "On the Second Baptism," 424.

6. "Unde inter cetera paenitentiae instituta monasterialis disciplina meruerit hanc praerogativam. Arbitror ob perfectam mundi abrenuntiationem ac singularem excellentiam vitae spiritualis, qua praeeminens universis vitae humanae generibus huiuscemodi facit. . . . Sed et quomodo in baptismo eruimur de potestate tenebrarum et in regnum transferimur claritatis aeternae, ita et in sancti huius secunda quadam regeneratione propositi, de tenebris aeque, non unius originalis, sed multorum actualium delictorum, in lumen virtutum evadimus, reaptantes nobis illud Apostoli: Nox praecessit, dies autem appropinquavit [Rom 13, 12]." Bernard de Clairvaux, *De praecepto et dispensatione*, in *Sämtliche Werke lateinisch/deutsch* I, 416, 418.

7. "Der wassertauff ist ein anheblich zaichenn, Ceremonj oder Teleta (auf kriechisch), gleich als wenn die Junngen sind jn die orden gstossen." Hubmaier, *Gespräch auf Zwinglis Taufbüchlein*, 188.

[I]f we had followed [the baptism of believers] until now and had employed it in the churches, then the vows and duties of all monks, priests, and nuns would have been unnecessary. But since the right Christian baptismal duty has been pushed out of the middle, Satan has imposed himself with his cloister commitments.[8]

Upon assuming the position of bishop at Nikolsburg in 1526, Hubmaier acknowledged his past conviction that ordination confers forgiveness of sins and renounced any comfort this belief once brought him:

Indeed, I declare that I place no value in the vows of monks, priests, and nuns. For if we lived according to the baptismal vow we would have enough to do day and night; however, we would still have to declare ourselves as unprofitable servants and would not put other burdens upon ourselves. However, because we did not know what water baptism means, and what the baptismal vow entails, Satan introduced monastic vows. . . . I consider it not only a mockery, but even an idolatry, for to it is ascribed forgiveness of sins; and he who receives it may not go to the baths nor dance nor gamble for a certain time.[9]

Likewise, in his catechism Hubmaier exhorts neophytes that believers' baptism, not holy orders, amounts to the real promise of discipleship: "This specifically is the right baptismal vow, which we have lost for a thousand years; in the meantime Satan has pushed his way in with his monastic vows and priestly vows and set them up in the holy place."[10] While the full implica-

---

8. Ibid., 187-88; the German is quoted in footnote 82, page 25.

9. "Ja ich bekhenn, das ich nichts halte auff münch, pfaffen vnd Nunnen glübt. Wann so wir der Tauffglübd nach lebten, hetten wir tag vnd nacht gnüg zeschaffen, müesten vnns dennocht vnnutz diener bekhennen, vnd wurden vns selbs ander burden nit aufflegen. Dieweil wir aber nit gewist, was der wassertauff bedeut vnd was die Tauffglübd erfordert, in dem hat der Satan die kloster glübd. . . . halte ich nit allain für ein gspött, ja, auch für ein Abgötterey, dann man ir verzeyhung der sünden zuschreybt, vnnd wölcher die entpfahet, der darff in etlicher zeit nit in das bad geen, nit tantzen oder spilen." Hubmaier, *Entschuldigung*, 274. The early modern practice of permanently forbidding public bathing, dancing, or gambling from those ordained (which Hubmaier shortens to a "certain time") is noted by Susan K. Wood, *Sacramental Orders* (Collegeville, Minn.: Liturgical Press, 2000), 60.

10. "Vnd das ist ebenn die recht Tauffglübd, die wir ob tauset iaren verloren haben, inn mitler zeyt hat sich der Satan mit seinen Kloster glübden vnd Pfaffen glübden eingetrungen vnd an die heiligen stat gesetzet." Hubmaier, *Eine christliche Lehrtafel*, 314.

tions of this quote will be elucidated later in the chapter, at this point we must note the decisive date at which Hubmaier places the downfall of the church—1,000 years prior to the sixteenth century, namely, the close of the patristic period. Such an opinion runs contrary to that of all other figures identified as early modern Anabaptists, who sought to restore the church to its New Testament roots, instead of trying to reform the church in accord with its old Catholic imperial heritage.[11] Consistent with the latter aim, Hubmaier was accused by Zwingli of "forcing baptism as if it were a monastic profession," a charge which Hubmaier not only refused to deny but proudly quoted.[12] For these reasons, the textual evidence both substantiates Hubmaier's pre-1525 appropriation of Bernard's sacramental theology concerning holy orders and points toward the former's possible conflation of the redemptive benefits dispensed by baptism and ordination into a novel concept of believers' baptism, to be discussed in the next chapter, after personally undertaking the rite on Easter Saturday of 1525.

Hubmaier commenced his theological pilgrimage under the assumption that his infant baptism regenerated him from original sin[13] while his vocation to the priesthood cleansed his soul from the much darker stain accumulated by a plethora of actual sins. As discussed in chapter two, the single area of disagreement in the respective fourfold *ordines salutis* of Bernard and Hubmaier concerned the second step, in which God, by virtue of his universal salvific will, provided all humans exercising their natural psychic freedom to yearn for righteousness with the voluntary opportunity to appropriately respond to the gospel. At this juncture, further examination of this variance between the two reformers is necessary. In addition to the conflict between Bernard's *testimonium internum Spiritus Sancti* and Hubmaier's preacher of the Word of God as the respective means preparatory to the seeker's decision, a twofold discrepancy arises as to what comprises an "appropriate response," and, derivatively, the identity of the *ratio praedestinationis*. For Bernard, regeneration occurs at the moment when a person trusts in Christ as

---

11. I borrow the label "Old Catholic Imperial Church" for the church between 100-500 C.E. from Earle E. Cairns, *Christianity through the Centuries*, 3rd rev. ed. (Grand Rapids, Mich.: Zondervan, 1996), 86.

12. "Jr . . . mit dem Tauff . . . zwinngen, sam es ein Münchische profession sey." In Hubmaier, *Gespräch auf Zwinglis Taufbüchlein*, 195.

13. That Hubmaier held this position as a Catholic (as expected from the medieval sacramental system) was admitted in 1525: "[I called] infant baptism an initial sign . . . *in remissionem peccatorum*, Acts 2:38, that is, in forgiveness of sins" (den kinder tauff ein anheblich zeychen . . . in remissionem peccatorum, Actorum am ij. cap. [V. 38], das ist in verzeyhung der sünden); *Von der christlichen Taufe*, 137.

a living person for forgiveness of sins and eternal life, which notion of saving faith makes up the factor that, excepting the handful of those redeemed by the *potentia absoluta*, determines one's divine election or reprobation.[14] However, as disclosed by Moore, Hubmaier embraced throughout his Catholic period the viewpoint of Eck on this score. According to Eck, reception of the sacrament of baptism must *ex opere operato* be looked upon by God as the *ratio praedestinationis ex parte praedestinati* (*i.e.* the ground of predestination on the part of the predestinate). Applied to the case of an infant, for example, Eck alleges that God predestines the child if she or he has been baptized; although she or he lacks faith and righteous works, a basis still exists for predestination within the infant, namely, her or his reception of the sacrament of regeneration. As Moore appropriately observes, "Infant baptism is not merely valid baptism, in Eck's view; it is significant enough to determine the child's eternal destiny."[15] To be sure, Hubmaier's Ingolstadt sermons reveal not only his adherence to this scheme, but a fine-tuning which reconciles it to the doctrine of purgatory. The controversialist's protégé hastened to point out (in what amounts in my assessment to a functional equivalent of backward causation) that the child, once grown to the age of discretion, could have her or his immediate admittance to heaven upon death (but not election) overturned by engaging in mortal sin.[16] In his reconceptualization of purgatory, Hubmaier, denying the existence of any distinct purgatory, postulated that baptized sinners are temporarily consigned to hell, conveying the character of purgatory, until they have been cleansed of all mortal sin. At this point the elect will enter paradise; however, the reprobate will remain in hell permanently. In his 1528 explication of his theological journey to King Ferdinand of Austria, Hubmaier summarizes the doctrine of purgatory he defended as a Catholic:

> Just as the kingdom of heaven is a place of peace for all persons who build on Christ with gold, silver, and precious stones, so the domain of hell is a purgatory for all who have built on Christ with wood, hay, and stubble. However, as for those who are utterly apart from Christ, there will be an eternal fire. But I know of no Scriptural grounds that, in addition to heaven and hell, there is a special purgatory.[17]

---

14. Leclerq, *Bernard*, 145.

15. Moore, "Catholic Teacher and Anabaptist Pupil," 80.

16. Ibid., 90. For a thorough discussion of backward causation see Alfred J. Freddoso, "Accidental Necessity and Power over the Past," *Pacific Philosophical Quarterly* 63 (1982): 54-68.

17. "Wie das himelreich allen den menschen, so auf Cristum gold, Silber vnnd Edlgestain gebauen, ein Statt der freyden ist, also ist das hellisch Reich

The purgatory of hell, in Hubmaier's theology, could be avoided in one of two ways, the former of which seems to bear striking resemblance to a partial indulgence and the latter to a plenary indulgence.

In accord with the 1439 Council of Florence,[18] the future rebaptizer argued that by partaking in the sacrament of penance, on the one hand, sanctifying grace is restored to the parishioner's soul for the time being until she or he commits another mortal sin. At this time, however, the process would need to be repeated: "When a person grieves and harms the church with a mortal sin . . . and now becomes reconciled to it again by confession, admission of blame, and acknowledgment of his sins, this church then has the authority by the order of Christ to forgive and absolve the same sins through its priests."[19] Surprising in itself, but explicable in light of the Hubmaier-Bernard literary dependence hypothesis, the former deemed unnecessary for the salvation of a religious what is necessary for that of a parishioner. Pressing the theology of the latter to its logical extreme, Hubmaier pronounced that holy orders rendered permanent the baptismal *ratio praedestinationis* and thereby absolved all past, present, and future actual sins of the ordained.[20] Even after forsaking Catholicism and embracing key Lutheran tenets, Hubmaier retained his faith in the eternal security which accompanies ordination; one common apologetic for this doctrine found throughout his pre-April 1525 works centers on the perceived symbolic significance of Jesus' turning water into wine at the wedding in Cana. Since holy orders entails marriage to the church, Hubmaier reasons that the water of baptism, instituted by John the Baptist, is transformed into the wine of salvation, received from the Lamb of God, in the spiritual wedding of ordination.[21] Less than two months before his rebaptism, Hubmaier wrote in a chain letter to the churches in Waldshut, Regensburg, Ingolstadt, and Freiburg:

---

allen denen ain fegfeur, so auf Cristum holtz, hew vnnd stupfflen gebauet haben. Welche aber gar ausserhalb Cristo sein, denselbenn wiert es auch ein ewig feur sein. Das aber ausserhalb himel vnnd hell ein sonnder fegfeur sey, des waiß jch in der Schrifft khainen grundt." Hubmaier, *Rechenschaft*, 473-74.

18. Johann Loserth, *D. Balthasar Hubmaier und die Anfänge der Wiedertaufe in Mähren* (Brünn: Verlag der histor.-statist., 1893), 72.

19. "Da ein mensch mit einer tödtsind die kirchen betriebt, verletzt . . . das er yetz durch peicht, schuldig gebung vnd bekanntnuß seiner Sunden sich widerumb mit jr versone, welche kirch alßdann auß dem Beuelch Cristi gwalt hat, durch jren priester . . . jm dieselbenn sund zuuerzeichen vnd nachtzelassenn." Hubmaier, *Rechenschaft*, 477.

20. Sachsse, *Hubmaier als Theologe*, 131.

21. Mabry, *Understanding of Faith*, 37-38.

> Since the water, in faith, becomes wine at the wedding, we must first
> put on John's rough coat before we may receive the soft, soothing, and
> gentle little lamb Christ Jesus. Now the [new religious] submits himself
> inwardly in the heart and will to a new life according to the rule and
> teaching of Christ, the physician who has made him whole, from whom
> he obtained life.[22]

Hence it seems probable that Hubmaier, when he left Regensburg and accepted the position of bishop at Waldshut in 1519, regarded himself as forever ontologically transformed into a new creature incapable of losing salvation, as the preliminary yet incomplete regeneration obtained through his
infant baptism was consummated in the second and entire regeneration of
holy orders.

Lutheran Influence on Hubmaier's Sacramental Theology

To be expected, as *Domprediger* (Cathedral Preacher) at Regensburg
from 1516-1519, Hubmaier virulently opposed the allegedly factious and
heretical Luther. This fact is nowhere more evident than in an October 1518
satirical poem sent to Pope Leo X, in which he went so far to suggest that
the Holy Father and the monarchs of Europe should join forces to eliminate
"the intolerable Luther."[23] It is clear, moreover, that Hubmaier's antipathy
was not uninformed, as he kept apprised of the Wittenberger's tracts and
even preached in direct rebuttal of the *Ninety-Five Theses*.[24] The turning
point for Hubmaier, however, materialized in 1519 shortly after his relo-
cation to Waldshut as a result of reading Luther's more elaborate doctrinal
formulations concerning Bible and sacraments. The recently appointed
bishop grew quite attracted to Luther's hermeneutics, which identified the
source of truth as *sola scriptura* plus faithful reason or rationality, along
with his doctrine that the sacraments cannot and must not be received with-

---

22. "Also würt das wasser im glauben zů wein auff der hochzeit, vnd můß
man zůuor den rauhen rock Joannis anlegen, ee vnd man das waich, lind vnd
senfftmütig lemblin Christum Jesum möge vberkommen. Vnd yetz ergibt sich
der mensch inwendig im hertzen vnd fürsatz in ain neu leben nach der regel vnd
leer Christi deß artzts, der in hat gsund gemachet, vnnd von dem er hatt das leben." Hubmaier, *Summe*, 111.

23. "den unerträglichen Luther." Balthasar Hubmaier, Untitled poem, in
Westin and Bergsten, *Schriften*, 14.

24. Sachsse, *Hubmaier als Theologe*, 130; Vedder, *Hübmaier*, 50.

out faith.[25] Operating in concert with one another, these newfound principles drove Hubmaier to undertake a systematic study of Erasmus' *Greek New Testament* and the Church Fathers, possible by virtue of his proficiency in Greek and Latin acquired at the University of Freiburg.[26] When a collection of Luther sermons was disseminated from Wittenberg later that year, Hubmaier, perusing them without delay, grew captivated by *Ein sermon von dem neuen Testament, das ist von der heiligen Messe*, which would henceforth remain his favorite of all Luther's works. Especially enamored by the following series of word-pictures, the Waldshut reformer would habitually quote them verbatim throughout his career: "Baptism and the Supper mean nothing without previous faith—they are like a sheath without a knife, a case without a gem, a hoop before an inn without wine."[27] Ignited by the fires of his "profoundly rational mind," which Mabry estimates as perhaps surpassing that of Calvin,[28] Hubmaier arrived no later than 1520 at the tentative deduction that infants, who presumably lack faith, should be prohibited baptism, regarding which inference he quickly drafted a letter seeking verification from Luther.[29] Strangely, and potentially revealing his own misgivings about pedobaptism,[30] Luther neglected to answer this epistle, an oversight which Hubmaier apparently interpreted in the best possible light.[31] On the

---

25. This is not to say that for Luther, reason could not be perverted to wrong uses; in that case, as Gerrish points out (*Grace and Reason*, 137), reason becomes "the devil's whore"; Mabry, *Doctrine of the Church*, 32; Eddie Mabry, *Balthasar Hubmaier's Understanding of Faith* (Lanham, Md.: University Press of America, 1998), 6-7.

26. Mabry, *Doctrine of the Church*, 1. Possessing an excellent facility for language, Hubmaier was competent in Hebrew as well by his master's graduation in 1506.

27. Martin Luther, "Ein Sermon von dem neuen Testament, das ist von der heiligen Messe," 6:363; the German is quoted in footnote 87, page 26.

28. Mabry, *Doctrine of the Church*, 102-03.

29. Ibid., 33; Loserth, *Hubmaier*, 49. In what the primary sources now reveal to be an understatement, Bergsten had speculated in 1961 *passim*, "It is not impossible that Luther himself, through his pamphlets . . . first caused Hubmaier to question the validity of infant baptism" (Es ist nicht ausgeschlossen, daß Hubmaier . . . durch das Lesen von Schriften Luthers den Anstoß empfing, über die Berechtigung der Kindertaufe nachzudenken); *Hubmaier*, 112.

30. On the topic of the unreciprocated correspondence, Mabry comments: "Luther had also apparently written at one time, in relation to this, that infants should, therefore, not be baptized without faith"; *Doctrine of the Church*, 32.

31. Sachsse, *Hubmaier als Theologe*, 132; Windhorst, *Täuferisches Taufverständnis*, 89.

basis of such a perceived tacit admission, Hubmaier diligently analyzed both the Bible and the Patristics, the latter of which he (in harmony with Luther's application of the "clear reason or rationality" hermeneutic) recognized as an authoritative commentary on the former, in search of evidence either for or against infant baptism.[32] These modest foundations of what would later heighten into a full-scale attack on infant baptism, however, quickly expanded following the publication of one of the Wittenberg reformer's most influential pamphlets.

Voicing his objections against Rome before the German populace, in October 1520 Luther circulated *The Babylonian Captivity of the Church* which, while supporting the continued practice of confirmation, marriage, ordination, and extreme unction, denied on Scriptural grounds that these four ceremonies amounted to sacraments. Only baptism, the Eucharist, and perhaps confession qualified, according to the recently excommunicated monk's standard, as (in the famous maxim of Augustine) "visible signs of an invisible grace,"[33] by virtue of their institution by Christ as divine promises consisting of both a word and a sign.[34] Such an analysis proved convincing to Hubmaier on two fronts: the Wittenberg reformer's evaluation that the sacraments formally comprise the vows God makes to humanity, which must be reciprocated by belief on the part of the recipients, and his curtailment of the number of sacraments to two, with penance playing an intervening role between baptism and the Mass. Hubmaier, consequently, would come to agree with Luther's following explication of the inextricably intertwined quality of sacred vows and personal trust:

> [T]hese two, promise and faith, are necessarily yoked together. No one can believe if there is no promise. If there is no faith, a promise is useless, as faith is its counterpart and completion. From these considerations, anyone can easily deduce that the mass, which is simply a promise, can only be attended and celebrated in faith.[35]

Thus, in his 1520 eucharistic liturgy, Hubmaier interpreted the Pauline self-examination clause (1 Cor. 11:28) in terms of belief in Christ's commitment of love:

> Now such inspection includes the following. First, one must believe fully and certainly that Christ gave his body and shed his rose-colored

32. Windhorst, *Täuferisches Taufverständnis*, 92.
33. Augustine, *City of God*, X.5.
34. Luther, *Babylonian Captivity*, 36:31.
35. Ibid., 36:77.

blood for him on the cross. . . . Let one also strengthen himself in gratitude, in order to be thankful . . . to God for the great, superabundant,
and unutterable love and goodness that he has shown him through his
all-beloved Son, our Lord Jesus Christ. . . . It is precisely to this fellowship and promise of love that the Supper of Christ testifies.[36]

Embracing Luther's equation of "sacrament" with the gracious form or
"promise of God" rather than its tangible matter,[37] Hubmaier, in a list of perceived Roman errors which his Waldshut congregation was ordered not to
perpetuate, maintained: "The third error: We have dubbed the baptismal water, like the bread and the wine of the altar, a sacrament, and regarded it as
such; however, not the water, bread, or wine, but the baptismal vow or the
promise of love [in the Supper] is truly and really a sacrament."[38] Concurring, in addition, with Luther that confession "is simply a means of reaffirm-
ing our baptism"[39] which affords the Eucharistic recipients with "the certi-
tude, as they eat, that their sins are forgiven,"[40] Hubmaier stresses penance
as an indissoluble bond linking baptism with the Lord's Supper:

> After the person has now submitted himself internally and in faith to a
> new life . . . then he allows himself to be baptized with external wa-
> ter. . . . But although the person knows . . . that he is a sinner and ad-
> mits himself to be guilty of the same, simultaneously he completely
> trusts that Christ has forgiven him his sins through his death . . . we

---

36. "Nun ist aber solhe erinnerung hierinn begriffen. Erstlich. Das der
mensch gentzlich vnd sicherlich glaube, das Christus seinen leib vnd sein rosen-
farb blůt dargeben vnd vergossen hab für in am creütz. . . . So bewere sich der
mensch in der danckbarkait also, das er . . . danckbar sey gegen Gott vmb die
grossen, vberreichlichen vnd vnaussprechenlichen lieb vnd gůthait, die er im
bewisen durch seinen aller geliebtesten Son, vnnsern herren Jesum Christ. . . .
Eben auff dise Gmainschafft vnd liebepflicht zeücht sich das Nachtmal Christj."
Balthasar Hubmaier, *Form*, in Geary Vessenmeyer, *Über Balthasar Hubmör,
einen der berühmtesten Wiedertäufer zur Zeit der Reformation—Kirchenhist.*
Archiv 4 (Halle, 1826), 240.
37. As explained on page 26; Luther, *Babylonian Captivity*, 36:36, 49, 55.
38. "Der drit Jrsal. Das wir das Tauffwasser eben wie auch brot vnd wein
des altars haben ein Sacrament gehaissen vnd es dar für gehalten, so doch nit das
Wasser, brot oder wein, sonder die Tauffglůbd oder Liebepflicht aigentlich vnd
recht ist ein Sacrament." Hubmaier, *Form zu taufen*, 352.
39. Luther, *Babylonian Captivity*, 36:133.
40. Ibid., 36:116.

should recall his goodness [in] the Supper, which is . . . a commemoration of the suffering of Christ.[41]

That auricular confession to a priest is intended here rather than simply personal confession to God is clarified in the 1520 liturgy: "Now let the priest sit down with . . . each person, [who] should start by accusing himself and confessing his sins and realizing his guilt."[42] Although verbally concurring with Luther's verdict that holy orders should not be classified as a sacrament, Hubmaier evaded the former's rejection of its transfiguring effect by arguing that the quasi-sacrament of penance entailed the existence of a priestly class empowered with "the authority by the order of Christ to forgive and absolve the same sins."[43] Moreover, Hubmaier argued that the rite of ordination, as the fulfillment of baptismal regeneration, is implied by the sacrament of baptism, from which it is thus validly derived.[44] At this point the query naturally arises: If penitential absolution presupposes the ontological power exerted by the clergy, what connection exists between this power and the sacraments of baptism and the Eucharist?

Surpassing the Catholic position that baptism, although validly performed by anyone "willing to do what the church does,"[45] should be administered by a priest, Hubmaier insisted from 1520 until his death that in order for God to "graciously impart to [the baptismal candidate] the grace and power of his Holy Spirit," the initial sacrament must be granted by the bishop.[46] It is plausible that Hubmaier so argued to prevent anyone in Waldshut from dispensing the rite other than himself. Without the power of the keys embodied by the bishop, argues Hubmaier, baptism is thus denuded of

---

41. "Nach dem vnd nun sich der mensch inwendig vnd im glauben in ain new leben ergeben hat . . . lasset sich tauffen mit dem außwendigen wasser. . . . Die weyl aber der mensch wayßt vnd bekennt, das er . . . ain böser, wurmstichiger vnd vergiffter baum ist . . . das er sey ain sünder, gibt sich deßelben schuldig. Doch darbey glaub er gentzlich, das Christus im sein sünd durch seinen tod verzigen hab . . . wyr billich ingedenck seyn [jn] das nachtmal . . . ist . . . ain widergedächtnuß deß leydens Christi." Hubmaier, *Summe*, 111-14.

42. "Nun setze sich der Priester mit . . . ein yedlicher mensch anfengklich sich selbs anklagen sole vnd sich seiner sünden . . . bekhennen vnd schuldig geben." Hubmaier, *Form*, 241.

43. Hubmaier, *Rechenschaft*, 477; the German is quoted in footnote 19, page 97.

44. Ibid., 478; Windhorst, *Täuferisches Taufverständnis*, 114.

45. Aquinas, *Summa Theologica*, 4:2408.

46. "das er disem menschen die gnad vnd krafft seines heiligen geysts gnediglich mittailen wölle." Hubmaier, *Form zu taufen*, 349.

its regenerative force.[47] While still demanding clerical dispensation, however, Hubmaier argued that either a bishop or priest possessed the power to consecrate the bread and wine.[48] Since we will be fully occupied with his eucharistic theology in chapter five, suffice it to say here that immediately after reading the *Babylonian Captivity*, Hubmaier accepted Luther's argument against transubstantiation and the sacrificial nature of the mass.[49] Three years later at the Second Zurich Disputation, Hubmaier would quote verbatim from Luther's 1520 treatise that "undoubtedly this is the key point of the abuses, that we construe the mass as a sacrifice," despite its true identity as "a testament of Christ," which entails that properly celebrating Mass "is to read a testament letter . . . in German" rather than Greek, Latin, or Hebrew.[50] As a rebaptizer, moreover, Hubmaier would persist in his denunciation, in harmony with Luther, of papists who proclaim: "As often as one performs the Mass a miracle occurs daily, that the attributes or the accidents remain without the substance. . . . as the dream and Thomistic interpolation of these wicked people contends."[51] Finding persuasive the Wittenberger's case for *sub utraque specie*, Hubmaier, as disclosed by his epistle to humanist Johann Adelphi, instituted lay reception of the Eucharist in both kinds at Waldshut no later than May 1521.[52] In a stunning liturgical innovation, Hubmaier, although retaining the prerogative of the priest to utter the words of consecration, tore down the altar, eliminated both the host and chalice, and substituted a standard dinner table with ordinary bread and individual cups of wine.[53] Hubmaier explains his new Supper model to Adelphi: "The table should be prepared with normal bread and wine. Whether the cups are silver, wood, or tin is irrelevant. But those who eat should be decently dressed and

47. Sachsse, *Hubmaier als Theologe*, 197.

48. Balthasar Hubmaier, *Eine Form des Nachtmals Christi*, in Westin and Bergsten, *Schriften*, 355-56.

49. Loserth, *Hubmaier*, 70.

50. "so müß on zwyfel diser der houptartickel sin des mißbruchs, das wir die meß für ein opffer ußrüffen. . . . ein testament Christi. . . . ist ein testamentbrieff lessen . . . in tütsch." Transcript of the Second Zurich Disputation, in *Zwingli Sämtliche Werke*, 2:786-87; *cf.* Luther, *Babylonian Captivity*, 36:47-48, 64.

51. "Derhalb als offt man Meeß halt, so geschehe ein teglich wunderzaychen, das die anheng oder accidentia on ein Matery enthalten werdent. . . . wie denn diser ellenden leütt traum vnnd Thomistischer zůsatz lauttet." Hubmaier, *Ein einfältiger Unterricht*, 290, 295.

52. Hubmaier, *Letter to Johannes Adelphi*, 232.

53. Rempel, *Lord's Supper*, 74.

should sit together in a disciplined manner without chattering and strife."[54] Striving to restore the "pristine purity" of the Last Supper in every respect, Hubmaier demanded that partaking of the elements be preceded by foot washing among the recipients.[55] Appended to his 26 October 1521 letter to the famous humanist Johann Sapidus, Hubmaier, reversing the anti-Luther stance of his poem three years earlier to Pope Leo X, sarcastically in a new poem compares Herod, the friend of Pilate, and the Roman pontiff, to whom he was no longer a friend. Just as Herod and Pilate engineered a judicial murder of Jesus, asserted Hubmaier, so Leo endeavored to do the same to Luther; further, in diametric opposition to Christ, "a poor, meek man who carried his cross," his so-called vicar is "proudly carried about by rapacious servants and holds all the riches of the world in his hands."[56] Hubmaier closes his correspondence by announcing his most profound religious transition to date—his formal break with Rome and allegiance to Luther—as he "now views with criticism" the Church that he "had previously served with such devotion" and rather "is sympathetic toward Luther."[57]

Hubmaier as Lutheran Rebaptizer in Waldshut and Regensburg: 1521-1522

Representing Waldshut, Basel, Baden, Schaffhausen, and the Black Forest region at the Second Zurich Disputation in October 1523, Hubmaier makes the following seemingly unremarkable, but upon historical analysis, significant revelation:

> I am not cognizant of having preached even a single statement in these two years that was not rooted in the Word of God. But this I admit and

---

54. "Alßdann sollen sy den tisch mit gmainem brot vnd wein beraitten. Ob aber das trinckgschir silbren, hültzen oder Zinen sey, ist gar nichts daran gelegen. Yedoch sollen die Essenden erberlich beklaydt sein vnd bey einander sitzen mit zucht, on alle klapperey vnd zanckhung." Hubmaier, *Letter to Johannes Adelphi*, 233.

55. Vedder, *Hübmaier*, 112; Rempel, *Lord's Supper*, 75.

56. "Christus sei ein sanftmütiger, armer knecht gewesen, der sein kreuz getragen habe. Der papst dagegen lasse sich hochmütig von habgierigen dienern tragen vnd halte alle reiche der welt in den händen." Hubmaier, *Der Brief an Sapidus*, ed. Bergsten (who has modernized Hubmaier's spelling), *Hubmaier*, 100.

57. "die Kirche, der . . . mit solcher hingabe gedient hatte, jetzt kritisch betrachtet vnd sympathien für Luther hegt." Ibid.

this pronounce myself guilty, that I have not implemented everything as fully as I knew; I have spared the weak in faith whom I had to raise at that time with milk instead of solid food.[58]

At this point the question immediately arises: To what is Hubmaier referring when he alleges, "I have not implemented everything as fully as I knew," and when he censures his lenience toward "the weak of faith"; in other words, what are the antecedents of "milk" and "solid food"? A surprising answer to this inquiry is provided by Hubmaier himself in August 1524, when he describes to Oecolampadius his new ceremony of infant dedication as a substitute for pedobaptism and the ensuing friction generated among parents fearful of damnation for their dying children:

I like to convene the church in the baptismal place, introducing the child. I expound the gospel text in the vernacular: "Children were brought . . . " (Matt. 19:13). Immediately after he has been given a name, the whole church prays for the child on their knees, committing him to Christ's hands, that he may increasingly draw nearer to the child and pray for him. If parents of a sick child are present at a given time, who with all anxiety desire the child to be baptized, I baptize him. In such a case, I share in sickness myself with the sick children, but just temporarily, until [the congregation is] better taught. But concerning the interpretation of the Word, I do not yield to them in the least respect. . . . For indeed we ourselves have already taught that according to the institution of Christ, the young children should certainly not receive baptism. In fact, who instituted baptism? Obviously, Christ. When? At the end of Matthew's gospel. With what words? "Go therefore and make disciples of all nations, baptizing them in the name of the Father and of the Son and of the Holy Spirit" (Matt. 28:19). Quite correct. Why, therefore, do we baptize the young children? Baptism, as my proverb affirms, is a naked sign [and] a type of vessel without wine.[59]

---

58. "Mir nit bewißt, das ich in zweien jaren nit ein einigs bûchstäblin gepredigt, das in dem wort gottes on grundt seye. Das bekenn ich vnd gib mich des schuldig, das ich es nit alles so gar vnd volkummenlich heruß gsagt, wie ich es den wol gewißt, ich hab aber verschonet der schwachen im glauben, die ich da zemal mit milch vnd nit mitt sterckerer speyß füren mûst." Transcript of the Second Zurich Disputation, in *Zwingli Sämtliche Werke*, 2:788.

59. "Loco baptismatis ego curo cenvenire ecclesiam, inducens infantulum, ac lingua vernacula interpretor evangelium: Oblati sunt parvuli (Mat. 19 [,13]). Subinde imposito nomine orat tota ecclesia flexis genibus pro parvulo, illum commendans in manus Christi, ut huic sit propitious, et oret pro eo. Si vero sunt

Notice that Hubmaier here claims to "indeed . . . have already taught" that "the young children should certainly not receive baptism," which appears to be the doctrine that he claimed at the 1523 Second Zurich Disputation to have preached for the past two years. Combining the testimony of these two accounts, then, we can infer that Hubmaier, excepting the sickly infants of (in his evaluation) the theologically undersophisticated "weak in faith," discontinued the "milk" of infant baptism and replaced it with the new ceremony of dedication as early as 1521. While not explicitly affirming that Hubmaier administered the "solid food" of believers' baptism, these sources at least illustrate his early conviction that only willing parishioners should be baptized and at best imply that some among the spiritually mature were rebaptized. Three other documents, all composed in January 1523, prove the latter suggestion to be correct. In tandem with the First Zurich Disputation between Zwingli and Fabri, Hubmaier defended his *Achtzehn Schlußreden* in an open forum intended for the clergy of Waldshut and its environs. Article eight, which admonishes the faithful to test their pastors against the Scriptural plumb line, presupposes believers' baptism as standard practice in Waldshut: "Since every Christian believes and is baptized for himself, every person should look and discern from Scripture whether he is being appropriately fed and watered by his shepherd."[60] In an explanatory note, Hubmaier draws the rebaptismal conclusion: "Anyone who believes and is not baptized, since infant baptism is not baptism, is obliged to receive baptism, even if he is already a hundred years old."[61] Reporting, in addition, on his meeting

---

parentes adhuc infirmi, qui volunt omnibus nervis baptisari prolem, hanc baptiso; in opere infirmus sum cum infirmiusculis ad tempus et, dum erudiantur melius, sed in verbo non cedo illis in minimo apiculo. . . . Palam quipped docuimus parvulos haudquaquam esse baptisandos. Enimvero quis instituit baptismum? Nimirum Christos. Ubi? Matthaei ultimo. Quibus verbis? Euntes docete omnes gentes, baptisantes eos in nominee patris et filii et spiritus sancti [Mt. 28, 19]. Recte quidem. Cur ergo baptisamus parvulos? Baptismus, aiunt, signum nudum est [et] haedera absque vino." Hubmaier, *Letter to Oecolampadius*, 1:342-43; this is one of only five extant letters Hubmaier composed in Latin rather than German.

60. "Wie ein yeder Christ für sich selbs glaubt vnd getaufft wirt, also soll ein yeder sehen vnnd vrteylen durch die geschrifft, ob er recht von seynem hyrten gespeyßt vnd getrenckt werde." Balthasar Hubmaier, *Achtzehn Schlußreden*, in Westin and Bergsten, *Schriften*, 73.

61. "Ein yeder mensch, der da glaubt vnnd ist nit täufft, wie dann der Kindertauff keyn tauff ist, schuldig sey, sich zûtäuffen lassenn, ob er schon hundert jar alt wer." Ibid. Hubmaier grew quite fond of this turn of phrase, not only quoting it in his classic 1525 *Von der christlichen Taufe der Gläubigen* (in

with Zwingli shortly before the Disputation, Hubmaier claims that the Zurich reformer openly endorsed the performance in Waldshut of what I will dub "catechetical rebaptism," where the former, instead of confirming catechized children (who had previously undergone infant baptism), baptized them again as believers.[62] That Zwingli so remarked is verified by the eyewitness testimony of Sebastian Ruckensperger, the prior at Sion in Klingau, who wrote a chronicle of the exchange: "Hubmör conferred with Zwingli in the Zurich Graben regarding the Scriptures on baptism; there Zwingli said Hubmör was right . . . to baptize children after they have been instructed in the faith."[63] In what appears to be an important discovery for Hubmaier scholarship in particular and Anabaptist historiography in general, the evidence furnished by these previously neglected five sources modifies a key presupposition of Anabaptist research—the time, place, and figures involved in the reinstatement of believers' baptism to the Christian tradition. The consensus view of Radical Reformation scholars, that the first adult rebaptism occurred at Zurich on 21 January 1525 at the home of Felix Manz when Conrad Grebel baptized George Blaurock (whereupon Blaurock proceeded to baptize all others present), seems to be mistaken both on the location and the group responsible for this act. Rather than the Swiss Brethren at Zurich (who would become the foremost exemplars of Evangelical Anabaptism),[64]

Westin and Bergsten, *Schriften*, 140), but devoted his entire 1526 treatise *Grund und Ursache* (in Westin and Bergsten, *Schriften*, 327-36) to defending this proposition.

62. This document, which is no longer extant, is quoted in full by Hubmaier against Zwingli in *Gespräch auf Zwinglis Taufbüchlein*, 186-87. While catechetical instruction for children followed by their confirmation was rare in Germany prior to Luther's revival of the tradition in 1528, Hubmaier learned the practice at Regensburg, where it had been carried out using Dederich's *Christenspiegel* since the 1470s, and transported it to Waldshut in 1519. It should be noted, moreover, that the first Reformation catechism was neither Luther's *Small* nor *Large Catechism*, but Hubmaier's *Eine christliche Lehrtafel*, first published in August 1524 and revised at Nikolsburg in 1526. For verification of these facts see Vedder, *Hübmaier*, 186-97, Sachsse, *Hubmaier als Theologe*, 136-37, Windhorst, *Täuferisches Taufverständnis*, 158, and Estep, *Anabaptist Story*, 96-97.

63. "Hubmör mit Zwingli conferiert die Schrifften vonn dem Tauff, auff dem Zürchgraben; da Zwingli sagt Hubmör recht geben, das man die Kinder Tauffen . . . nach im glauben vnderricht seyent." Sebastian Ruckensperger, *Biechlen*, in J. C. Füsslin, *Beiträge zur Erläuterung der Kirchen-Reformationsgeschichte des Schweizerbundes*, 5 vols. (Zürich, 1741), 1:252-53.

64. Williams, *Radical Reformation*, 221-23.

the Magisterial Radical Reformer Balthasar Hubmaier, not at all representative of the Anabaptist movement or even any sect therein, was actually the initiator of sixteenth-century believers' baptism, which is shown to have first transpired at Waldshut by January 1523 and more probably sometime in 1521.

At least nine months before the October 1523 Second Zurich Disputation, at which time those whom Zwingli considered his "extremist disciples," Conrad Grebel and Felix Manz, parted company from their theological mentor, Hubmaier imparted the sacrament of baptism to parishioners who had been first instructed in the faith, and he displayed extreme reluctance to perform the rite for infants. But which sources, we may ask, led Hubmaier to the conclusion that believers' baptism comprised the practice of the early church? While this topic will be explored in much greater detail in the next chapter, as it exerts an enormous impact on his baptismal theology, we will simply point out here that Hubmaier was brought to this inference as much, if not more, from the writings of the second through fourth century Church Fathers than from the New Testament. Among the numerous patristic sources cited revealing that believers' baptism amounted to either the exclusive or majority practice up to the time of Augustine (whom Hubmaier, contrary to Luther, Zwingli, and later Calvin, vilifies as the instigator of the foremost papal abomination of "child-washing") include Clement, Tertullian, Origen, Athanasius, Eusebius, Cyril, Basil the Great, and Jerome.[65] Ironically, therefore, upon the three pillars of Luther's 1519 premise that baptism ought not be received by those without faith, his hermeneutical presupposition of *sola scriptura* plus sound reason, and his supposed agreement with Hubmaier's doubts on infant baptism, the Waldshut reformer was driven to search the Scriptures and Church Fathers and finally arrive at the non-Lutheran conclusion (unbeknownst to Hubmaier at the time) that, using Luther's own analogy, infant baptism "is the same . . . as hanging a barrel hoop at Easter in anticipation of future wine which is not to be casked until fall, and of which one has no idea whether it will be ruined beforehand by hail, frost, or another type of bad weather."[66] The pivotal role of Luther in shaping Hubmaier's views is depicted by Rollin Stely Armour:

---

65. Balthasar Hubmaier, *Der uralten und gar neuen Lehrer Urteil, Ausgabe* I, in Westin and Bergsten, *Schriften*, 230-34.

66. "Es ist eben ein ding . . . als ein reyff vmb Ostern außstecken auff künfftigen wein, der im herbst erst solle gefasset werden, vnnd man noch nit weyß, ob er vorhyn durch hagel, reyffen oder ander vngewitter verderbt würdet." Balthasar Hubmaier, *Von dem Ampt der Apostelen*, in Westin and Bergsten, *Schriften*, 137.

He himself claimed that the first direct stimulus toward a reexamination
of baptism came from Luther, specifically from Luther's . . . *Ein Sermon von dem neuen Testament, das ist von Heiligen Messe,* in which
Hubmaier found Luther stressing the importance of faith for the sacraments. . . . Although Luther did not intend what Hubmaier attributed to
him, it is probably true that Hubmaier's first questions about baptism
did arise from Luther's doctrine.[67]

At this time, the Regensburg City Council recalled Hubmaier to preach at
the chapel *zur Schönen Maria,* an invitation that he provisionally accepted
without resigning his bishopric at Waldshut.

Upon learning that the old dispute between the Dominicans and the city
council had been settled through the intervention of the Duke of Bavaria
(who conferred upon the office of bishop spiritual jurisdiction over the
church, the right of confirmation and investiture of all foundations, and an
indemnity in ready money), Hubmaier returned to Regensburg, where he
was greeted on Advent Sunday 1522 with a splendid welcome from leaders
in both church and civic affairs.[68] In spite of his commission to sing three
masses a week, arrange processions, and preach as often as the provost required, which he faithfully carried out, the newly appointed joint bishop of
both Regensburg and Waldshut marched forward with his pastoral and liturgical reforms. As rightly noted by Vedder, "There is no doubt that he was
now strongly inclining to the new doctrine and that his preaching was of the
evangelical type, though he practised the rites of the Church."[69] During his
first week in the pulpit, Hubmaier began preaching a series of expository
sermons from the Gospel of Luke.[70] In a letter written 17 January 1522 to a
friend in Ulm, he reports that Christ is preached in unadulterated Lutheran
fashion in Nürnberg, despite the opposition of Frederick of Austria, and
adds, "Likewise among us in Bavaria is the gospel preached."[71] While re-
fraining from his probably established Waldshut practice of rebaptizing
adults, in fear of the Catholic city council, Hubmaier, while retaining for the
most part the liturgies of baptism and confirmation, substituted the respec-

---

67. Armour, *Baptism,* 24.
68. Loserth, *Hubmaier,* 98; Windhorst, *Täuferisches Taufverständnis,* 164.
69. Vedder, *Hübmaier,* 56.
70. Sachsse, *Hubmaier als Theologe,* 135.
71. Balthasar Hubmaier, *Letter to a Friend in Ulm,* trans. William R. Estep,
Anabaptist Beginnings: A Source Book (Nieuwkoop: B. de Graaf, 1976), 88.
The original Latin document is preserved in the Stadt-und Universitätsbibliothek, Hamburg, Germany.

tive acts of infant dedication and baptism in their stead.[72] When Hubmaier, quite probably due to theological ignorance on the part of parishioners, received no objections to the innovation, he lauded his flock in a March 1522 letter to Rychard for fully standing "with us in proclaiming the evangelical faith."[73] At the same time, Hubmaier connected himself with a Lutheran circle in Regensburg, which was organized by the dyer Laien Blabhans, in order to keep apprised of the latest tracts of Luther.[74] It was in this group, however, that another dramatic turn in Hubmaier's theology transpired, which sprang from his reading of *Vom Anbeten des Sacraments des heiligen Leichnams Christi* shortly after Christmas 1522.[75] Such a transformation, to be dealt with at length in the next section, caused Hubmaier to leave the city and return to Waldshut immediately after the turn of the new year. Contra the supposition by Bergsten that the reformer must have resigned his second bishopric because he "was not a success during his second period in Regensburg,"[76] the primary sources reveal that such a verdict is incorrect. In fact, the City Council commemorated Hubmaier's departure by drawing up a special resolution which promised their permanent friendship and presenting him with an honorarium of fifteen guilders on 1 January 1523.[77] Notwithstanding his annulment of infant baptism and implementation of catechetical (and probably adult) believers' baptism, as well as his "Lutheran" preaching, there was no known complaint against Hubmaier from the Catholic Church up to the time of his return to Waldshut.[78]

Hubmaier's 1523 Break with Luther over Libertarian Free Will and Infant Baptism

As a result of his participation in the Luther reading group led by Blabhans, Hubmaier encountered in *Vom Anbeten des Sacraments* what he took to be a fundamental revision in the Wittenberg reformer's original views of faith and baptism. Actually, however, the late 1522 treatise revealed Hub-

---

72. Loserth, *Hubmaier*, 102; Sachsse, *Hubmaier als Theologe*, 137.
73. "mit vns vnd verkündigten die evangelische Lehre." Balthasar Hubmaier, *Brief an Rychard*, in Bergsten, *Hubmaier*, 105.
74. Windhorst, *Täuferisches Taufverständnis*, 165.
75. Sachsse, *Hubmaier als Theologe*, 132.
76. "Es heißt darin, daß es Hubmaier während seines zweiten Aufenthaltes in Regensburg nicht geraten wollte." Bergsten, *Hubmaier*, 105.
77. *Special Resolution of the Regensburg City Council*, in Loserth, *Hubmaier*, 24.
78. Bergsten, *Hubmaier*, 106; Sachsse, *Hubmaier als Theologe*, 133.

maier's original misunderstanding of Luther's *fides*, owing to the fact that the latter appears to have never furnished a clear definition in his earlier writings.[79] From his anthropological starting point of libertarian free will, Hubmaier interpreted *fides* as the product of natural human capacity, namely, a form of belief (*glaub* or *glauben*). Therefore, when Luther affirmed in 1519 that the sacraments are invalid apart from faith, Hubmaier drew the inference that *glaub* was necessary for the reception of both baptism and the Eucharist.[80] For instance, Hubmaier stated that valid baptism is predicated upon a recognition of one's condition as a sinner as well as one's *glaub* in the promise of the Word of God that one's sins will be forgiven through Christ.[81] He also affirmed that water baptism (*tauffen im wasser*) encompasses a public recognition and confession of one's *glaub*.[82] In both these cases, Hubmaier evidently means by *glaub*, in Mabry's definition, "faith as belief, or the act of giving mental assent to the truth, as an act of human ability."[83] It seems to have come as quite a shock to Hubmaier when Luther, in his theological defense of infant baptism, proved in the December 1522 treatise not to embrace this same concept.[84] Here Luther wrote:

> Contrary to this, we maintain, according to Christ's words, "Whoever believes and is baptized, etc.," that faith must be present prior to or at the time of baptism, or the rite becomes a sheer mockery of the attending Divine majesty, and it offers grace that no one receives. Accordingly we maintain that by the faith and prayer of the church the young children are purified from unbelief and the devil, and faith is conferred upon them. Hence they are baptized, as this gift was also conferred upon the children by circumcision of the Jews. Otherwise Christ would not have said, "Let the little children come to me . . . for of such is the kingdom of heaven." Matt. 19. However, no one has the kingdom of heaven apart from faith.[85]

---

79. Mabry, *Understanding of Faith*, 34-35.

80. Hubmaier, *Ampt der Apostelen*, 139-40; Mabry, *Doctrine of the Church*, 32-33.

81. Hubmaier, *Summe*, 112.

82. Hubmaier, *Eine ernstliche christliche Erbietung*, 83.

83. Mabry, *Doctrine of the Church*, 37.

84. Sachsse, *Hubmaier als Theologe*, 134; Windhorst, *Täuferisches Taufverständnis*, 170.

85. "Da gegen halten wir nach den wortten Christi 'Wer da gleubt vnnd getaufft wirt' u. das zuvor odder ihr zu gleich glaube da sein muss, wenn man teufft, oder ein lauter spott Gottlicher maiëstat drauss werde, als die da kegenwirtig sei vnd gnade anbiete und niemandt neme sie on. Darumb achten wir, die

In this passage, Luther presupposes *fides* to be a gift of God's grace, apart from any human ability. As such, the faith of the church could be imparted by God to an infant, enabling him or her to be properly baptized. Somewhat inconsistently with this quote, moreover, Luther proceeded to argue that the validity of the sacraments did not depend upon faith by drawing a distinction between proper reception and valid reception.[86] While faith was necessary for proper reception of baptism and the consequent bestowal of sanctifying grace, baptism may be validly administered without the grace of baptism being necessarily received. Luther gives the analogy of a Turk who, if she or he were baptized, would be validly baptized but not properly baptized, since she or he possessed no faith.[87] A theologian with the ability to see the logical relationship between doctrines, Hubmaier further realized that Luther both did not identify *fides* with *glaub* and could not equate them by virtue of his late-Augustinian anthropology, which shone forth in this writing.[88] According-ing to the Wittenberg reformer, in the Fall humanity paradoxically employed its *liberum arbitrium*, defined as the faculty supplying the potentiality to choose between the performance of spiritual good and evil, so as to destroy its *liberum arbitrium*, thereby leaving the will miserably enslaved.[89] In-cluded in this monergistic faith is the Holy Spirit's transformation of, in the oft-quoted words of Ezekiel 36:25-27, the elect's "heart of stone" (*i.e.* one lacking *liberum arbitrium*) into a "heart of flesh" (*i.e.* one enjoying *liberum*

---

jungen kinder werden durch der kirchen glauben vnnd gebet vom vnglauben und teuffel gereinigt und mit dem glauben begabt und alsso getaufft, Weil solch gabe auch durch beschnettung der Juden den kinder geben wortt, sonst hette Christus Matt. 19. nicht gesagt 'Last die kinder zu mir kamen, solcher ist das himelreich.' On glauben aber hatt niemant das himelreich." Martin Luther, *Vom Anbeten des Sacraments des heiligen Leichnams Christi*, in *D. Martin Luthers Werke*, 7:693.

86. Robert W. Jenson, *Visible Words: The Interpretation and Practice of Christian Sacraments* (Philadelphia: Fortress Press, 1978), 43.

87. Luther, *Vom Anbeten des Sacraments*, 7:695.

88. Sachsse, *Hubmaier als Theologe*, 135. Such was also perceived by Erasmus, which, coupled with his disquiet concerning related statements made in Luther's December 1520 *Assertio omnium articulorum M. Lutheri per Bullam Leonis X novissimam damnatorum*, provoked him to compose his 1524 *Diatribe de Libero Arbitrio*. See A. N. Marlow and B. Drewery, "The Lutheran Riposte," in *Luther and Erasmus: Free Will and Salvation*, ed. E. Gordon Rupp and A. N. Marlow (Philadelphia: Westminster, 1969), 12-15.

89. But note that Luther alleges that humans possess free will in matters pertaining to earthly affairs while not in those pertaining to salvation. See Luther, *Vom Anbeten des Sacraments*, 7:698-99.

arbitrium); hence for Luther, *fides* is the cause of *assensus*, not vice versa.[90] At this point, a combination of two factors prompted Hubmaier to resign his Catholic bishopric at Regensburg and return to Waldshut. First, Hubmaier understood that the irreconcilable anthropological differences between himself and Luther logically entailed a model of the sacraments with which the former was uncomfortable, meaning that the rebaptizer could no longer in good conscience style himself an exponent of Luther's doctrine.[91] Second, Hubmaier, in spite of the Catholic city council, had felt somewhat secure in his supposed "Lutheran" reforms in doctrine and ritual because of the powerful Nikolsburg Lutheran burgher contingent, the support of which Hubmaier deemed necessary to counterbalance the city council and advance his program of reformation.[92] Fearing that he would face stiff resistance on both popular and civic fronts, Hubmaier returned to Waldshut, where he enjoyed *carte blanche* to initiate change, shortly after the turn of 1523.

On taking up his work anew at Waldshut, Hubmaier almost immediately gave attestation of his theological separation from Luther. It seems likely that such a break constituted the primary reason why Hubmaier called for the Waldshut Disputation in January 1523. This appraisal is substantiated by the *Achtzehn Schlußreden* drawn up for the debate, the opening two articles of which respectively affirm *sola fides* and then qualify the doctrine in a libertarian way by equating *fides* with *glaub*: "1. Faith alone makes us just before God. 2. This faith is the knowledge of the mercy of God, which he manifested to us by offering his only begotten Son."[93] Concerning the dialogue, Vedder argues that its first two articles are "deliberate, calculated, willful" and "can be accounted for only on one ground, that Hübmaier was anxious to mark clearly his divergence from Luther in some matters that the latter reckoned cardinal in the Protestant theology."[94] In February 1523, Hubmaier emphasized from the pulpit "that Luther was without doubt only human like themselves" and warned them "against depending on the teachings . . . of Luther."[95] Nevertheless, out of gratitude for Luther, whom he

90. Spitz, *Protestant Reformation*, 91; Pelikan, *Reformation*, 153-55.

91. Sachsse, *Hubmaier als Theologe*, 136; Loserth, *Hubmaier*, 63.

92. Bergsten, *Hubmaier*, 105; Windhorst, *Täuferisches Taufverständnis*, 171.

93. "1. Der eynig glaub macht vns frumm vor Gott. 2. Diser glaub ist die erkantnyß der barmhertzigkeyt Gottes, so er vns in der darstreckung seyns eingebornen süns erzeygt hat." Hubmaier, *Achtzehn Schlußreden*, 72.

94. Vedder, *Hübmaier*, 201.

95. "Luther sei ohne zweifel ein mensch wie sie . . . sich auf Luthers . . . lehren zu verlassen." Balthasar Hubmaier, *Predigt*, in Johann Loserth, *Die Stadt*

regarded as his foremost predecessor in the proclamation of the risen Christ, Hubmaier continued to freely describe himself in his writings using the "Lutheran" moniker.[96] It should be noted at this point that during the remainder of his theological career, Hubmaier never considered himself an Anabaptist, but rather an evangelical reformer.[97] Following as a logical corollary from his non-Lutheran conception of faith, Hubmaier hastened to expand in a series of sermons the doctrine of justification implicit in his tripartite anthropology and precisely how it differed from that articulated by Luther.

Salvation, in Hubmaier's theology, encompasses a process in which fallen humans are reconciled to God; however, it is not a matter of God's declaring them righteous as if they were, in fact, righteous before him. To the contrary, redemption, for Hubmaier, amounts to a progression which transforms fallen humans so that they truly become acceptable before God and thus, in the words of 2 Peter 1:4, participate in the divine nature.[98] Hence, through a process very much resembling the Eastern Orthodox notion of θέωσις or divinization, the sinner literally is recreated and made acceptable by sharing in the "godness" of God.[99] Commencing with an inner regeneration experience (which is more precisely defined as a recreating experience) at the moment when a person appropriately responds to God's Word, such a participatory divinization continues under the shepherding of the church until she or he is converted into a totally righteous person. In a July 1523 homily Hubmaier explained his definition of justification as follows:

> On the order of Christian justification: [The sinner] lets himself be enlisted in the congregation of the Christian church . . . to live according to the Word, will, and rule of Christ, to order and focus his action

---

Waldshut und die vorderösterreichische Regierung 1523-26 (Vienna: C. Gerold's Sohn, 1891), 108.

96. "Lutherische"; Ibid., 109. As Bergsten points out, Hubmaier would reaffirm his admiration but partial disagreement with Luther at Nikolsburg in 1526 (*Hubmaier*, 138). In fact, Hubmaier reports in 1526 that his "detractors accuse me publicly to be the most evil of all Lutheran archheretics, a Lutheran heretic" (mein vngnedig mißgönner für den aller bösten Luterschen Ertzketzer außrüeffen, Lutherischer Ketzer); *Entschuldigung*, 279.

97. This verdict, affirmed by Mabry (*Doctrine of the Church*, 39) and Sachsse (*Hubmaier als Theologe*, 219), is evinced in Hubmaier, *Entschuldigung*, 275 and Hubmaier, *Ein einfältiger Unterricht*, 289.

98. Sachsse, *Hubmaier als Theologe*, 171-73.

99. Mabry, *Doctrine of the Church*, 101-02; Mabry, *Understanding of Faith*, 48-50.

and inaction according to him, and also to fight and strain under his banner until death. . . . The flesh must be killed each day because it wants only to live and rule after its own desires. At this point the Spirit of Christ triumphs and attains the victory. This leads the person to yield good fruits that bear witness of a good tree. He carries out day and night all those things pertaining to the praise of God and brotherly love. In this way, the old Adam is martyred, killed, and carried to the grave. This is a summary and right order of an entire Christian life which starts in the Word of God.[100]

The doctrine of justification, in my judgment the most important doctrine of the Reformation period (the Eucharist ranks as a close second), was typically construed by the Magisterial Reformers as a gift of God from beginning to end. While "justification (Rechtfertigung) by faith alone"[101] became the rallying call of Luther's reformation, wherein faith itself is a gift of God given to the sinner through grace, Hubmaier intentionally avoids the forensic term *Rechtfertigung* and replaces it with the ontological term *Frombmachung* (occasionally *Rechtmachung*).[102] On this score Mabry contends, "Hubmaier wished to set forth a completely different understanding of the doctrine of justification . . . in order to dissociate himself from Luther's concept of this principle."[103] In contrast to the Lutheran *simul justus et peccator* (at the

---

100. "Von der ordnung einer Christenlichen frombmachung. [Der sünder], vor der Christenlichen kirchen, inn dero gemeynschafft er sich lasset verzeychnen . . . nach dem wort, willen vnnd regel Christi zůleben, sein thůn vnd lassen nach jm schlichten vnnd richten, auch vnder seinem fenlin kempffen vnd streyten biß inn den todt. . . . Da můß das fleysch täglich getödt werden, vnd will es aber nun leben vnd regieren nach seinen lüsten. Hye ligt ob vnd siget der geyst Christi, vnnd bringt der mensch gůt früchten, die nun zeügknůß gebent eins gůtten boums, vnd yebt sich tag vnd nacht inn allem dem, so das lob Gottes antrifft vnnd brüderliche liebe. Dardurch würdt der alt Adam gemartert, tödtet vnnd zů grab tragen. Das ist ein summ vnnd rechte ordnung eins gantzen Christenlichen lebens, das da anfahet im wort Gottes." Balthasar Hubmaier, *Von der ordnung einer Christenlichen frombmachung*, in Westin and Bergsten, *Schriften*, 157, 160-61.

101. Martin Luther, *Commentary on Galatians*, in Pelikan, *Luther's Works*, 1:246; Sachsse, *Hubmaier als Theologe*, 173.

102. For some representative examples see Hubmaier, *Achtzehn Schlußreden*, 72 and Hubmaier, *Eine christliche Lehrtafel*, 316. Windhorst, *Täuferisches Taufverständnis*, 31; Loserth, *Hubmaier*, 119.

103. Mabry, *Doctrine of the Church*, 103.

same time righteous and a sinner),[104] Hubmaier employs the adjective *fromm*, which typically means "pious, devout, or religious."[105] Instead, Hubmaier modifies the term in the sense of *gerecht* (right or just), making justification far closer to *Gerechtmachung* (making right or just) than Luther's forensic version.[106] From mid-1523 until the end of his life, therefore, Hubmaier utilized the terms *fromm*, *Frombmachung*, and *Rechtmachung* to emphasize his understanding that justification is the act of making a person intrinsically holy before God.[107]

Hubmaier's employment of the aforementioned theological terms drastically shaped his translation and subsequent interpretation of Scripture in his 1523 and 1524 sermons. A skilled Greek exegete, Hubmaier most frequently preached using Erasmus' *Greek New Testament* and rendered it in the vernacular for his congregation.[108] Delivering a series on the Pauline epistles, Hubmaier chose 1 Timothy 1:15 as his theme, which notes that Christ came into the world "to save sinners" ($\dot{\alpha}\mu\alpha\rho\tau\omega\lambda o\dot{v}s$ $\sigma\hat{\omega}\sigma\alpha\iota$), which he rendered in German as "den sünder gerecht und fromb zemachen."[109] Here $\sigma\hat{\omega}\sigma\alpha\iota$ is translated as *gerecht und fromb zemachen* (to make aright and just or pious), thus equating personal holiness with the condition of salvation. This use of *fromm* is also seen in his translation of Romans 4:25, which alludes to Christ's death and resurrection "for our justification" ($\delta\iota\alpha$ $\tau\dot{\eta}\nu$ $\delta\iota\kappa\alpha\dot{\iota}\omega\sigma\iota\nu$ $\dot{\eta}\mu\hat{\omega}\nu$); as expected, Hubmaier renders the phrase as "von unsere frombmachung."[110] Later in the same sermon, he amplifies *Frombmachung* by substituting the descriptive medical term *Gesundmachung* (making healthy)[111]:

> By means of these comforting words, the sinner again becomes rejuvenated, comes to himself or herself, grows joyful, and commits himself or herself from that time on freely and completely to Christ the physician, entrusts him with all his or her sickness, and gives them to him, thereby desiring, as much as it is possible for a wounded person to de-

104. Martin Luther, *Scholia on the Epistle to the Romans*, in *Luthers Werke*, 56:272; Spitz, *Protestant Reformation*, 93.

105. Brunotte and Weber, *Kirchenlexikon*, 1:880.

106. Ibid., 1:1501; Windhorst, *Täuferisches Taufverständnis*, 25-26; Mabry, *Understanding of Faith*, 46-47.

107. Sachsse, *Hubmaier als Theologe*, 173.

108. Windhorst, *Täuferisches Taufverständnis*, 39-41.

109. Hubmaier, *Summe*, 111.

110. Hubmaier, *Von der ordnung*, 157.

111. Brunotte and Weber, *Kirchenlexikon*, 1:669, 1417.

sire, to submit himself or herself to Christ's will, and call on him each day for justification and purification.[112]

This quote indicates precisely what Hubmaier intended by *Frombma-chung*—namely, that one is made healthy again. Such a state of health, in the reformer's anthropology, denotes that the spiritual freedom of counsel restored by the Holy Spirit through regeneration will be progressively enhanced by an increased somatic freedom of pleasure as one perseveres in holiness, to be fully consummated in the general resurrection at the end of the world.[113] Hence the words *fromm* and *Frombmachung* indicate an actual change in a person's nature, not Luther's unmerited favor of God whereby one who was still a sinner, due to the special work of Christ, is accepted before God as a saint.[114] For Hubmaier, therefore, *Frombmachung* literally means *machen fromm* (to make right or just), in which the spirit of the fallen human is immediately restored through regeneration and the body gradually restored through sanctification to their originally created condition.

It follows from the foregoing discussion that Hubmaier's doctrine of justification relegates faith to a less dominant role in the *ordo salutis* than was common during the Magisterial Reformation. If God makes one into a righteous person, then one's individual righteousness forms the basis of one's acceptance by God rather than faith.[115] This point is underscored well by Mabry:

> Even though it is by faith, through grace, that one is made acceptable, faith still plays a lesser role in Hubmaier's doctrine of justification. The faith is necessary to enable the transformation to take place, but the acceptance is on the basis of the transformation (which is really just natural wholeness and health), and not upon faith.[116]

---

112. "Durch solche trost wort würdt der sünder widerumb erkückt, kumpt zů jm selbs, würt frölich vnd ergibt sich füran gantz vnd gar an disen artzt Christum, also das er jm all sein kranckheit befilcht, heymsetzt vnd vertrauwet, will sich auch, als vil einem verwundten moglich, inn seinen willen ergeben vnd rüfft jn an vmb täaglich gsundmachung vnd reynigung." Hubmaier, *Von der ordnung,* 159.
113. Sachsse, *Hubmaier als Theologe,* 179-80; Loserth, *Hubmaier,* 126.
114. Windhorst, *Täuferisches Taufverständnis,* 42; Pelikan, *Reformation,* 320-21.
115. Loserth, *Hubmaier,* 127.
116. Mabry, *Doctrine of the Church,* 119.

The role of faith in justification, according to Hubmaier, comprises that by which the sinner turns toward God for help and which enables one to obey God's commands. By performing the divine will, the person whose nature has been restored to health is made intrinsically acceptable to God and therefore justified. Faith alone is not the ground of justification; rather, it is simply the second step, following the sinner's natural hungering and thirsting for righteousness unaided by grace, in the transformation process.[117] In diametric opposition to Luther, Hubmaier draws this conclusion quite poignantly: "Although faith alone (der glaub allain) makes us God-fearing (fromb), it alone does not save."[118] Elsewhere Hubmaier reiterates the same sentiment: "Mere faith (Der bloß glaub) is not sufficient for salvation."[119] This unique Magisterial Radical, then, equates justification and personal righteousness in a manner designed to significantly distance himself from his Magisterial precursor Luther.

Hubmaier's Relationship to Zwingli and his Radical Disciples

Since the publication of his 1961 biography *Balthasar Hubmaier, Seine Stellung zu Reformation und Täufertum*, the majority of Anabaptist historians have followed Torsten Bergsten in his thesis that Hubmaier, originally a follower of Zwingli who later sided with Grebel, Manz, and Blaurock, launched a reformation at Waldshut which comprised a branch, or offshoot, of the Zurich reformation.[120] I aim to demonstrate, however, that such a position is untenable on two counts: the primary sources provide no evidence for and furnish strong evidence against the notion that Hubmaier was ever converted to Zwinglianism, and the same can be said for his support of the founding members of the Swiss Brethren. As we have already illustrated, Hubmaier's adherence to Lutheranism ceased in January 1523; but shortly

---

117. Mabry, *Understanding of Faith*, 33-35.

118. "Ob wol der glaub allain fromm macht, so macht er doch allain nit selig." Hubmaier, *Eine christliche Lehrtafel*, 316.

119. "Der bloß glaub nit gnug ist zu der Seligkait." Hubmaier, *Rechenschaft*, 462.

120. Bergsten, *Hubmaier*, 110. For a representative sample of scholars who embrace Bergsten's assessment see Armour, *Anabaptist Baptism*, 19-21; Friedmann, *Theology of Anabaptism*, 94; Windhorst, *Täuferisches Taufverständnis*, 57; Pipkin, "Baptismal Theology," 34-35; Williams, *Radical Reformation*, 228-33; Estep, *Anabaptist Story*, 87-89; and Hans-Jürgen Goertz, *The Anabaptists* (New York: Routledge, 1996), 39-40.

thereafter, Hubmaier acquired a high interest in the reform activities at Zurich. Later that same month, after his return from Regensburg, Prior Ruckensperger vom Klaster Sion, from Klingau, arrived at Waldshut with a request that Hubmaier, who was already a prominent evangelical pastor, should travel with him to St. Gall.[121] Hubmaier concurred on the condition that Ruckensperger would also take him to Zurich, and the two men lodged at St. Gall for three days, during which time Hubmaier met some of the evangelical leaders there.[122] Nevertheless, Hubmaier was barred from preaching due to some of his evangelical doctrines.[123] While there, Joachim von Watt, the director of the evangelical reformation in St. Gall, handed Hubmaier a letter to deliver to Zwingli upon his arrival at Zurich.[124] When Ruckensperger and Hubmaier finally reached Zurich, the Prior introduced the Waldshut reformer to Zwingli, marking the first meeting between the two. It was at this Zurich exchange, as previously shown, that Zwingli endorsed Hubmaier's already established practice to rebaptize children after their instruction in the faith.[125] It should be emphasized that this encounter was not one where the established reformer Zwingli took an upstart Hubmaier under his wing, as most scholars suggest;[126] to the contrary, the meeting featured two already established evangelical reformers coming together to discuss matters theological and practical. Hubmaier, who was converted to the Magisterial Reformation no later than 1521 through the writings of Luther, had been conducting branches of that reformation first in Waldshut and then in Regensburg, and was previously recognized as an eminent evangelical preacher, cannot be dubbed a disciple of Zwingli in any sense, much less that he was a student who initiated a Zwinglian reform movement.

Due to this preliminary conversation, Zwingli invited Hubmaier to attend the First Zurich Disputation of January 1523, where Hubmaier supported Zwingli on the matter of *sola scriptura* but opposed Zwingli's Antiochene Christology and the sacramentarian position on the Eucharist derived

---

121. Ibid., 108-10.

122. Hubmaier, *Eine ernstliche christliche Erbietung*, 82; Hubmaier, *Summe*, 110.

123. The primary sources supply no hint as to precisely which doctrines the authorities at St. Gall objected.

124. Loserth, *Hubmaier*, 132; Mabry, *Doctrine of the Church*, 40-41.

125. Hubmaier, *Gespräch auf Zwinglis Taufbüchlein*, 187; Ruckensperger, *Biechlen*, 1:253.

126. For instance, see Yoder, "Turning Point," 133; Clasen, *Anabaptism*, 103-04; Windhorst, *Täuferisches Taufverständnis*, 60; Pipkin, "Baptismal Theology," 34-35; Williams, *Radical Reformation*, 222; and Estep, *Anabaptist Story*, 81.

therefrom.[127] Accusing the Zurich reformer of theological double-talk regarding the words of institution, *Hoc est [enim] corpus meum*, Hubmaier insisted upon some form of real presence (to be disclosed in chapter five):

> Hence I implore and warn you, dear Zwingli, for the sake of God, that you from now on withhold such glosses and worthless discourses as you employed, for instance, in the words of Christ concerning the Supper where you gratuitously turned an *est* into a *significat*. . . . If you had preserved the straightforward understanding of the words spoken by Christ, then much harm would have been prevented.[128]

Thus we see that even when the two reformers were on the best of terms, they were not in agreement on every matter. When Zwingli invited Hubmaier to represent Waldshut, Basel, Baden, Schaffhausen, and the Black Forest at the Second Zurich Disputation, Hubmaier revealed that he no more supported the radical disciples of Zwingli than their mentor. In opposition to Grebel, Manz, and Blaurock, Hubmaier supported Zwingli on matters pertaining to the liturgy of the Mass and images of the Catholic Church, thereby securing the support of the city council,[129] and advocated a gradual reform in Zurich which would eventually rather than immediately lead to consonance between biblical theology and ecclesiastical practice.[130] Analyzing the proceedings of the First and Second Zurich Disputations, therefore, it seems apparent that the Waldshut reformer acted independently of both Zwingli and his radical followers and was not necessarily a proponent of either side. Aside from his anachronistic use of the confessional designations "Anabaptist" and "Zwinglian," Mabry makes this point quite well: "Instead of being a disciple of either party, Hubmaier seems more to have had his own positions on the various issues, on the basis of which he acts independently of each group. By 1523, at least, Hubmaier seems not to be any more an Anabaptist [sic] than a Zwinglian."[131] Since there is no evidence that Hubmaier

---

127. Loserth, *Hubmaier*, 134; Sachsse, *Hubmaier als Theologe*, 139.

128. "Doch bitte vnd ermane ich dich vmb Gottes willen, lieber Zwingle, das du für an solher glossen vnnd Tannten miessig gangest. Als du namlich inn den wortenn Christi, das Nachtmal betreffennde, auch gethon hast, da du on alle not ein Est für Significat außrieffest. . . . Liesssts du bey dem ainfeltigen verstand der wort bleiben, wann Christus hat ainfaltigklich geredt, so belibe vil vnratt vermitten." *Transcript of the Second Zurich Disputation*, 2:786.

129. Bergsten, *Hubmaier*, 110-12; Vedder, *Hübmaier*, 58-59.

130. Loserth, *Hubmaier*, 136-40; Vedder, *Hübmaier*, 61-64.

131. Mabry, *Doctrine of the Church*, 50.

had any further contact with the Zurich radicals until 1525, it is to this year of the former's own rebaptism that we now turn.

Based on the fact that Hubmaier was rebaptized by Wilhelm Reublin, branded by his adversaries as the "most rabid" of the Zurich radicals,[132] Bergsten suggests that the former's movement amounted simply to an extension of the Swiss Brethren.[133] However, it is critical to remember that before 1524, the point at which infant baptism first became an issue in the Zurich Reformation, Hubmaier was already refusing to administer the rite, of which he served as a leading opponent since at least 1523, and was baptizing mostly believers from that point forward. However, the final blow to Bergsten's theory, in my judgment, was dealt by the following discovery of Leonhard von Muralt and Walter Schmid: when some Anabaptist converts from Zurich came to Waldshut in February 1525 and insisted that Hubmaier join their cause by allowing himself to be rebaptized, he flatly refused.[134] Such a rejection stood in spite of the fact that Hubmaier, at first glance paradoxically, had issued the following challenge on 2 February 1525:

> Whoever wills, let him demonstrate that one should baptize infants, and let him do this with German, plain, clear, and unambiguous Scriptures relating only to baptism without any addition. On the other hand, Balthasar Fridberger pledges to prove that the baptism of infants is a work without any foundation in the divine Word.[135]

Such a situation is highly significant, for it exposes a crucial theological disconnect in Hubmaier's thinking between the rebaptism of the laity and his own rebaptism as a cleric. Recall that Hubmaier, after reading Luther's *Babylonian Captivity of the Church* in 1520, agreed that only baptism and the Lord's Supper constituted sacraments, with penance playing a key medi-

---

132. Goertz, *Anabaptists*, 25-26; Estep (*Anabaptist Story*, 50-53) lists several cases where Reublin's zeal may have exceeded his judgment.

133. Bergsten, *Hubmaier*, 118-19.

134. Leonhard von Muralt and Walter Schmid, *Quellen zur Geschichte der Täufer in der Schweiz* (Zürich: S. Hirzel, 1952), 2:319; this point is confirmed by Mabry, *Doctrine of the Church*, 52.

135. "Wer da wölle, solle anzeygen, das man die jungen kinder täuffen solle vnnd das thůe mit teütschen, hällen, claren, eynfeltigen schrifften, den Tauff alleyn betreffende, on allen zůsatz. Balthazar Fridberger erbeůt sich herwiderumb zůbeweysen, das der Kindertauff ein werck sey on allen grundt des Göttlichen worts." Hubmaier, *Öffentliche Erbietung*, 106. It should be noted that Hubmaier, since he was born in Fridberg near Augsburg, took from there the second surname Fridberger; Vedder, *Hübmaier*, 24.

ating role between the two. Nonetheless, Hubmaier retained his regenerative doctrine of ordination, probably derived from Bernard of Clairvaux, by ontologically grounding this ceremony in the power intrinsic to the sacrament of baptism and necessary for the reconciliation of penance, the restoration of grace flowing from which is a requirement for worthily partaking of the Eucharist. Relying upon his holy orders, therefore, it seems clear that Hubmaier fully believed that both the temporal and spiritual punishment for his past, present, and future actual sins had been remitted through his Bernardian spiritual "second baptism," relieving him of any need to engage in a physical second baptism. However, the evidence may suggest that the salvific confidence of the Waldshut reformer suffered a major blow in April 1525, leading to the most drastic and groundbreaking theological changes in his career.

Apparently unconvinced that Waldshut had embraced the Anabaptist message, the fiery missionary Wilhelm Reublin journeyed from his Zurich home to Waldshut for an audience with the city's renowned evangelical reformer.[136] The two most recent historical studies of Reublin, by Hans-Jürgen Goertz and George Huntston Williams, have reached similar conclusions regarding the content of his theology. According to Goertz, the theme of practically all Reublin's sermons revolved around anticlericalism, and in particular, an "extremist version" of Luther's priesthood of all believers which asserted the impotence of ordination to render any person specially qualified to perform ministerial tasks forbidden to the ordinary believer.[137] This hypothesis finds support in the research of Williams, who furnishes several case studies of Reublin's homilies. In 1524, Reublin preached to "audiences up to four thousand" against the sacrament of holy orders and, notably, "against the bishop himself."[138] When the Zurich radical attempted to delegitimize Zwingli from his authority as people's priest at the pivotal 17 January 1525 First Zurich Disputation on Baptism, the teacher summarily rebuked his former student as "simple of mind, foolishly bold, garrulous, and unwise."[139] Since there is no reason to believe Reublin preached anything different at Waldshut from what he asserted throughout the rest of his career, it seems likely that this "hostile Anabaptist" inveighed against the validity of Hubmaier's ordination. Three pieces of evidence indicate that Reublin may have convinced Hubmaier of the inability of holy orders to

---

136. Windhorst, *Täuferisches Taufverständnis*, 76-80; McClendon, "Balthasar Hubmaier: Catholic Anabaptist," 22-24.

137. Goertz, *Anabaptists*, 36-42.

138. Williams, *Radical Reformation*, 178.

139. Ibid., 215.

wash away sin, thereby shattering the latter's certainty of salvation. First, Hubmaier, after hearing the message of Reublin, expressed fear before the congregation that he would be consigned to hell at best temporarily (which is consistent with his conception of purgatory) and at worst permanently,[140] and immediately requested that Reublin baptize him "publicly in the pulpit" and in the presence of many witnesses on Easter Saturday, 15 April 1525.[141] Second, in an act perhaps inexplicable apart from his repudiation of holy orders, Hubmaier renounced his ordination as bishop and the corresponding benefice before the congregation and then asked to be elected to the bishopric and its material remuneration, which his parishioners did without delay.[142] Third, Hubmaier proceeded to rebaptize the concelebrating priests by affusion out of a milk pail,[143] which suggests that he feared for their damnation as well. For these reasons, we can accept as quite plausible the thesis that the anticlerical Reublin persuaded the Waldshut reformer that his ordination was devoid of any salvific power, which led a fearful Hubmaier to both demand personal rebaptism and rebaptize his subordinate priests in order to guarantee his and their salvation. We will see that such a rejection of holy orders coupled with the acceptance of rebaptism congealed into an innovative sacramental theology of believers' baptism, which will occupy the attention of the next chapter.

One must not be misled into thinking, however, that Reublin won Hubmaier over to the Anabaptist cause. Rather, since Hubmaier, believing he was not validly baptized as an infant, depended on his rebaptismal ordination for eternal security, and the former likely persuaded him that his ordination neither constituted a rebaptism nor bestowed eternal spiritual rebirth, he naturally decided to be rebaptized, but displayed no evidence of embracing any other distinguishing tenet of the Swiss Brethren.[144] Summarizing the events of Easter 1525, Mabry concludes: "[While] Hubmaier readily accepted Reublin's preaching, and allowed himself to be baptized. . . . this . . . was not necessarily a conversion to Anabaptism as a whole movement. He

---

140. Sachsse, *Hubmaier als Theologe*, 157-58.

141. "hin an offner Kanzel in der kirch vnd im beisein vieler zeugen getaufft." Balthasar Hubmaier, *Waldshut an Straßburg*, in *Quellen zur Geschichte der Täufer* (Gütersloh: C. Bertelsmann, 1955), 4:391.

142. Bergsten, *Hubmaier*, 304; Windhorst, *Täuferisches Taufverständnis*, 82.

143. As reported by Huldrych Zwingli, *Antwort über Doktor Balthasar's Taufbüchlein*, in Egli and Finsler, *Sämtliche Werke*, 4:591, who declared that Hubmaier thereby "divided the pious folk and brought them into danger" (fromme Volk geteilt und in Gefahr gebracht).

144. Loserth, *Hubmaier*, 142.

simply agreed with them on that one point."[145] Bearing in mind the foregoing analysis, it seems plausible that Hubmaier's reformation was not significantly influenced by either Zwingli or his erstwhile past disciples. It follows,
without even analyzing his sacramental theology, that no positive reason
exists for the widespread proposition that Hubmaier was an Anabaptist in
any meaningful sense.[146] If the term "Anabaptist" is trivially defined as a
practitioner of believers' baptism as opposed to infant baptism, then Hubmaier merits the distinction; however, as illustrated in chapter one, in view
of a more substantive definition rooted in the findings of contemporary
scholarship, Hubmaier emerges scarcely more an Anabaptist than Luther or
Zwingli. During that era, however, his rejection of pedobaptism and adherence to believers' baptism was enough for his opponents to mislabel him as
an Anabaptist, with all its derogatory overtones.

Synopsis of Hubmaier's Theological Pilgrimage

Before launching into an extended analysis of the Magisterial Radical's
distinctive sacramental theology, a brief summation of the variegated threads
of his intellectual journey is warranted. The dogmatic structure of Hubmaier's theology, featuring patristic and medieval undercurrents, assumed its
shape through his academic training under John Eck at the universities of
Freiburg and Ingolstadt. Quite influential among the medieval doctors in
Hubmaier's thinking, as for Luther and Calvin, proved to be Bernard of
Clairvaux. In particular, Hubmaier embraced Bernard's doctrine of ordination, according to which ordination serves as a "second baptism" consum-
mating the purification from original sin bestowed through the *sacramentum
initiationis* by releasing the soul from all eternal and temporal penalties of
past, present, and future actual sins, and attempted to strengthen it through a
reassessment of the *ratio praedestinationis* and reconceptualization of purgatory. In contrast to Bernard's view that conversion, defined as repentance
from wrongdoing and trust in Christ as a living person for remission of iniquity and everlasting life, forms the basis of predestination (which Hubmaier
regarded as problematic in light of Bernard's theory of holy orders), Hubmaier, inspired by the writings of Eck, subdivided the predestinary ground
into the *ratio praedestinationis ex parte praedestinati* and its divine approval
for immediate access to the beatific vision. Although the former *ratio* ac-

---

145. Mabry, *Doctrine of the Church*, 52.
146. This deduction is proposed but finally dismissed in Robert A. Mackoskey, "The Life and Thought of Balthasar Hubmaier, 1485-1528" (Ph.D. dissertation, University of Edinburgh, 1956), 40-42.

quired at baptism guarantees that the recipient will eventually be admitted into paradise, she or he first must undergo purging of all mortal sins in hell, figuratively called "purgatory" because the baptized sinner will not forever remain there. The latter, conferred through holy orders, absolves one of any purgation and assures the religious entrance to paradise at the moment of death. By the time he graduated as *doctor theologiae* from Ingolstadt in 1512, therefore, Hubmaier reposed full confidence in his ordination as guaranteeing that he, in his gloss on John 8:12, would never come into judgment, but would forever have the light of life.[147]

During the next four years, Hubmaier, as professor of theology at Ingolstadt and priest at the Church of our Beloved Lady, amassed an excellent reputation for his scholarship and preaching, which led the Regensburg City Council to offer him the prestigious post of *Domprediger*. Such an invitation was too appealing for the young preacher to resist, and he occupied this position with his characteristic flair and Catholic piety from 1516-1519. When Luther's *Ninety-Five Theses* stirred up passion in Germany, Hubmaier was among the first to lash out against them not only from the pulpit,[148] but by going so far as to request the anathema of the allegedly heretical monk in a satirical poem to Pope Leo X in 1518. However, upon his promotion to bishop of Waldshut in 1519, a revolutionary turn in Hubmaier's religious thought began to materialize, motivated in part by his misperception of Luther's *sola fides* as *assensus*, or in German, *glaub*. Reading the Wittenberger through the metaphysical categories of his tripartite libertarian anthropology, Hubmaier devoured Luther's pamphlets relating to the sacraments and the authority of Scripture as interpreted by patristic "sound reason." As a theological synergist, Hubmaier found Luther's claim that the sacraments could not be validly received without faith (which the former took to mean belief) very attractive, quoting often the "hoop before an inn without wine" analogy from the latter's 1519 homily on the Mass. Reasoning that infants lack *glaub* and equating *glaub* with *fides*, Hubmaier derived from Luther a conclusion that the Wittenberg reformer would not anticipate, namely, the invalidity of infant baptism. When Hubmaier wrote to Luther for verification of his conclusion, he was greeted by silence, serving to underscore perhaps Luther's own suspicion that infant baptism might not be supported by the sacred text; Hubmaier, however, interpreted this non-response as a tacit response in denial of "child washing."[149] Such a development moved Hubmaier to under-

---

147. Hubmaier, *Form des Nachtmals Christi*, 356.
148. Bergsten, *Hubmaier*, 76.
149. Vedder, *Hübmaier*, 115. Hubmaier derisively comments, "What is [my] opinion of the infant baptism which the water-priests use? Nothing other

take a directed study of Erasmus' 1516 *Greek New Testament* and the Church Fathers on the question of baptism. Persuaded by much of Luther's 1520 *Babylonian Captivity of the Church*, moreover, Hubmaier instituted communion *sub utraque specie* and removed the Waldshut altars by May 1521.[150] While accepting Luther's sacramental reduction from seven to technically two and functionally three, Hubmaier preserved his belief in the power of ordination by ontologically grounding its authority as derivative from baptism and prerequisite to penance. Nevertheless, a greater sacramental innovation, previously unnoted, was established by Hubmaier in partial form at Regensburg in 1522 and in complete form at Waldshut no later than 1523.

The same event which met with excommunication and charges of treason from the Zurich ecclesiastical and political authorities in January 1525, namely, the baptism of believers, appears to have gone largely unnoticed in Waldshut by the Swiss and Austrian authorities from 1523-1524, as it sparked no upheaval either religious or civil. The evangelical reformer of Waldshut, who always enjoyed the support of his city council, abolished infant baptism as "a mocking casuistry" (*spöttlich gehandelt*)[151] and instituted two forms of believers' baptism. Lay adults were exhorted to be baptized regardless of age, and their children received the *sacramentum initiationis* in place of the confirmation rite after learning the basics of the faith. This finding, which modifies the standard dating of the first adult rebaptism at Zurich on 21 January 1525, raises a host of queries, for which only tentative answers will be attempted here. Why, we may ask, was infant baptism regarded as the cornerstone of the Christendom church-state amalgam by the Zurich authorities, where it was accordingly deemed as indispensable,[152] and not by the Waldshut authorities, who viewed the act as solely religious and carrying no political import whatsoever?[153] The explanation may lie in the respective relationships between the principal reformer and local government of each city, for in both Waldshut and Zurich, the city council trusted

---

than the adult child bathing the young child, in this way depriving the latter of the real water baptism of Christ" (Was [halte] denn von dem Kindertauff, den die Wasserpfaffen brauchen. Nicht anders, denn das das altt kind wasserbadet das Jung khindlen, dardurch es des rechtenn Wassertauffs Christj beraubt wirdt); *Eine christliche Lehrtafel*, 314.

150. Windhorst, *Täuferisches Taufverständnis*, 16.
151. Hubmaier, *Von der ordnung*, 137.
152. Baylor, *Radical Reformation*, xvii; Yoder, "Turning Point," 136.
153. Windhorst, *Täuferisches Taufverständnis*, 57.

the judgment and followed the lead of their reformer.[154] Ironically, perhaps the Zurich council would never have linked infant baptism with treason had it not been for Zwingli's equation of the two, and suggestively, there is no evidence for the council's fear that abolition of infant baptism would undermine the cohesiveness of society until Zwingli made this argument at the 17 January 1525 First Zurich Disputation on Baptism.[155] Thus it appears that Zurich's religious authority may have convinced the political authorities, unconcerned with the point at which baptism occurred, that believers' baptism constituted a grave political threat, predictably causing them to side with Zwingli against his erstwhile disciples. However, since neither religious nor political authorities in Waldshut viewed the replacement of infant with believers' baptism as problematic,[156] the transition seems to have created no controversy and was viewed as just another in a long series of reforms initiated by Hubmaier. A second question follows from this: If Zwingli had, like Hubmaier, advocated believers' baptism in 1525 instead of the former's "overly zealous" followers,[157] would the city council have embraced it? This inquiry, it seems to me, should be answered affirmatively, since, as Hubmaier hastened to remind the readers of his famous antipedobaptist polemics, article eighteen of Zwingli's *Sixty-Seven Articles*, which the city council accepted in January 1523, endorsed the practice of believers' baptism.[158] Finally, is believers' baptism intrinsically incompatible with a state church? As we shall see in the next chapter, this does not seem to be the case, as suggested by Hubmaier's successful state churches of believers in both Waldshut and Nikolsburg. When Hubmaier returned to Regensburg for a brief preaching stint in 1522, he implemented "catechetical rebaptism" but avoided the more extreme measure of adult rebaptism, assuming that he would encounter opposition from its Catholic city council, which did not,

154. Robert Walton, *Zwingli's Theocracy* (Toronto: University of Toronto Press, 1967), 185-88; Oskar Vasella, "Zur Geschichte der Täuferbewegung in der Schweiz," *Zeitschrift für Schweizerische Kirchengeschichte*, XLVIII (1954): 184; John H. Yoder, *Täufertum und Reformation im Gespräch* (Zürich: EVZ-Verlag, 1968), 117-28; Bergsten, *Hubmaier*, 258; Sachsse, *Hubmaier als Theologe*, 145.

155. Walton, *Theocracy*, 193; Vasella, "Geschichte," 188; Yoder, *Täufertum*, 132.

156. Bergsten, *Hubmaier*, 270; Sachsse, *Hubmaier als Theologe*, 148.

157. Clasen, *Anabaptism*, 11.

158. Hubmaier, *Von der christlichen Taufe*, 155; Hubmaier, *Gespräch auf Zwinglis Taufbüchlein*, 186.

like those in Waldshut and Zurich, generally submit to religious authority but appears to demand that clerics follow its desires.[159]

From October 1521 until December 1522, Hubmaier believed that his reforming program, featuring as its *sine qua non* a libertarian anthropology which manifested itself in the practice of (at least catechetical) believers' baptism, was in full accordance with the thought of Luther. This perception was soon shattered, however, when Hubmaier, as part of a Luther reading group of burghers led by the dyer Laien Blabhans, encountered the complete exposition of the Wittenberger's views on faith as a monergistic gift of God and pedobaptism as both proper and valid in *Vom Anbeten des Sacraments des heiligen Leichnams Christi*. No longer able to honestly dub himself a follower of Luther's doctrine, Hubmaier, who feared losing the popular support from the burgher contingent needed to counterbalance any possible hostility from the Catholic city council, departed from Regensburg just after New Year's of 1523 and returned to a joyful congregation in Waldshut.[160] While preserving the appellation "Lutheran" out of deep respect and gratitude for his predecessor's "tireless efforts to advance the kingdom of God,"[161] Hubmaier displayed no hesitation in disputing Luther's views from the pulpit and advancing his own in their stead. In defense of his doctrine of *liberum arbitrium* over against Luther's *servum arbitrium*, Hubmaier argued that faith constituted the natural capacity of the human soul to believe the salvific promises of God.[162] Purposely distancing himself from Luther's forensic theology of justification and its corollary *simul* doctrine, Hubmaier, in harmony with his synergism, insisted that justification was not *Rechtfertigung* but *Frombmachung*, thereby equating justification with sanctification. Since one, in Hubmaier's view, must be made into a righteous person through virtuous living and the performance of good works, the preacher translated key biblical terms, including $\delta\iota\kappa\alpha\iota\omega\sigma\iota\nu$ and $\sigma\omega\sigma\alpha\iota$, as *Frombmachung, Rechtmachung,* and *fromb machen.* Hence for Hubmaier, faith is a necessary but not sufficient condition for salvation.

The theological independence of Hubmaier, who was able to unite seemingly contradictory religious modalities into a coherent system, reveals itself throughout Hubmaier's contact with both Zwingli and his radical followers from 1523 to 1525. At the First Zurich Disputation, for example, Hubmaier freely alternated between support and rejection of Zwingli's *Sixty-Seven Articles*. While concurring with Zwingli on the authority of Scripture,

---

159. Vedder, *Hübmaier*, 45-46.
160. Bergsten, *Hubmaier*, 120.
161. Vedder, *Hübmaier*, 79.
162. Sachsse, *Hubmaier als Theologe*, 180-82.

he upbraided the Zurich reformer for "sophistry" in exegeting the Eucharistic words of institution through his lens of sacramentarianism.[163] In a similar vein, Hubmaier decried the future Swiss Brethren at the Second Zurich Disputation for injudicious radicalism concerning the liturgy of the Mass and images. For Hubmaier, who appears to have still considered his ordination as a rebaptism of sorts in February 1525, there was no need to be physically rebaptized, causing him to spurn the request of the nascent Anabaptists to do so. However, the most profound theological transformation in Hubmaier's career transpired in April 1525 when Wilhelm Reublin likely persuaded Hubmaier that holy orders lacked any salvific power, thus putting the latter in the same position as the laity whom he had exhorted for at least two years to undertake believers' baptism. In accord with his newfound adherence to a radical form of the priesthood of all believers, then, a worried Hubmaier immediately asked Reublin to baptize him before the entire congregation, temporarily renounced his bishopric, and successfully requested his parishioners to vote him back into the office. On this basis, the majority of Radical Reformation historians generalize that Hubmaier converted to Anabaptism; however, the evidence seems to suggest that he remained an evangelical reform theologian throughout the duration of his life who was convinced by Reublin to abandon none of his beliefs with the sole yet important exception of the validity of ordination. As we will see in the next two chapters, moreover, Hubmaier's rebaptism served as the culminating factor in a host of influences which gave rise to his sacramental theology, interweaving his reconceptualized doctrines of believers' baptism, church discipline, and the Lord's Supper into a consistent framework. Since Anabaptists, by definition, regarded the great Christian symbols as ordinances rather than sacraments, the forthcoming demonstration that Hubmaier developed a genuinely sacramental theology will decisively render impossible any identification of this reformer as an Anabaptist.

Chapter 4

Hubmaier's Doctrine of the Sacrament of Believers' Baptism

As a corollary to his anthropological starting point of libertarian free will, which he acquired from Bernard of Clairvaux, Hubmaier inclined from his earliest days as *doctor theologiae* toward a voluntaristic model of Christianity springing out of *fides humana*, in which *fides* is understood as *glaub* or *assensus* (*i.e.* belief) rather than the Lutheran *fides caritate formata* (*i.e.* faith informed by love).[1] Failing to grasp this dissimilarity, however, Hubmaier was driven by his libertarian presupposition to embrace a misinterpretation of Luther that reception of the sacraments must be conditioned by personal faith. Armed with the requisite linguistic tools, Hubmaier, doubting that infants possessed faith, undertook a careful search of Erasmus' *Greek New Testament* and the patristic sources to discover the original baptismal practice of the church. Once he concluded that believers were often baptized until a decree requiring infant baptism, inspired by the late Augustine, was issued by Pope Innocent I in 407,[2] the Waldshut reformer demanded no later

---

1. Sachsse, *Hubmaier als Theologe*, 171; Pelikan, *Reformation*, 253.

2. Hubmaier, *Von der christlichen Taufe*, 155; Hubmaier, *Der Lehrer Urteil* I, 232; Hubmaier, *Von der Kindertaufe*, 261. In all of these references, Hubmaier quotes from Augustine's letter to Innocent I, entitled *De consecratione* (in Aemilius Friedberg, *Corpus iuris canonici* [Graz: Akademische Druck-und Verlagsanstalt, 1959], 1:1402), where Augustine justifies infant baptism on the basis of his doctrine of original sin after it had been revised due to the Pelagian controversy. Hence Hubmaier can say concerning baptism: "We have failed . . . so miserably for such a long time, namely for the past thousand years, Augustine being not a little to blame for this" (Wir . . . so lannge zeyt her, namlich ob Tauset Jaren, Augustinus ist nit wenig darann Schuldig); *Gespräch auf Zwinglis Taufbüchlein*, 171.

than 1523 that his parishioners submit to rebaptism, excepting himself and his subordinate clergy, whom he regarded as already rebaptized through the divine ceremony of ordination. When Wilhelm Reublin, a Zurich Anabaptist reputed for his anticlerical hallmark, persuaded Hubmaier of the salvific impotence of holy orders, the frightened pastor solicited Reublin to rebaptize him before the congregation and subsequently rebaptized his subordinate clerics on 15 April 1525. This event served as the crowning influence which coordinated a multiplicity of loose doctrinal threads fabricated throughout his Lutheran (1519-22) and post-Lutheran (1523-25) stages into a coherent framework distinctly positing believers' baptism as a sacrament, or a means of grace that bestows the grace it signifies, contra the Anabaptist non-salvific view of the rite as a mere ordinance. This chapter provides a thorough analysis of Hubmaier's baptismal theology, which is subdivided for the sake of elucidation into four logically successive and cumulative steps: the conception of believers' baptism as a sacrament, including the pivotal role of the early Church Fathers (as opposed to Scripture) in its development; the salvific role of believers' baptism both for the remission of personal sins and in the divine predestinary scheme; the inventive formulation of believers' baptism as the key to the entrance door to the kingdom of heaven; and the inextricable relationship between this baptismal key and its corresponding door, provocatively identified as the initial stage of church discipline. Details concerning the liturgy and mode of believers' baptism will be appropriately treated within this fourfold model.

The Sacramental Identification of Believers' Baptism and Its Patristic Support

In his 1991 *MQR* article on Hubmaier's baptismal theology, H. Wayne Pipkin, although perpetuating the incorrect assumption that "Hubmaier had avoided using the term 'sacrament' in his discussion of baptism," highlights that Hubmaier's treatises surprisingly create "an overwhelming impression of a self-conscious identification with the ancient church," where "the faith affirmed is that of the Apostles' Creed."[3] This latter point cannot be too strongly underscored, for Hubmaier, while employing Scriptural arguments to undermine the veridicality of pedobaptism in his 1525 polemics, does not cite the sacred text in constructing his doctrine of baptism; rather, he attempts to weave several distinct doctrinal strands from the patristic sources together into a unified framework. As Bergsten points out, far from basing

---

3. Pipkin, "Baptismal Theology," 51-52.

his doctrine almost exclusively on the Bible, Hubmaier "was giving increasing importance to the Fathers of the Church and to decisions of the Church Councils."[4] Moreover, contra the notion that Hubmaier refused to accept believers' baptism as a sacrament, the Waldshut reformer, on the authority of St. Jerome, explicitly declares in his 1526 *Gespräch auf Zwinglis Taufbüchlein*: "For the body should not receive the sacrament of baptism (das Sacrament des Tauffes) unless the soul has previously received the truth of faith."[5] As noted in chapter one, Hubmaier defined the term "sacrament" at the Second Zurich Disputation in 1523 as "an outward, visible sign and seal through which we are completely assured of the forgiveness of our sins."[6] Moreover, in his liturgical elaboration of this definition, Hubmaier emphasizes that sacraments constitute means of grace, which are received so that God will "graciously communicate to [the recipient] the grace and the power of his Holy Spirit."[7] That Hubmaier regarded baptism and the Eucharist as grace-conveying sacraments is further disclosed by the fact that his liturgies for both ceremonies contain this blessing explaining the divine benefit bestowed through the external act: "May the Lord communicate his grace to us. . . . May he himself impart to all of us the power and the strength that we may worthily assume [the Christian life] and bring it to its saving completion according to his divine will."[8] In volume 1 of his two-volume historico-theological exposition of believers' baptism, *Der uralten und gar neuen Lehrer Urteil*, Hubmaier praised the verdict of Cyprian and the Fourth Synod of Carthage (255 C.E.) that baptism encompassed "God, Spirit, gospel, sacrament, and grace,"[9] from which he concluded "that only believers

---

4. "Die drei Schriften, an denen Hubmaier im Herbst des gleichen Jahres arbeitete, lassen aber erkennen, daß er den Kirchenvätern und den Konzilienbeschlüssen eine immer größere Bedeutung . . . beimaß." Bergsten, *Hubmaier*, 361.

5. "Wann es mag nit sein, das der Leib das Sacrament des Tauffes entpfahe, es hab denn die Seel zůuoran entpfangen die warhait des Glaubens." Hubmaier, *Gespräch auf Zwinglis Taufbüchlein*, 206.

6. Transcript of the Second Zurich Disputation, in *Zwingli Sämtliche Werke*, 2:786; the German is quoted in footnote 94, page 28.

7. "Er disem menschen die gnad vnd krafft seines heiligen geysts gnediglich mittailen wölle." Hubmaier, *Form zu taufen*, 349.

8. "Der Herr mittaile vns sein gnad. . . . Derselb verleyhe vns allen macht vnd sterckhe, das wirs nach seinem göttlichen willen wirdigklich mit hail verbringen vnd vollenden." Hubmaier, *Form des Nachtmals Christi*, 362; *cf.* Hubmaier, *Form zu taufen*, 349.

9. "Gott, Geist, Ewangelium, Sacrament vnd genad." Hubmaier, *Der Lehrer Urteil* I, 244.

[should] receive, desire, and seek the sacrament"[10] of baptism. Hubmaier reinforces this point in volume 2 by explicitly stating that the candidate receives grace in the rite of baptism: "The baptizand has previously been instructed in the faith and is therefore brought believing to baptism, in order that he may know what grace he receives in baptism and to whom he henceforth owes obedience."[11] It is evident that for Hubmaier, classifying baptism and the Lord's Supper as sacraments rather than as Anabaptist ordinances amounted to far more than a terminological divergence, namely an indicator of the numinous power mediated from God to the believer through these Christ-appointed channels.

Frequently Hubmaier ties the sacramental character of baptism and the Eucharist to the ethical dimension of the Christian life. With regard to baptism, Hubmaier insists that there exists an indissoluble bond between this sacrament and church discipline, to be explored fully later in the chapter. Hubmaier postulated that all those who either affirmed the validity of infant baptism (Catholics, Luther, Zwingli) or denied the sacramental quality of believers' baptism (Anabaptists) did so in an attempt to evade accountability for their Christian commitment.[12] That the reformer could so argue concerning the Anabaptists, as we will see, betrays his surprising ignorance of the paramount emphasis placed by Anabaptists upon church discipline, yielding further corroboration that Hubmaier was not an Anabaptist. In light of the perceived corruption in the Roman church, Hubmaier alleges that the so-called "papal antichrist" fears the reinstatement of believers' baptism, as it would render him guilty of transgressing his faith. This is why, Hubmaier insists after moving to Nikolsburg in 1526, the Catholic imperial authorities are attempting to forestall his reforms:

> Hence, day and night, the antichrist has exerted such a tremendous effort to drain out for himself the water baptism of Christ and replace it with his fraudulent, despicable anti-Christian infant baptism. In this case, if someone would faithfully remind him of his sacramental bap-

---

10. "das die Sacrament nur die glaubigen solten empfahen, begeren vnnd suchen." Ibid., 245.

11. "Der Taufling im glauben zû vor vnderwisen werd vnd also gelaubig zum Tauff gelassen werde, darmit das er wisse, was genaden er darinnen empfach, vnnd wem er darnach gehorsam schuldig sey." Hubmaier, *Der Lehrer Urteil* II, 248.

12. Hubmaier, *Strafe*, 345-46.

tismal vow and commitment, he could quickly exempt himself and say, "I was a child then."[13]

Here Hubmaier, as indicated in the previous chapter, follows Luther by classifying the form and not the matter of baptism as sacramental. This form, however, not only consists of the divine promise of salvation, but also the reciprocal human vow to follow Christ in discipleship. Ironically, the radical insists that baptism and the Eucharist are sacraments rather than signs in his denunciation of Anabaptists (his "dear brethren") who hold the view that modern scholars erroneously attribute to Hubmaier himself:

> But to all those who scream: "What's the big deal about water baptism? What's the big deal about the Lord's Supper? After all, they are just outward signs! They're nothing but water, bread, and wine!". . . . They have never learned enough in their entire life to know [that] our water baptism [is] a sacramental oath before the Christian church and all her members, gathered bodily in part and completely in the Holy Spirit, or in the power of our Lord Jesus Christ (which is all the same power), and surrendering oneself to her in hand-pledged commitment. Observe, dear brethren, that if this were not so . . . then our water baptism and bread-breaking would merely be an illusion and a sham as well, nothing better than what the idiotic child baptism and infant-feeding were before.[14]

---

13. "Auß der vrsach hat der Antichrist tag vnd nacht so mercklichen fleyß fürkhert, Christo seinen Wassertauff auß zegiessen vnd seinen erdichten, ellenden vnnd Antichristischen Khindertauff an die stat zesetzen. Auff das, so er seiner Sacramentlicher Tauffglübde vnd handglobter trew ermanet vnd erinnert wurde, er sich bald enschuldigen möcht vnd sagen: Jch bin ein khind gwesen." Hubmaier, *Strafe*, 345.

14. "Darumb alle die so da schreyen: Ey was ist es vmb den Wassertauff. Was ist es vmb das Nachtmal. Seind es doch nun eüsserliche zaichen. Da ist nichts denn wasser, brot vnd wein. . . . Die selben haben ir leben lang nye so vil geleernt, das sy wißten vnnser Wassertauff [ist] einem Sacramentlichen ayd vor der Christenlichen Kirchen vnd vor allen iren glidern, so zum tail leiblich vnd gar im geyst bey ein ander seind, auff die krafft Gotes vaters vnd Sons vnd heiligen geists oder auff die krafft vnsers herren Jesu Christj (wöhles alles ain krafft ist) offentlich bezeügen, vnnd sich ir mit hanndtglobter trew ergebenn. Darauff secht, ir liebenn brüeder . . . ob wol vnnser Wassertauff vnd Brotbrechung auch nun ein schein vnd Spiegelfecht ist, ja nichts bessers denn wie der torechtig Khindertauff vnd Khindlen pappen bißher gwesen." Ibid., 346. As Hubmaier indicates earlier in this treatise (340), the "infant-feeding" (Khindlen

For this reason, Hubmaier asserted in an apologetic for his baptismal theology, "I have never taught Anabaptism."[15] Hubmaier had occasion to publicly express his disquiet with the Anabaptist perspective when Hans Hut, a prominent South German radical, visited Nikolsburg in 1527 and taught in his sermons that "the baptism which follows preaching and faith is not the true reality by which man is made righteous, but is only a sign . . . a likeness, and a memorial of one's dedication."[16] In response, Hubmaier vigorously opposed him and accentuated the sacramental character of baptism:

> Concerning this baptism and sacrament, I am extremely incensed by the way Hans Hut and his followers taught and administered [it] and plan to stand against it in my teaching and writing my entire life as God gives me strength. . . . Moreover, I have no doubt that, with the help of God, I could quickly invalidate his baptism. . . . This is why the baptism that I taught and the baptism that Hut endorsed are as far apart as heaven and hell, east and west, Christ and Belial.[17]

Therefore, the primary sources from the period following the reformer's own rebaptism permit no doubt that Hubmaier regarded baptism as a sacrament over against the notion of a mere sign or ordinance.

Because of their perceived indispensability for Christian discipleship, Hubmaier castigated those who dishonored the sacraments, which could occur either by neglecting them or failing to live up to the baptismal vow, the content of which will be elucidated later in this chapter. In his discussion of the sacraments with Oecolampadius in 1525, Hubmaier excludes from the church those with faith alone but who avoid reception (a probable allusion to those refusing to undergo believers' baptism): "I announce that we do not regard believers as Christians, so long as they do not accept the Christian

---

pappen) refers to the reception of the Eucharist by those who are spiritual, not literal, infants and are in his thinking not ready for the solid sacramental food.

15. "Khainen widertauff hab ich nye geleert." Hubmaier, *Entschuldigung*, 275.

16. Hans Hut, "The Mystery of Baptism," trans. Rollin Stely Armour, in *Baptism*, 83.

17. "Mit dem tauff vnd Sacramennt, wie Johann Hut mit seinen Anhenngern gelert vnd praucht hat, bin jch vast vbl daran, will auch darwider sein mit leren vnd schreibenn, als vil mir gott Crafft gibt, mein lebenlanng. . . . Mir ist auch kain . . . seinen tauff . . . wolt jch mit der hilff gottes pald abstellen. . . . Darumb ist der tauff, so jch gelert, vnnd der tauff, den Hutt furgeben hat, souerr von einannder als himel vnnd hell, oriennt vnd occident, Cristus vnd Belial." Hubmaier, *Rechenschaft*, 486-87.

symbols, no matter how holy they are otherwise. For Christ wanted to gather a people to himself through the sacramental symbols."[18] On the other hand, Hubmaier reinforced to his Nikolsburg congregation in 1526 the necessity of personal fidelity to their "spiritual marriage" contracted at baptism:

> Be heedful of your baptismal vow . . . which you swore to God and the church publicly and certainly not unknowingly when receiving the water. . . . Make sure you bear fruit worthy of your baptism . . . so that you may, in the power of God, fulfill your vow, promise, sacrament, and sworn commitment. God sees it and knows your hearts.[19]

Violation of this oath, accordingly, renders all miscreants as

> wicked persons [who] should be summarily excluded and banned, who have become unfaithful, who violate the sacraments and perjure, who have not maintained their vow, duty, loyalty, honor, or faith in . . . our Lord Jesus Christ, despite being his all-beloved bride. . . . Those who truly violate the sacraments are those who do not keep their baptismal vow.[20]

Hubmaier's understanding of the baptismal vow, then, seems to imply that the sinner must both make an inward surrender to God and promise henceforth to lead a new life according to the law of Christ in order to be validly baptized.

Such a sacramental understanding of baptism was given substance by Hubmaier's knowledge of the history of Christian thought, which insight is

---

18. "Jch bekhenn das die glaubigen, so lang sy die Christenlichen zaichen nit annemen, wie heilig sy sunst seind, halten wir sy nit für Christen. Dann Christus hat also durch die Sacramentlichen zaichen im ein volckh wollen versamlen." Balthasar Hubmaier, *Von der Kindertaufe*, in Westin and Bergsten, *Schriften*, 268.

19. "Seyd ingedenckh eürer Tauffglübd . . . die ir in entpfahung des wassers . . . Gott vnd der Kirchen offentlich vnnd wol bedechtlich gethon habt. Lügent, das ir wirdig fruchten des Tauffs . . . bringent, auff das ir in der krafft Gottes eürer glübd, zůsagung, Sacrament vnnd aydspflicht genüeg thůend. Gott sicht es vnd erkent eüre hertzen." Hubmaier, *Form des Nachtmals Christi*, 364.

20. "die bösen mennschen kurtzlich außschliessen vnd verbannen soll, die da treüloß, Sacramentbrichtig vnd mainaidig worden, ja weder glübd, pflicht, trew, eer, noch glauben an . . . vnserm herren Jesu Christo, auch an seiner aller liebsten Praut. . . . Die seind die rechten Sacramenttbrichel, die jr Tauffglübd . . . nit halten." Hubmaier, *Bann*, 375.

manifested through *Der uralten und gar neuen Lehrer Urteil* exploring "the opinion of the ancient and new teachers" on believers' baptism. This *tour de force* analyzes the baptismal theologies of no less than twenty church fathers from the late first to the early fifth centuries, including Clement, Tertullian, Origen, Cyprian, Athanasius, Eusebius, Cyril, Basil the Great, Ambrose, and Jerome, to argue for the numinous quality of baptism and its dispensation to mostly believers until the Pelagian controversy.[21] Paradoxically, Hubmaier selectively applied Luther's practice of citing many of the Church Fathers as authoritative expositors of the sacred text:[22] while Luther utilized this strategy largely to appropriate the theology of the late Augustine,[23] Hubmaier endorsed the patristic sources up to, but not including, Augustine. In diametric opposition to Luther, Hubmaier militates against Augustine as the most notorious deviser of "blue answers" (blawen antwurten),[24] or lies, concerning free will and (in his view) derivatively infant baptism.[25] As Torsten Bergsten points out, "Hubmaier . . . maintains that Augustine and many since his time had been mistaken about baptism. In *Judgment I* Hubmaier's attitude toward the great Father of the Church is also unmistakably nega-

---

21. Windhorst, *Täuferisches Taufverständnis*, 78; Bergsten, *Hubmaier*, 377.

22. While Luther's attitude toward the Church Fathers in general is still a matter of controversy among Reformation scholars, Heiko Oberman (*Luther: Man Between God and the Devil* [New York: Doubleday, 1992], 247-48) points out that Luther regarded the writings produced by the first four ecumenical councils along with the Fathers whose thought they encapsulated as authoritative.

23. Pelikan, *Reformation*, 139-42; Spitz, *Reformation*, 87-89.

24. Hubmaier, *Der Lehrer Urteil* I, 232.

25. In Hubmaier's reading, Augustine's change of perspective on human freedom from libertarian freedom before the Pelagian controversy to compatibilist freedom afterwards determined his stance on baptism. If humans possess *liberum arbitrium*, as held by the early Augustine, then Augustine's dictum that "foreign faith is not sufficient for water baptism" (*Ante Baptismum*, in Friedberg, *Corpus iuris canonici*, 1:1383) entails according to Hubmaier that only believers, who successfully employed their natural capacity to generate *glaub*, can be baptized. On the other hand, if humans possess *servum arbitrium*, as held by the late Augustine, then the same dictum is for Hubmaier irrelevant to the question of baptism, since faith would be the result of irresistible grace independent of free will and could thus be bestowed on infants. Further, since original sin entailed the transmission of actual guilt rather than the mere inclination toward concupiscence, infants required baptism in order to be saved. Hubmaier enunciates fully his opinion of Augustine in *Der Lehrer Urteil* II, 244-45.

tive."[26] Thus the very hermeneutic employed by Luther (and later Calvin) to draw upon Augustine was turned against the *doctor gratiae* and used to refute his arguments in behalf of infant baptism. However, it becomes clear from volumes 1 and 2 of *Der Lehrer Urteil* that, while Hubmaier's historical motive for quoting the Ante-Nicene and Nicene Fathers was to show that believers were often baptized for the first four centuries of the common era, his doctrinal incentive for citing these Fathers was to provide evidence supporting baptismal regeneration. What makes this ironic is that baptismal regeneration is a doctrine typically associated with the late Augustine and his post-Pelagian perspective on original sin.[27] In Augustine's thought, the only way for infants to be saved from the guilt inherited from Adam was if God regenerated them at the moment of baptism.[28] Hubmaier thus seems to have taken the concept of baptismal regeneration out of its usual Augustinian compatibilist and infant baptismal context and redistricted it to a libertarian and believers' baptismal context by appealing to selected pre-Augustinian Fathers who taught both *liberum arbitrium* and salvation through baptism.

Therefore, Hubmaier contends that sins are remitted at the moment that a believer, having first naturally hungered and thirsted for righteousness and assented to the facts of the gospel, undergoes believers' baptism: "Baptism . . . is to make alive and whole again the confessing sinner with the fire of the divine Word by the Spirit of God. This occurs through the forgiveness of his sins."[29] At this time, the spiritual marriage is completed, as Christ's vows of eternal life are personally accepted by the believer, who reciprocates to the divine spouse by vowing "that he will believe and live according to [Christ's] divine Word from this day forth, and if he should stumble in this undertaking, he will accept brotherly admonition, according to Christ's

---

26. "Hubmaier . . . hält . . . daß Augustin und viele nach ihm sich hinsichtlich der Taufe getäuscht hätten. Auch im *Urteil 1* ist Hubmaiers Haltung zu dem großen Kirchenvater noch unverkennbar negativ." Bergsten, *Hubmaier*, 364.

27. Roger E. Olson, *The Story of Christian Theology* (Downers Grove, Ill.: InterVarsity Press, 1999), 266-67.

28. Augustine, *Enchiridion*, trans. Albert C. Outler (Philadelphia: Westminster Press, 1955), 52; Augustine, *On Nature and Grace*, trans. John A. Mourant (Washington, D.C.: Catholic University of America Press, 1992), 9.

29. "Täuffen . . . ist den bekennenden verieher seiner sünden mit dem feür des Göttlichen worts durch den geyst Gottes widerumb erklicken vnd gsundt machen. Das geschicht, so im verzeyhung seiner sünden." Hubmaier, *Von der christlichen Taufe*, 121.

order."[30] In volume 1 of *Der Lehrer Urteil*, Hubmaier quotes approvingly the pronouncement of Origen, "The person who stops sinning receives baptism for the forgiveness of sins. That is why I admonish you not to come to baptism without mindfulness and careful prior deliberation, but that you first produce fruits worthy of the restoration of your life."[31] Without any reference to the standard Anabaptist proof-text 1 Peter 3:20-21, which could have been used to make the same argument, Hubmaier cites Basil the Great to compare the salvific indispensability of baptism to the need for the antediluvians to enter into Noah's Ark: "He also compares water baptism with the flood from which no one was saved except those who entered the ark in faith."[32] On the authority of Cyril, Hubmaier bolsters the argument by declaring that anyone currently receiving instruction in the faith but not yet baptized is lost: "It is not enough that one believes, but he must also be baptized. For whoever believes and is not baptized, but is a catachumen, is not now saved."[33] In contradistinction to his treatment of all the previous Church Fathers, Hubmaier inveighs against Augustine for trying to convince Pope Boniface, a supporter of believers' baptism, that infant baptism should be the official practice of the church, despite its seemingly dubious character evident in the confession of faith by godparents rather than the children:

> Pope Boniface disputes with Bishop Augustine. The pope says that godparents, when they bring the child to baptism, may not truthfully answer in place of the child that it renounces the devil or that it believes. For they have no idea whether their child will be pure or impure, pious or a criminal. To this Augustine gives a blue answer.[34]

---

30. "das er fürhin nach seinem Göttlichen wort glaubenn vnd lebenn wölle. Vnnd wo er sich darinn vbersehe, wölle er sich alsdann brüderlich straffen lassen, nach der Ordnung Christi." Hubmaier, *Eine christliche Lehrtafel*, 314.

31. "Der mennsch enpfahet den Tauff zů verzeyhung der sünden, der auffhortt sünnden. Darumb so bit ich euch, das ir nit on fürsichtigkayt vnd on fleyssige vorbetrachtung zů dem Tauff kument, sunder das ir erzaigent zum ersten wirdig früchten der neüerung ewers lebens." Hubmaier, *Der Lehrer Urteil* I, 230.

32. "Er vergleicht auch den wassertauff dem sündfluß, auß wölchem nyemant erredt war, wenn der im glauben in die Arch eingieng." Ibid.

33. "Es ist nit gnůg, das ainer glaubt, sunnder er můß auch getaufft werden. Dann wölcher glaubt vnd nit taufft wirt, sunder ist ein Catechumenus, ist yetz nit sälig." Ibid., 231.

34. "Hat der Babst Bonifacius ein span wider den Bischoff Augustinum, vnd sagt der Babst, das die Gefattern, so das kind zum Tauff halten, nymmermer mit warhait an statt des khinds antwurten mügend, das es den Teüffel widersag,

Such vituperation against Augustine is reiterated in Hubmaier's 1525 dialogue with Oecolampadius on pedobaptism: "Augustine greatly erred in his canon *Firmissime* [Most Firmly]. . . . If he had written *Impiissime* [Most Impiously] instead he would have been nearer to the truth."[35] At the close of volume 1, Hubmaier summarizes the *ordo salutis* gleaned from his selected patristic sources, in which he explicitly places salvation after baptism: "You see here even more clearly how one should first preach; second, believe; third, be baptized; fourth follows salvation."[36] However, such a model raised two practical issues: first, the fate of unbaptized infants quite significant to parents; and second, the compatibility of believers' baptism with a state church. Both of these would be addressed by the Magisterial Radical in volume 2 of *Der Lehrer Urteil*.

Recall that Hubmaier, as disclosed in his August 1524 letter to Oecolampadius, instituted the practice of infant dedication in place of pedobaptism in an attempt to comfort worried (and, in his judgment, doctrinally underinformed) parents.[37] Those whom Hubmaier characterized as theologically astute, nevertheless, realized that the new ceremony in reality carried no more salvific efficacy than the "child washing" it replaced.[38] This is because, as the reformer admits elsewhere, Christian parents bear righteous and unrighteous children alike: "Dear friends, [dedication] is nothing, since it often happens that the same father and mother bring both good and bad fruit into the world. For example, take Abel and Cain or Esau and Jacob. It depends on God, not on the father and mother."[39] Contrary to Conrad Grebel's stance that "all children who have not yet come to the discernment of the knowledge of good and evil, and have not yet eaten of the tree of knowledge, they are surely saved by the suffering of Christ, the new Adam, who

---

oder das es Glaub. Die weyl sy nitt wissen, ob das khind wird keüsch oder vnkeüsch, frumb oder ein dieb werdenn. Darauf gibt im Augustinus ein blawe antwurt." Ibid., 232.

35. "Augustin hat groblich gejrret in seinem. c. Firmissime. . . . Het er Jmpijssime dafür geschriben, wer im baß angestanden." Hubmaier, *Von der Kindertaufe*, 261.

36. "Sichstu hye noch klärer, wie man zum ersten predigen solle, zum andern Glauben, zum dritten taufft werden, zum vierdten folget die säligkayt." Hubmaier, *Der Lehrer Urteil* I, 238.

37. Sachsse, *Hubmaier als Theologe*, 200; Loserth, *Hubmaier*, 179.

38. Windhorst, *Täuferisches Taufverständnis*, 98; Vedder, *Hübmaier*, 202.

39. "Lieber fründ, es ist nichts, dann es geschicht offt, das vatter vnd müter gůt vnnd böß frucht bringent. Nymm für ein exempel Abel vnd Chayn, Esau vnd Jacob. Es ligt an Gott, nit an vatter vnd müter." Hubmaier, *Von der christlichen Taufe*, 156.

has restored their vitiated life . . . through an infused faith,"[40] Hubmaier objected that this supposition was theologically arbitrary and lacked Scriptural justification: "But some greatly boast about an infused faith which God imparted to the children and by which they are saved; I know nothing about that. . . . about that I have no Scripture. For this reason I refuse to let it stand . . . as a theology."[41] Unable to bring himself to the conclusion that infants are damned, Hubmaier appealed to his Bernardian distinction between God's *potentia ordinata* and his *potentia absoluta*. Although the *ordo salutis*, whereby salvation follows believers' baptism, constitutes the prevailing spiritual law, the divine lawgiver, according to Hubmaier's divine-command theory of ethics, may graciously override that law by his *potentia absoluta* if he so chooses. In a conclusion which proved unacceptable to distraught parents in both Waldshut and Nikolsburg,[42] Hubmaier confesses ignorance as to the eternal destiny of infants and assigns their salvation or condemnation to the secret and hidden will of God:

> I am not embarrassed not to know what God did not want to reveal to us in clear and simple words. He tells me as he told Peter, "What concern is it of yours as to what I choose to do with infants? Follow me, look to my word and will," John 21:22. However, still I will humbly and sincerely entreat God to be a merciful Father to them. I commit this matter into his hands. His will be done; with this I am content to leave it. For if God does not choose to save infants, then even if one were to toss them into the water a thousand times, it still would not help.[43]

------

40. Conrad Grebel, *Letter to Thomas Müntzer*, trans. George H. Williams and A. M. Mergal, *Spiritual and Anabaptist Writers* (Philadelphia: Westminster, 1957), 81.

41. "Das aber ettlich mit einem eyngossen glauben hoch da her brangen, denn jnen Gott eyngiesse, vnd inn dem selben werden sye behalten. Jch weyß nichts darumb. . . . hab ich keyn schrifft darumb. Derhalb lasse ichs . . . nit ein Theology seyn." Hubmaier, *Von der christlichen Taufe*, 156.

42. Vedder, *Hübmaier*, 116; Bergsten, *Hubmaier*, 368.

43. "Vnd schame mich auch nit, nit zů wissen, was vns Gott nit mit einem klaren vnd hellen wort hat wöllen offenbaren, sonder er hat zů mir gesagt wie zů Petro: Was gadt es dich an, was ich mit den jungen kindlin thůn will? Volg du mir nach, syhe auff mein wort vnnd willen, Johan. Am xxj. [V. 22]. Doch will ich jn vnderthenigklich vnd ernstlich bitten, das er jnen wölle ein gnädiger vatter sein. Jnn sein händ will ich jms befelhen, sein will geschehe. Darbey lasse ichs bleyben. Dann so er nit wille, ob mans zů tausent malen ins wasser stiesse, würdt es dennocht nit helffen." Hubmaier, *Der Lehrer Urteil* II, 248.

Hubmaier reiterates the same point in his written debate with Zwingli:

> For being children of God does not depend on blood, the will of the
> flesh, or a man's will, but God has given the right of becoming his
> children to all those who believe in his name. . . . Thus whether God
> saves little children or how he handles them, I leave to him; I entrust
> the children to his hands. But I have no Scripture about it, and therefore
> I do not want to know.[44]

In fact, Hubmaier, foreshadowing his doctrine of eternal security rooted in
predestination (to be discussed later in this chapter), draws a potentially devastating implication from the view, here attributed to Zwingli, that all infants
are saved:

> I cannot say whether the young children are saved or damned. I leave it
> to the judgment of God. However, if your argument were valid, then
> everyone baptized in childhood would necessarily be of God and there-
> fore saved, since no one could tear them out of God's hand. Then, from
> this group come the spiritual and earthly thieves, murderers, and ty-
> rants, all of whom even before their infant baptism, according to your
> logic, were in the kingdom of God."[45]

In that case, insists Hubmaier, the divine justice would be violated.[46] Apparently, Hubmaier, while unable to yield his theological convictions, was
moved by pastoral concerns to establish the rite of infant dedication, which
he hoped would satisfy troubled yet in his mind doctrinally unsophisticated

---

44. "Dann Khinnder Gottes seinn ist nit auß dem blůt oder auß dem willen
des fleischs oder auß dem willen des mannes, sonder allen denen hat Gott gewalt
geben seine Khinnder zů werden, die da glauben inn seinen namen. . . . Ob aber
Gott die Jungen Khindlin selig mache, oder wie er mit jnen handle, das setz ich
jm haim. Jch befilhe jms in sein hennd. Jch hab kain schrifft daruon, derhalb
beger ichs nit zů wissenn." Hubmaier, *Gespräch auf Zwinglis Taufbüchlein*, 193.

45. "Ich die Jungen Kinder weder Sälig sprechen kan, noch verdammen. Jch
laß es steen in dem vrtail Gotes. Ja, wo dein Argument gerecht wer, so müstent
doch alle menschen, die in jr Kindthait taufft seind, Gotes sein vnd Sälig werden. Wann niemandt mag Got die seinen auß der hand reissen. Wann her kummen denn die Geystlichen vnnd Weltlichen Dieb, Mörder vnnd Tyrannen, dere
aller ja vor jrem Kindertauf, nach deiner red, das reych Gotes auch gewesen ist."
Ibid., 201.

46. Ibid., 202.

parents, who failed to understand that the pedobaptism of Catholics and Magisterial Reformers would not secure paradise for their children.

While the principal reason that sixteenth-century European governments opposed the elimination of infant baptism was its perceived anti-statist thrust, Hubmaier avoided this anti-statist implication through his practice of infant dedication. Since infant baptism typically served as the cornerstone of the church-state Christendom amalgam, whereby the child was enrolled in the census and granted citizenship, marriage privileges, and inheritance rights, most magistrates found the abolition of this practice quite threatening to civil stability and wished to punish rebaptizers.[47] Notably, the historical records show that in both Waldshut (1523-25) and Nikolsburg (1526-28), children were enrolled in the census and granted full rights as citizens through infant dedication, the ceremony of which looked exactly like the prior ceremony for infant baptism but with a different underlying theology.[48] By thus divesting sacramental power from the consecration of infants without eradicating the ceremony, Hubmaier was able to keep the cornerstone of the church-state amalgam intact while practicing believers' baptism. In his 1524 treatise *Von Ketzern und ihren Verbrennern*, the first early modern treatise defending religious liberty,[49] Hubmaier had already proclaimed his conviction that each person should be free to choose whether or not to submit to baptism and thereby join the ranks of the *Gemeinde der Christenheit*, the visible assembly of Christendom.[50] But the occasion arose to articulate the practical outworkings of such a model, which had first successfully put in place at Waldshut from 1523-25 by virtue of Hubmaier's leadership coupled with an acquiescent city council, when the Magisterial Radical was forced to relocate to Nikolsburg in 1526 after Austrian troops captured Waldshut and reclaimed the city for Catholicism. Quickly becoming perhaps the most tolerant rulers in Europe,[51] Leonard and Hans von Lichtenstein

---

47. James D. Tracy, *Europe's Reformations: 1450-1650* (Lanham, Md.: Rowman and Littlefield, 1999), 68.

48. Bergsten, *Hubmaier*, 108-09, 406-07; Windhorst, *Täuferisches Taufverständnis*, 139.

49. This designation is often incorrectly given to Sebastian Castellio's 1554 *Concerning Heretics and Whether They Should Be Punished by the Sword of the Magistrate*, which did not go nearly as far as *Von Ketzern*. While Castellio argues that someone could be executed for heresy only if that person undermined (or threatened to undermine) the commonweal, Hubmaier claims that secular authority cannot execute or even punish someone for heresy under any circumstances.

50. Bergsten, *Hubmaier*, 379-80.

51. Williams, *Radical Reformation*, 334.

constituted the most likely potential converts to Hubmaier's free state church concept, which he defended in volume 2 of *Der Lehrer Urteil*. While agreeing with Luther and Zwingli that the reformation should be supported on the local level by magistrates, Hubmaier insisted that the magistrates must leave unpunished and unbanished those not wishing to embrace the state religion: "If they refuse to yield to statements of authority or gospel evidences, then avoid them and allow them to continue ranting and raging (Titus 3:10) so that those who are filthy may become more filthy still (Rev. 22:11)."[52] Appealing to the Sermon on the Mount and the Johannine discourses, Hubmaier argues that Jesus himself would have advocated religious tolerance: "For Christ did not come to murder, execute, or burn, but for those who live to live even more abundantly. . . . Thus while burning heretics appears to be following Christ, it is rather to deny him indeed and be more abominable than Jehoiakim, the king of Judah."[53] Here Hubmaier seems to be suggesting a theological basis for religious freedom more profound than is generally recognized: to persecute a person for heresy amounts to an implicit denial of the incarnation, since the God revealed in Christ is the God of the invitation, not of coercion. The accuracy of this inference is verified by Hubmaier's analysis of the relationship between the character of God and libertarian human freedom:

The heavenly Father, who now views humanity afresh through the merit of Jesus Christ our Lord, blesses and draws each person with his life-giving Word which he speaks into the person's heart. This drawing and call is like an invitation to a marriage or to an evening meal, through which God gives power and authority to all people inasmuch as they themselves want to come; the free choice is left to them. . . . But those who do not want to come, such as Jerusalem and those who purchased oxen and houses and took wives, he excludes as unworthy of this evening meal. He desires to have uncoerced, willing, and joyous

52. "Ob sy sich mit gwaltsprüchen oder Euangelischen vrsachen nit wöltind weisen lassen, so gang iren müssig vnd laß sy die weil toben vnnd wütten, Tit. 3 [V. 10], damit die so ietz psudlet sind, noch baß psudlet werdind. Apoc. vlt. [V. 11]." Hubmaier, *Der Lehrer Urteil* II, 253.

53. "Dann Christus ist nit kommen, das er metzge, vmbringe, brenne, sonder das die, so da lebend, noch reychlicher lebind. . . . Darumb ketzer verbrennen ist Christum im schein bekennen, aber in der that verlöügnen vnd greülicher sin dann Joachim, der könig Juda." Ibid., 254.

guests and givers—these he loves, as God does not force anyone. . . .
Similarly, Lot was not coerced by the two angels in Sodom.[54]

This passage reveals that from the theological foundation of libertarian free
will, Hubmaier can deduce that God, who created humans with the faculty to
choose either spiritual good or evil, would not himself violate that very faculty. If not even God compels people into his kingdom but offers them an
invitation which they can freely accept or deny, then, it follows that humans
have no right to compel people into the heavenly kingdom either. Like his
conviction that only believers may receive baptism, therefore, Hubmaier's
commitment to religious freedom appears to be a direct corollary from his
libertarian anthropology.

Without separating church and state, Hubmaier proceeds to set the
boundaries for the religious and civic authorities in the treatment of dissenters. As one of the preeminent debaters of his day,[55] Hubmaier instructs
priests and deacons to employ apologetics in an attempt to win people who
rejected the state church. Moreover, he forbids these clerics from handing
dissenters over to the civic government:

> Those who disagree should be overcome with holy instruction, not
> quarrelsomely but gently, even though the Holy Scripture also contains
> wrath. But the wrath of Scripture is truly a spiritual flame . . . it is not
> an excuse for them . . . to turn the godless over to the secular authority,

---

54. "Des himelischen vaters beschehen vnd erlangt werden, der nun den
menschen durch das verdienen Jesu Christi vnsers herrens auff ein neües ansehe,
begnade vnd in ziehe mit seinem lebend machenden wort, wölhes er dem menschen in das hertz redt, durch welhe ziehung vnd eruordrung einer ladung auff
ein hochzeit oder zů einem nachtmal vergleichet, gibt got macht vnd gwalt allen
menschen, so ferr vnd sy selbs wöllen (es ist inen freye waal haimgesetzt) zek-
hummen. . . . Welher mensch aber nit will, wie Hierusalem vnd die, so ochsen
vnd dörffer gekaufft vnd weyber genomen, auch nit khummen wolten, die selben lasset er auß bleiben wie die vnwirdigen diß nachtmals. Er will vngezwun-
gen, willig vnd frölich gest vnd geber haben, die selben hat er lieb. Wann Gott
zwingt anders niemant . . . nit annders gezwungen. . . . Deß gleich Loth die zwen
Engel in Sodoma." Hubmaier, *Von der Freiheit*, 394.

55. Due to his perceived successes, among other debates, at the Waldshut
Disputation (January 1523) and in Zurich against Zwingli (December 1525),
after which a seemingly embarrassed Zwingli felt compelled to torture Hubmaier into recanting on the wheel, Mabry reports that Hubmaier was recognized
"as a kind of apologist *par excellence*"; *Understanding of Faith*, vii. For details
about each of these debates see Vedder, *Hübmaier*, 69-75 and 125-41.

for anyone who turns someone over in this way is even more guilty of sin.[56]

Such reasoning is grounded upon Hubmaier's belief in the sovereignty of God, who alone can determine the difference between wheat and tares. Consequently, God has not placed in human hands the right to burn heretics, be they truly heretics or not. From this it follows that the grand inquisitors are themselves the greatest heretics in burning alleged heretics contrary to the teaching and example of Christ, thereby uprooting the wheat with the tares before the harvest.[57] This recalls Hubmaier's more comprehensive explication of these same points in *Von Ketzern*:

> The greatest deception of the people is the type of zeal for God which, apart from Scripture, is carried out concerning the salvation of souls, the honor of the church, love for truth, good intentions, traditions and customs, episcopal decrees, and the suggestions of reason, all of which have been pleaded from the light of nature. These are lethal errors, when they are not ruled and guided by Scripture. . . . The result of these words will not be indifference but a battle as we fight constantly, not against human beings, but against their godless teachings. . . . This is why they are carried away with sighs, as the righteousness of God (for whose judgment they are held) will either convert or harden them, so that the blind will continue leading the blind and both the seducers and the seduced will keep descending further into wickedness. . . . Indeed we should pray and hope for repentance as long as a person lives in this wretchedness.[58]

---

56. "Welche söllich sind, sol man mit hailigen kuntschafften, nit zänckisch sonder sennfftlich überwinden, obgleich wol die hailig gschrifft auch zorn innhalt. Aber dieser zorn der gschrifft ist warlich ain gaystlich feür. . . . Ja es würt sich auch nit entschuldigen . . . das sy die gotloßen weltlichen gwalt vbergebend, dann welcher der massen übergibt, sündet noch schwärer." Hubmaier, *Von Ketzern*, 96-97, 100.

57. Bergsten, *Hubmaier*, 174.

58. "So ist nun deß volcks der größt betrug der yfer gottes, der on gschrifft fürgwent wirt, der selen hail, eer der kirchen, liebe der warhait, güte mainung, der brauch oder gwonhait, die bischoflichen satzungen vnd dz anweisen der vernunfft, welches erbetlet ist von dem nateürlichen liecht har. Dann sy sind tödliche pfil, wo sy nit nach der gschrifft gelaittet vnd gericht werden. . . . Vnd aber dise wort bringend vns nit ayn müssiggang, sonder ayn streyt, so wir on vnderlaß nit zwar den menschen, sonder iren gottlosen leeren widerfechtend. . . . Darumb wurdind sy mit sünfftzen hingenommen, so die gerechte gotes (deß gricht sy vorbehalten sind) sy aintweders bekert oder verhettet, damit blinden

This quote makes clear that in Hubmaier's assessment, God has set definite limits on the jurisdiction of secular authorities and clearly prescribed the methods of evangelism for Christians, and that any transgression of this divinely established order constitutes grave sin.[59] Contra the widespread sixteenth-century notion that heretics amounted to spiritual murderers who must (even more than physical murderers) be executed by the state for the common good,[60] Hubmaier convicts of spiritual murder precisely those who demand the execution of heretics. This is because the latter condemn potential heretics to perdition before the end of the suspects' lives, which God granted to furnish them further opportunities to repent and be saved, had naturally elapsed.[61]

Even when conversing with the Lords von Lichtenstein, Hubmaier is direct in his denunciation of "holy violence," maintaining that any judgment upon religious dissenters lies outside the domain of government: "The authorities judge the evildoers but not the godless, who are unable to harm either body or soul but instead are profitable, since, as we know, God can turn evil into good."[62] As highlighted by Carl Sachsse, we find here a further refutation by Hubmaier of Aquinas' notion that the godless are harmful to society: the power of God is manifested more abundantly when a notorious opponent of the faith is freely converted, thereby possibly drawing other outsiders into the church.[63] Ironically, Hubmaier employs the same argument, which was used by Luther and Zwingli in an attempt to extinguish the Anabaptist zeal to purify the visible church,[64] to forestall the magistrates'

---

blinden fûrind, vnd allzeit baide die verfûrten vnd verfûrer hinfarind in ergers. . . . Ja man sol ouch bitten vnnd hoffen vmb bûßwirckung, so lang der mensch in disem ellend lebt." Hubmaier, *Von Ketzern*, 97-100.

59. Estep, *Anabaptist Story*, 86.

60. Olson, *Story*, 417-18.

61. Sachsse, *Hubmaier als Theologe*, 9-10.

62. "Der gwalt richtett die boßhafften, aber nit die gotloßen, welche da weder leyb noch seel schaden mögend, sonder vil meer nûtz sind, also weislich kan got auß dem bösen gûts ziehen." Hubmaier, *Der Lehrer Urteil* II, 254.

63. Sachsse, *Hubmaier als Theologe*, 11.

64. Unlike Hubmaier and the Anabaptists, who believed that the true church was necessarily visible, Luther and Zwingli drew the distinction between the visible church (*i.e.* the temporal body of those who belong to the ecclesiastical institution) and the invisible church (*i.e.* the community of those who will be saved which is known only to God). Both cite approvingly Augustine's comparison of the church to the net described by Matthew 13:47-50, which held both good and bad fish until the Last Judgment (*City of God*, XVIII.49), in order to show that sometimes the evil members of the church could be useful to the

desire to Christianize society. Rather than sincere and insincere believers coexisting in the church, as maintained by Luther and Zwingli, Hubmaier posited that Christians and non-Christians should live together peacefully in society until the day of the Lord's judgment.[65] Appealing once again to the wheat and tares analogy, Hubmaier declares that religious differences between citizens must not undermine social tranquility:

> That is exactly what Christ meant when he said, "Let both grow up together until the harvest, so that in gathering the tares you do not uproot the wheat together with them". . . . [The tares] must not be destroyed until Christ orders the reapers, "Gather the tares first and tie them in bundles to be burned."[66]

This conviction, first acquired at Waldshut no later than 1524,[67] effected a tremendous conversion in Hubmaier's attitude toward the Jews. As noted in the first chapter, Hubmaier, during his first stint as Regensburg *Dompredi-ger*, directed persecution against the Jewish citizens, eventually resulting in their expulsion and Catholic annexation of their synagogue. But as an evangelical reform theologian, Hubmaier reversed his opinion and championed Christian adoption of a philo-Semitic stance: "Indeed, truly I should show friendship toward Jews and heathen . . . so that they might be drawn by a Christian example to Christian faith (which gives rise to such friendly works)."[68] Jews, Catholics, those considered by Hubmaier as "unbiblical followers" of Luther and Zwingli, and pagans, it is affirmed again and

---

church and to its real members, as teachers and interpreters of the Scriptures; see Martin Luther, *Response to the Book of Master Ambrosius Catharinus*, in *Luthers Werke*, 8:715 and *Against the Antinomians*, in *Luther's Works*, 47:117; Huldrych Zwingli, *Explanation and Proof of the Conclusions or Articles*, in *Zwingli Sämtliche Werke*, 2:58.

    65. Windhorst, *Täuferisches Taufverständnis*, 145; Estep, *Anabaptist Story*, 85.

    66. "Eben das selb hat Christus gewölt, sprechende: Lassends baide mitainandern auffwachsen biß zůr ärndt, auff das, so ir das vnkraut samlend, auch nit zůsampt den waitzen außrauffind. . . . Welch . . . sy doch nit außglöscht, so lang biß Christus sagen wirt den schnittern: samlend vonerst dz vnkraut vnd bindens in büscheli, die zů verbrennen." Ibid., 255.

    67. Windhorst, *Täuferisches Taufverständnis*, 152.

    68. "Ja auch freündtschafft solle ich erzaygenn gegen Juden vnnd Hayden . . . auff das sy durch ein Christennlich Exempel zů dem Christenlichen glauben (der solhe freüntliche werck würckhet) auch noch gezogen Regulen." Hubmaier, *Bann*, 374.

again,[69] must be won by spiritual means, that is, by the careful use of Scripture, patience, prayer, and a credible witness.[70] For Hubmaier, therefore, it follows that "the law that consigns heretics to death by fire is founded upon Zion in blood and Jerusalem in wickedness."[71] The significance of Hubmaier's reconception of civil-ecclesiastical relations cannot be overemphasized, as he forged a new religious modality heretofore unknown in early modern, if not church, history. Seemingly two hundred years ahead of his time, Hubmaier heralded a revolutionary transformation of the role of magistrates from the enforcers of religious decrees to those who, through righteous governance, would provide an environment amenable to the free spread of the gospel.[72] In his exegesis of Luke 22:25 Hubmaier fleshes out his concept of a Christian magistracy:

> A Christian, if he is in the government, refuses to domineer and does not want to be called "gracious lord" or "prince." Instead, he regards himself as a servant of God and watches carefully that he acts according to the order of God, so that the righteous are protected and the evil punished. . . . Yet I ask, admonish, and warn everyone at whose side God has hung the sword, in the name of Jesus Christ and his final judgment, not to use it against . . . heretics . . . through arresting, pursuing, beating, placing in the stocks, hanging, drowning, or burning. . . . For whoever sheds human blood (namely, against the order of divine justice), that person's blood, declares God, will itself also be shed.[73]

---

69. For a few representative excerpts see Hubmaier, *Eine ernstliche christliche Erbietung*, 81-83; *Summe*, 110; *Entschuldigung*, 280-81; and *Eine christliche Lehrtafel*, 324.

70. Estep, *Anabaptist Story*, 85.

71. "Vnd das recht, so die ketzer zům feür verurtailt, bawt auff baide, Syon im blůt vnnd Hierusalem im boßhait." Hubmaier, *Von Ketzern*, 97.

72. Loserth, *Hubmaier*, 48-55; Vedder, *Hübmaier*, 88-89.

73. "Aber ein Christ, so er schon in der Oberkhait ist so hörscht er nit. Er begeert auch nit, das man jm gnad herr oder Junckher sage. Sonder er betracht, das er ist ein diener Gottes, vnd fleysset sich, das er der ordnung Gottes nach handle, darmit die frommen beschützt vnd die bösen gestrafft werdent. . . . Yedoch bitte, ermane vnd warne ich durch Jesum Christum vnd durch sein Jüngst gericht alle die, denen got dz schwert an die seytten gehenckt, das sy es nit brauchen wider . . . ketzern . . . weder mit fahen, verjagen, stöcken, blöcken, hencken, ertencken oder verbrennen. . . . Dann wölcher menschen blůt vergeůst (verstand wider die ordnung götlicher gerechtikayt), des blůt, sagt got, selber solle auch vergossen werden." Hubmaier, *Von dem Schwert*, 452.

As implied in his parenthetical remark concerning the order of divine justice, Hubmaier did not, like most Anabaptists, completely reject capital punishment.[74] Rather, he felt that capital punishment, while granted by God to the government in order to punish criminals and protect the remainder of the populace from their wickedness, could not legitimately be used against heretics.[75] Remarkably, in the early modern period, an era remembered for civil intolerance toward nonconformists who refused to submit to what rulers held to be the "one true religion,"[76] Hubmaier's "quasi-enlightenment" model[77] gave birth to successful believers' state churches in both Waldshut and Nikolsburg, as their respective magistrates embraced the reformer's program and submitted to rebaptism at his hands.[78]

Believers' Baptism as the Ordained *Ratio Praedestinationis*

Merging the patristic assertion of baptismal necessity for salvation with his *sine qua non* of libertarian free will, Hubmaier forged an elaborate covenant theology of believers' baptism, entailing reciprocal divine and human stipulations, in the context of a revised Bernardian model of God's prescience. Unlike Zwinglian covenant theology, where God constitutes the sole actor, Hubmaier maintained that God and humanity played distinct yet interdependent roles in the calculus of salvation. On the one hand, the triune God mercifully offers redemption by the work of the second divine person and faithfully sends preachers to those who adequately prepare themselves

---

74. Clasen, *Social History*, 174.

75. Hubmaier, *Von dem Schwert*, 449-51.

76. This stance is epitomized not only in the 1555 Peace of Augsburg, which stipulated the principle of *cuius regio eius religio* (lit. "whose region, his religion") giving each magistrate the right to determine the religion (either Catholic or Lutheran; in the 1648 Peace of Westphalia expanded to include Calvinism) in his territory, but also the various Wars of Religion (*e.g.* Schmalkaldic Wars, Thirty Years' War) as well as the persecution of Huguenots in France. See Tracy, *Europe's Reformations*, 92, 138-40, 145-67.

77. I call Hubmaier's model "quasi-enlightenment" because its precepts would not again be articulated until the Enlightenment by philosophers such as Voltaire; see his *Treatise on Tolerance*, trans. Simon Harvey (Cambridge: Cambridge University Press, 2000), 24-27, 49-53, 64-71.

78. Bergsten, *Hubmaier*, 306; Vedder, *Hübmaier*, 151.

for the gospel by seeking righteousness.[79] On the other hand, the believing individual, after placing trust in the gospel message, appropriately responds by entering into a covenant with God and his church through baptism. In his exegesis of Romans 10:9-10, a passage which predicates salvation upon right belief and confession of faith, Hubmaier contends that the confession described by Paul refers to baptism.[80] This means, contrary to Luther,[81] that faith alone, while engendering reverence for God, is not sufficient for salvation, but must be supplemented by the confession of believers' baptism:

> On what is the Christian church built? On the . . . confession of faith that Jesus is the Christ, the Son of the living God. This external confession is what creates a church, and not faith alone. . . . Although faith alone makes us God-fearing, it alone does not save, for it must be accompanied by public confession. . . . Baptism in water in the name of the Father, and the Son, and the Holy Spirit . . . [is] the public confession and testimony of internal faith and commitment.[82]

Implicit to this claim is the following undercurrent: just as human freedom is the *sine qua non* of theology, so believers' baptism is the *sine qua non* of the church. Hubmaier makes this deduction explicit in *Von der christlichen Taufe*: "Where there is no water baptism, there is neither church nor minis-

---

79. Hubmaier, *Von der Freiheit*, 388-90; Moore, "Catholic Teacher and Anabaptist Pupil," 88-89.

80. Contemporary New Testament scholarship suggests that Hubmaier may have indeed been right, as Rudolf Bultmann and Vernon Neufeld argue on form critical grounds that Romans 10:9 was originally a baptismal creed, whereby the candidate announced his belief in and allegiance to Christ. See Bultmann, *Theology of the New Testament*, 2 vols., trans. Kendrick Grobel (New York: Scribner's, 1951), 1:312 and Neufeld, *The Earliest Christian Confessions* (Grand Rapids, Mich.: Eerdmans, 1964), 62, 68, 144.

81. Martin Luther, *Avoiding the Doctrines of Men*, in *Luther's Works*, 35:141.

82. "Warauff ist die Christenlich Kirch gebaut. Auff die . . . bekantnuß des Glaubens, das Jesus seye Christus, ein Son des lebendigen Gottes. Dise eüsserlich bekandtnuß macht eben ein Kirchen, vnnd nit der Glaub allain. . . . Ob wol der glaub allain fromm macht, so macht er doch allain nit selig, dann die offenlich bekantnuß můß auch darbey sein. . . . Täuffen im wasser inn dem nammen des vatters vnd süns vnd des heyligen geysts . . . [ist] offenliche bekantnůß vnd zeügnůß des inwendigen glaubens vnd pflichten." Hubmaier, *Eine christliche Lehrtafel*, 315-16; cf. Hubmaier, *Von der christlichen Taufe*, 122.

ter, neither brother nor sister."[83] Such an equation of confession of faith with baptism is strengthened when Hubmaier appropriates Luther's interpretation of Matthew 16:18, according to which the church is built not on Peter but his confession of faith,[84] and indicates that believers make this same declaration of faith through baptism. Hubmaier explains his argument in syllogistic form, advancing from step to step:

> For this we have outstanding evidence, Matt. 16:18. There Christ says, "You are Peter, and on this rock (in other words, that which you confess) I will build my church" . . . Moreover, Paul affirms, "For one confesses . . . and so is saved," Rom. 10. . . . We confess the universal Christian church, the fellowship of the saints, and forgiveness of sins with external baptism. . . . To summarize: Where water baptism according to the institution of Christ is not reestablished and practiced . . . there is no church . . . nor anything that resembles the Christian position and nature. God lives; thus it must be, or heaven and earth will perish.[85]

Thus for Hubmaier, Peter's confession leads neither to the Catholic doctrine of apostolic succession nor to Lutheran solafideism,[86] but to the authenticity of believers' baptism. In his dialogue with Oecolampadius, Hubmaier conjoins Matthew 16 with the Markan Appendix to show the necessity for believers, rather than infants who cannot believe, to be baptized: "The Christian church is built on the confession of its own faith, Matt. 16:18. Whoever himself believes and is baptized is saved, not the person for whom one be-

---

83. "Wo der Wassertauff nit ist, da selbs ist keyn Kirch, keyn diener, weder brüder noch schwester." Hubmaier, *Von der christlichen Taufe*, 145.

84. Luther, *Sermon on Matthew 16*, 7:281-82.

85. "Deß haben wir schöne zeügknuß. Mat. Am 16 [V. 18]. Da sagt Christus: Du bist Petrus, ein felser, vnd auff den felsen, (verstee, den du bekennest) wird ich bauen mein Kirchen. . . . Vnd Paulus: Mit die bekanndtnuß zu der seligkayt. Ro. 10. . . . Da man glaubet ein allgmaine Christliche Kirchen, ein gmainschafft der heiligen vnd ablassung der sünden mit dem außwendigen Tauff. . . . Ja in Summa: Wo der Wassertauff nach der Ordnung Christj nit widerumb auffgericht vnnd gebraucht wirdt . . . da ist khayn Kirch . . . noch nichts, das einem Christenlichen stand vnd wesen gleych sehe. Got lebt. Es ist also. Oder himel vnnd erden müß zů stucken brechen." Hubmaier, *Eine christliche Lehrtafel*, 315-17.

86. Pelikan, *Reformation*, 262-74; Tracy, *Europe's Reformations*, 16-19.

lieves, Mark 16:16."[87] Hubmaier, consistent with his reliance on the patristic sources, further links this notion with remission of sins by turning to the relevant clause in the Niceno-Constantinopolitan Creed.

As previously indicated, Hubmaier championed the doctrine of baptismal regeneration, namely, that forgiveness of sins and spiritual rebirth occur at the moment of baptism. The radical appeals for this notion to an Ecumenical Council, the verdict of which he considers authoritative:

> This is the interpretation and edict issued in a Christian manner by the Nicene Council [sic—actually Constantinopolitan], in these words: I confess one unique baptism for the remission of sins. Peter assigns to it the same meaning: "Let each of you be baptized in the name of Jesus Christ for the remission of your sins," Acts 2:38.[88]

Notice here, in opposition to the biblicism of the Anabaptists,[89] Hubmaier quotes Scripture on the basis of a creedal formula, not vice versa. Based on the Latin text of the Niceno-Constantinopolitan Creed, Hubmaier justifies the practice of believers' baptism, which he again equates with public confession:

> That is why water baptism is called a baptism *in remissionem peccatorum*. . . . Here everyone with eyes must see, and everyone with ears must hear, that it is not enough for a person to confess his sins and improve his life, but it is necessary for a person to go beyond this by submitting to baptism in the name of Jesus Christ. . . . for the forgiveness of sins. In this way, people must testify publicly that they are Jesus' disciples.[90]

---

87. "Auff die bekanntnuß des aignen glaubens wird gebauet die Christenlich Kirch, Mat. 16 [V. 18]. Wölher selbs glaubt vnd getaufft wirdt, wirt selig. Nit für wöhlen man glaubt, Mar. 16 [V. 16]." Hubmaier, *Von der Kindertaufe*, 266.

88. "Das ist eben der verstand vnd beschluß im Concilio Niceno Christenlich außgangen, mit disen worten: Jch bekhenn ein ainigen tauff zů ablassung der sünden. Vnd Petrus hayst in auch also, da er sagt: Vnd ein yedlicher werde getaufft in dem namen vnsers herren Jesu Christj, zů verzeihung der sünden. Act. 2. c. [V. 38]." Hubmaier, *Eine christliche Lehrtafel*, 315.

89. Friedmann, *Theology of Anabaptism*, 20-21.

90. "Auß dem grundt würdt der wasser tauff genent ein tauff in remissionem peccatorum. . . . Hye sehent alle die, so augen habend, vnnd hörend, die da habend oren, das es nit genůg ist, das der mensch sich seiner sünden bekennet vnd sein leben besseret, sonder über das als ist von nöten, das er sich täuffen lasse auff den nammen Jhesu Christi. . . . zů vergebung der sünden. Das ist, sye

Hence Luther's practice of interpreting Scripture through the lenses of patristic creedal affirmations[91] is abundantly evident in the theology of Hubmaier. Accordingly, Hubmaier reinforces his Niceno-Constantinopolitan conclusion with articles nine and ten of the Apostles' Creed, which links baptism to the church in such a way that Cyprian's formula, "extra ecclesiam nulla salus,"[92] serves, at least according to God's *potentia ordinata*, as the salvific standard:

> Water baptism is given for the forgiveness of sins, Acts 2; 1 Pet. 3. It is also recognized in the ninth and tenth articles of the Christian faith, in which we confess the universal Christian church, communion of saints, and remission of sins. All of this is also the perspective and conclusion of the Council of Nicea [sic—actually Constantinople], which ended in a Christian manner with these words: "I confess one unique baptism for the remission of sins." Therefore, as much as the communion of God the Father, and of the Son, and of the Holy Spirit, yes, also the communion of the entire heavenly host and the whole Christian church, and also as much as the forgiveness of sins is important to a person, equally important is water baptism through which the person enters, and which is exemplified in, the universal Christian church, outside of which there is no salvation.[93]

The logic is clear that for Hubmaier, then, relationship with the trinitarian deity, the living saints on earth, and the departed saints in heaven after death

---

müßten offenlich bezeügen, das sye auch deren jünger weren." Hubmaier, *Von der christlichen Taufe*, 137, 141.

91. These included the Apostles' Creed, the Niceno-Constantinopolitan Creed, and the Chalcedonian Definition; Pelikan, *Reformation*, 176-77; Gerrish, *Grace and Reason*, 165-66.

92. Cyprian, *Letters*, 72:21.

93. "Der Wassertauff wirdt geben zů verzeihung der sünden, Act. 2, 1. Pe. 3. Er ist auch begriffen in dem neündten vnd zehenden Artickel des Christenlichen glaubens, dar inn wir bekhennen: Ein allgmaine Christenliche kirchen, ein gmainschafft der heiligen, vnd ablassung der sünden, wölchs eben auch der verstand vnnd bschluß ist im Concilio Niceno, Christenlich außgangen mit disen worten: Jch bekenn ein ainigen tauff zů ablassung der sünden. Darumb als vil dem menschen an der Gmainschafft Gottes vatters vnd des Sons vnd des heiligen geysts, ja, auch an der Gmainschafft alles himelischen höres vnd der ganntzen Christennlichen Kirchen, auch an der verzeihung seiner sünden gelegen ist, als vil solle im an dem Wassertauff gelegen sein, durch wölhen er eingeet vnd eingeleibet wirdt der allgmainen Christenlichen Kirchen, ausserhalb der khain hayl ist." Hubmaier, *Grund und Ursache*, 335.

is predicated upon pardon for sins and admission to the Community of Christendom (*Gemeinde der Christenheit*),[94] which is contingent upon water baptism. But at this point the question immediately arises: what about all those throughout church history who did not receive believers' baptism? Are they saved or condemned? Hubmaier applies his quasi-Bernardian model of divine foreknowledge in formulating a coherent answer to this quandary.

Recalling the doctrinal context surrounding the question, Hubmaier, as illustrated in chapter three, maintained that believers' baptism serves as the *ratio praedestinationis* that God has ordained. Since God is bound to his own promises by virtue of his *veracitas*, he must, simultaneous with his divine creative decree, predestine all those whom he already knew, in his counterfactual knowledge, would freely submit to baptism were he to actualize the world which he in fact selected. Consequently, in a seeming taunt toward Lutherans and Zwinglians, Hubmaier argues that anyone having the opportunity to be baptized as a believer but yet refuses to do it due to salvific reliance on *sola fides* is damned:

> But to those who say, "Yes, we believe, yes, some of us have already received the Holy Spirit as well. We have no need of baptism; faith saves us." Not at all! The person who believes submits to baptism and does not keep arguing, for where water and a person to baptize him are available, he has the command of Christ before his eyes. . . . which Christ demands and wants us to fulfill. Otherwise we will have no share with him in his kingdom.[95]

Hubmaier, in a document signaling the end of friendly relations between himself and Oecolampadius, clearly propounds the doctrine of baptismal regeneration while not too subtly calling into question the salvation of his former compatriot and the other preachers in Basel:

> All of you shout out together again and say: "Whoever believes is saved. What need do we have of water baptism?" Answer: Thus states Christ: "Whoever believes and is baptized will be saved," Mark 16:16.

---

94. Hubmaier, *Eine christliche Lehrtafel*, 315.

95. "Warlich sye . . . sagen: Ja, wir glauben, ja, wir haben zum teyl auch den heyligen geyst schon empfangen, was bedürffen wir des tauffs, der glaub macht vns selig. Neyn nit also. Sonder welcher glaubt, der laßt sich täuffen vnd disputiert nit weytter, dann er sycht die ordnung Christi vor augen, vnd das, wo wasser vnnd der täuffer mögen gehabt werden. . . . den eruordert er vnd will jn von vns haben, oder wir werden keyn teyl bey jm überkommen inn seinem reich." Hubmaier, *Von der christlichen Taufe*, 142-43, 145.

Similarly Peter declares, "Change your ways, and let each of you be baptized in the name of our Lord Jesus Christ for the forgiveness of sins," Acts 2:38. If now faith alone were sufficient for salvation, then Christ and Peter would have added baptism in vain.[96]

However, owing to the divine mercy, Hubmaier claims that God, in his *potentia absoluta*, saves those who have faith but lack the chance to receive the sacrament as believers. Hubmaier supplies the following counterfactual illustration based on Acts 8:

Where [water and a baptizer] are not available, then faith is sufficient for salvation. Consider an example. If the treasurer who sat beside Philip in the chariot and who had come to faith had died suddenly before they reached the water, then he would not have been saved less than after baptism. Christ implies this when he says, "He who believes and is baptized will be saved. He who does not believe will be damned". . . . When now the treasurer had both the baptizer and the water available, then according to the dictate of Christ, he was required to be baptized. If he had not done so, then Christ would have regarded him as a scorner and violator of his words, and he would have been punished accordingly.[97]

In his dialogue with Zwingli, who accused Hubmaier of consigning to hell many great saints throughout church history, Hubmaier bolsters his aforementioned claim by referring to the thief on the cross, to whom Christ de-

96. "Das jr abermals all zesamen stimment vnd sagt: Wölher glaubt der wirt selig, was bdürffen wir des Wassertauffs. Antwurt. So redt Christus: Wölher glaubt vnd taufft wirdt, wirdt selig, Mar. 16 [V. 16], deßgleich Petrus: Besserent euch, vnd werde ein yedlicher getaufft in dem namen vnsers herren Jesu Christi zů verzeyhung der sünden, Act. 2 [V. 38]. Were nun der glaub allain gnůg, so het doch Christus vnd Petrus den Tauff vergeblich hin zů gsetzt." Hubmaier, *Von der Kindertaufe*, 268.
97. "Wo man aber [wasser vnnd der täuffer] nit überkummen mag, da ist der glaub gnůg. Nymm ein exempel. So der Schatzmeyster, auff dem wagen neben dem Philippo sitzend, vnd glaubend, gehling gestorben wer, ee sye zů dem bach kamen, wer er nit weniger selig worden, dann nach dem tauff. Das will Christus, da er sagt: Welcher glaubt vnnd täufft würdt, der würdt selig, welcher nit glaubt, würdt verdampt. . . . Da nun der Schatzmeyster den täuffer vnnd das wasser hett bey einander, ward er schuldig nach dem beuelch Christi, sich zů täuffen lassenn. Wo er das nit thon, hätte jn Christus für ein verschmeher vnd übertretter seiner worte gehalten, vnd wer also gestrafft worden." Hubmaier, *Von der christlichen Taufe*, 143.

clared salvation. Nevertheless, all those declining the opportunity to identify themselves with Christ through baptism stand self-condemned:

> But I say to you. . . . The thief on the cross believed and was in Paradise with Christ on the same day, but he was absolutely not baptized. . . . The person who has the same excuse as the thief on the cross is absolutely at peace with God even though he has never been baptized in water. But when one does not have this excuse, then let the person examine the reality of his own faith, since the Word . . . says: "Whoever believes and is baptized is saved," Mark 16:16. This passage proves that one must always link faith and baptism together.[98]

Therefore, unlike most Anabaptists who, although assigning no redemptive function to believers' baptism, tended to relegate anyone either past or present perceived as outside their sect (*i.e.* most people from the second to the sixteenth centuries) to damnation,[99] Hubmaier firmly believed that the church continuously existed since its founding by Christ.[100] Although the sixteenth-century church was in need of reform, not restoration, the historic church has always performed its redemptive function, such that thousands have legitimately been saved down through church history: "Undoubtedly many thousands have been saved who were not baptized, since they had no opportunity to be baptized."[101] Such a conclusion stands firmly in the tradition of Luther, who insisted that the Roman church possessed at all times

---

98. "Aber ich sage dir. . . . Der Schacher am Creützt hat glaubt, vnd ist des selben tags mit Christo in Paradeyß gewesen, vnnd gar nicht Getaufft mit kainem eüsserlichen Tauff. . . . Wölcher Mensch die entschuldigung hat des Schächers am Creützt, der ist mit Got wol zů friden, ob er schon nymmermer Wassertauff wirdt. Wo aber dise entschuldigung nicht ist, da lüge ein yegklicher zů jm selber. Wann wie das wort . . . bestat: Welcher glaubt vnd Taufft wirdt, wirdt Sälig, Mar. 16 [V. 16]. Hie můß man ye glauben vnd Tauffen auch bey ein ander bleiben lassen." Hubmaier, *Gespräch auf Zwinglis Taufbüchlein*, 185.

99. While acknowledging this point (*Theology of Anabaptism*, 18-19), Friedmann goes even one step further: "Anabaptists and Spiritualists reached beyond Paul, back to the Gospel of Jesus" (159); for a fine summary of the dominant Anabaptist view of church history see Walther Köhler, *Dogmengeschichte als Geschichte des christlichen Selbstbewusstseins*, Vol. II: *Zeitalter der Reformation* (Leipzig: M. Niehan, 1951), 85-358.

100. Sachsse, *Hubmaier als Theologe*, 185-91.

101. "Dann on zweyffel vil tausendt selig worden, die nit taufft seyndt, dann sye haben nit mögen darzů kümmen." Hubmaier, *Von der christlichen Taufe*, 143.

word and sacraments and remained, by virtue of this, a true church, while, as Hubmaier concurred,[102] the papacy was obscuring the gospel.[103]

The Sacrament of Believers' Baptism as the Key into the Kingdom of Heaven

Among the most creative contributions made by Hubmaier to sixteenth-century sacramental theology was his identification of the two sacraments as the keys described in Matthew 16:18. Following his scholastic forebears Peter Lombard, Bonaventure, and Aquinas, the radical fixed the number of keys at two; but unlike these medieval thinkers, who regarded the keys as the divinely bestowed priestly powers to determine appropriate penance for and subsequently remit sin,[104] Hubmaier shifted the disciplinary function from the keys to their two respective doors, one leading into and the other leading out of the kingdom of heaven.[105] For Hubmaier, then, Christ handed the power of the keys, which he administered during the entirety of his earthly ministry to forgive sins, over to the *ecclesia universalis* after his resurrection:

> When Christ says . . . "I will give you the keys of the kingdom of heaven". . . . he indicates (with the word "you") the unity of the church. . . .

---

102. "O God, spare us from these glossers! The old pope has until this time used the same glosses for such words as head, church, keys, rock, spiritual, etc., whereby . . . the whole Bible [is] confused" (O Got, behüt vns vor solchem Glasieren. Der alt Bapst hatt bißher auch der gleychen Glosen gebrauchet in den wörtern Haupt, Kirch, Schlüssel, Felß, Gaystlich etc., dardurch . . . die gantz Bibel [ist] verwirrt); Hubmaier, *Gespräch auf Zwinglis Taufbüchlein*, 184.

103. Luther writes in his *Lectures on Galatians*, "Although the city of Rome is worse than Sodom and Gomorrah, nevertheless there remain in it Baptism, the Sacrament, the voice and text of the Gospel, the Sacred Scriptures, the ministries, the name of Christ, and the name of God. Whoever has these, has them; whoever does not have them has no excuse, for the treasure is still there. Therefore the Church of Rome is holy, because it has the holy name of God, the Gospel, Baptism, etc."; in *Luther's Works*, 26:24.

104. Peter Lombard, *Quatuor Libri Sententiarum*, trans. Elizabeth F. Rogers (New York: S.U.I., 1917), XVIII.1.2; Bonaventure, *Breviloquium*, trans. Erwin Esser Nemmers (St. Louis: Herder, 1946), 203-04; Aquinas, *Summa Theologica*, 3:84.

105. Windhorst, *Täuferisches Taufverständnis*, 26-27; Loserth, *Hubmaier*, 133.

The church never possessed this power before Christ's resurrection of
Christ, for while John and Christ's disciples preached and baptized before Christ's resurrection, they never pointed those who were baptized
to the church for the forgiveness of their sins, since at that time the
church had not received the keys from Christ. Instead, they pointed,
pushed, and brought to Christ the born-again and baptized disciples
(whom they had guided to an awareness of their sins). Christ himself
received them, forgave their sins, opened up to them the doors of Christian fellowship, and took them into his holy communion.[106]

This concept of the keys has three crucial implications. First, Matthew 16:18
is regarded as a prophetic text describing literally what Christ "will give"
(future tense) rather than "give" (present tense) to "you," interpreted not as
Peter but the church, after Christ left this world. Accordingly, the church did
not receive the keys at Caesarea Philippi, but at the ascension:

This authority is given to the Christian church by Christ Jesus her
spouse and bridegroom . . . [who] utilized them in teaching and in action, when he physically walked among us. However, when he ascended into heaven and sat at the right hand of his almighty Father, no
longer physically remaining with us on earth, at this moment he hung
this authority and these keys at the side of his most beloved spouse and
bride . . . as he promised to her, Matt. 16.[107]

---

106. "Jn dem das nun Christus sagt . . . ich wird dir geben die Schlüßden
des reichs der himelen. . . . bedeut Christus die ainigkhait der Kirchen. . . . Disen
Gwalt hat die Kirch vor der vrsteend Christi nye gehabt, dann ob wol Johannes
vnd die Junger Christj gepredigt vnd wassertaufft vor der vrsteend Christi, habend sy doch denen getaufften nye zaigt oder sy gewisen zů der Kirchen zů verzeyhung irer sünden. Wann die Kirch hat dannzmal noch kainen Schlüssel von
Christo entpfangen, sonder sy habend die new gebornen vnd taufften Jungern
(wölhe sy yetz in erkantnuß irer sünden eingefiert) gewisen, triben vnd bracht zů
Christo, der selb hat sy angenommen, Jnen ire sünnden verzigen, die porten der
Christennlichen Kirchen auff gespört, vnd sy hin ein in sein heilige Gmainschafft angenommen." Hubmaier, *Bann*, 368-69.

107. "Diser gwalt der Christenlichen Kirchen von Christo Jesu irem
Gesponß vnd eegmahel herkumbt vnd geben ist . . . den selben mit der leer vnnd
werckh gebraucht, als er bey vns leiblich hatt gewandlet. Aber da er inn die
himeln auff faren wolt, vnnd sich setzen zu der gerechten seins allmechtigen
vatters, vnnd nit mer leiblich bey vns auff erd beleyben, dannzmal hat er seiner
aller liebsten Gesponß vnnd Gmahel . . . wie er Jr denn verhaissen, Math. Am
16." Ibid., 368.

The fact that Jesus forgave sins after Peter's confession at Caesarea Philippi, for Hubmaier, necessitates the prophetic interpretation of this text:

> Now we see why he dealt with the sinful woman . . . by declaring to her, "Your sins are forgiven," and with the thief on the cross hanging to his right, "Today you shall be with me in Paradise." However, there was a tremendous difference concerning the keys . . . before Christ's resurrection and . . . after his resurrection. . . . As I maintained concerning the keys, first Christ himself utilized the keys by loosing and binding sinners according to the command of his heavenly Father. Afterwards, he turned these same keys over to the Christian church and let her handle, apply, dispense, and permit, since she possesses this authority and will possess it and utilize it until the coming of the Lord.[108]

Since the close of Christ's earthly ministry, the second implication entails that Christ no longer (except in cases of emergency) forgives the sins of human beings; rather, he has entrusted the church with the power to forgive their sins. Hence the forgiveness of sins, in *potentia ordinata*, now stands at the discretion not of God but the church: "It follows that the Christian church itself possesses the power to forgive and to retain sin."[109] Third, such authority to forgive sins is exercised through water baptism in the neophyte's initial incorporation into the church, and, as we will see later, through church discipline in subsequent cases of fall and repentance. Accordingly, Hubmaier proceeds to equate the first key with water baptism, which unlocks the entrance door to salvation: "Christ gave and commanded the church . . . to baptize [believers] in water, thereby with the first key opening to them the door, the portals of the Christian church, admitting them

---

108. "Also hat er gehandlet mit der Sünderin . . . da er zů ir sagt: Dir werdent nachgelassenn dein sünd, vnd zů dem Schacher zur rechten seytten am kreütz hangende: Heüt wirstu bey mir sein in dem Paradeys. Demnach ist der Schlüssen halb gar ein grosser vnderschid gewesen . . . vor der vrsteend Christi vnd . . . nach der vrsteennd. . . . Aber ich hab gesagt (Der Schlüßlen halb): Wann vor hat Christus die Schlüsselen selbs gebraucht, die sünder auffgelößt vnd gebunden nach dem beuelch seins himelischen vatters. Darnach hat er die selben der Christenlichen Kirchen vberantwurttet vnd sy darmit schaffen, machen, schalten vnd walten lassen, wie sy die denn noch hat vnd wirdts behalten vnd brauchen biß zů der zůkunfft des Herrens." Ibid., 369.

109. "Eruolgt, das die Christenlich Khirch eben disen Gwaltt hat zů verzeihen vnd zubhalten die sünnd." Ibid., 370.

to the forgiveness of sins."[110] In traditional language, therefore, it seems that baptism, which is administered after the candidate has convinced the congregation that she or he has *glaub*, in fact functions *ex opere operato* to open the doors of the church and of heaven to one who was baptized.[111] This means, in Hubmaier's words, "Anyone whose sins the Christian church forgives on earth, these very sins are already forgiven in heaven as well, and anyone whose sins she does not forgive here on earth, these very sins are not forgiven in heaven as well."[112] Moreover, Hubmaier explains to Zwingli that just as baptism serves as the key of loosing, the Eucharist constitutes the key of binding: "While in water baptism the church uses the key of admitting and loosing, in the Supper it uses the key of excluding, binding, and locking away."[113] As implied by his formulation, Hubmaier attaches a sacramental significance to John 20:23, "If you forgive anyone his sins, they are forgiven; if you do not forgive them, they are not forgiven," by construing the first conditional clause as the conferral of believers' baptism and the second as the withholding of the Lord's Supper. Hubmaier furnishes his exegesis of the first clause:

> We have certainly known for a long time that a Christian life must start with teaching, out of which flows faith, and that accordingly water bap-

---

110. "Christus der Kirchen geben vnd zů gestelt. . . . die [glaubige] nachmals im wasser tauffen, vnd mit dem ersten Schlüssel Jr die porten der Christenlichen Kirchen auff schliessen, vnd sy einlassen zů verzeihung irer sünden." Ibid., 368.

111. Interestingly enough, Hubmaier never treated the following dilemma, to be considered later in more detail, which seems to flow from his conception: If the church forgives sins through baptism, and it makes a mistake as to whether or not someone has faith, does God also include the sinner or exclude the saint from heaven? Mabry points out that for Hubmaier, this was not a real problem because he "believed that there was no difference between what was taught about the saintly life in the New Testament, and the church's interpretation of it. The Scriptures clearly stated that which one has to do, and the Holy Spirit guided the saints in their decisions"; *Doctrine of the Church*, 86-87.

112. "Das wölhen menschen die Christenlich Kirch verzeyhet ire sünden auff erden, denselbigenn seinnd sy schon verzygen auch in den himeln, vnd wölhen sy ire sünden nit verzeihet hye auff erden, den selben seind sy nit nach gelassenn auch in den himelen." Hubmaier, *Von dem Schwert*, 442.

113. "Wann in disem Wassertauff braucht die Kirch den schlüssel der einlassung vnnd auff lösung, jn dem Nachtmal aber den schlüssel der außschliessung, bindung vnnd versperrung." Hubmaier, *Gespräch auf Zwinglis Taufbüchlein*, 171.

tism follows afterward in compliance with its institution by Christ, where a person, by public confession of his faith, enters for the first time and is initiated into the holy, universal Christian church (outside of which there is no salvation) for the forgiveness of his sins. Therefore, with the first key that Christ promised and gave his church, John 20:23, he is admitted and enrolled into the communion of the saints.[114]

While the Eucharist will be dealt with in depth by the next chapter, we will here cite the exegesis of the second clause: "What is the ban? It is an exclusion [from] the communion of the Lord's Supper. . . . Where does the church derive this authority? Out of the command of Christ, John 20:23."[115] We can understand why then, for Hubmaier, the sacraments are indispensable to the church: the first allows her expansion, while the second ensures her purity.

Strikingly reminiscent of Luther's declaration in *The Babylonian Captivity of the Church* that "the mass is a part of the gospel, nay the sum and substance of the gospel. . . . for if we do not hold firmly [to] the mass . . . we shall lose the whole gospel, and all its comfort,"[116] Hubmaier advances one step further by identifying the two sacraments as the garments with which Christ has clothed his bride. The removal of these garments debases the pure assembly to a shameful adulteress that ceases to be the church:

> O my Lord Jesus Christ, institute once again the two bands, namely water baptism and the Supper, with which you have outwardly girded and bound your bride. For unless these two elements are again instituted and practiced according to your appointment and order, we have among

---

114. "Seytmal vnns ye vast wol bewist, das ein Christenlich leben erstlich an der leer anfahen müß, auß wölher der Glaub herfleüset, vnd dar nach der Wassertauff in halt der einsetzunng Christi hernach volget, durch wölchen der mensch in der offenntlichen bekanndtnüß seines glaubens seinen ersten eingang vnd anfang thût in die heiligen, allgmainen Christennlichen Kirchenn (ausserhalb der khain hail ist) zû verzeyhunng seiner sünden, vnd yetz wirdt er durch den erstenn schlüssel, den Christus seiner Kirchen zûgesagt vnd geben, Joan. Am 20 c. [V. 23], eingelassen vnnd angenommen in die Gmainschafft der heiligen." Hubmaier, *Eine christliche Lehrtafel*, 307.

115. "Was ist der Ban. Er ist ein außschliessung [von] der Gmainschafft des Nachtmals Christi. . . . Wannher hat die Kirch disen gwalt. Auß dem beuelch Christi, Joan. 20 [V. 23]." Ibid., 316-17.

116. Luther, *Babylonian Captivity*, 36:66, 62.

us neither faith, love, church covenant, fraternal admonition, ban, nor exclusion, without which it may never again be well in your church.[117]

It should be emphasized that Hubmaier's listing of faith and love as the first two sacramental results is intentional, for it discloses a deep theological point: baptism amounts to the consummation of the recipient's faith, while withholding the Supper to a miscreant is the fulfillment of a filial love which encourages him or her to repentance. In his Eucharistic liturgy, Hubmaier proclaims, "Just as water baptism is a public testimony of Christian faith, so is the Supper a public testimony of Christian love,"[118] which sentiment is echoed in his debate with Oecolampadius: "Whoever correctly teaches baptism and the Supper correctly teaches faith and love."[119] While the Eucharist will be analyzed in the next chapter, these quotes seem to imply that believers' baptism amounts to nothing less than incorporation into the community of the saints. This point is reinforced by Hubmaier's demand that in order to be a true sixteenth-century believer, during which time believers' baptism was available, one must necessarily

> let himself or herself be outwardly registered, enrolled, and inducted by water baptism into the communion of the church, according to the institution of Christ. . . . For with outward baptism the church opens her doors to all believers who confess their faith orally before her and takes them into her lap, fellowship, and communion of saints for the forgiveness of their sins.[120]

---

117. "O mein herr Jesu Christe, richte widerumb auff die zway band, namlich den Wassertauff vnd das Nachtmal, mit wölhen du dein Praut außwenndig vmbgürtet hast vnd gebunden. Wann es sey denn sach das die zway stuckh nach deiner einsetzung vnd ordnung wider auffgericht vnd gebraucht werdent, haben wir vnder vns weder Glauben, liebe, Kirchenn glübd, Brüderliche straff, Ban noch auß schliessung, on wölhe dinng es nimmer mer wol steen mag in deiner Kirchen." Hubmaier, *Die zwölf Artikel*, 219.

118. "Dann wie der Wassertauff ein offenlich zeügknuß ist eins Christenlichen glaubens, also ist das Abent essen ein offentliche kundtschafft Christenlicher liebe." Hubmaier, *Form des Nachtmals Christi*, 358-59.

119. "Wölher den Tauff vnnd das Nachtmal recht leert, der leert recht den glauben vnnd liebe." Hubmaier, *Von der Kindertaufe*, 262.

120. "Last er sich auch eüsserlich verzichnen, ein schreyben, vnnd also mit dem Wassertaüff einnleyben in die Gemainnschafft der Kirchenn, nach der einsetzunng Christj. . . . Dann mit dem außwendigen Tauff schleüst die Kirch auff ire portenn allenn glaubigenn, die iren glauben mündtlich vor ir bekennen, vnd

It follows from the foregoing discussion that the visible church in Hubmaier's sacramental theology bears a profound importance, no less than in Catholicism, for in both cases the church constitutes a kind of admissions office to heaven. Hubmaier seems at this point to create an unrecognized paradox regarding the infallibility of the church. On the one hand, he acknowledges that "the particular church may err," and that the local church "as the daughter has exactly the same power to bind and loose on earth as her mother, the universal church."[121] On the other hand, he asserts, by virtue of its direction by the Spirit, the infallibility of the *Gemeinde der Christenheit*: "But the universal church cannot err. She is without spot, without wrinkle, is governed by the Holy Spirit, and Christ is with her until the end of the world."[122] Since Hubmaier made no distinction between being admitted to the particular church and being admitted to the universal church, such that entrance into the first was entrance into the second,[123] then the possibility remains that the particular church could mistakenly baptize unrepentant sinners and thereby incorporate them into the universal church and heaven. That Hubmaier failed to see this tension in his doctrine of the visible church is evident from his confident oath, "For as truly as God lives, those whom the church admits or excludes on earth are also admitted or excluded in heaven."[124] Such a dilemma appears to be exacerbated by Hubmaier's belief that when the sinner willingly receives baptism at the hands of the church, God responds to the sinner with the grace of regeneration and thereby purifies the heart.[125] Could the particular church, then, by virtue of its power of the keys force the hand of God to bestow regenerating grace and spiritual purification upon a person falsely professing faith? While this problem was never recognized, much less solved, by Hubmaier, we will now turn to the liturgical mechanisms he put in place which he apparently thought would

---

nimbt sy an in ir schoß, gesellschaft vnd gemainschafft der heilgen zů verzeyhung irer sůnnden." Hubmaier, *Eine christliche Lehrtafel*, 313-15.

121. "Die sonderlich Kirch mag gar irren. . . . als die tochter hat eben gleichen gwalt zebinden vnd auffzelösen auff erden, wie die allgmain Kirch ir můtter." Ibid., 315.

122. "Aber die allgmainn Kirch mag nit irrenn. Sy ist on mackel, on runtzlen, wirdt regiert von dem heiligen geyst, vnd Christus ist bey ir biß zů enndt der welt." Ibid.

123. Sachsse, *Hubmaier als Theologe*, 187-89.

124. "Denn als waar Gott lebt, was die Kirch also einlasset oder versperret auff erdenn, das ist eingelassen oder dauß verspert auch in den himelen." Hubmaier, *Eine christliche Lehrtafel*, 316-17.

125. Mabry, *Doctrine of the Church*, 137.

forestall any conflict between internal belief and the external sacrament of baptism.

Commensurate with his theological innovations into the meaning of baptism, Hubmaier devised a new baptismal liturgy, first published at Waldshut in 1524 and then reissued at Nikolsburg in 1526, in an attempt to manifest the ceremony's numinous significance to his parishioners. Not surprisingly in light of Hubmaier's reliance upon the Church Fathers, his liturgy attempts to recapture the catechetical praxis of the early church.[126] In Volume 1 of *Der Lehrer Urteil* Hubmaier admits this point:

> I am fully aware, as the Fathers emphasized, that from primitive times . . . one taught [believers] publicly in a group after they acquired understanding of the word of salvation, which is why they were called "catachumens," namely, the instructed. After they committed themselves to an unshakable faith in their hearts and confessed it with their mouths, they were baptized. . . . Hence let us first take up the task with word and teaching.[127]

Although Hubmaier, as we have illustrated, drew up a catechism to instruct children before baptism, he sensed the need to ensure that adult candidates were thoroughly trained as well. Rather than subjecting adults to catechism, in a manner similar to Calvin's later practice of lifelong oral catechism in Geneva,[128] Hubmaier insisted that adults learn on their own from his written catechism, *Eine christliche Lehrtafel*, the fundamentals of the faith, upon which they would be examined before the entire congregation.[129] This procedure, which Hubmaier dubbed the *Christenliche erbiettung* (Christian challenge), was apparently designed to impose upon adults not a little sociological pressure to learn well the essentials of Christian belief, lest they suffer humiliation in the company of their peers.[130] Hubmaier furnishes the fol-

---

126. Windhorst, *Täuferisches Taufverständnis*, 155.

127. "Wie wol ich wayß (als die alten anzaygent), das man von alter her . . . man hat sy offenlich miteinander gleert, als sy zů uerstentnuß khumen sind, (dannen her sy auch Catechumenj hand gehaissen, das ist, die berichten), des worts des hayls. Vnd so sy dem festen glauben jm hertzen geben habend vnd mit dem mund veriehen, hat man sy getaufft. . . . So lassent vns die sach mit wort vnd leer erstlich angreyffen." Hubmaier, *Der Lehrer Urteil* I, 234, 240.

128. Spitz, *Reformation*, 197.

129. Recall from chapter three that this catechism was first published at Waldshut in August 1524 and then revised and reprinted at Nikolsburg in 1526. Loserth, *Hubmaier*, 204.

130. Hubmaier, *Form zu taufen*, 349.

lowing detailed list of elements in which the successful candidate would display proficiency:

> He should be questioned to see whether he is sufficiently educated in the articles of the law, gospel, faith, and the doctrines pertaining to a new Christian life. Moreover, he should demonstrate that he can pray and explain the articles of the Christian faith [*i.e.* the Apostles' Creed]. These factors must necessarily be proven first if one wants to be received into the congregation of Christians through outward baptism for the forgiveness of his sins.[131]

In Hubmaier's version of Christianity, then, forgiveness of sins in a real sense depends on knowledge; unless one can articulate basic Christian doctrine before the congregation, it is impossible for one to receive believers' baptism and thereby (at least in *potentia ordinata*) be saved. Only if the candidate passes this test, "the bishop presents him to the church, exhorting all brothers and sisters to fall on their knees and ask God with great affection to graciously impart to this person the grace and power of his Holy Spirit and complete in him what he has started through his Holy Spirit and divine Word."[132] It appears that for Hubmaier, grace amounts not to the unmerited favor of God, as for Luther and Zwingli,[133] but instead a quasi-substance that empowers one to share in the life of God himself by enlightening the mind and strengthening the will to do good and avoid evil. Hubmaier virtually admits this point in his explication of the results of grace: "God will . . . be with [the baptizand] and his spirit . . . increase his faith . . . and supply him

---

131. "Darmit er in verhöre, ob er in den Articklen des Gesatzs, Euangelions, Glaubens vnd leeren, ein new Christenlich leben betreffende, gnůgsamlich vnderricht sey. Auch wie er betten künd vnd mit verstand außsprechen die stuckh des Christenlichenn glaubens, wölhes alles vor an nott ist ze wissen dem menschen, der durch den eüsserlichen tauff zů verzeyhung seiner sünden in die gemain der Christenheit wille eingleibt werden." Ibid.

132. "Stelt in der Bischoff für sein Kirchen, ermanet alle brüeder vnd schwestern auff ire knye nider zefallen, mit hertzlichem andacht zů Gott zeschreyen, das er disem menschen die gnad vnd krafft seines heiligen geysts gnediglich mittailen wölle vnd volbringen, das er in im durch seinen heiligen geyst vnd götlich wort hat angefangen." Ibid.

133. Martin Luther, *A Treatise on the New Testament*, in *Luther's Works*, 35:89; Zwingli, *Exposition*, 268-70.

with all strength and endurance so that he will always persevere."[134] Although he does not specifically mention Bernard, Mabry observes that Hubmaier's concept of grace "exhibits definite parallels with medieval mysticism,"[135] and Alvin J. Beachy affirms that "the mystical components of Hubmaier's doctrine of grace have been firmly established."[136] Given our probable verification of the Hubmaier-Bernard dependence theory in chapter two, it would be profitable to compare their respective concepts of grace. In *De gratia et libero arbitrio*, Bernard defined grace as the divine power which suggests good thoughts to the soul and generally concurs with the soul to convert such ideas into meritorious works.[137] Hence grace, "by suggesting the good thought . . . and by supplying consent with faculty and ability," enables "the work that we perform."[138] Therefore, Hubmaier concurs with Bernard that grace is a strengthening agent which in some way makes righteous living possible.

We have called attention to the fact that, following Luther in the *Babylonian Captivity*, Hubmaier attaches the sacramental power of baptism not to its matter but to its form. The mode of baptism administered by Hubmaier is affusion, or the pouring of water over the candidate: "Baptism in water is to pour outward water over the confessor confessing his or her sins, according to the divine command, inscribing him or her among the number of sinners out of his or her own knowing and willing."[139] Hubmaier provides no theological or biblical reason for adopting this method; nowhere in his writings does he concern himself with the mode of baptism, which implies that in all probability he simply adopted the most convenient practice.[140] Because the grace of baptism resides in its form, Hubmaier emphasizes, in order to distance himself from the Catholic position, that sins are pardoned not by the

---

134. "Got . . . sey mit ihm vnd mit ihrem geyst . . . den glauben meeren wölle . . . vnd das ihn endtlich in einem Christenlichen glauben verharren." Ibid., 350.

135. Mabry, *Doctrine of the Church*, 114.

136. Alvin J. Beachy, *The Concept of Grace in the Radical Reformation* (Nieuwkoop: B. D. Graaf, 1977), 201.

137. Evans, *Mind of St. Bernard*, 161-62.

138. "Siquidem immitendo bonam cogitationem . . . ministrando et consensui facultatem vel facilitatem . . . apertum opus nostrum." Bernard, *De gratia*, 240.

139. "Täuffen im wasser ist den bekennenden verieher seiner sünder auss dem Götlichen beuelh mit eüsserlichen wasser übergiessen vnd den in die zal der sündern auss eygner erkantnüss vnd bewilligung enschreiben." Hubmaier, *Von der christlichen Taufe*, 121.

140. Vedder, *Hübmaier*, 142-43.

water, but by the keys which actualize the covenant: "Forgiveness of sins is not an attribute of the water, but an attribute of the power of the keys, which Christ, by the authority of his Word, hung at the side of his bride and spotless spouse, the Christian church, and commanded her to use in his physical absence."[141] Due to his conflation of infant baptism and confirmation into believers' baptism, as observed in chapter three, Hubmaier administers the laying on of hands associated with in practice but divorced theologically from confirmation:

> Let the bishop again order his church to pray for the baptized novice. . . . After the church has finished this prayer, the bishop lays his hands on the head of the novice and says: "I testify to you and give you authority that from this day forward you shall be considered a member of the Christian communion."[142]

This quote raises two important issues: given Hubmaier's doctrine of purgatory, what is the theological significance of being in the *ecclesia universalis*; and given his stress upon church discipline, what is the practical significance of incorporation into the church? An analysis of these queries will comprise the thrust of the next section.

Relationship between the Key of Baptism and the Door of Fraternal Admonition

During his Catholic days, Hubmaier maintained that infant baptism comprised the *ratio praedestinationis ex parte praedestinati*, which guaranteed its recipient, after possibly some time in hell to purge his or her sins, eventual entrance into the heavenly kingdom. However, by virtue of the sacrament of holy orders, clerics were guaranteed full remission of all temporal and spiritual penalties due for past, present, and future sins, thus furnishing

---

141. "Nit das die nachlassung der sünden dem wasser zügeaignet werde, sonnder dem gwalt der Schlüsselen, die Christus in krafft seins worts seiner Gesponß vnd vnuermailigtem Eegmahel, der Christenlichen Kirchen, in seinem leiblichen abwesen beuolhen vnd an die seytten gehenckt hat." Hubmaier, *Grund und Ursache*, 335.

142. "Yetz ermane der Bischoff sein Kirchen zum andern mal zübetten für den getaufften Newlinng. . . . Nach dem nun die Kirch das gebeet volpracht, legt der Bischoff dem Newlinng die hennd auff das haubt vnd sagt: Jch gib dir zeückhnuß vnd gwalt, das du füran vnder die Christenlichen Gmainschafft sollest gezelt werden." Hubmaier, *Form zu taufen*, 350.

the forensic basis for immediate entrance into paradise. Surprisingly, following his rebaptism Hubmaier retained the same soteriological structure, never abandoning his doctrine that purgatory was a metaphorical term for a finite time spent in hell, but modified some of the variables within the system. The initial change made by Hubmaier consisted in substitution of believers' baptism, the first of the two keys, for pedobaptism. However, Hubmaier defined the portion of the baptismal vow in which the candidate submitted to *brüderliche Strafe* (fraternal admonition), which admonition amounted to the opening stage in his twofold plan of church discipline, as the liminal door through which one must pass to move from what Mircea Eliade termed the "profane state" of damnation to the "sacred state" of redemption.[143] Consequently, Hubmaier identified acquiescence to fraternal admonition as the "right door of Christian election" (rechte thür der Christenlichen waal).[144] By submitting to *brüderliche Strafe*, the believer "renounces Satan and all his conceptions and deeds, [for] the church opens her door to all believers . . . and takes them into her lap, fellowship, and communion of saints for the forgiveness of their sins. . . . She opens the door of heaven to them."[145] Thus, placing oneself under the authority of the congregation amounts to entering into the door of the church, which is equivalent to the door of heaven.

Hubmaier declares the baptismal vow, in which such submission takes place, to be the human aspect in a reciprocal covenant between God and the believer. Like Bernard and Luther,[146] Hubmaier explains this covenant in terms of a spiritual marriage. As the divine husband, God vows "the forgiveness and remission of the candidate's sins through the death and resurrection of our Lord Jesus Christ,"[147] which is accepted in the act of baptism. As the human bride, the recipient

vows and promises publicly and orally by the power of God, Father, Son, and Holy Spirit, that he or she intends to believe and live hence-

---

143. Mircea Eliade, *Rites and Symbols of Initiation: The Mysteries of Birth and Rebirth* (New York: Harper and Row, 1965), 117.

144. Hubmaier, *Eine christliche Lehrtafel*, 309.

145. "Er widersagt dem Satan, allen gespensten vnnd wercken, [da] schleüst die Kirch auff ire portenn allenn glaubigenn . . . vnd nimbt sy an in ir schoß, gesellschaft vnd gemainschafft der heiligen zů verzeyhung irer sünnden. . . . Schleüsset im auff den himel." Ibid., 314-15, 17.

146. Bernard, *De diligendo Deo*, 130; Luther, *Commentary on Galatians*, 51:246.

147. "verzeyhunng der selben, durch den todt vnd vrsteend vnsers herrens Jesu Christj." Hubmaier, *Eine christliche Lehrtafel*, 313.

forth according to the divine Word . . . and when one does not do this, one promises the church hereby that he or she will virtuously receive from its members fraternal discipline.[148]

By water baptism the candidate thus pledges to the church to live a saintly life according to the rules of Christ and vows that if she or he should stray from this intent, she or he will voluntarily submit to fraternal discipline by the church. Thus, in the act of baptism, believers give the church the right to discipline and excommunicate them if the church deems this necessary.[149] Nowhere is this more evident than in Hubmaier's baptismal liturgy, where the bishop's lines are marked "B" and the recipient's lines "R":

Here the bishop lays out the baptismal vow to the baptizand in the following manner:
[Statement of faith in the Father, Son, and Holy Spirit from the Apostles' Creed]
B: Will you lead your life and walk according to the Word of Christ from this day forward, as he gives you grace? If so, speak:
R: I will.
B: If now you sin and your brother is aware of it, will you allow him to admonish you once, twice, and the third time before the church, and voluntarily and submissively accept fraternal admonition? If so, speak:
R: I will.
B: Do you now desire, in light of your faith and vow, to be baptized in water according to the institution of Christ, and to be inducted and thus enrolled in the visible Christian church for the forgiveness of your sins? If so, speak:
R: I desire it in the power of God.
B: I baptize you in the name of the Father and of the Son and of the Holy Spirit for the forgiveness of your sins. Amen, so let it be.[150]

---

148. "offentlich vnd münndtlich Got angelobet vnnd zůsagt auff die krafft gottes vatters vnnd Sons vnd heyligen geysts, das er fürhin nach seinem Göttlichenn wort glaubenn vnd lebenn wölle . . . vnd wo er das nit thůt, verspricht er hiemit der Kirchen, das er von iren glidern, vnd von ir brůderliche straff wölle tugentlich annemen." Ibid., 314-15.

149. Mabry, *Doctrine of the Church*, 141.

150. "Hie helt der Bischoff dem menschen für die Tauffglubd vnnd also. . . . Wiltu füran dein leben vnd wandel fieren nach dem wort Christj, als vil er dir gnad verleyhet, so sprich: JCH WJL. So du nun füran sündest vnd dein brüeder waiß es, wilt du dich von im zum ersten, andern vnd zum dritten mal vor der Kirchen straffen lassen vnd brüederliche straff willigklich vnnd gehorsamlich auff nemen, so sprich: JCH WJL. Begerstu nun auff disen glauben vnnd pflicht

Therefore, baptism amounted not simply to a personal matter by which neophytes confessed their faith; it was also a symbol of submission to the congregation to which they would adhere and, as we will see, a necessary condition for receiving the Eucharist.

The content of *brüderliche Strafe* consisted in the threefold warning of Matthew 18:15-20, which, like Bernard's steps of pride in his *De gradibus humilitatis et superbiae*,[151] showed sinners, without penalty, that they were progressively moving further from discipleship to Christ (*Nachfolge Christi*)[152] and closer to exclusion from the Lord's Supper. Displaying pastoral sensitivity, Hubmaier attempts to expound the Matthean text in a manner consistent with Christian charity:

> But let every Christian watch out for himself that this reprimand . . .
> springs up out of love and not out of jealousy, hate, or anger. . . . [First]
> sins should be reprimanded privately according to the order of
> Christ. . . . If he refuses to listen to you, then take one or two others
> with you for the purpose of testimony. If he refuses to listen to them either,
> then tell it to the congregation. . . . gently and respectfully.[153]

In order for any of the three reproofs to be valid, demands Hubmaier, it must be preceded by the following reminder of the miscreant's baptismal vow:

> Now dear brother, you swore a baptismal vow to Christ Jesus our Lord.
> You surrendered yourself to him, which included your public promise
> before the church to desire to lead and govern your life from that point
> forward according to his Holy Word (in the way that Scripture indicates);
> and that if you failed to do so, you would voluntarily allow
> yourself to be admonished according to the order of Christ. On this ba-

---

im wasser nach der einsetzung Christi getaufft, eingeleibt vnd also in die eüsserlichen Christenlichen Kirchen eingeschriben werden zů verzeyhunng deiner sünnden, so sprich: Jch begeers auff die krafft Gottes. Jch Tauff dich in dem namen des Vatters vnd Sons vnd des heiligen geysts zů verzeyhung deiner sünden. Amen, das werde war." Hubmaier, *Form zu taufen*, 349-50.

151. Bernard, *De gradibus*, 14.

152. Hubmaier, *Strafe*, 339.

153. "Doch hab ein yedlicher Christ sich selbs in gůter acht, darmit dise straff . . . auß liebe vnd nit auß neyd, haß oder zorn herfliessent. . . . [Zuerst] sünnden soll man auch nach dem beuelh Christj haimlich straffen. . . . Hört er dich nit, so nim noch ainen oder zwen zů dir, von der zeügkhnuß wegen. Hört er die aber auch nit, so sag es der Gmaine. . . . gůettiklich vnd tugentlich." Ibid., 342.

sis you received water baptism and were enrolled in the membership of the Christian communion.[154]

It seems clear from this admonition that, for Hubmaier, baptism was not merely a symbol of individual discipleship but of corporate discipleship as well. However, a congregation could only uphold the disciplinary system made possible by baptism if the pastor himself submitted to fraternal discipline, or the "right door of Christian election." All pastors refusing to place themselves under the discipline of their congregations are denounced by Hubmaier in the strongest possible terms as guilty of spiritual murder.

> Unquestionably, it is in many cases obvious what incompetent shepherds and pastors have been imposed upon us by popes, bishops, provosts, abbots, and also by worldly emperors, kings, princes, and nobles, by their bulls and mandates, such as courtisans, donkey groomers, fornicators, adulterers, simonizers, gamblers, drunkards, and idiotic rogues, whom we honestly would never trust to herd our pigs and goats, but yet we were forced to accept them as shepherds of our souls. They are nothing but robbers and murderers, since they did not enter through the right door of Christian election.[155]

We discern from this quote that Hubmaier insisted upon fraternal discipline not only to safeguard the purity of the laity, but also to procure spiritual accountability for their shepherds, without which all manner of sin might abound among the clergy.

---

154. "Nun hastu, lieber Brüeder, ein Tauffglübd gethon Christo Jesu vnserm herren, Jm dich der massen verpflicht vnd offentlich vor der Kirchen angelobt, das du dein leben füran nach seinem heiligenn wort (das zeugkhnuß in der Schrifft hat) richten vnnd regiern wöllest, wo du aber solchs nit thůest, dich nach dem beuelch Christi willigklich straffen lassen. Darauff hastu den Wassertauff entpfangen vnd bist also in die zal der Christenlichen Gmainschafft eingschriben worden." Ibid., 344.

155. "Ja, es ist auch menigklich vnuerborgen, was vns die Bebst, Bischoff, Probst, Abbt vnd auch die weltlichen Khayser, Künig, Fürsten vnd herren durch jre Bullen vnd Mandaten für kunstloß hirten vnd seelsorger eingetrungen, als namlich Cortisanen, Eselstrigler, Hůrer, Eebrecher, Kupler, Spiler, Sauffer vnd Schalckßnarren, denen wir fürwar die Sauen vnd Gayssen zehietten nit vertraut hetten, noch můsten wirs für vnnser seelhirten annemen. Darauß seinnd nichts denn dieb vnnd mörder worden, wann sy seind zů der rechten thür der Christenlichen waal nit einganngen." Hubmaier, *Eine christliche Lehrtafel*, 308-09.

At this point Hubmaier appears to make two further substitutions in his former Catholic soteriological structure: he replaces ordination with the state of being in the church, and he replaces its permanent guarantee of immediate access into heaven with a provisional guarantee of immediate entrance to paradise conditioned upon a person's belonging to the church at the moment of death.[156] Therefore, while it is true that the sacrament of believers' baptism assures one eventual entry to heaven, which could never be annulled even by exclusion from the Eucharist (to be discussed in chapter five), one may have to spend time in hell before entering heaven if one is separated from the church, which suffering would be averted if one remained in good standing with the visible body. Accordingly, Hubmaier distinguishes between "eternal life . . . prepared from the foundation of the world for all believers in Christ,"[157] in which believers' baptism serves as a prerequisite for one's election, and "the shortest path of all to eternal life,"[158] or faithful adherence to *brüderliche Strafe* so that one would never be subject to the second stage of ecclesiastical discipline, the *Bann*. In Hubmaier's conception, then, fraternal discipline forms a help mechanism or "spiritual safety-net" which enables one to freely persevere on the shortest path to the beatific vision.[159] Conversely, breaking one's baptismal vow by not heeding fraternal discipline amounts to nothing less than dishonoring baptism and the Eucharist, for which one will be punished accordingly:

> Those who are faithless, who violate the sacraments and perjure, who have not maintained their vow, duty, loyalty, honor, or faith in the Almighty God and his only begotten Son, our Lord Jesus Christ, as well as to his all-beloved bride, the holy universal and Christian church . . . must be summarily excluded and banned, [as] those who truly violate the sacraments are those who do not keep their baptismal vow.[160]

---

156. Sachsse, *Hubmaier als Theologe*, 175; Loserth, *Hubmaier*, 214.

157. "Das ewig leben . . . wölchs von anfang der welt berayttet ist allen Christglaubigen." Hubmaier, *Strafe*, 325.

158. "der aller nechst weg, durch den man eingeet in das ewig lebenn." Ibid.

159. Windhorst, *Täuferisches Taufverständnis*, 164.

160. "Die da treüloß, Sacramentbrichig vnd mainaidig worden, ja weder glübd, pflicht, trew, eer, noch glauben an dem allmechtigen Gott vnd an seinem aingebornen Son vnserm herren Jesu Christo, auch an seiner aller liebsten Praut der heiligen allgmainen vnd Christenlichen Kirchen nit gehalten haben . . . kurtzlich außschliessen vnd verbannen soll, [als] die seind die rechten Sacramenttbrichel, die jr Tauffglübd . . . nit halten." Hubmaier, *Bann*, 375.

Drawing together the threads of all that occurs within the sacramental liturgy, Hubmaier presents the baptismal ceremony throughout his treatises as an act of confession, obedience, individual discipleship, and church membership. Since the first three of these qualities require a voluntary decision, the ceremony therefore undermines the validity of infant baptism. All of this is displayed in the following quotation:

> Now when a man confesses that he is a sinner, believes in the remission of sins, and has committed himself to a new life, he must then testify outwardly before the church of Christ . . . that he accepts the word of Christ in his heart, and is minded to surrender himself to live in [the] future according to the word, will, and law of Christ. . . . Then he must be baptized in water, by which means he publicly professes his faith and purpose [through] his sacramental baptismal confession. . . . If he should in the future bring reproach or blame upon the name of Christ through public or grievous sins, he promises to submit to punishment by his brethren, according to the command of Christ (Matt. 18). From all this it is easy to see that infant baptism is a deception, invented and introduced by men.[161]

In his 1526 treatise on fraternal admonition, Hubmaier insisted upon the necessity of fraternal discipline for the existence of the church, since its application reveals who is and is not a faithful Christian: "Where this is lacking, there is certainly also no church, even if water baptism and the Supper of Christ are practiced."[162] Here we perceive that Hubmaier, in effect, delineates baptism, discipline, and the Eucharist as the three necessary marks of a

---

161. "Auff das, so sich nun der mensch ein sunder bekennt, nachlassung der sünden glaubt vnd aber sich inn ein new leben ergeben hatt, bezeügt er auch das selb außwendig, offentlich vor Christenlichen kirchen . . . das er der maßen im wort Christi inwendig vnderricht vnd gesynnet sey, das er sich schon ergeben hab, nach dem wort, willen vnnd regel Christi züleben. . . . Vnd lasset sich täuffen mit dem außwendigen wasser, inn welchem er offentlich bezeügt seinen glauben vnnd fürnemen [durch] seiner Sacramentlicher Tauffglübde. . . . Vnnd ob er furan mit offentlichen oder ergerlichen sünden den glauben vnd nammen Christi beschwertzen oder taddelen wurde, das er sich hyemit vnderwerffe vnd ergebe inn brüderliche straff nach der ordnung Christi, Matthei am xviij. Cap. Hye sycht menglich, das der Kindertauff ein gaugkel wreck ist, von den menschen erdicht vnnd eyngefüret." Hubmaier, *Von der ordnung*, 160.
162. "Wo die nit ist, da ist gewißlich auch khain Kirch, ob schon der Wassertauff vnd das Nachtmal Christj daselbs gehaltenn werdent." Hubmaier, *Strafe*, 338.

true church.[163] Hubmaier makes the indispensability of discipline as the centerpiece of discipleship dramatically clear: "The sum of a Christian life: Where there is no fraternal admonition, there is no church either."[164] Returning to the flood analogy borrowed from Basil the Great, Hubmaier asserts that the ark of the church must be entered through the door of church discipline:

> [When] by means of fraternal admonition . . . the people commit themselves to practice and to submit to the same, [they are] registered, enrolled, and inducted into the fellowship of the holy universal Christian church—outside of which there is no salvation, just as no salvation existed outside of Noah's Ark.[165]

As long as the believer remains within the ecclesial ark, he or she is guaranteed immediate access to heaven at the moment of death. Moreover, Hubmaier's system of church discipline enables the believer to rest assured that he or she cannot be "tossed overboard," so to speak, apart from his or her conscious decision to thrice violate the external warnings of fellow believers. Such a synergistic soteriology, bound together in practice by the adhesive of *brüderliche Strafe*, evades the perennial conflict between God's sovereignty and human assurance of salvation by predicating all divine predestinary decisions, including eventual and immediate entrance to paradise, upon the respective tangible acts of baptism and membership within the physical, external church.

---

163. In his early writings (*e.g. Reply to Sadoleto*, in Peter Barth and Wilhelm Niesel, eds., *Johannis Calvini opera selecta*, 5 vols. [Munich: C. Kaiser, 1926], 1:467), Calvin attempted to institute a similar trichotomy which defined the marks of the church as faithful preaching of the Word of God, correct administration of the sacraments, and church discipline; however, church discipline was later dropped, reducing the number of marks to two (*Institutes*, 4.1.9). Pelikan summarizes this development well in *Reformation*, 215.

164. "Die Summ eins Christenlichen lebens. Wo khainn Brüederliche straff ist, da ist auch kain Kirchen." Hubmaier, *Strafe*, 339.

165. "[Solhs] durch die brüederlichen strafe . . . zethon vnd volbringen hat sich das volckh . . . in die gmanischafft der heiligen, allgemainen vnd Christenlichen Kirchen einschreiben, verzaichnen vnd einleiben lassen, ausserhalb dero kain hay list, wie ausserhalb der Arch Noha." Hubmaier, *Strafe*, 339.

Summary of Hubmaier's Doctrine of Baptism

Like the hub of a wheel, the baptismal theology formulated by Hub-maier drew together the four distinctive spokes of patristic thought, the divine method of predestination, the power of the keys, and church discipline into one integrated system based upon the anthropological foundation of libertarian human freedom. Since Hubmaier's conception of the relation between *glaub* and regeneration included a voluntaristic element, as neophytes had to freely believe (assuming the particular church did not err) prior to their reception of the baptismal *ratio praedestinationis ex parte praedestini*, the discussion of baptism thus flowed out of his tripartite conception of free will. Upon partaking in the sacrament of believers' baptism, which serves to consummate one's faith, God graciously acts through his life-giving Spirit to regenerate the person so that the spirit has restored to it the freedom of counsel and is, like the pre-Fall Adam, able to generate good thoughts in and of itself. In developing this concept, Hubmaier enlisted the aid of ancient patristic statements, especially those of Origen, Cyril, Basil the Great, and Jerome, to reveal both that individual faith is necessary to a valid and efficacious sacrament and that faith without baptism cannot save.[166] This latter point raised two pressing questions: what is the eternal destiny of children who die without baptism; and have the vast majority of Christians down through church history, who had no opportunity to receive the sacrament as believers, been damned? Utilizing his differentiation between God's *potentia ordinata*, providing a reliable set of covenantal principles guaranteeing that he will save those who are baptismally regenerated, and his *potentia absoluta*, according to which he can do anything not ruled out by the terms of his covenant with humanity, Hubmaier attempts a consistent solution to both quandaries. With regard to the first, Hubmaier, while confessing ignorance as to whether all unbaptized children are saved, offers to bereaved parents the possibility that God could mercifully extend his *potentia absoluta* to save their children.[167] Concerning the second, however, Hubmaier departed from the widespread Anabaptist view, which denied legitimacy and thus soteriological potency to the post-Constantinian church, by arguing that all believers lacking the opportunity for rebaptism are saved, just like the thief on the cross, simply on the basis of their faith. However, the fate of those with the opportunity to enter into the rebaptismal covenant and, in Hubmaier's judgment, stubbornly refusing is quite another matter indeed.

---

166. Armour, *Baptism*, 51.
167. Ibid., 35.

Preserving in attenuated form the Catholic doctrine of the keys, Hubmaier insists that in *potentia ordinata,* one must belong to the visible, universal church in order to receive salvation. But distancing himself from Roman dogma, conversely, the radical removed the keys from the penitential realm and redistricted them to the sacramental realm. Accordingly, the first key of believers' baptism unlocked the entrance door to the church, which Hubmaier often interchanges with the kingdom of heaven, for association with the first guarantees immediate admission into the second at the moment of death. As the earthly successor to the incarnate Christ, the church possessed the power of forgiving sin, which power it dispensed by enrolling sinners within its charge through baptism. When a person receives baptism, Hubmaier insists, one enters the true ship of salvation by which alone one can escape the floods of sin. Since the church can typically be entered only through water baptism, the ceremony is thus raised from the ordinance level of a mere confession of faith to the sacramental level of redemptive necessity, with cases of inaccessibility constituting the only exception. It follows, therefore, that anyone who could be rebaptized, most notably the followers of Luther and Zwingli, but declined due to solafideism is condemned.[168] Hence water baptism was necessary for the forgiveness of sins and admission to salvation. Such baptism, in Hubmaier's Waldshut and Nikolsburg parishes, was always accompanied by the vow of faithfulness, which constituted the formal sacramental ground. Via the candidate's pledge to the Christian life, the congregation obtains the authority to exercise its disciplinary power over him or her, thereby preserving the purity of the church. In Hubmaier's imagery, the baptizand enters into the church through the entrance door of submission to church discipline, which door was unlocked by the baptismal key. To provide believers a tangible means of salvific protection, averred Hubmaier, Christ instituted *brüderliche Strafe,* which prohibits disconnection from the congregation unless a person has freely and deliberately rejected one individual, one judicial, and one ecclesial admonition to turn from sin. In sum, while divine predestination ensured final salvation to anyone baptized as a believer, although a temporary but painful purgation in hell was not ruled out, obedience to fraternal discipline guaranteed, in a way compatible with his or her free will, that the believer would never experience darkness but was entitled immediate access to the beatific vision upon his or her departure. To the faithful, this system was surely a heartening thing, as baptism and church discipline comprised two visible marks of the saints by which they could recognize each other and find objective assurance that they themselves were among the redeemed.

---

168. Williams, *Radical Reformation,* 231.

Chapter 5

Hubmaier's Doctrine of the Sacrament of the Eucharist

Due to its central role in his sacramental and ethical thought, Hubmaier devoted three treatises to the Eucharist, *Etliche Schlußreden vom Unterricht der Messe, Ein einfältiger Unterricht*, and *Eine Form des Nachtmals Christi*, between 1524 and 1526. As the second key given by Christ to his followers, which unlocks the exit door to the church (and, derivatively, to the kingdom of heaven), the Eucharist discloses, in Hubmaier's theology, who would and would not be admitted to heaven at the present moment. Participation in the intimate meal afforded the recipient tangible evidence that she or he was currently entitled to the beatific vision, while exclusion from the meal guaranteed that if the outsider died in the existing state of affairs, she or he would, in *potentia ordinata*, be consigned to hell, either temporarily (if the person received believers' baptism) or permanently (if the person was never baptized as a believer). From this salvific configuration it follows that the essence of *christliche Bann*, Hubmaier's second stage of church discipline, consisted of excommunication from the Lord's Supper unless and until the miscreant displays proof to the local congregation of true repentance, desistance from sin, and definite steps of self-improvement.[1] As is the case with Calvin,[2] the antithetical relationship of the Eucharist and the expelling stage of church discipline furnishes a hallmark of Hubmaier's thought. However, unlike Calvin and all other sixteenth-century proponents of an Antiochene

---

1. Mabry, *Doctrine of the Church*, 83.
2. Robert M. Kingdon, "The Control of Morals in Calvin's Geneva," in Lawrence P. Buck and Jonathan W. Zophy, eds., *The Social History of the Reformation* (Columbus: Ohio State University Press, 1972), 11.

Christology, including Zwingli, the Anabaptists, and Heinrich Bullinger,[3] Hubmaier championed an Alexandrian Christology and extended this concept to its logical limits in order to devise an original and radically incarnationist doctrine of the real presence of Christ which, as Rempel observes, "completely broke with the conventional Eucharistic schema as it had been formulated since the time of Augustine."[4] In this chapter I will argue that Hubmaier, upon the joint foundation of his libertarian anthropology and Christology, constructed a sacramental edifice in which the congregation itself is ontologically transformed into the physical body of Christ while partaking of the Eucharist and thus manifest within itself a historical continuation of the Incarnation. Furthermore, this edifice is composed of several key doctrinal and practical building blocks, such as the doctrine of *communicatio idiomatum*, the Anselmian dichotomy between the definitive and repletive presence of God,[5] and the tremendous magnitude of the moral conduct exhibited by the church in general and its members in particular. Through the "consubstantiation," in the literal sense of the congregation simultaneously possessing both Christ's human *Wesen* (essence or substance) and their own human *Wesen* during the Supper,[6] Hubmaier crafts a positive theology of the Eucharist which was greater than the sum of its parts.

The Sacramental Identification of the Eucharist

Like believers' baptism, Hubmaier recognized the Eucharist as a sacrament in the classical sense of the term, *i.e.* the visible sign which communicated the invisible grace that it signified.[7] This fact is revealed by his description of what happens when the congregation partakes of the elements coupled with his explicit classification of the Eucharist as "the sacrament" (*das Sacrament*) and "the sacrament of the altar" (*das Sacrament des Alltars*). In his Eucharistic liturgy, *Eine Form des Nachtmals Christi*, Hubmaier

---

3. Calvin, *Institutes*, 4.17.31; Huldrych Zwingli, *On the Lord's Supper*, in Bromiley, *Zwingli and Bullinger*, 212-13; Friedmann, *Theology of Anabaptism*, 138-39; Heinrich Bullinger, *Of the Holy Catholic Church*, in Bromiley, *Zwingli and Bullinger*, 305.

4. Rempel, *Lord's Supper*, 52.

5. Anselm, *Proslogium*, in *Proslogium, Monologium, An Appendix in behalf of the Fool by Gaunilon, and Cur Deus Homo* [hereafter abbreviated *PMAC*], trans. Sidney Norton Deane (Chicago: Open Court, 1926), 18, 24-26; Anselm, *Monologium*, in *PMAC*, 59.

6. Hubmaier, *Messe*, 103.

7. This definition was originally formulated by Augustine, *City of God*, X.5.

directs the celebrant, who could either be a bishop or a priest,[8] to inform the congregation both before and after consuming the bread and wine that they respectively are about to receive and have just received the grace of God. Immediately before breaking the bread, the minister instructs his flock, "Now eat and drink with one another in the name of God, the Father, the Son, and the Holy Spirit. . . . May the Lord communicate to us his grace. Amen."[9] Similarly, after everyone has drunk the wine, the cleric instructs the congregation to be seated in order to hear his "conclusion": "Arise and depart in the peace of Christ Jesus. The grace of God be with us all. Amen."[10] Here we see that for Hubmaier, the dispensation of grace in the Eucharist amounted to more than simply a theological point, but a living reality which the laity needed to appreciate. Indeed, Hubmaier insisted that only church members "with reverence and hearts desiring grace"[11] could participate in the sacred meal. Such a prerequisite entailed that one must first submit to believers' baptism before being allowed to receive the Eucharist: "Just as faith precedes love, so water baptism must precede the Lord's Supper."[12] That Catholics and the followers of Luther and Zwingli take part in the Eucharist without the regenerating grace of believers' baptism, Hubmaier asserted, was "another conspiracy" hatched by "the relentless Satan . . . to hold us in his snare."[13] This is because, unlike believers' baptism (which seemingly imparted grace *ex opere operato* to anyone who willingly participated in the ceremony),[14] reception of the "new grace and drawing of the heavenly Father" communicated through the Eucharistic channel depended upon the Father's "looking at humanity afresh by the merit of Jesus Christ

---

8. Balthasar Hubmaier, *Form des Nachtmals Christi*, 355, 362.

9. "So essent vnd trinckent mit ein ander in dem namen Gottes vaters vnd des Sons vnd des heiligen geysts. . . . Der Herr mittaile vns sein gnad. Amen." Ibid., 362.

10. "den Beschluß. . . . Steend auff vnd geend hin in dem frid Christj Jesu. Die gnad Gottes sey mit vns allen. Amen." Ibid., 363-64.

11. "mit andacht vnd gnadbegirigem hertzen." Ibid., 361.

12. "Dann wie der glaub vorgeet der liebe, also soll der Wassertauff dem Nachtmal vorlauffen." Ibid., 364.

13. "der vnrůewig Satan einen andern ranckh." Ibid.

14. Although candidates were supposed to first demonstrate the authenticity of their faith by passing the *Christenliche erbeittung* prior to baptism, the reception of regenerating grace of baptism did not appear to be contingent upon this test; the only prerequisite clearly articulated by Hubmaier for receiving such grace was that candidates submitted to baptism of their own free will, thus precluding infant baptism.

our Lord,"[15] which merit was appropriated through believers' baptism. Just as infant baptism served in Hubmaier's judgment as a sham which gave people a false sense of security that hindered them from obtaining the salvation found in believers' baptism,[16] the Eucharist of Catholicism, Luther, and Zwingli was analogously deemed a counterfeit which provided its recipients no power to live the Christian life.[17] Therefore, Hubmaier vilifies both the "sacrificers (Catholic priests) and consecrators (Luther and Zwingli)"[18] as perpetrators of a monstrous blasphemy:

> Nevertheless, it pleased the heavenly Father who saw the error of this disgusting idolatry from the beginning of time, that is to say, that we would not only worship Ceres, or an idol of bread, as the pagans, or an idol of wine, Bacchus, or a water idol, Neptune, but that we would construct of these three idols a complete trinity . . . which is the worst abomination on earth before the face of God. . . . Whoever does not want to see and hear undoubtedly desires to be blind and deaf. May God open our ears and eyes and loosen our tongues, so that we hear, see, and speak accurately from this point forward, that this idolatry will no longer grow, and that this triune idol and abomination will be ousted from the holy throne.[19]

---

15. "ein neüe gnad vnd ziehung des himelischen vaters . . . den menschen durch das verdienen Jesu Christi vnsers herrens auff ein neües ansehe." Hubmaier, *Von der Freiheit*, 394.

16. Hubmaier, *Grund und Ursache*, 334-36.

17. Sachsse, *Hubmaier als Theologe*, 204.

18. "Sacrificierer vnd Consecratisten." Hubmaier, *Ein einfältiger Unterricht*, 299; cf. Sachsse, *Hubmaier als Theologe*, 205.

19. "Aber also hatt es gefallen dem Himelischen Vatter, der von anbegin der Welt den Jrrsal diser greülichen Abgötterey gewist hatt, namlich das wir nit allain eine Ceserem, das ist ain Abbgöttin des brots, anbetten wurden, wie die Hayden, oder ein Abgott Bachum des Weins, oder ein Wasser Got Neptunnum, sonder wie wir wurden auß disen dreyen Abgötteren ein gantze Triualtigkeit machen . . . wölches der gröst Grewel ist vor dem Angesicht Gottes auff Erden. . . . Wer nit sehen vnnd hören will, der will mit gwalt blind vnd khörloß sein. Got wölle vns vnsere Oren vnd Augen auff thon, vnd vnsere Zungen lösen, damit wir für an recht hörn, Sehen vnd Reden, auf dz nit mer solche Abgötterey erwachse vnd diser triueltig Abgot vnd Greüel auß dem Hayligen Stůl abgestossen werde." Hubmaier, *Ein einfältiger Unterricht*, 299.

Since the infant baptism and Eucharist practiced by his opponents possessed no salvific power, then, Hubmaier deems their constitutive elements of water, bread, and wine as a false trinity of idols.

Contrary to the widespread view that Hubmaier, like his supposed Anabaptist brethren, rejected the application of the term "sacrament" to the Lord's Supper,[20] an examination of the reformer's three treatises on the subject along with many of his other writings reveal that Hubmaier displayed no qualms in either assigning sacramental nomenclature to the Eucharist or overtly claiming that the participants in some way shared in the body and blood of Christ. In *Der Lehrer Urteil* II, for example, Hubmaier calls the Eucharist Christ's body and blood, in which its recipients participate, as well as "the sacrament": "The baptized members of Christ should also participate in the body and blood of Christ. For he wants only believers to receive, desire, and seek the sacrament, for only they belong to the confessors and followers of Christ."[21] In *Der Lehrer Urteil* I Hubmaier, while discussing the alleged heresy of allowing children to partake of the Supper, refers to the Supper as "the sacrament" twice in passing:

> They brought young children as well to the sacrament of bread and wine, despite its having no basis in the Word of God. Such people give no other rationale or defense for their actions than that we Germans also baptize our children. For this reason they deem it appropriate to let their children eat and drink of the sacrament since baptism and the breaking of bread are two comparable ceremonies, both instituted in the New Testament by Christ.[22]

---

20. Vedder, *Hübmaier*, 208-10; Windhorst, *Täuferisches Taufverständnis*, 200-01; Mabry, *Doctrine of the Church*, 165-66; Rempel, *Lord's Supper*, 50; Estep, *Anabaptist Story*, 252.

21. "Die getaufften glider Christi, die solten auch des Leibs vnd Plůts Christi tailhafftig sein. Dann er will, das die Sacrament nur die glaubigen solten empfahen, begeren vnnd suchen, dann sy nur den bekenten vnd nachfolgern Christi zů hören." Hubmaier, *Der Lehrer Urteil* II, 245.

22. "Das sy die jungen khinder auch zů dem Sacrament (wie mans genennt) des brots vnd weins gefieret, wölcher doch im wort gotes khaynen grund hat. Derhalb die selben khain ander beschönung, noch entschuldigung irer thaten fürwenden, dann das wir Teütschen vnsere khinder auch tauffen. Auff solchs jnen wol gebüre die jren, mit dem Sacrament zů speysen vnd trencken, die weyl doch der Tauff vnd die Brotbrechung eben zwů gleich Ceremonien seyend, im Newen Testament von Christo auffgesetzet." Hubmaier, *Der Lehrer Urteil* I, 227.

Moreover, Hubmaier, in opening *Ein einfältiger Unterricht* with a historical survey of various positions on the real presence, describes the Eucharist as "the sacrament of the altar": "From ancient times there has always been tremendous discord concerning the sacrament of the altar."[23] While the significance of the Eucharist as a "living commemoration" will be discussed later in this chapter, suffice it to say here that Hubmaier's *Eine Form des Nachtmals Christi* declares that this concept follows from the fact that the Supper constitutes a sacrament in which the recipient shares in the divine grace and power made available by the atonement: "The person is now celebrating . . . a sacrament [and] a living commemoration in the breaking of bread and the distribution of the cup . . . in the grace and power of the passion and the shedding of blood by our Lord Jesus Christ."[24] In his summary of this position in the twenty-sixth article of *Eine Rechenschaft des Glaubens*, Hubmaier not only dubs the Eucharist "the sacrament" but also posits that Christ gave us the Supper "out of love for the remission of our sins."[25] Hence the Supper plays some role (to be later determined) in the calculus of salvation. For these reasons, the primary sources permit no doubt that Hubmaier regarded the Eucharist as a grace-conveying sacrament.

The Christology of Hubmaier

Hubmaier's Eucharistic theology, which centers around the real presence of Christ, is predicated upon an Alexandrian Christology as opposed to an Antiochene Christology. These christological approaches, dating back to fourth and fifth century Alexandria and Antioch (the two foremost schools of thought in the Patristic church), were grounded in two distinct views of Jesus.[26] Following the explicit Johannine portrayal of Christ's deity and implicit portrayal of his humanity, the Alexandrian perspective starts with the Λόγος as the second person of the Trinity who humbles himself by assuming from the Virgin Mary an anhypostatic human nature (*i.e.* one having no sub-

---

23. "Nach dem bey den vralten ye vnnd allwegen grosse vnainigkayt gewesen in dem Sacrament des Alltars." Hubmaier, *Ein einfältiger Unterricht*, 290.

24. "Der mensch yetz . . . ein Sacrament [vnd] ein lebendige gedechtnuß hellt mit diser Brotbrechung vnd außtailung des Kelchs . . . auff die gnad vnd krafft des leydens vnnd blůt vergiessens vnnsers herren Jesu Christj." Hubmaier, *Form des Nachtmals Christi*, 358.

25. "dem Sacramennt. . . . auß liebe zuuertzeichung vnnserer Sunden." Hubmaier, *Rechenschaft*, 486-87.

26. Reinhold Seeberg, *Text-book of the History of Doctrine*, 4 vols., trans. Charles E. Kay (Grand Rapids, Mich.: Baker, 1956), 1:248.

sistence or person in and of itself), which he personalizes in the Incarnation.[27] Such a view is also called a "Christology from above" or a "Word-Flesh Christology," because it begins with the person of the Λόγος and then attempts to account for Christ's humanity.[28] By contrast, following the explicit Synoptic portrayal of Christ's humanity and implicit portrayal of his deity, the Antiochene perspective starts with the man Jesus of Nazareth who possesses a freestanding (*i.e.* complete rather than anhypostatic) human nature, which the divine Λόγος then indwells, or with which the Λόγος sets up a moral union.[29] Such a view is also called a "Christology from below" or a "Word-Man Christology," because it begins with Jesus as a human person and then attempts to account for the divine aspects of Christ.[30] Of the many theological corollaries springing from each model, the respective doctrines concerning the relationship between the divine and human natures of Christ proved most significant to early modern Eucharistic debates.[31] The Alexandrian view, the sixteenth-century advocates of which included not only Hubmaier but also the Roman church and Luther, carries with it the doctrine of *communicatio idiomatum* (communication of attributes). This doctrine postulates that every necessary attribute of the divine Λόγος, such as omniscience, omnipotence, and (most importantly) omnipresence or ubiquity, are transferred over to the human nature of Jesus, such that the humanity of Jesus was also omniscient, omnipotent, omnipresent or ubiquitous, and the like. If Jesus' humanity, like his divinity, is present everywhere, then no theological barriers prevent that humanity from being specially present in the Eucharist.[32] However, the Antiochene view denies any flow of attributes from Christ's divine to his human nature.[33] As a result, the sixteenth-century advocates of this latter Christology, including Zwingli, the Anabaptists, and Calvin, maintained that for Christ to be fully human, his human nature must be finite in knowledge, power, and presence. Since Christ's human nature can only be locally present (*i.e.* existing at any one moment at one place and one time) on this model, therefore, upon his ascension Jesus' physical body resides solely in heaven at the right hand of God the Father and cannot be

27. Pelikan, *Emergence of Tradition*, 230, 247-49.
28. John N. D. Kelly, *Early Christian Doctrines*, 2nd ed. (New York: Harper, 1960), 281.
29. Pelikan, *Emergence of Tradition*, 231, 251-55.
30. Kelly, *Doctrines*, 281.
31. Pelikan, *Reformation*, 160-62.
32. Robert S. Franks, *A History of the Doctrine of the Work of Christ*, reprint (Eugene, Ore.: Wipf and Stock, 2001), 291.
33. Pelikan, *Reformation*, 158-59.

specially present in the Eucharist.[34] Accordingly, the ubiquity of Christ's human nature played a vital role in Hubmaier's conception of the Lord's Supper.

In his three Eucharistic treatises, Hubmaier develops the implications of Christ's ubiquity in a polemical fashion against the views of his Catholic, Magisterial, and Anabaptist contemporaries. Rempel perceives that these figures serve for Hubmaier as "foils" and "stepping-stones toward convictions that transcended all of them."[35] Not surprisingly in light of his Christology, Hubmaier rejected the sacramentarianism[36] of Zwingli and the Anabaptists and denounced their metaphorical interpretation of the Eucharistic words of institution, *Hoc est [enim] corpus meum*, as sophistry:

> [They] employ the little word *est* for *significat*, that is, *is* for *signifies*, so that: "The bread signifies my body." Such an opinion can never be forced with clear and proper Scriptures. . . . It fails to satisfy the human conscience; it gives more cause for erring and confusing the whole Bible than to satisfying or overcoming the opponents. For if this is the practice, then no one would be sure where *est* (is) stands in the Scripture for *significat* (signifies) or for itself.[37]

However, despite his common adherence to an Alexandrian Christology with Catholicism and Luther, Hubmaier repudiated both the Roman and Lutheran doctrines derived from it. Hubmaier first denies the Catholic doctrine of transubstantiation[38] as an unbiblical invention of Aquinas:

> The dream and Thomistic interpolation of these wicked people contends. . . . that the bread in its essence is transformed into Christ's flesh

---

34. Franks, *Work of Christ*, 314-16.

35. Rempel, *Lord's Supper*, 45.

36. The sacramentarian view teaches that the Supper is a symbolic reminder of Christ's passion and death in which Christ is not physically present; Spitz, *Reformation*, 147.

37. Hubmaier, *Ein einfältiger Unterricht*, 291; the German is quoted in footnote 101, page 30.

38. The doctrine of transubstantiation maintains that when the words of consecration are spoken by the officiating priest over the bread and wine, their substances are transformed into the respective substances of the physical body and blood of Christ, with only the accidents of bread and wine remaining. Hence, the elements still looks, feels, and tastes like bread and wine, although the "breadness" and "wineness" have been eliminated. Pelikan, *Reformation*, 57-59.

and the wine in its essence into his blood through the words of institution . . . but the bread and wine cease to be essentially bread and wine . . . the nature and matter of the bread and wine have absolutely no further existence, are annihilated, and vanish. Therefore, neither the matter nor the essential forms of the bread or wine remain, but only the two kinds of attributes. [They] say that indeed, it is true that as often as one performs the Mass a miracle happens daily, namely, that the attributes or the accidents remain without the matter. . . . If you had forever, you could not prove this with the Scripture.[39]

In a play on words between "monstrance" and "monster," Hubmaier castigates the perceived idolatry of worshiping the consecrated host in the monstrances as God:

They are well called . . . monstrances, from monstrosity, from the sea monster that emerges out of the sea, as John describes in Revelation. For how can a disgusting monster or sea monster be created and presented to us so that we view and worship an earthly thing as a heavenly good, a perishable thing as an eternal, a creature as the Creator and regard God himself as in the monsters and monstrances? *O monstra, monstra, monstrastis nobis monstruosa monstra* (O monster, monster, present to us the monstrous monsters).[40]

Employing apocalyptic overtones, Hubmaier thus separates himself decisively from medieval Catholic Eucharistic theology. The Radical Reformer

---

39. "Diser ellenden leütt traum vnnd Thomistischer zůsatz lauttet. . . . das Brot werde wesentlich verwandelt in das fleysch durch die wort, vnd der wein wesenlich in das blůt . . . sunder brot vnd wein hören auff zůsein wesenlich brot vnd wein . . . das wesen vnnd Matery des Brots vnd weins werdent gar zenichtig, anihiliert vnnd verschwindent. Also das weder matery noch wesenliche form des brots oder weins da bleybe, sunder allain dero bayderlay gestallten. [Die] sagent, ja, jm sey also, derhalb als offt man Meeß halt, so geschehe ein teglich wunderzaychen, das die anheng oder accidentia on ein Matery enthalten werdent. . . . Welcher in die ewigkeit mit der schrifft nit mag erhalten werden." Hubmaier, *Ein einfältiger Unterricht*, 290, 295.

40. "Es hayssen wol . . . Monstranntzen, a Mönstro, von eim mör wunnder, das auß dem mör kumbt, wie Johannes schreibt in der Offenbarung. Wann wie mag ein greülicher Monstrum oder Mörwunder gemacht vnnd vns angezaigt werden, dann so wir ein jrrdisch ding für ein Hymmelisch gůtt, ein zergengklichs für ein ewigs, ein creatur für den schöpffer vnnd für Gott selber in den Monstern vnnd Monstrantzen sehen vnd anbetten. O monstra, monstra, monstrastis nobis monstruosa monstra." Ibid., 302.

then proceeds to charge Luther's doctrine of consubstantiation[41] with mis-representing the sacred text: "[That] bread and wine do not pass out of exis-tence, but . . . the flesh and blood are hidden under the forms of bread and wine. . . . one must not toy with the Scriptures haughtily in this manner, or we might as well let the ark of God quickly fall into the mud with the mali-cious oxen."[42] As we will see, Hubmaier rejected the Catholic and Lutheran positions because he believed that both had misplaced that which bears the real presence of Christ and mistaken the vehicle of the real presence for the bearer of that presence.

In erecting the doctrinal pillars necessary for what he perceived as cor-rectly identifying that which bears the real presence, Hubmaier turned to *die Schülen* (the schools)[43] and reappropriated their distinction between the de-finitive presence of God and the repletive presence of God. This dichotomy, originally formulated by Anselm in his *Proslogium* and *Monologium*,[44] maintained that God, who is by nature a timeless and spaceless spiritual be-ing, is differently present in various realms of existence depending on the quality of his power of operation manifested therein.[45] For Anselm, God's definitive presence denotes his omnipotent and unapproachably glorious dwelling in the heavenly realm of spirits.[46] Conversely, God's repletive presence signifies his filling of all space-time locations (*i.e.* all points within

---

41. The doctrine of consubstantiation holds that when the words of institu-tion are spoken over the bread and wine, they simultaneously contain, respec-tively, the substance of the physical body of Christ coupled with the substance of bread and the substance of the physical blood of Christ coupled with the sub-stance of wine. By way of explanation, Luther (*Babylonian Captivity*, 36:43-44) gave the famous analogy of a piece of hot iron: just as every part contains simul-taneously the substance of heat and the substance of iron, so Christ is "in, with, and under" the elements. Pelikan, *Reformation*, 200-01.

42. "Brot vnd wein hören nit also auff, sunder . . . vnder den gstalten des Brots vnd weins sey fleysch vnd blůt verborgen. . . . es gilt nit also mit der schrifft gaylen, oder wir wurden die Arch Gotes gar bald mit den můtwilligen Ochsen in das kott fellen." Hubmaier, *Ein einfältiger Unterricht*, 290, 292.

43. Hubmaier, *Das andere Büchlein*, 417.

44. I am not claiming that Hubmaier was literarily dependent on Anselm for this concept, as Peter Lombard, Bonaventure, Aquinas, and several other Scho-lastics with whom Hubmaier was familiar made use of it; rather, I am simply pointing out that Hubmaier employed an Anselmian distinction. See Etienne Gilson, *History of Christian Philosophy in the Middle Ages* (London: Sheed and Ward, 1955), 126-30.

45. Anselm, *Proslogium*, 18, 24-25.

46. Ibid., 26.

the universe) without being restricted in any way by space or time.[47] On Anselm's view, in much the same way as the human soul or mind is not spatially located but is wholly present at all points in its physical body, so God, the Supreme Mind, is not spatio-temporally located but is wholly present at all points within the universe.[48] Synthesizing this Anselmian taxonomy with his Alexandrian belief in the *communicatio idiomatum*, Hubmaier argues that since Christ is the second person of the Godhead and his human nature possesses the same attributes as his divine nature, the categories of definitive and repletive presence equally apply to Christ's divinity and humanity after the ascension.[49] Thus, while Christ's physical body is definitively present at the right hand of God the Father, his body is repletively present at all points in the space-time universe without being limited by it. Hubmaier summarizes his twofold model of the presence of Christ "bodily according to his humanity": on the one hand, "he has a definite place 'in heaven, in heaven,' and not everywhere"; on the other hand, "because the Godhead is everywhere . . . the Lord Jesus is with [the visible church] himself . . . bodily . . . until the end of the world."[50] At this point, Hubmaier discloses that which bears the real presence in his doctrine of the Eucharist through an exegesis of Paul's Mars Hill sermon at Athens. From Acts 17:24, "The God who made the world and everything in it is the Lord of heaven and earth and does not live in temples built by hands," Hubmaier formulates one negative and one positive inference. Equating the Catholic tabernacles and monstrances, in which the consecrated hosts were stored and venerated, with the "temples built by hands," Hubmaier declares, "One cannot enclose Christ in the small stone-houses or in the monstrances."[51] From this inability to contain Christ,

---

47. Anselm, *Monologium*, 59.

48. Justo L. Gonzalez, *A History of Christian Thought: From Augustine to the Eve of the Reformation* (Nashville: Abingdon, 1971), 163.

49. Sachsse, *Hubmaier als Theologe*, 206-07.

50. "Er nach der menschhait leiblich. Er hat ein bstimbte stat (jm himel, Jm himel) vnd mit allenthalb . . . denn die Gothait allenthalb ist . . . der Herr Jesu ist durch [der eüsserlichen Kirchen] sein . . . leiblich . . . biß zů end der welt." Hubmaier, *Bann*, 370. As illustrated by Brunotte and Weber (*Kirchenlexikon*, 1:1163), *bstimbte stat* is a sixteenth-century German translation of the Latin *praesentia definitiva* (definitive presence). Note that in *Ein einfältiger Unterricht*, 290, Hubmaier uses the term *gsättigt stat*, which Brunotte and Weber (*Kirchenlexikon*, 1:1164) show to be a sixteenth-century German translation of the Latin *praesentia repletiva* (repletive presence), to delineate the mode in which Christ's body is present "everywhere."

51. "Man Christum nit inn stainene heüßlin oder in Monstrantzen beschliessen müge." Hubmaier, *Ein einfältiger Unterricht*, 302.

Hubmaier reasons, it follows "plainly and explicitly that the bread is bread and the wine is wine rather than flesh and blood, as people have so long believed."[52] However, Hubmaier then positively identifies the human partakers of the bread and wine as the bearers of the real presence: "In temples built by hands, etc. Here you see again that God will not live in temples built by hands, but in temples built out of living stones. As Paul writes, 'Do you not know that you are the temple of God?'"[53] In some sense, then, the church, the members of which constitute living stones who are being built into a temple, are filled in a special sacramental way with the physical presence of Christ at the Supper. Hubmaier proceeds to reinforce this conceptual framework with doctrinal substance by directing his attention to the Johannine account of the Last Supper.

Theological Development of Hubmaier's Eucharist

Whereas Luther, Zwingli, and the Anabaptists found the exegetical substantiation for their conceptions of the Eucharist largely (if not exclusively) in the Synoptic Gospels,[54] Hubmaier elucidated his view of Christ's presence in the Eucharist by appealing primarily to the more lengthy version of Jesus' final meal with his disciples in the Gospel of John (chapters 13-17), with which he harmonized the Pauline form of the words of institution and instructions concerning the Supper (1 Cor. 11:23-34). Rempel, in his analysis of Hubmaier's Eucharistic doctrine, observes, "Hubmaier was trying to actualize a Christianity whose main tenets were put forth in certain thought patterns originating in the Fourth Gospel. . . . It is the Johannine world and spirit which left their mark on him and gave him the structures of his thought."[55] Hubmaier begins with an exegesis of John 17:26, "I have made you known to them, and will continue to make you known in order that the love you have for me may be in them and that I myself may be in them."[56]

---

52. "wol vnd aigentlich, das hie brot brot vnnd wein wein sey vnd nit fleisch vnd blût, wie man lange zeit gelaubt hat." Hubmaier, *Form des Nachtmals Christi*, 361.

53. "Jn Templen mit Henden gmacht etc. Da sihestu abermals, das Gott nit in gemaurten Templen wonen wil, sunder in denen, so auß lebendigen stainen gemacht sind. Als Paulus schreibt: wißt jr nit, das jr der Tempel Gottes sind." Hubmaier, *Ein einfältiger Unterricht*, 302.

54. Luther, *Babylonian Captivity*, 36:33-48; Zwingli, *Lord's Supper*, 188-98, 235-38; Friedmann, *Theology of Anabaptism*, 138-42.

55. Rempel, *Lord's Supper*, 84-85.

56. Hubmaier, *Form des Nachtmals Christi*, 356.

Since this quote from the so-called high priestly prayer comprised the last words the Johannine Jesus spoke at the Last Supper, Hubmaier contends that it not only directly pertains to the Supper, but also describes precisely what takes place when the Eucharist is celebrated. The reformer explains, "So the bread that we break means and commemorates the communion of Christ's body with us, that he is our own," and "he gave himself for us through the drink of the communion of his blood"; hence "the body and blood of Christ communes with us all."[57] Here Hubmaier, appearing to distance himself from the Zwinglian and Anabaptist position that the Eucharist solely commemorates Christ's presence, maintains that the Supper is both a commemoration and far more than a commemoration. It also means the communion of Christ's body with the recipients; that is to say, through participation in the bread and wine, the recipients literally commune with the physical body and blood of Christ. This communion, as we shall see, entails an ontological change in the participants, which Hubmaier attempts to justify by combining the preceding exegesis of John 17:26 with his interpretation of the Pauline words of institution.[58]

Hubmaier's most precisely formulated definition of the meaning of the Eucharist springs from his viewing the Pauline words of institution, "This is my body given for you; do this in my remembrance" and "This cup is the new covenant in my blood; do this, as often as you drink it, in my remembrance" (1 Cor. 11:24-25), through Johannine lenses. This is the crucial formulation: "the body of Christ in remembrance" (*der leib Christi in der gedechtnuß*) and "the blood of Christ in remembrance" (*das blůt Christi in der gedechtnuß*), that is, "a living remembrance" (*ein lebendige gedechtnuß*).[59] To grasp the subtleties of this conception fully, we need to examine all three of his Eucharistic treatises at once, since they all follow the same logical order.[60] Moreover, it should be noted that his two doctrinal treatises

---

57. "Dann das brot, das wir brechen, ist inn der bedeůtung vnd inn der widergedechtnůß die gemainschafft des leybs Christi mit vns, das er vnser aygen sey . . . er ye den selben fůr vns hab dar geben durch das tranck dz gemainschaffts seins blůts. . . . der leyb vnd dz blůt Christi vns allen gemain ist." Hubmaier, *Messe*, 103.

58. Rempel, *Lord's Supper*, 53.

59. Hubmaier, *Ein einfältiger Unterricht*, 293, 298; Hubmaier, *Form des Nachtmals Christi*, 358, 362.

60. This may be due to the fact that the first drafts of *Ein einfältiger Unterricht* and *Eine Form des Nachtmals Christi*, both published at Nikolsburg in 1526, were composed along with *Etliche Schlußreden vom Unterricht der Messe* in 1524. This is suggested by a comment Hubmaier made in his 1524 letter to Oecolampadius regarding two drafts not yet meant for print: "We have written

on the Mass (a term which he uses interchangeably with Eucharist and Lord's Supper), *Etliche Schlußreden vom Unterricht der Messe* and *Ein einfältiger Unterricht*, finds practical outworking in *Eine Form des Nachtmals Christi*, a liturgy which often amplifies theological points made in the two doctrinal treatises. The first thing to be underscored regarding the words of institution is their placement in his liturgy. In contrast to the historic ecclesiastical practice of consecrating each element before the congregation receives it,[61] Hubmaier instructs the president to utter the sacramental formulas ("This is my body . . . " and "This cup is the new covenant . . . ") immediately after the congregation has respectively eaten the bread and drunk the wine.[62] Hubmaier defends this change with a rare citation of Matthew 26 and Mark 14, in which Jesus declared, "This is my blood," after the disciples drank the wine:

> Here we observe, that just as Mark relates the words of Christ, so Matthew records them in the same way. We must consider this fact alone: that in Matthew, Christ ordered his disciples to all drink from the cup before he spoke the words of consecration over the cup. Likewise, Mark reports that only after they all drank from the cup did Christ say, "This is my blood."[63]

As to the power exerted by the sacramental formulas, Rempel observes that Hubmaier retained the traditional understanding of the word as the primal agency of God's action;[64] thus Hubmaier concurred with Augustine's maxim, "When the word is joined to the sign (*signum*), the sacrament is ef-

---

twenty theses on the Eucharist (an accurate description of *Ein einfältiger Unterricht*), also several rules on preparing the table of the Lord (an accurate description of *Eine Form des Nachtmals Christi)*" (Scripsimus de eucharistia viginti conclusions, item aliquot regulas de paranda mensa Domini); Hubmaier, *Letter to Oecolampadius,* 342.

61. Pelikan, *Emergence of Tradition,* 236-38.

62. Hubmaier, *Form des Nachtmals Christi,* 362.

63. "Hie est zů mercken, wie Marcus die wort Christi beschreibt, also sinnd sy auch durch Matheum anzaygt. Allainn das eben zů ermessen ist, das Christus beuolhen hat seinen Jungern, das sy all trincken sollent, ee vnnd er die wort der Consecrierung vber den Kelch gesprochen im Matheo. Also bezeügt da Marcus, das sy all darauß getruncken haben, vnd darnach hat Christus erst gsagt: Das ist mein Blůt." Hubmaier, *Ein einfältiger Unterricht,* 299.

64. Rempel, *Lord's Supper,* 46.

fected."[65] Consistent with his Alexandrian Christology, Hubmaier regarded the Eucharistic *res* as the physical body of Christ: "When Christ commands, 'Take and eat, this is my body which is given for you,' he means his mortal body, as he himself suffered for us."[66] However, the reformer departed from previous sacramental thought by proposing that the *signa* were the recipients of the Supper while partaking of the bread and wine rather than the elements themselves: "We all are one bread and one body—we all, who have communion in one bread and one drink . . . and not the bread on the table which he gave them to eat . . . and not the wine in the cup."[67] Such language seems to imply that the transformation which takes place in Hubmaier's new order of the Supper is that of the congregation rather than of the elements.[68] This inference is strengthened by the fact that three times in Hubmaier's liturgical comments and prayers, the participants are referred to as "the body of Christ" (*der leib Christi*), while the description is avoided in reference to the bread.[69]

Proceeding to his exegesis of the words of institution, one of Hubmaier's crucial hermeneutical decisions is to give priority to the Pauline version, which contains the longer ending ("do this in my remembrance"), over the shorter Synoptic versions. In light of Luther's hermeneutical principle that obscure passages must be interpreted in light of plain ones, which found wide acceptance throughout the Radical Reformation,[70] Hubmaier insists that it is the totality of Christ's words, interpreted by the longer ending, which yields their true meaning:

> Where several Scriptural passages are cryptic or treat a topic quite briefly, which often lead to disputes, one should resolve these by appealing to other Scriptural passages that are clearer or more apparent, albeit concerning the same topic, and placing them alongside the cryptic or brief passages insofar as this is possible. One should ignite these passages together, allowing them to burn like a bundle of several wax

---

65. Hubmaier, *Messe*, 103; Augustine, *Exposition of the Psalms*, in *Corpus christianorum, Series latina* (Turnhout, Belgium: Brepols, 1953), 38:8.

66. "So Christus Pott: nement, essend, das ist mein leyb, der für etlich geben wirt, bedeüt er seinen sterblichen leyb, dann er selb . . . für vns gelitten hat." Hubmaier, *Messe*, 102.

67. "Wir vil sein ain brot, vnd wir vil seind ain leyb, wir alle, so in ainem brot vnd inn ainem tranck gemainschafft halten . . . vnnd nit das thüsch brot, das er inen zü essen darbot . . . vnd nit den wein im trinckgeschir." Ibid., 102-03.

68. Rempel, *Lord's Supper*, 51.

69. Hubmaier, *Form des Nachtmals Christi*, 363-64.

70. Williams, *Radical Reformation*, 338.

candles in order that a shining and clear light of the Scriptures burst forth. Now all people must confess that Matthew and Mark, in their presentation of Christ's words when he handled the bread, were *micrologi*, namely, indicating his words in the briefest way. . . . [But] Paul, by the special providence of God, set forth Christ's words at the Supper far more completely. This is why we want to . . . place them together and, then after doing so, draw from them a perfect conclusion.[71]

Hubmaier combines the Pauline words "in remembrance" with the standard "this is my body/blood" to arrive at his Eucharistic conception of "the body/blood of Christ in remembrance."[72] To explain what this formula means, Hubmaier appeals to his Anselmian dichotomy between the definitive and repletive presence of Christ's physical body. At the respective moments that believers, in the act of remembrance, eat the bread and drink the wine, Christ, whose humanity is definitively present (*bstimbte stat*) in heaven, fills the believers with the repletive presence (*gsättigt stat*) of his body and blood in a special sacramental way.[73] However, Hubmaier refuses to elaborate on how this sacramental repletive presence differs from the typical repletive presence of Christ's humanity except to confess that such a matter is a mystery that no human can fathom: "Since you discern that this matter of the Supper is so lofty and significant, we can neither apprehend nor understand it with human reason."[74] Reinforcing his model of the real presence in the Supper, Hubmaier writes, "The eating of bread is the body of Christ really,

---

71. "Wo etlich Sprich der Schrifften dunckel sein oder mit gar kurtzen worten fürgetragen, darauß spen erfolgen mechten, soll man die auff zůlösen annder geschrifften, so etwas hayters oder Klarers sind, doch in gleicher sach, neben den tuncklen oder verkürtzten redden setzen, als vil man jr gehaben mage, vnnd soll man sy gleich wie vil wachs liechter zůsamen gwunden mit ainander anzinden vnd brinnen lassen, so wirdt ein heller, klarer schein der gschrifft herfür brechen. Nun můß aber ye Mennigklich bekennen, das Matheus vnnd Marcus in disen worten, die Christus gebraucht, als er das brot in die hannd genommen, Micrologj seyendt, das ist, sy habent sein wort auff das kürtzest anngezaigt. . . . [Aber] Paulus, die seind auß sunderer fürsehung Gotes in disen worten des Nachtmals vil reychlicher, derhalb wir jr . . . zůsamen setzen wöllen vnnd darnach ein volkhommen vrtayl darauß beschliessenn." Hubmaier, *Ein einfältiger Unterricht*, 292.

72. Ibid., 293.

73. Ibid., 290; Hubmaier, *Bann*, 370.

74. "Die weyl jr sehet, das dise Materj von dem Nachtmal so hoch vnnd schwer ist, das wir sy auß menschlicher vernunfft nit ergründen noch begreyffenn mügent." Hubmaier, *Ein einfältiger Unterricht*, 303.

but just in the celebrated remembrance . . . and the drinking of wine . . . [is] the blood of Christ in the celebrated remembrance."[75] Notice here that not the bread but the person engaged in the sacramental act of bread-eating bears the body of Christ, and not the wine but the person engaged in the sacramental act of wine-drinking bears the blood of Christ. For this reason Hubmaier declares, "Just as we now have communion with one another in this bread and wine of the Christ meal . . . the body and blood of Christ communes with us all."[76]

At this juncture in his three Eucharistic treatises, Hubmaier emphasizes that the transformation which occurs at the Supper is ontological. Unlike Zwingli and the Anabaptists, who refer to the church as the body of Christ in a symbolic sense,[77] Hubmaier employs theologically precise linguistic handles, such as the noun *Wesen* (nature or essence) and the adjective *wesentlich* (essentially or substantially), to argue that an ontological shift followed the consumption of the respective elements. Upon this consumption, the members of the visible church became the *res*, the physical body and blood of Christ, to which the *signa* of bread and wine were pointing.[78] Concerning the relationship between the external elements and Christ's human nature, of which the faithful internally partake, Hubmaier writes, "We maintain that the bread and wine of the Christ meal are outward word symbols of an inward Christian nature (*inwendigen Christenlichen wesens*) here on earth, in which . . . the body and blood of Christ is my body and blood."[79] To make the identity of this nature explicit, Hubmaier goes on to define the *inwendige Christenliche wesen* as the state where Christ's person "is essentially and bodily present" (*mensch wesenlich vnnd leiblich ist*).[80] Therefore Hubmaier clearly affirms that the bread and wine are outer signs of the human essence of Christ present on earth. In order to distance himself from the possible objection that the participants at the moment of reception, who

75. "Das Brotessen der Leib Christi sey wesenlich, sonder allain in der gehaltnen Gedechnuß . . . vnnd das trannck trincken . . . [ist] das Blût Christi in der gehaltnen gedechtnuß." Ibid., 297-98.

76. "Wie wir nun in disem brot vnd tranck deß christmal mit ainander gemainschafft haben . . . der leyb vnd dz blût Christi vns allen gemain ist." Hubmaier, *Messe*, 103.

77. Zwingli, *Lord's Supper*, 237; Clasen, *Social History*, 114-15.

78. Hubmaier, *Messe*, 104; Hubmaier, *Ein einfältiger Unterricht*, 303.

79. "Beschlieslich volgt, dz das prot vnd der wein des christmals vßwendig wortzaichen seind ains inwendigen Christenlichen wesens hie auff erden, inn welchem . . . der leyb vnd dz plût Christi mein leyb vnd main plût . . . ist." Hubmaier, *Messe*, 104.

80. Hubmaier, *Ein einfältiger Unterricht*, 300.

share in Christ's human essence, could, like the Catholic host, be worshiped as divine,[81] Hubmaier again draws upon the distinction between the definitive and repletive presence of Christ's physical body. Only the definitive presence of Christ's body, which is in heaven and from which the repletive presence emanates, is for Hubmaier worthy of worship: "Christ Jesus ascended into heaven and is seated at the right hand of God his heavenly Father. . . . since Stephen saw him there, it is there that we desire to seek, reverence, and worship him."[82] Hubmaier repeats the same sentiment in his commentary on the Apostles' Creed: "Hence it is unnecessary, my merciful Christ, to worship you either here or there, as indeed you are present neither in bread nor in wine, since you are found seated at your heavenly Father's right hand, where the saintly Stephen also saw you and worshiped you."[83] However, the repletive presence, of which the sacramental presence in the Supper is a mode, is qualitatively lower and therefore not appropriately worshiped.[84] To worship the repletive presence of Christ at all, much less in a believer, Hubmaier denounces as an "abominable idolatry" which must be avoided "so that the Word of God will not thereby be blasphemed as a result of you."[85] To further illustrate the difference between the definitive and repletive presence, Hubmaier uses two biblical metaphors: the Johannine analogy of the vine and the branches and the Pauline analogy of the head and the remainder of Christ's body.

Central to Hubmaier's conception of the real presence is his novel exegesis of the parable of the vine and the branches (John 15:1-8). Since this parable was spoken by the Johannine Jesus at the Last Supper, Hubmaier contends that it discloses the meaning of what takes place as the faithful partake of the Eucharistic wine: "John 15: All these words, which Christ spoke

---

81. As the Council of Trent pronounced concerning the host, "There is, therefore, no room left for doubt that all the faithful of Christ . . . offer in veneration the worship of *latria* which is due to the true God, to this most Holy Sacrament"; Waterworth, *Canons and Decrees*, 268.

82. "Christus Jesus auffgefaren sey in die himmel, sitze zů der gerechten Gottes seins Himmelischen vatters. . . . dasselbs hat in Stephanus gesehen, daselbs wöllen wir Jn suchen, eeren vnnd anbeten." Hubmaier, *Ein einfältiger Unterricht*, 303.

83. "Derhalben ist on nott, mein sennfftmůtiger Christe, dich weder hye noch dortt, ja, weder in brott noch weinn, annzebetten, denn da finndt man dich sitzennd zů der gerechtenn deinns hymelischen Vatters, wie dich auch der heilig Stephanus gesehen hat, vnd dich anbettet." Hubmaier, *Die zwölf Artikel*, 217.

84. Windhorst, *Täuferisches Taufverständnis*, 246.

85. "diser greülichen Abgötterey. . . . darmit das Götlich wort durch dich nit also gelestert." Hubmaier, *Bann*, 370, 372.

at the Last Supper, indicate this . . . a pointer to the spiritual significance of the pouring out of the wine."[86] The vine, which is the source of existence for the branches, alludes to Christ as he is definitively present in heaven.[87] The branches, which are distinct from the vine but still bear the physical nature of the vine, symbolizes the sacramental mode of the repletive presence.[88] Hubmaier declares that as churches collectively and believers individually drink the wine, they respectively become branches, which Christ "brings to life so that they begin to live, turn green, and bear fruit,"[89] and the grapes on those branches.[90] Just as each particular grape and its corresponding branch possess the same physical nature as the vine itself but are distinct from the vine, Hubmaier reasons, so each individual recipient and the church in general possess the physical nature of Christ in the Eucharist but are distinct from Christ himself.[91] Hubmaier supplements this point by appealing to Paul's imagery of the church as a body, the head of which is Christ (1 Cor. 10:14-17). Accordingly, Hubmaier posits that the head of the body, without which the remainder cannot live, represents the definitive presence of Christ's humanity at the right hand of God the Father, while the remainder of the body denotes the sacramental form of the repletive presence.[92] Hence as Hubmaier explains in his liturgy, believers share in the physical presence of the body of Christ, although the head of that body is in heaven: "All-beloved brothers and sisters in the Lord: By thus eating the bread, we now . . . have all become one body, and our head is Christ . . . who is there in heaven."[93] In the same way that he connected the parable of the vine and branches with the sacramental wine, Hubmaier links the metaphor of the body with the sacramental bread by appealing to 1 Corinthians 10:16-17, "And is not the bread that we break a participation in the body of Christ? Because there is one loaf, we, who are many, are one body, for we all par-

---

86. "Joan. 15. Darauff geent alle wort, die Christus ob dem letzen Nachtmal geredt hat . . . außgiessung des weins geystlich bedeüttet vnd anzaigt." Hubmaier, *Form des Nachtmals Christi*, 358.

87. Windhorst, *Täuferisches Taufverständnis*, 248-49.

88. Sachsse, *Hubmaier als Theologe*, 207-08.

89. "lebendig, das sy anfahen leben, grünen vnd frücht bringen." Hubmaier, *Summe*, 111.

90. Hubmaier, *Messe*, 103.

91. Windhorst, *Täuferisches Taufverständnis*, 250.

92. Sachsse, *Hubmaier als Theologe*, 208.

93. "Jr aller liebsten brüeder vnd schwester in dem herren. Wie wir nun yetz all mit dieser essung des brots...[wir] seind all . . . ain leib worden, vnd vnser haubt ist Christus . . . der da ist in den himelen." Hubmaier, *Form des Nachtmals Christi*, 363.

take of the one loaf."[94] In his exegesis of this text, Hubmaier seems to indicate that the loaf signifies the sacramental presence of the physical body of Christ in which the church participates:

> One should always pay greater attention and render more seriousness to the things symbolized by the word symbols than to the symbols themselves . . . as we . . . remember by the bread how he, Christ, was our Christ, and how we . . . all are one bread and one body—we all, who have communion in one bread and . . . the communion of the body of Christ with us.[95]

When the church consumes the one loaf, of which each member of the church eats a fragment, the unified church shares in the nature of the one physical body of Christ, in which each member comprises a unique "little kernel" (*kernlin*).[96] Since every body part and combination of parts (excluding the head) has the same nature as the head but is distinct from it, every believer and church share the same human nature as Christ but are distinct from him.[97] Hubmaier substantiates his doctrine of the real presence by appealing to the Pauline consequences of unworthily partaking the Eucharist. The Radical Reformer maintains that Paul refers to the bread as bread and the wine as wine both before and after their consecration in order to show that the consecration effected no change in the elements. But since unrepentant sinners who consume the bread and wine bear the physical body and blood of Christ, thereby literally abusing the human nature of Christ and provoking the divine wrath, Paul declares them guilty of the body and blood of Christ and accuses them of failing to discern the fact that they are participating in the body of the Lord.

> Observe how plainly and clearly Paul writes, "Whoever now eats this bread and drinks the cup of the Lord unworthily is guilty of the body and blood of the Lord." Look here, all who want to see, that . . . the drink [is] called a fruit of the vine before and after the words of consecration. So Paul calls the bread bread and the cup a drink as well, and

---

94. Ibid., 358; Hubmaier, *Messe*, 103.

95. "Soll man inn allweg mer vnnd ernstlicher achtnemen der ding, so durch die wortzaichen bedeüt seind, dann die zaichen . . . alls brot . . . dabey wir gedencken, wie er, Christus, vnser Christus gewesen, vnd wir auch . . . vil sein ain brot, vnd wir vil seind ain leyb, wir alle, so in ainem brot gemainschafft halten vnd . . . die gemainschafft des leybs Christi mit vns." Hubmaier, *Messe*, 103.

96. Ibid.

97. Windhorst, *Täuferisches Taufverständnis*, 251.

states that whoever eats this bread and drinks this drink unworthily is guilty of the body and blood of the Lord, rather than being guilty of the bread and wine. . . . "As he does not discern the body of the Lord": O dear pious Christians, the bread is not the body of Christ and the wine is not his blood, however, because we are the true body and blood of Christ . . . at the Supper of Christ, we shall be concerned . . . that the physical presence of Christ is not held with contempt or heedlessness, but rather with the utmost sincerity, devotion, and zeal according to the order of the institution of Christ. For truly, where we fail to differentiate the Supper of Christ from other eating and drinking, we eat and drink judgment upon ourselves, just as Paul harshly rebuked the Corinthians for the same offense. Let each one examine himself at this point and consider the holy and solemn institution of the Supper of Christ, since it is not child's play. Thus anyone who scorns or abuses the ceremonies of the new covenant scorns and abuses Christ himself.[98]

As the foregoing evidence indicates, Hubmaier applied the Anselmian dichotomy of definitive and repletive presence to the Johannine and Pauline analogies to craft a doctrine in which the faithful share the human nature of Christ in the Supper without being deified and without surrendering their own distinctive characters or natures. Insofar as each recipient, while partaking of the Eucharist, has both Christ's human nature and his or her own hu-

---

98. "Sihe wie gar haytter vnnd klar schreibt Paulus: Wölcher nun vnwirdigklich von disem Brot esset vnd von dem Kelch des Herren trinckt, der ist schuldig an dem leyb vnnd Blůt des Herrens. Hie merck, wer mercken will, wie . . . das Tranck ein gewechß des Weinstocks vor vnnd nach den worten der Consecrierung genent. Also haisset auch Paulus das Brot Brot, vnd den Kelch ein Tranck, vnd wölcher vnwirdigklich von disem Brott esse vnd von disem Tranck trincke, der sey schuldig an dem leib vnd blůt des Herrens, vnd sagt nit am Brott vnnd am Wein. . . . Das er nit vnnderschaidet den leib des herrens. O lieben frommen Christen, wiewol das Brot nit der Leyb Christi ist, noch der weinn sein Blůt, yedoch als vnns ist dem waren leyb vnnd blůt Christi . . . ann dem Nachtmal Christi, vill soll vnns gelegenn sein . . . darmit dasselb nit mit spott oder leüchtfertigkayt, sunder mit grossem Ernst, andacht vnnd innbrünstigkait gehalten werde, nach ordnung der einsetzung Christi. Oder fürwar, wo wir nit vnderschayden das Nachtmal Christi vonn dem anndern esenn vnnd trincken, werdend wir vnns selbs das gericht essen vnnd trincken, wie auch Paulus derhalb die Chorinther strenngklich gestrafft hatt. Lůg ein yedlicher mensch da zů jm selbs vnnd betracht die Hochwirdigen ernstliche einsetzunng des Nachtmals von Christo, wann es ist nit Kinnds Spil. Wann wölcher die Ceremonien des newen Testaments veracht oder mißbraucht, der verachtet vnnd mißbraucht Christum selber." Hubmaier, *Ein einfältiger Unterricht*, 300-01.

man nature simultaneously, Hubmaier's doctrine of the Eucharist is a literal consubstantiation (*i.e.* the possession of two natures at once), in which each recipient is consubstantiated into the humanity of Christ. Contra Luther's doctrine of consubstantiation, in which the Eucharistic elements are consubstantiated into Christ's humanity,[99] Hubmaier maintains that believers in particular and the church in general are consubstantiated into Christ's body and blood as they partake of the bread and wine.

Ethical Implications of the Lord's Supper

As a result of their being the bearers of the human nature of Christ in a special sacramental way, the church in general and its members in particular assume a profound ethical responsibility in Hubmaier's conception of the Lord's Supper. Just as Hubmaier's Alexandrian Christology furnishes the basis for the doctrine of the real presence, so his Bernardian doctrine of the interaction between grace and free will furnishes the basis for the ethical dimension of his Eucharist. Alongside of the reformer's Christological emphasis in the Supper, Rempel observes that "Hubmaier had a second preoccupation, the human response to grace and the freedom of the will," a conviction which turned him perhaps even further away from Luther and Zwingli than from his former synergistic brand of Catholicism.[100] Contrary to the Lutheran and Zwinglian doctrine of intrinsically efficacious grace, in which God's grace premoves the human will to perform spiritual good,[101] Hubmaier insisted that divine grace was extrinsically efficacious, such that grace empowers the person to perform spiritual good if she or he freely wills to do so: "[God] does nothing without your consent so that your goodness would not be from compulsion but from your own free will."[102] Because human nature possesses a free will, it is possible for people to accept and fruitfully use the grace given to them. When applied to the Eucharist, Hubmaier's understanding of grace leads to a difference between what I will call "potential grace" and "actual grace." During the time that believers share in Christ's human nature, Christ grants them a measure or supply of grace

---

99. Luther, *Babylonian Captivity*, 36:43-44.

100. Rempel, *Lord's Supper*, 44.

101. Martin Luther, *Commentary on Galatians* (1519), in Pelikan, *Luther's Works*, 2:503; Huldrych Zwingli, *Treatise on Providence*, in Fritz Blanke, Oskar Farner, and Rudolf Pfister, eds., *Zwingli-Hauptschriften* (Zürich: Zwingli-Verlag, 1940), XI: 266-68.

102. "An deinen willen wolt [Gott] nichts thon, auf das dein giette nit wer genöttigt, sonder selbs willig." Hubmaier, *Rechenschaft*, 469.

which Hubmaier dubs "die salbung Gottes" (the anointing of God),[103] conceived as a divine substance (rather than God's unmerited favor toward sinners) which cannot operate in and of itself.[104] Such "potential grace" is converted by recipients into "actual grace" when they choose to carry out works of charity toward God and neighbor. Upon this conversion, the actual grace supplies the faithful with the divine energy needed to carry out the works they choose to undertake.[105] Hubmaier summarizes this perceived harmony between grace and free will: "One stands in total freedom to will and to work good or evil. The good one can work is through the anointing of God. . . . [While] believers [are] free and independent by themselves. . . . God works such working in his believers through the inward anointing."[106] Hence we see that for Hubmaier, the Eucharistic elements exhibit, in addition to their Christological symbolism, a deep ethical symbolism. Just as the physical food of bread and wine is transformed by the body into the energy necessary for physical life, so the spiritual food of potential grace dispensed through the vehicles of bread and wine is transformed by the soul into the energy necessary for spiritual life.[107] This is why, in Hubmaier's assessment, reception of the Eucharist, while not necessary for salvation as was believers' baptism, is necessary for living the Christian life and progressing toward sanctification. Thus, no one wanting to live consistently as a disciple of Christ can avoid the Supper.[108] Expressing these sentiments forcefully, Hubmaier writes:

> Now the person who does not want . . . to keep the Supper, he wants neither to believe in Christ nor to live out Christian love and does not want to be a Christian. The degree to which a person is concerned about the flesh and blood, namely, about the suffering and death of Christ Jesus, about the shedding of his rose-colored blood, about the forgiveness of sins, about brotherly love and communion with God the Father, the Son, and the Holy Spirit, yes, the communion of the whole heavenly host and the universal Christian church outside of which there

---

103. Hubmaier, *Form des Nachtmals Christi*, 360.
104. Sachsse, *Hubmaier als Theologe*, 209.
105. Loserth, *Hubmaier*, 275.
106. "Der mensch da steet in aller freyhait ze wöllen vnd wircken gûtes oder böses. Das gût auß der salbung Gottes. . . . den glaubigen selber frey vnd ledig. . . . Gott wirckt solhs wircken in seinen glauigen, durch die innerlichen salbunng." Hubmaier, *Form des Nachtmals Christi*, 360.
107. Windhorst, *Täuferisches Taufverständnis*, 246-47.
108. Mabry, *Doctrine of the Church*, 73, 169.

is no salvation, to precisely the same degree he should be concerned about the bread and the wine of God's table.[109]

Therefore, for Hubmaier the Eucharist assumed a preeminent place in the life of the church. It is probably for this reason that Hubmaier's churches in Waldshut and Nikolsburg practiced the Eucharist weekly,[110] a practice that Calvin desired to adopt in Geneva but was prevented from implementing by the Genevan city government.[111]

The strong ethical thrust in Hubmaier's Eucharist is exemplified by the liturgical details leading up to the reception of the elements. Indeed, Hubmaier subdivided his 1526 liturgy, *Eine Form des Nachtmals Christi*, into two sections: the preparatory gathering, which centered around the *Liebespflicht* (pledge of love), and the Supper itself.[112] Unlike the Anabaptists,[113] Hubmaier retained a fixed liturgical form for the celebration of the Eucharist. The liturgy begins with a call to brothers and sisters to gather around the *Tisch Gottes* (table of God), just as Jesus had arranged with his disciples for the Last Supper.[114] As previously noted in chapter three, Hubmaier replaced the altar with a standard dinner table, at which the faithful would partake of ordinary bread and individual cups of wine. An emphasis on the human disposition in the Supper finds pointed expression throughout the text. For example, the worshipers are exhorted not to chatter frivolously but rather call to mind and confess their sins: "But those who eat . . . should sit together in a disciplined manner without chattering and strife. . . . Every-

---

109. "Wölher sich nun . . . das Nachtmal nit halten, der will Christo nit glauben noch Christenlicher lieb pflegen vnd will nit ein Christ sein. Als vil nun dem menschen gelegen an dem fleisch vnd blūt, ja, an dem leyden vnd sterben Christi Jesu, an seiner rosen farben blūt vergiessung, an verzeihung der sünden, an brüederlicher liebe vnd an der Gmainschafft Gottes vatters vnd Sons vnd des heiligen geyst, ja, an der gemainschafft alles himelischen höres vnnd an der allgmainen Christenlichen Kirchen, ausserhalb der kain hail ist, so vil solle im gelegen sein an dem brot vnnd wein des dischs Gottes." Hubmaier, *Form des Nachtmals Christi*, 359.

110. As seen from the Waldshut period in Hubmaier, *Messe*, 102, and from the Nikolsburg period in Hubmaier, *Form des Nachtmals Christi*, 356. This fact is confirmed by Rempel, *Lord's Supper*, 75.

111. Robert M. Kingdon, "The Genevan Revolution in Public Worship," *Princeton Seminary Bulletin* XX.3 (1999): 279.

112. Hubmaier, *Form des Nachtmals Christi*, 355, 361-62.

113. Rempel, *Lord's Supper*, 74; Friedmann, *Theology of Anabaptism*, 139-40.

114. Hubmaier, *Form des Nachtmals Christi*, 355.

one should start by accusing himself and confessing his sins and realizing his guilt before God."[115] Afterwards Hubmaier, taking great care to ensure that the participants know what they are doing, directs the celebrant to explain one of the Pauline or Johannine Eucharistic passages:

> At this point the priest should sit down with the people and speak to them, expounding the Scriptures regarding Christ, in order that the eyes of all who are assembled together may be opened, which were still somewhat darkened or shut. . . . The minister of the Word may select the 10th or 11th chapter of Paul's First Epistle to the Corinthians, or the 13th, 14th, 15th, 16th, or 17th chapter of John.[116]

The result of this explication should be the stirring up of the hearts of those gathered around the table to a response of devotion, love, and gratitude to Christ: "Now the priest must be diligent to fully proclaim the death of the Lord, in order for the people to envision the infinite goodness of Christ, and the church may be taught, edified, and directed in heartfelt fervent and brotherly love."[117] At this point the priest reads and amplifies Paul's warning in 1 Corinthians 11 for believers not to eat or drink damnation on themselves. Such an amplification consists in admonishing the congregation to examine their souls individually as to whether they have an inner hunger and thirst for the bread which comes from heaven, due to the Johannine demand that the heavenly bread and wine be consumed in spirit, faith, and truth: "Let a person search himself to see if he has a true inner and fervent hunger for the bread that comes down from heaven, from which one truly lives, and thirst for the drink which springs up into eternal life, to both eat and drink in the spirit, faith, and truth, as Christ instructs us in John 4, 6, and 7."[118] Here

---

115. "Yedoch sollen die Essenden . . . bey einander sitzen mit zucht, on alle klapperey vnd zanckhung. . . . Ein yedlicher mensch anfengklich sich selbs anklagen solle vnd sich seiner sünden vor got bekhennen vnd schuldig geben." Ibid.116. "Nun setze sich der Priester mit dem volck nider vnd thüe auff seinen mund, erklere die schrifften von Christo, darmit die augen der beysitzenden auffgethon werdent, die noch etwas tunckels vnnd zübachen seind. . . . Neme der Diener des worts für sich das 10. oder 11. c. der ersten Epistlen Pauli zü den Corinthern, oder das 13., 14., 15., 16., 17. c. Joannis." Ibid., 355-56.

117. "Allain khere man fleyß an, darmit nun der tod des herrens ernstlich verkhündet, dem volckh die vberschwengklich güthait Christi eingebildet vnd die Kirch in hertzlicher, jnbrünstiger vnd brüderlicher liebe vnderricht, erbauen vnd gefiert werde." Ibid., 356.

118. "Probiere sich der mensch, ob er einen rechten inwendigen vnd inbrünstigen hunger vnd durst hab nach dem brot, das herab steygt vom himel, in wöl-

Hubmaier's appeal to and reinterpretation of John 6 are remarkable, since John 6 was a classic proof-text used by Catholic polemicists to defend the doctrine of transubstantiation and was thus avoided altogether by Luther and Zwingli in their doctrines of the Eucharist.[119] In Hubmaier's exegesis of John 6, as suggested by the previous quote, the bread and wine, while not transformed into the body and blood of Christ, are still considered the "bread that comes down from heaven" and the "drink which springs up into eternal life." This is because they are the channels through which Christ mediates his "potential" grace to believers: "It is not that this bread and wine are anything other than bread and wine," although they effect "the significant mysteries . . . for the sake of which Christ therefore instituted [the Eucharist]."[120] Due to the supreme importance of partaking such sacred elements in a worthy fashion, Hubmaier closes the preparatory gathering with the pledge of love, which he insists must be avowed by each participant as a prerequisite for Eucharistic reception.

In order to ensure that human acts of commitment to Christ are carried out in response to the grace received at the Supper, Hubmaier requires its recipients to take the *Liebespflicht*. This lengthy and comprehensive pledge constitutes an ethical summons to imitate Jesus' surpassing act of self-giving by loving brother and sister and, if necessary, disciplining them. Only after assent is there the distribution of the elements. The text of the pledge reads as follows:

> Brothers and sisters, if you desire to love God before, in, and beyond all things, to serve him only through the power of his sacred and living Word, to reverence and pray to him and follow his name forever, to submit your fleshly and sinful will to his divine will which he has

---

chem warlich der mensch lebt, vnd nach dem tranck, das da fleüßt in das ewig leben, sy bayde zeessen vnd trincken im geyst, glauben vnd warhait, wie vnns Christus leert, Joan. 4, 6, 7." Ibid., 357.

119. Pelikan, *Reformation*, 195-96; Luther claimed that "John 6 is to be totally set aside, on the ground that it does not utter a syllable about the sacrament" (*Babylonian Captivity*, 36:32). With this verdict Zwingli concurred: "[I]n John 6, when Christ referred to eating his flesh and drinking his blood he simply meant believing in him as the one who has given his flesh and blood for our redemption and the cleansing of our sins. In this passage he is not speaking of the sacrament, but preaching the Gospel under the figure of eating and drinking his flesh and blood" (*Lord's Supper*, 199).

120. "Nit das hie brott vnnd wein etwas anders dann brot vnnd wein seyend, sonnder . . . bedeütlichen haimlichaiten . . . darumb es denn Christus also eingesetzt hat." Hubmaier, *Form des Nachtmals Christi*, 359.

wrought in you by his living Word, both in life and in death, then let each one say individually: I WILL.

If you desire to love your neighbor and serve him with works of brotherly love, to lay down your life and shed your blood for him, to obey father, mother, and all civic authorities according to God's will, doing all these things in the power of our Lord Jesus Christ, who laid down his flesh and shed his blood for us, then let each one say individually: I WILL.

If you desire to carry out fraternal admonition (brüederliche straff) among your brothers and sisters, to bring peace and unity between them, and to reconcile yourselves to everyone you have wronged, to forsake all jealousy, hatred, and ill will toward everyone, to voluntarily desist from any deed or behavior that brings harm, difficulty, or offense to your neighbor, to love your enemies as well and do good to them, and to exclude according to the Rule of Christ, Matthew 18, anyone who refuses to do so, then let each one say individually: I WILL.

If you desire to confirm publicly before the church this pledge of love (liebepflicht) which you have just made, through the Supper of Christ, by eating bread and drinking wine, and to bear witness to it in the power of the living memorial of the passion and death of Jesus Christ our Lord, then let each one say individually: I DESIRE IT IN THE POWER OF GOD.[121]

---

121. "Jr brüeder vnd schwestern, wöllent ir Got in der kraft seins heiligen vnd lebendigen worts vor, in vnd ob allen dingen liebhaben, im allain dienen, eeren, anbetten vnd seinen namen füran heiligen, auch eüren fleischlichen vnd sündigen willen seinem götlichen willen, den er durch sein lebenndig wort in euch gewirckt hat, vnderwirflich machen zum leben vnd tod, so sag ein yedlicher insonderhayt: JCH WJLL. Wöllent ir eüren nechsten lieb haben vnd die werckh brüederlicher liebe an im volbringen, eür fleisch vnd blůt für in darstrecken vnd vergiessen, auch vater, můter vnd aller Oberkait, nach dem willen Gottes gehorsam sein, vnd das auff die krafft vnsers herren Jesu Christi, der auch sein fleisch vnnd blůt für vns dargestreckt hat vnd vergossen, so sag ein yedlicher in sonderhait: JCH WJLL. Wöllent ir brüederliche straff brauchen gegen eüren brüedern vnd schwestern, fridvnd ainigkhait zwischen jnen machen vnd auch euch selbs mit allen denen, die ir belaydigt habt, versönen, neyd, haß vnd allen bösen willen gegen menngklich fallen lassen, alle hanndlung vnnd handtierung, so eurem nechsten zů schaden, nachtail vnnd ergernuß raichet, willigklich abstellen, auch eure feind liebhaben vnnd jnen wolthon, vnd alle die, solchs nit thon wöllen, nach der Ordnung Christi, Mat. 18. c., außschliessen, so sag ein yedlicher in sonderhait: JCH WJL. Begeert ir hierauff in dem Nachtmal Christj mit der essunng des brots vnnd trinckung des weins solhe liebepflicht, die ir yetz gethon, offentlich vor der Kirchen zebestetigen vnd zů bezeügen auff

Such a pledge demands that the faithful conform to Christ, the head of the church, and to be, as he was, a person who lives for others. Hubmaier reasons that if believers vow to appropriate the divine grace bestowed in the Eucharist by living a life of love, then unbelievers can assess their own faith against the standard of how believers live. Since their lives are the book which the world reads, believers are obliged to discipline each other in love.[122] It should be noted, furthermore, that the *Liebespflicht* presupposes a theory of the atonement in which Christians are accordingly made to be willing and able to act as Jesus acted. Hubmaier makes this point explicit in *Messe*:

> Just as the body and blood of Christ became my body and blood on the
> cross, in the same way my body and blood must become the body and
> blood of my neighbor, and his must become my body and blood during
> my time of need, or we cannot profess to be Christians at all. This is the
> will of Christ in the Supper.[123]

Christ's will can be so identified, insists Hubmaier, since sacraments signify, consistently with the reformer's covenant theology, both a divine and a human occurrence. Along with the divine sacramental presence, Hubmaier contends that the Eucharist signifies sanctified human nature, or a continuation of the earthly life of the second person of the Trinity, as the believer who bears that life is literally brought into the physical body of Christ.[124] Consequently, the believer who realizes the penultimate transformation which transpires and the "potential" grace given in the Eucharist will submit his or her will wholly to Christ, which may lead to death:

> The person who observes the Supper of Christ in this way and medi-
> tates on the passion of Christ with a strong faith will thank God for this
> grace and goodness as well. He will submit himself to Christ's will,
> namely, that we must do for our neighbors the same thing that he has

---

die krafft der lebendigen gedechtnuß des leydens vnd sterbens Jesu Christi vnsers herrens, so sag ein yedlicher in sonderhait: JCH BEGERS auff die krafft Gottes." Ibid., 362.

122. Rempel, *Lord's Supper*, 78.

123. "Also wie der leyb vnd dz plüt Christi mein leyb vnd main plüt am Creütz worden ist, dergleichen soll auch mein leyb vnd plüt meins nechsten leyb vnd plüt, vnd dasselbig herwiderum inn neten mein leyb vnd plüt werden, oder wir söllen vns christen zü sein gar nit berüemen. Das ist der will Christi im nachtmal." Hubmaier, *Messe*, 104.

124. Rempel, *Lord's Supper*, 80-81.

done for us and lay down our bodies, lives, properties, and blood for their sake.[125]

However, Hubmaier realizes that humans cannot so live in their own strength: "A person who loves his neighbor as himself is a rare bird, indeed, like an Indian phoenix on earth. . . . You claim that such is humanly impossible. My answer: It undoubtedly is for the Adamic human nature."[126] Therefore, the "potential" grace given by God in the Eucharist, without which grace believers stand powerless to actualize the divine will, is imperative for *Nachfolge Christi* (discipleship to Christ).[127] For this reason, it is vital for the believer through the channel of the Eucharist to approach

> God diligently for grace and strength (or, in my terminology which stresses the relationship Hubmaier postulates between these two elements, potential and actual grace), so that he might impart them to us and thus enable us to perform his will. For if he does not impart grace to us, we are lost already, since we are human, we were human, and we will be human until death.[128]

In Hubmaier's thought, then, the Lord's Supper proves to be the mediator of the supreme sacramental and ethical reality to an otherwise helpless humanity.

While Hubmaier denounces as blasphemous the Catholic notion that Christ is literally sacrificed by the priest celebrating the Eucharist,[129] the

---

125. "Welcher mensch nu das nachtmal Christi dermassen begeet vnd betracht das leyden Christi in ainem vesten glauben, derselb würdt auch Got vmb dyse genad vnnd gůthayt dannck sagen, sych in den willen Christi ergeben, der dann ist, wie er vns gethon hab, das wir auch also vnserem nächsten thůn sollen vnd vnser leyb, leben, gůt vnd blůt von desselben wegen dar spannen." Hubmaier, *Summe*, 114.

126. "Ein mensch, der seinen nechsten als lieb wie sich selbs habe, ein seltzamer vogel ist, ja, gar ein Jndianischer Phenix yetz auff erdenn. . . . Sprichstu: Das ist dem menschen zethon vnmůglich. Antwurt: Ja, dem Adamischen menschen." Hubmaier, *Form des Nachtmals Christi*, 359.

127. Hubmaier, *Ein einfältiger Unterricht*, 303-04.

128. "Got emssigklich vmb gnad vnd krafft, das er vns die mitteyle, auff das wir also seinen willen verbringen mögen. Dann wo er nit gnad gibt, so ist es vmb vnns schon verlorn, wie seind menschen vnd waren menschen vnd werden menschen byß in den tod bliben." Hubmaier, *Summe*, 114.

129. Hubmaier declares, "When one wants to restore and appropriately keep the Supper of Christ, I absolutely insist on destroying the altars on which we,

reformer affirms that Christ's body is figuratively sacrificed in a new way. It should be pointed out that for Hubmaier, the time period in which believers bear the real presence of Christ begins when they partake of the elements and ends at the close of the Supper service.[130] However, *salbung Gottes*, or the measure of "potential grace" mediated through the vehicles of bread and wine, continues with the believer for an indefinite period of time following the Supper.[131] With this in mind, Hubmaier exhorts the faithful upon their dismissal from the Eucharist, "Arise and depart in the peace of Christ Jesus. . . . Make sure that you bear fruit worthy of . . . the Supper of Christ, so that you, in the power of God, satisfy your vow, pledge, [and] sacrament."[132] Moreover, it was certainly possible for those baptized believers who become sharers in the physical body of Christ at the Supper to be sacrificed in martyrdom for their radical version of Christian faith.[133] Such was an experience Hubmaier knew all too well, as he was forced to flee Waldshut when the Austrian imperial government captured the city in December 1525, upon fleeing to Zurich suffered prison and torture at the hands of Zwingli from December 1525 to April 1526, and subsequently faced the impending threat of Austrian King Ferdinand I during his ministry at Nikolsburg.[134] Thus,

---

insofar as we have participated, have crucified and killed Christ Jesus again until the present time" (Die Altär hayß ich ja abbrechen, auff den mann Christum Jesum, als vil an vnns gewesen, bißher widerumb gecreütziget vnd tödtet hat, wo man anders das Nachtmal Christi auffrichten vnd recht halten will); *Entschuldigung*, 276.

130. Hubmaier quite clearly delineates that "the body and blood of Christ is shared with us all . . . only . . . when we eat and drink together" (der leyb vnd dz blüt Christi vns allen gemain ist . . . nur . . . so wir mit ainander essen vnd trincken); *Messe*, 102-03.

131. Hubmaier, *Form des Nachtmals Christi*, 360.

132. "Steend auff vnd geend hin in dem frid Christj Jesu. . . . Lůgent, das ir wirdig fruchten des . . . Nachtmals Christj bringent, auff das ir in der krafft Gottes eůrer glůbd, zůsagung, Sacrament." Ibid., 364.

133. Estep, *Anabaptist Story*, 73-75.

134. Vedder, *Hübmaier*, 122-29, 219-21. As to his maltreatment by Zwingli, Hubmaier relates: "He tried to instruct me in the faith by public law and trial before his own government, before the confederates, and before the emperor himself, and by capturing, imprisoning, and torturing me and threatening me with the executioner. But faith is a work of God and not of the Heretics' Tower, where one sees neither sun nor moon and lives on nothing but bread and water" (Der mich über offenliche rechtbot vnd Appellation für sein aigne Obrigkait, für gmayn Aydgnossen, auch für den Khaiser selbs wolt mit fahen, thürnen, martern vnd mit dem hencker den glauben leeren. Aber der glaub ist ein werckh gottes

insofar as those who are the body of Christ in the Eucharist are martyred, Christ is figuratively sacrificed not in, but as a result of, the Eucharist:

> Because we now, as a result of eating the bread and drinking the wine in memory of the passion and shed blood of our Lord Jesus Christ for the forgiveness of our sins . . . have all become one loaf and one body, and our Head is Christ, we ought to fully conform ourselves to our Head . . . by each of us offering his own flesh and blood.[135]

In this reconceptualization of the Eucharistic sacrifice as the self-offering of the worshiping community empowered by the Eucharist, Hubmaier maintains that Christ's sacrifice for humanity becomes the transforming power of history when those who appropriate it for themselves imitate its sacrifice.[136] Here we perceive that an evangelistic thrust underlies Hubmaier's doctrine of the Supper: as believers figuratively become Christ to others, the reformer argues that nonbelievers will be attracted to his radical form of Christianity, enter the church through baptism, and ultimately come into ontological communion with Christ in the Eucharist.[137] The sacraments thus enable God the Son to be salvifically at work in the church. For these reasons, Hubmaier claims that if all one had of Christianity was a right understanding of its sacraments, one would possess all things spiritual: "Now if we possessed no other word or Scripture, but only possessed an accurate understanding of water baptism and the Supper of Christ, we would possess God and all his creatures, faith and love, the law and all the prophets."[138] Specifically with regard to the Eucharist, the church can only operate

---

vnd nit des Ketzer thurns, darjnn man weder Son noch Mon sihet vnd nichts den von wasser vnd brot gelebet); *Entschuldigung*, 279-80. It should also be pointed out that Hubmaier was burned at the stake at the decree of Ferdinand in Vienna on 10 March 1528 (Vedder, *Hübmaier*, 242-44).

135. "Wie wir nun yetz all mit dieser essung des brots vnd trinckung des trancks in der gedechtnuß des leidens vnd blůtuergiessens vnsers herrens Jesu Christj zů nachlassung vnserer sünden . . . vnd seind all ain brot vnd ain leib worden, vnd vnser haubt ist Christus, also sollen wir billich vnserm haubt gleichförmig werden . . . einer . . . sein fleisch und blůt darspannen." Hubmaier, *Form des Nachtmals Christi*, 363.

136. Windhorst, *Täuferisches Taufverständnis*, 248.

137. Sachsse, *Hubmaier als Theologe*, 208.

138. "Wo nun yetz ein mensch kain ander wort oder schrifft hette denn allain den rechten verstand des Wassertauffs vnnd Nachtmals Christj, so hat er doch schon Gott vnd all Creaturen, glauben vnd liebe, Gesatz vnd all Propheten." Hubmaier, *Form des Nachtmals Christi*, 359.

through the grace dispensed through its celebration; therefore Rempel declares, "In its role as the embodiment of the church's outward life, the Lord's Supper is the *sine qua non* of the church."[139] Further, the grace received in the Supper enables the perpetuation of the power that the incarnate Christ exhibited and the kingdom which he instituted throughout history:

> From this fact it follows and becomes transparently obvious that the Supper . . . does not transpire out of human powers or abilities, since that would be conceitedness or human pride. Instead, it transpires . . . in the name of our Lord Jesus Christ, that is, in the grace and power of God. Therefore, it is a power. . . . [Through it the believer can] live according to the Word and command of Christ from that point forward. However, he must not attempt this out of human ability, in order that what happened to Peter will not happen to him, since Christ states that "apart from me you can do nothing, and you can do nothing without the power of God the Father, Son, and Holy Spirit." At this point the person breaks out in speech and action, proclaiming the name and exalting the worship of Christ, in order that others will be healed and saved through us, just as we previously came to faith through people who proclaimed Christ to us, causing the kingdom of Christ to be enlarged.[140]

This quote encapsulates the inextricable interrelationship in Hubmaier's thought between the power of God made possible by the Eucharist, the performance of good works, and the advancement of the gospel. In sum, the Eucharist, whose worthy consumption was made possible by the Christian's right relationship with God, encompasses three historical points of reference, as it points backward to the suffering of Christ, to the present in the sharing

---

139. Rempel, *Lord's Supper*, 88.

140. "Hierauß eruolget vnd würdt grundtlich erlernet, das das nachtmal . . . nit auß menschlichen krefften oder vermögen, dann das wer ain vermůttung oder mennschliche vermessenhayt, sonder . . . in dem namen vnsers herren Jesu Cristi, dz ist, in der gnad vnd krafft Gotes. . . . Derhalb hab er . . . nach dem wort vnd beuelch Chrysti füran zeleben, aber das nit auß menschlichem vermögen, darmit im nit beschehe wie Petro, dann on mich mögt ir nichts thůn, spricht Christus, sonder in der krafft Gotes, vatters vnd deß sons vnd deß hailigen gaists. Yetz bricht der mensch auß im wort vnd werck, verkündet vnd macht groß den namen vnd lob Christi, darmit auch ander durch vns haylig vnd selig werden, wie wyr durch ander, die vns Christum vor gepredigt, auch seynd zům glauben komen, auff das das reych Christi gemeert werde." Hubmaier, *Summe*, 112, 114.

of Christ's *Wesen* by the church, and forward to the righteous living, evangelism, and possible suffering of Christ's people. For Hubmaier, the Lord's Supper proves to be the sign that the incarnation is being carried on in the church.[141]

The Door of Excommunication and its Eucharistic Key

The direct link between Jesus' incarnation and earthly ministry and the life of the church is further underscored in Hubmaier's doctrine of the keys. As indicated in the previous chapter, the first of the two keys bequeathed by Christ to the church at his ascension was the sacrament of believers' baptism, and the second key comprised the sacrament of the Eucharist. Rempel summarizes the reformer's understanding well: "In baptism, the church uses the key of initiation; in the Lord's Supper, it applies the key of excommunication."[142] The door unlocked by this excommunicatory key amounted to the second stage in Hubmaier's program of church discipline, which he denominated the *christliche Bann* (Christian excommunication).[143] Adhering to the Matthean schema, Hubmaier insisted that the ban could not be inflicted until three previous attempts had been made to persuade a straying sheep to return to the flock: "Now after a sinner has been first rebuked and warned by his brother in secret, then in the presence of two or three witnesses, and finally before the whole church according to the order of Christ . . . but still neither wants to better his life nor to refrain from this sin, then he shall be banned."[144] Although the Anabaptists employed the term *Bann* (without the adjective *christliche*) to describe their disciplinary model, Hubmaier's version of the *Bann* proved to be far less severe than that practiced by his "dear brethren."[145] In the ban depicted by the *Schleitheim Confession*, the miscreant was entirely excluded from the Anabaptist community, considered irredeemable, and treated as if she or he was dead.[146] As Estep recounts, such a conception led many Anabaptists, such as Menno Simons and Dirk Philips, to demand that shunning be practiced between married partners to the extent

---

141. Rempel, *Lord's Supper*, 72.
142. Ibid., 68.
143. Hubmaier, *Bann*, 367.
144. "Nach dem nun der Sunder durch seinen Bruder erstlich ermanet vnd gstrafft ist in der gehaim, darnach vor zwayen oder dreyen zeügen, zum dritten vor der gantzen gmain nach der ordnung Christj . . . vnd er aber sein leben nit bessern will, noch diser sünden absteen. Als dann soll man verbannen." Ibid.
145. Mabry, *Doctrine of the Church*, 54-55, 85.
146. Sattler, *Schleitheim Confession*, 36-37.

of denying the excommunicated member "bed and board," either culminating in marital separation at best or divorce at worst.[147] By contrast, Hubmaier's ban entailed none of these things.[148] Banned members of Hubmaier's Waldshut and Nikolsburg congregations were neither excluded from the church, nor viewed as eternally damned,[149] nor regarded as dead. Moreover, Hubmaier actually insisted that marital relations, which he calls "die werckh der notturfft" (the works of necessity) in reference to 1 Corinthians 7:3-4, continue between a banned spouse and a spouse in good standing: "The works of necessity, these should and indeed must be shared with a person under the ban."[150] Rather, Hubmaier, employing the medieval understanding of *Bann*,[151] defined *der christliche Bann* as exclusion from the Eucharist: "What is the ban? It is an exclusion [from] the communion of the Lord's Supper."[152] Such was a severe penalty in the reformer's theology due to the indispensability of receiving the Supper weekly to continually replenish one's store of grace necessary to living the Christian life.[153] Concerning the afterlife, moreover, if one died while banned, then one would not immediately be granted access to the beatific vision; instead, one would first be purged of the unrepented sin during a temporary period in hell (Hubmaier's redefined concept of "purgatory") before entering heaven.[154] In Hubmaier's thought, therefore, the Eucharist was antithetically related to the Christian ban.

Such an antithetical relationship between the Lord's Supper and the excluding stage of church discipline is also found in the thought of John Calvin, who can on this subject be profitably compared with Hubmaier. In book four of his *Institutes of the Christian Religion*, Calvin maintained that since sharing the sacramental meal is an intimate experience which represents a moral community, only people who have correct belief and follow proper Christian behavior should receive the Eucharist: "It is received only by true believers who accept it with genuine faith and heartfelt gratitude. . . . [who]

---

147. Estep, *Anabaptist Story*, 171-72.

148. Vedder, *Hübmaier*, 212-14.

149. Such a notion was precluded by Hubmaier's doctrine of believers' baptism, which ensured that anyone who received the sacrament would eventually reach heaven.

150. "Die werckh der notturfft, die selben sollent vnnd mügendt den verbantten wol mitgetaylt werdenn." Hubmaier, *Bann*, 373-74.

151. Kremer, *Reallexikon*, 1:429, 7:2, 7-9, 14.

152. Hubmaier, *Eine christliche Lehrtafel*, 316; the German is quoted in footnote 115, page 163.

153. Sachsse, *Hubmaier als Theologe*, 208-09.

154. Loserth, *Hubmaier*, 264.

will aim wholeheartedly for holiness and perfect purity."[155] With this sentiment Hubmaier would have concurred but perhaps also heightens the ethical
bar for "worthy reception" in the consciences of the faithful:

> Who can sit down at the Supper with a good conscience? My answer: A
> person who has taken it to heart, thereby molding himself in mind and
> heart, and inwardly perceives that he truly can say with his heart, "The
> love of God which he has lavished upon me through the sacrifice of his
> only begotten and all-beloved Son to pay the penalty for my sins, of
> which I have heard and received unwavering assurance through his
> holy Word, has stirred, softened, and permeated my spirit and soul in
> such a way that I intend and am prepared to offer my flesh and blood
> by ruling over and ultimately conquering it, so that it must obey me
> against its own will and refrain from manipulating, tricking, injuring, or
> harming my neighbor at all in body, soul, respect, possessions, wife, or
> children, but instead be burned in the fire and die for him, just as Paul
> wanted to be anathema for his brethren and Moses wanted to be blotted
> out of the book of life on behalf of his people." This type of person
> may with a good conscience and merit sit down at the Supper of
> Christ. . . . In this way all Christian persons must act and think to wor-
> thily eat and drink at the Lord's Table.[156]

Through such a lofty ethical standard, which the radical never attempted to
enforce through church discipline but realized could only be inwardly en-

---

155. Calvin, *Institutes*, 4.1.17, 4.17.2.
156. "Wer mag nun mit güter gewissen sich an das Nachtmal setzen. Antwurt: Wölher mensch sich also gehertzigt, auch in seinem geyst vnd gmiet
gestaltet, jnnerlich entpfindet, das er warlich vnd von hertzen sagen mag: Die
lieb Gottes, so er mir in darstreckhung seins aingebornen vnd allerliebsten Sons
zů bezalung meiner sunden bewisen, als ich in seinem heiligen wort gehört vnd
gwißlich versichert bin, hat dermassen meinen geyst vnd seel bewegt, erwaicht
vnd durchtrungen, das ich auch also gesynnet bin vnd bewilligt meinem fleisch
vnd blůt zebietten, darüber, hörschen vnd also maistern, das er mir můß wider
seinen aygen willen gehorsam sein, füran meinen nechsten nit vortailen, be-
triegen, beschedigen noch in ainigerlay weg in an leib, seel, eer, güt, weib oder
kind belaidigen, sonder vil mer für in in das feür geen vnd sterben, wie auch
Paulus begeert für seine brüeder ein flůch zesein vnd Moses für sein volckh auß
dem bůch der lebenndigen außgetilgt ze werden. Ein solher mensch mag sich
wol mit güter gwissen vnd wirdikait an das Nachtmal Christj setzen. . . . Also
handelt vnd thůt ein yedlicher mensch, der ein Christ ist, darmit er wirdigklich
esse vnd trinckh von dem Tisch des herrens." Hubmaier, *Form des Nachtmals
Christi*, 359-60.

forced by each individual believer,[157] Hubmaier employed moral suasion in an attempt to foster in the minds of the Eucharistic recipients high expectations, according to which they should govern their lives. Accordingly, both reformers decried as sacrilege any administration of the Supper in which heretics or malefactors partake. If the unworthy consume the elements, Hubmaier admonishes,

> then the external breaking of bread, eating and drinking constitutes a killing letter, hypocrisy, and the type of food and drink by which one eats judgment and drinks death, as Adam did with the forbidden fruit of the tree in Paradise. . . . The external breaking of bread is then nothing but an Iscariotic and damning hypocrisy.[158]

Calvin agrees:

> The Church is the body of Christ (Col. 1:24) and cannot be defiled without disgracing Christ, her Head. So that nothing in the Church may bring disgrace on his sacred name, the erring member must be expelled. This is true too of the Lord's Supper, which would be spoiled by someone taking part wrongly.[159]

Hence for both Hubmaier and Calvin, appropriate administration of the Supper was contingent upon the enforcement of morality.

Although Hubmaier and Calvin employed dramatically different methods to maintain discipline, the end result of both methods was practically identical. Unlike Hubmaier's three-warning system of *brüderliche Strafe*, at the heart of Calvin's disciplinary system stood the Genevan consistory. Calvin insisted on the creation of this structure, which Robert M. Kingdon identifies as "the most controversial single institution established by the reformation in Geneva,"[160] upon his 1541 return to Geneva following a three-year

---

157. Bergsten, *Hubmaier*, 412-13.

158. "da ist das eüsserlich brot brechen, essen vnd trincken ein todtender büchstab, heüchlerey vnd ein solhe speyß vnd tranckh, dar an man das vrtail isset vnd den todt trinckt, wie Adam an der verbotnen frucht des holtz im Paradeyß thet. . . . das außwendig Brot brechen nichts denn ein Jscariotische vnd verdamliche gleichßnerey sein." Hubmaier, *Form des Nachtmals Christi*, 357-58.

159. Calvin, *Institutes*, 4.12.5.

160. Robert M. Kingdon, "Was the Protestant Reformation a Revolution? The Case of Geneva," in *Studies in Church History 12: Church, Society and Politics*, ed. Derek Baker (Oxford: Oxford University Press, 1975), 218.

hiatus in Strasbourg.[161] The consistory, made up of all the elders and city pastors with one syndic (who was also an elder) as its presiding officer, acted as a morals court which met every Thursday. At this time the twelve elders, each representing one of the city's twelve districts, would report to the consistory names of residents who did not behave properly, who persisted in their former Catholic practices, and whose religious beliefs were suspect. A high percentage of their cases consisted of people engaged in domestic quarrels and sexual promiscuity.[162] The consistory analyzed each case. On the one hand, if the sin was minor and the miscreant contrite, she or he might be dismissed with a scolding. On the other hand, if the sin was major and the miscreant unrepentant, she or he could be excommunicated, which amounted to barring the person from the Lord's Supper. Strikingly resembling the significance of this same punishment in Hubmaier's Waldshut and Nikolsburg, Kingdon reports that such was in Calvin's Geneva "a terrible penalty in a day when regular receipt of Communion was regarded as an essential sign of the operation of God's saving grace."[163] Despite their divergence over the real presence of Christ in the Eucharist, Calvin proved to be in accord with Hubmaier concerning the character and effect of grace mediated by the bread and wine.

Throughout the *Institutes*, Calvin uses the term "grace" equivocally: when discussing exegetical matters, grace refers, as in the Lutheran maxim *sola gratia*, to the unmerited favor of God; when teaching his flock how to live as faithful servants of God, however, grace alludes to a divine quasi-substance which empowers believers to perform works of righteousness.[164] Since the sacraments fall for Calvin into the realm of practical theology, his doctrine of the mediation of grace through the Eucharist is predicated upon the latter instead of the former definition. Thus Calvin compares the liquids of wine and oil to the grace bestowed in the Supper, which must be poured into the open vessel of a faithful soul: "[The elements] offer Christ to us, and in him, the treasures of grace. They are useless if not received in faith just as wine and oil, when poured out, will go to waste unless they are poured into an open vessel. If the vessel is not open, it will remain empty even if the liquid is poured onto it."[165] While Hubmaier shared this conception of the

---

161. This hiatus was induced by the Genevan city government, which forced Calvin and William Farel out of the city in 1538; for a detailed account of this incident see Kingdon, "Genevan Revolution in Public Worship," 271.

162. Kingdon, "Reformation a Revolution," 218.

163. Kingdon, "Control of Morals," 11.

164. Pelikan, *Reformation*, 152-53.

165. Calvin, *Institutes*, 4.14.17.

character of sacramental grace, the two reformers differed concerning the means by which God transmitted it to the believer. As previously indicated, Hubmaier held that grace flowed through the divinely ordained channels of bread and wine. For Calvin, however, the Holy Spirit proved to be the vehicle communicating substantive grace to the soul.[166] In book four, chapter seventeen of the *Institutes*, Calvin proceeds to amplify his concept of Eucharistic grace by equating it with the omnipresent divinity of Christ, such that "the soul partakes of Christ in reality [and] by his energy it may grow spiritually."[167] In this way, Calvin turns Christ's ubiquitous divine nature into a spiritually life-giving and nourishing substance which the Spirit transmits into the believer's soul as she or he consumes the physically nourishing substances of bread and wine:

> Christ feeds our souls, just as bread and wine support our bodily life. There would be no point in the signs, if our souls did not find their nourishment in Christ. . . . Although it seems an incredible thing . . . we have to remember the immense inward power of the Holy Spirit and how stupid it is to try to measure its immensity by our feeble efforts. What our minds cannot grasp, faith must engender—that the Spirit really does unite things separated by space. Christ transfuses his life into us by that sacred communion of flesh and blood. . . . because of it, believers have Christ living in them. In the same way, Christ chose to call himself the bread of life (John 6:51), not only to teach that our salvation is treasured up in the faith of his death and resurrection, but also, because of real communion with him, his life passes to us and becomes ours, just as bread gives strength to the body.[168]

Such a conflation of grace with the omnipresence of Christ yielded Calvin's doctrine of the virtual or spiritual presence of Christ in the Supper, according to which the "stuff" of Christ's divine nature fills the believer's soul.[169] However, unlike Hubmaier's doctrine that the Eucharistic participants essentially possess both their own nature and Christ's human nature, Calvin avoids any suggestion that this "filling" allows the faithful to essentially possess Christ's divine nature. Rather, this "filling" functions in the same way as when the Holy Spirit is said to "fill" the believer, without the believer sharing in his deity; in the Supper "our souls are fed by Christ, just as

---

166. Brian Albert Gerrish, *Grace and Gratitude: The Eucharistic Theology of John Calvin* (Minneapolis: Fortress, 1993), 132-33.

167. Calvin, *Institutes*, 4.17.5.

168. Ibid., 4.17.5, 10.

169. Gerrish, *Grace and Gratitude*, 176-78.

the bodily life is sustained by bread and wine," while at all other times the Spirit "continues to act as a caring parent, providing the food which keeps us spiritually alive."[170] This analysis discloses a deep difference between the Eucharistic doctrines of Hubmaier and Calvin: in Hubmaier's Supper, the believer is "consubstantiated" into the body of Christ, which presence is qualitatively different and ontologically higher than the daily infilling of the Spirit; whereas in Calvin's Supper, although the believer is filled with the divine presence of Jesus, this infilling is qualitatively and ontologically equal to the daily infilling of the Spirit.[171] For Hubmaier, the Eucharistic presence is different both qualitatively and personally from the presence of the Holy Spirit (*i.e.* the second rather than the third trinitarian person fills the believer in the Supper). For Calvin, by contrast, the Eucharistic presence is only personally different but not qualitatively different from the Spirit's presence, as Christ performs the role in the Supper played on a daily basis by the Spirit.

Despite the fact that Hubmaier and Calvin differ as to how the quality of the divine presence in the Eucharist compares with the divine presence daily accessible to the faithful, both reformers concur that the quality of assurance regarding salvation is much higher in the Eucharist than ordinarily available. As already suggested, Hubmaier taught that any baptized believer was as-sured immediate entrance into heaven if she or he died in a state of being worthy to receive the Eucharist, but would have to spend a temporary period in hell before reaching heaven if she or he died in an unworthy sacramental state.[172] Such a dichotomy appears to be a modification and softening of the Catholic idea of being or not being in a state of grace at the moment of death. Late medieval Catholic theology, into which Hubmaier was steeped at Freiburg and Ingolstadt,[173] posited that if a person died in a state of grace, meaning that one's soul lacked the stain of mortal sin, then one was assured eventual acceptance into paradise, preceded by a probable spiritual cleansing in a purgatory distinct from heaven or hell. If that person died without being in a state of grace, then she or he would be eternally consigned to hell.[174] What Hubmaier does, in effect, is to replace the "state of grace" with the

---

170. Calvin, *Institutes*, 4.17.1.

171. Pelikan, *Reformation*, 190-91.

172. Christof Windhorst, "Das Gedächtnis des Leidens Christi und Pflicht-zeichen brüderlicher Liebe: zum Verständnis des Abendmahls bei Balthasar Hubmaier," in Hans-Jürgen Goertz, ed., *Umstrittenes Täufertum 1525-1975* (Göttingen: Vandenhoeck & Ruprecht, 1977), 126-27.

173. Bergsten, *Hubmaier*, 70-75.

174. Pelikan, *Reformation*, 35-38.

"state of being worthy to receive the Eucharist," eliminate the prospect of purgatory for those who die worthy to receive, and reduce for the unworthy an eternal hell to a temporary purging in hell before beholding the beatific vision. Although Calvin repudiated the existence of "purgatory" in any sense and believed that at the moment of death, persons are eternally consigned to either heaven or hell, the Supper in his thought furnished its recipients with a tremendous amount of confidence that they were among the elect:

> Believers derive great assurance and joy from this sacrament, as proof that they are part of the body of Christ, so that everything which is in him also belongs to them. It follows that we can confidently assure ourselves that eternal life, of which he himself is the heir, is ours, and that the kingdom of heaven into which he has entered can no more be taken from us than from him. We cannot be condemned for sin because he absolves us from guilt, having taken it on himself. This is the marvelous transaction he has made in his amazing goodness! Having become, like us, a son of man, he has made us, like him, sons of God.[175]

Calvin's language seems to imply that the Eucharist furnishes us with the best earthly approximation of the invisible church; this conclusion is reinforced by his exegesis of 1 Corinthians 11, in which he argues that God makes to the partakers "promises by which consciences may be roused up to an assurance of salvation."[176] Calvin also declares in the *Institutes* that the aim of the Supper is to confirm Christ's promise of salvation for the faithful: "The chief object of the sacrament is to seal and confirm his promise by which he testifies that his flesh is our food and his blood our drink, feeding us to eternal life. He is the bread of life and whoever eats it shall live forever."[177] Because the Eucharist of Hubmaier and Calvin respectively revealed the precise and the approximate content of the sanctified elect at the moment in which it occurred, both took pains to ensure that former miscreants seeking readmission to the Supper had truly repented of their ways.

Hubmaier affirms that when straying members return to the fold, the church must welcome them back with open arms. However, much visible effort needed to be made by miscreants, insisted Hubmaier, to convince the church they had truly returned to the fold. When such effort was exerted, the ban was lifted and the offender allowed to return to the Eucharist. All this is summarized in Hubmaier's catechism, where he describes the lifting of the

---

175. Calvin, *Institutes*, 4.17.2.
176. Calvin, *Commentary on Corinthians*, 1.11.25.
177. Calvin, *Institutes*, 2.17.4.

ban and readmission to the Supper as the door of the ban, which keeps the miscreant out of heaven, being unlocked by the key of the Eucharist:

> Leon: If he ceases his sin, stays away from the influences and paths that might lead him to fall again, and improves himself, what outlook does the church take of him? Hans: She joyfully receives him again, just as the father received back his prodigal son, and just as Paul received back the Corinthians. She unlocks the door of heaven for him and allows him to return to the communion of the Lord's Supper.[178]

Here we see that the banned member was to be truly repentant, cease the sin in question, forestall future temptations to commit that sin, and better herself or himself. In his treatise on the ban Hubmaier further spells out the steps necessary to self-improvement:

> True repentance and remorse over sin consists in this: that one forsakes all performance of the relevant sin and thereafter flees, lays aside, and refrains from anything that might entice him and draw him again into it, including gluttony, drunkenness, gambling, anger, sexual immorality, and bad company. The contrition of any person who refuses to do this stems not from the heart, regardless of the mouth might utter. For he who claims to be sorry about his sins but does not flee enticements to those sins is a liar. He is acting like someone who claims he wants to avoid being dirty but spends all his time with coal and old kettles. However, the father receives the prodigal son with great joy when he returns wholeheartedly and admits that he sinned against both heaven and his father. Although he realizes that he no longer deserves to be called his son, he asks for forgiveness. He will never commit it again, which is the best repentance. [To] never commit [the sin again] is the best repentance.[179]

---

178. "Leon. So er nun der sünden absteet, vermeydet steg unnd weg, dardurch er widerumb fallen möcht, vnd bessert sich, wie hellts die Kirch mit im. Hanns. Sy nimbt in wider auff mit freüden, als der Vatter seinen verlornen Son, vnnd wie Paulus den Corinther, Lu. 15 [V. 20], 2 Cor. 2 [V. 10], schleüsset im auff den himel, vnd last in widerumb khummen zü der Gmainschafft des Nachtmals Christi." Hubmaier, *Eine christliche Lehrtafel*, 317.

179. "Das ist aber ein rechte büß vnnd rew vber die sünd. So der mensch der selben sünden mit der that absteet vnd fürhin alles fleücht, hinweg thüt vnd meydt, als vberessen, trunckenhait, spill, zorn, hürerey, böse gselschafft vnd alles das, dardurch er widerumb in die sünd mecht geraitzt vnd gezogen werden. Wölher aber das nit thüt, den selben rewen sein sünd nit von hertzen, geb was er mit dem mund schwetze. Dann wölher redt, jm seyend sein sünd layd, vnd ver-

When the change in the miscreant seemed apparent to the church, such that she or he met all the quoted requirements and convinced the church that the relevant sin would never be committed again, the community forgave the sin, opened the door of the church (and thus of heaven) to the person again, and allowed her or him to return to the Eucharist, which Hubmaier classified as the sign of a moral community itself.[180] In Calvin's Geneva, measures were taken by the consistory to ensure that, before it readmitted those under temporary excommunication to the Eucharist, the excommunicants had remedied their relevant faults to an adequate degree. A few representative examples from the Genevan consistory registers will suffice to show the institution's general pattern of dealing with those it barred from the sacrament. On 23 February 1542, the pack-saddler Jaques Emyn, who knew neither the Lord's Prayer nor the Apostles' Creed, was "remanded to learn his faith and creed before coming to Holy Communion, and ordered to come recite them here before taking it. Here in three weeks."[181] In this case, the consistory, which refused the Supper to Emyn because of his religious ignorance, would only readmit him if he knew the essentials of the faith three weeks later. Similarly, before the mason Pierre Calabri, who was absent from sermons and could not recite the creed, was allowed the Supper, the consistory ruled on 20 July 1542 "that he come present himself before the next Holy Communion to show how he has profited" from frequenting "the sermons" and attending "catechism every Sunday . . . before [the Eucharist] is given to him."[182] When Besanson Fouson, who was accused of fornication, was hauled into the consistory on 6 April 1542, the consistory declared "that he be forbidden to receive Holy Communion" and that he not be allowed to receive "until it is evident that he has improved."[183] Whether or not Fouson was making improvements was to be monitored by the consistory every Thursday until it deemed his sexual conduct as acceptable, whereupon he

---

meydt aber die vrsachen der sünnden nit, der ist ein Lugner vnd thût gleich wie ainer, der sich nit verromigen will vnd doch sein gsellschafft teglich hat mit kolen vnd allten kösslen. Ja den verlornenn Son nimbt der vater an mit grossen fretiden, der von hertzen widerkhert vnd bekennt sich, das er in den himel vnd in Jn gstind hab. Er sey nit wirdig sein Son genennt zù werden. Aber er solle jm verzeihen. Er wölle es fürbaß nymmer thon, wölhes die höchst bůß ist. Nimmer thon die gröst bůß." Hubmaier, *Bann*, 377.

180. Mabry, *Doctrine of the Church*, 83.

181. Robert M. Kingdon, gen. ed., *Registers of the Consistory of Geneva in the Time of Calvin, Volume 1: 1542-44* (Grand Rapids, Mich.: Eerdmans, 2000), 11.

182. Ibid., 95-96.

183. Ibid., 37.

would be readmitted to the Supper. Likewise, when Pierre Sermod was convicted of playing dice games on 21 December 1542, the Consistory judged "that he be given good remonstrances and forbidden the next Communion until he is better disposed and worthy of receiving it and makes more improvement."[184] Under the oversight of Calvin, then, the consistory functioned as "a compulsory counseling service"[185] which first reformed the offender and only then permitted her or him to again partake of the Eucharist. Although both Hubmaier and Calvin took definitive measures to ensure that only the truly repentant and restored would be received back to the Supper, one major difference surfaces at this point between the programs employed by the two reformers. For Hubmaier, restoration was an individual effort which required significant personal initiative on the part of the offender; no ecclesiastical institution which assisted the offender was ever put in place at Waldshut or Nikolsburg. On the contrary, restoration was conceived by Calvin as a process which must be supervised and evaluated by the consistory; at every stage the offender, through varieties of moral suasion, including admonitions and chastisements (often at the hands of Calvin himself), was encouraged to better herself or himself by the disciplinary arm of the Genevan church.

Stemming from his concept that the true church was necessarily visible and public, Hubmaier insisted that both its admission, through baptism and its corresponding vow, and exclusion, by banning from the Eucharist, must be visible and public. In particular, moreover, the ban was made public so that a sin may be seen as publicly disapproved and disciplined, thereby discouraging weaker members of the church from straying:

> Let us observe that the ban must be . . . openly proclaimed, in order that the Word of God and the entire Christian church will not be shamed, slandered, and hated, and that the neophytes and the weak are not led to stumble by the sinner's wicked example or be degraded, but instead that, due to this punishment, they will be distressed, fearful, and know better how to guard themselves from sins and vices from that point forward.[186]

---

184. Ibid., 160.

185. Robert M. Kingdon, "The First Calvinist Divorce," in Raymond A. Mentzer, ed., *Sin and the Calvinists: Morals Control and the Consistory in the Reformed Tradition* (Kirksville, Mo.: Sixteenth Century Journal Publishers, 1994), 1.

186. "Jst zů merckhen, das der Bann ist . . . offentlich auß gerůeffet, dar mit das wort Gottes vnd die gantz Christenlich Kirch von seinen wegen nit geschennt, gelöstert vnd veracht, ja auff das auch die Neuling vnnd schwachenn an

Such public shaming techniques were also employed by Calvin, whose liturgy for the Eucharistic celebration included reading the names of all who were barred from the sacrament along with the reasons why they were barred.[187] Hubmaier affirmed that due both to our sinful nature, which needs to be restrained, and to the continuation of the sanctification process, the ban was absolutely necessary for the order and purity of the church:

> For this reason, o you pious Christians, it is always obligatory, because humans are by nature children of wrath, sinful and corrupt, to treat them with wholesome medicine . . . so that the whole body would not thereby be warped, embarrassed, and ruined, but rather that Christian people mature and persevere in the new Christian life which they have started.[188]

Likewise, Calvin claims that discipline is essential for the church's survival:

> Some people hate discipline so much that they object to the very name, but we must remind them that no society or household can be controlled without it. It is even more necessary in the Church, which ought to be run in the best possible way. As the saving doctrine of Christ is the life of the church, discipline is the sinews of the church (*disciplina nervus ecclesiae*) which hold the parts together in the correct position. All who want to get rid of discipline will bring about the downfall of the Church.[189]

Thus, withholding the Eucharist from miscreants proved to be a central mechanism in Hubmaier's Waldshut and Nikolsburg and Calvin's Geneva for the inculcation of new habits which the reformers viewed as compliant with their respective Radical and Reformed faiths.

---

seinem bösenn Exempel nit geergert noch verbösert werdendt, sonnder vil mer ab diser straff erschreckent, sich fürchtent, vnd sich vor den sünden vnd lastern wissent für an noch baß zů verhietten." Hubmaier, *Bann*, 367-68.

187. Kingdon, "Genevan Revolution in Public Worship," 278-79.

188. "Hierauff, o ir frommen Christen, ist ye nott, die weil doch die menschen von natur her Khinder des zorns seind, böß vnd vntüchtig, jnen mit hailsamer ertzney zu begegnenn . . . darmit nit der gantz leib dar durch vngestaltet, geschent vnd verderbt werde. Sonder auff das die Christenlichen menschen in irem angefangnen, newen vnd Christenlichen leben fürfaren vnd verharren." Hubmaier, *Strafe*, 339.

189. Calvin, *Institutes*, 4.12.1.

Summary of Hubmaier's Doctrine of the Eucharist

Through an integration of his Alexandrian (and Johannine) doctrine of Christ with his Pauline doctrine of the church, Hubmaier constructed a theological system whose consequence was a radically new conception of the Eucharist. In this quite philosophically realist doctrine, the church is the extension of the incarnation, collectively and individually. When believers partake of the Supper, they ontologically share in the human nature or essence (*Wesen*) of Christ without sacrificing their own human natures.[190] Such a "consubstantiation" of the faithful seems to be grounded in Hubmaier's reinterpretation of the medieval principle, common in popular and scholarly thought, that a sacrament was an analogue of the incarnation.[191] Stemming from the Seventh Ecumenical Council of Nicea (787),[192] the notion arose in medieval sacramentology that since God had revealed himself in flesh, any material thing consecrated for that purpose could be the instrumental cause for the mediation of spirit.[193] However, Hubmaier employed similar argumentation to suggest that the material objects of bread and wine were the instrumental cause not of the mediation of Christ's spirit, but of Christ's repletively present humanity. Due to the Alexandrian doctrine of *communicatio idiomatum*, Hubmaier contended that the divine attribute of omnipresence or ubiquity transferred over to his human nature. He then proposed, in Anselmian fashion, that the distinction between the definitive and repletive presence of Christ's divine nature was also, in effect, transferred over to his human nature. Thus the definitive presence of Christ's physical body is at the right hand of God the Father, while the repletive presence of that same body fills the universe. Drawing on Paul's metaphor of the one body comprised of many members and John's imagery of the vine and the branches, Hubmaier identified the body's head and vine as the definitive physical presence of Christ and the body's remainder and branches as the physical presence available to the church in the Supper. Upon these metaphysical and exegetical pillars, Hubmaier asserted that the real presence of Christ in the Eucharist constitutes a special sacramental mode of the ubiquitous repletive bodily presence of Christ in which believers physically participate. Thus, the Supper proved for Hubmaier not only to be the primal meeting point be-

---

190. Hubmaier, *Messe*, 103.

191. Rempel, *Lord's Supper*, 67.

192. Philip Schaff and Henry Wace, eds., *Nicene and Post-Nicene Fathers*, 14 vols. (New York: Scribner's, 1900), 14:551-53.

193. Gary Macy, *The Theologies of the Eucharist in the Early Scholastic Period* (Oxford: Clarendon Press, 1984), 132.

tween God the Son and the church, but an expansion of the incarnation itself. Echoing a Bernardian theme,[194] the Eucharist constitutes the event in which humanity is made, just as during Christ's earthly life, into a means of divine self-disclosure, thereby acquiring a foretaste of its final redemption at the general resurrection. Hence Rempel declares that for Hubmaier, "the Lord's Supper becomes the medium of the church as incarnation."[195] As a result, such a radically anthropocentric Eucharist becomes for Hubmaier the sur-passing symbol of Christian discipleship.

The breaking of bread and drinking of wine, indicates Hubmaier, is a reaffirmation and strengthening of the reciprocal covenant forged by God and each believer at baptism, marked by the *Tauffglübde* (baptismal vow).[196] Likewise, Hubmaier composed a *Liebespflicht* (vow of love) to precede the consumption of the elements.[197] On the human side, the faithful vow to make good use of the grace to be transmitted through the vehicles of bread and wine, thereby making the divine power present in the world. On the di-vine side, God promises to physically identify with them in the Eucharist, wherein a "potential grace" is imparted for the faithful to actualize as they serve as salt and light to the world. In Hubmaier's conception, the kingdom of Christ becomes the transforming power of history when those who sacra-mentally claim his grace use it to imitate his sacrifice. Believers not only remember Christ's sacrifice, but also desire to suffer as Christ suffered, both for the cause of Christ and for the needs of the members of the commu-nity.[198] This is one of the reasons the ecclesial exit door, the *Bann*, proved so important in Hubmaier's theology. In order not to profane the sacrament, those unworthy to receive, which unworthiness was defined as having ex-hausted the threefold discipline in Matthew 18 *sans* repentance, must be prevented from bearing the physical essence of Christ.[199] By constructing the ban as prohibition from the Supper, Hubmaier declares in a visible way that the person has been put out from the divine life of the community. Denial of such life or grace, mediated by the Eucharistic elements, means that the mis-creant lacks any source of empowerment or nurturing to righteousness, and is thus precluded from advancing on the path to sanctification.[200] Moreover, if the offender died in such a state, she or he would first have to suffer a

---

194. Sommerfeldt, *Spiritual Teachings*, 31-38.
195. Rempel, *Lord's Supper*, 70.
196. Hubmaier, *Strafe*, 345.
197. Hubmaier, *Form des Nachtmals Christi*, 361-62.
198. Mabry, *Doctrine of the Church*, 171.
199. Hubmaier, *Bann*, 375.
200. Rempel, *Lord's Supper*, 71-72.

temporary period in hell before entering heaven, which period was entirely averted by the sacramentally worthy. Similar to Calvin's position concerning those admitted to the Supper, such an antithetical relationship between the Eucharist and the *Bann* revealed that the partakers of the sacred meal, for Hubmaier, amounted to the exact composition at that moment of the true church. For these reasons, the ban proved very effective as a means of church discipline. However, the Eucharistic doctrine with which it was juxtaposed stands at variance with the sacramental and ordinance-based theologies of Hubmaier's predecessors and contemporaries. While affirming a doctrine of real presence, in contradistinction to Zwingli, Calvin, and the Anabaptists, neither the Fourth Lateran Council (1215) nor early modern Catholicism nor Luther would have dared identify the bearer of that real presence as the human recipients themselves. Although Hubmaier draws upon various aspects of patristic, medieval, and early modern sacramental thought, these seem to be minor notes in the score of a symphony composed with quite different themes in mind. All of this suggests that while various lines of theology may have provided Hubmaier with the necessary doctrinal springboard for his thought, he was essentially an independent thinker and, as such, he formulated a Eucharistic theology which was truly his own.[201]

---

201. Mabry, *Doctrine of the Church*, 177.

Chapter 6

The Free State Ecclesiology of Hubmaier

In the realm of church-government relations, Hubmaier displays perhaps his most conspicuous departure from the *Schleitheim Confession*, the 1527 doctrinal statement subscribed to by most Anabaptists. While Michael Sattler and his compatriots vilified the state as "the abomination" and "the kingdom of Satan" from which no spiritual good could result,[1] due largely to the persecution they had suffered at the hands of Catholic, Lutheran, and Zwinglian magistrates, Hubmaier sharply rebuked the adherents of the *Confession*, whom he regarded as theologically undersophisticated, for aiding Satan by attempting to engineer the downfall of "the Christian magistracy" (die Christennliche Oberkayt).[2] Behind this conflict lie two competing interpretations of the doctrine, common to Hubmaier and the Anabaptists, that the spiritual and temporal worlds comprised two independent realms which should not interfere with one another. On the one hand, the Anabaptists held that the civil authority was at best a subset of and at worst equivalent to the temporal world. On the other hand, Hubmaier asserted that the government constituted a *tertian quid*, instituted by God for the protection of the good and the punishment of the wicked, which could not be consigned to either the spiritual or temporal realm. During his second successful experiment with a "free state church," Hubmaier delineated and defended the principles of his ecclesiology in his 1527 treatise *Von dem Schwert*, designed as both an apologetic for his Nikolsburg church to the Margraviate of Moravia and a polemic against the Anabaptist exegesis of the Sermon on the Mount. Accordingly, this chapter seeks both to disclose the structure of Hubmaier's doctrine of church and government, in which the two are mutually complementary rather than contradictory, and to illustrate how such an ecclesiology

---

1. Sattler, *Schleitheim Confession*, 37-38.
2. Hubmaier, *Von dem Schwert*, 435.

was implemented at Waldshut (1523-25) and Nikolsburg (1526-28), with particular emphasis on Hubmaier's balance between the service of Christians in government and the principle of religious tolerance. Although Hubmaier maintained, in diametric opposition to the *Confession*, that obedience to Christ entails wielding the sword as soldiers and magistrates, the reformer decried any exertion of force to compel dissenters into the church or preserve doctrinal conformity among the faithful. By developing the unique sixteenth-century historical modality of a believers' state church, Hubmaier, in effect, put the finishing touches on the cumulative case for his identification as a Magisterial Radical Reformer.

The Role of the Church in the World

While Hubmaier insisted that the main goals of the church were to reconcile individuals to God in the sacrament of believers' baptism and nurturing them to righteousness through physical fellowship with Christ in the Eucharist, he realized that the church, although not essentially of this world, was very much in the world. Therefore, it was necessary for the church to understand its relationship to the world and the proper role to play therein:

> The Christian church . . . has the authority and power to seal all people with water baptism who are willing to receive, believe, and order their lives according to [Christ's] teaching, and to inscribe and receive them into her Holy Communion. . . . But, sadly, we mourn unto God . . . that we are in the kingdom of the world, which is a kingdom of sin, death, and hell. But Father, help us out of this kingdom, we are stuck in it over our ears, and will not be free from it until the end. : . . So Solomon prayed and was given great wisdom by God . . . to rule according to his Word and will.[3]

As indicated by this quotation, Hubmaier looked to Solomon's kingship over God's chosen people in the Ancient Near Eastern world as a model for

---

3. "Der Christenlichen Kirchen . . . sy gwalt vnd macht habe alle die menschen, so solhe leer annemendt, glaubent vnd füran ir leben darnach richten vnd fieren wöllent, mit dem Wassertauff zů verzaichnen, auch die selben in ir heilige Gmainschafft ein zůschreiben vnd auffzůnemen. . . . Aber laider, Gott sey es klagt . . . welchs ein reych ist der sünden, tods vnd der hellen. Aber vater, hilff du vns auß dem reich, wir steckhen darinn biß vber die oren vnd mugen hie auff erden nit ledig werden. . . . Also hat Salomon gebetten, vnd ist jm grosse weyßhayt von Gott geben worden . . . nach seinem wort vnnd willen zůfieren vnd regieren." Hubmaier, *Von dem Schwert*, 436-37, 442.

Christian rulers in the early modern world. Like the Anabaptists, Hubmaier believed that the church and world were opposing forces in the saga of salvation history, such that the former would only be despoiled by integration with the latter.[4] Despite his conception of the true church as visible and existing in a visible world, Hubmaier argues that its focus should remain on spiritual and eternal things; however, such a precarious balance can for the reformer only be maintained through a mutual interaction between church and civil government. To engender this interaction, Hubmaier proceeds one step further than the Anabaptists by distinguishing between the world and the government based on their respective motives for inflicting harm:

> The orderly government . . . punishes the wicked according to the command of God for the good of the pious and innocent. But the devil and his minions do nothing for the good or peace of people, but everything to their injury and harm with an envious and vindictive mind. But the government has a special sympathy for all those who have transgressed; it wholeheartedly wishes that it had not happened, while the devil and his followers wish that all people were miserable. Do you see, then, brothers, how far separated from one another these two servants are, the devil and orderly government?[5]

Thus, while the government punishes only criminals in order to protect the good, the world, under demonic control, attempts to injure both good and evil alike. Hubmaier contends that since those of the kingdom of God yet live in the kingdom of Satan, or the evil world which is alien to the will of Christ, God has instituted civil government in the world. For Hubmaier, God has ordained that the government, like the church, would be his servant in the world, and that it would accomplish his desire, seen most evidently in the Old Testament prophets, for social justice.[6] So that the government may protect the good and defenseless from the depravity of the world, God has

---

4. Mabry, *Doctrine of the Church*, 187.

5. "Der ordennlichen Oberkayt . . . strafft auß dem beuelch Gottes die bösen, zů gůttem den frommen vnd vnschuldigen. Aber der Teüfel mit seinen hauffen, der thůt nichts zů gůttem oder friden den mennschen, sonder alles nun zů nachtail vnd schaden mit neydigem vnd rachgyrigem gmůet. Die Oberkayt aber tregt ein sonder mitleiden mit allen denen, die sich vbersehen haben. Sy wolte von hertzen, das es nit beschehen were. So wolt aber der Teüfel vnd sein anhang, das alle menschen vnglückhafftig werent. Sehent ir da, Brüeder, wie weyt dise zwů dienstbarkaitten des Teüfels vnd der ordenlichen Oberkaiten von ein ander geschaiden seyent." Hubmaier, *Von dem Schwert*, 439.

6. Bergsten, *Hubmaier*, 454.

placed the sword at the magistrate's side and authorized him to wield the sword for its ordained purpose: "The government is also bound to rescue and release all oppressed and persecuted people, widows, orphans, friends, and strangers without any respect of persons according to the will and most earnest command of God, as found in Isaiah 1, Jeremiah 21, 22. . . . This is why God has hung the sword at the side of the government and has made it to be his servant."[7] The duty of the government, then, is to free and protect all innocent and peaceful people, which Hubmaier would exploit in his vision of a complementary interrelationship between the civil and ecclesial servants of God.

Far from the Anabaptist notion that the government stands in opposition to the church, Hubmaier postulates that the government works to further the cause of the church. While the church is reconciling fallen humanity to God by removing them from the domination of the world, the government possesses the task of protecting the church from the evils instigated by the world in order for the church to bring its divinely assigned task to completion. Hence the civil authority provides the church with the security necessary to do its work:

> For the sake of the evil [the government] is ordained in this way by God for the protection and defense of the pious. . . . Therefore, it is most necessity, O pious Christians, with greatest diligence and most earnest devotion to pray to the omnipotent God for a pious, just, and Christian government on earth under which we can live a peaceful and quiet life in all godliness and honesty. When God gives this to us, we ought to receive it with special thanksgiving.[8]

In Hubmaier's theology, the civil authority is not viewed as a necessary evil, but a friend and guardian of the church. The church, in return for such public

---

7. "Die Oberkait ist schuldig zů handthaben vnd erledigen all vndertruckt vnd gezwungen menschen, witwen, waysen, erkant vnd fremdling on alle ansehung der Personen nach dem willen vnd ernstlichen beuelch Gotes. Esa. Am 1., Hiere. 21. 22. . . . Darumb hat Jr Got das schwert an die seyten gehenckt vnd sy zů seiner dienerin eruordert." Hubmaier, *Von dem Schwert*, 438.

8. "Wann von der bösen wegenn ist es also von Gott geordnet zů bschütz vnnd schirm der frommen. . . . Demnach ist von grossen nötten, O ir frommen Christen, den allmechtigen Got mit hohem fleyß vnd mit ernstlichem andacht zůbiten vmb ein fromme, grechte vnnd Christenliche Oberkhayt auff erden, darmit wir ein fridlichs vnd stilles leben in aller gotseligkhait vnd redlicheit vnder ein ander fieren mügen. Wo vns Gott nun die gibt, gebůrt vns die selben mit sonderlicher dancksagung anzůnemen." Ibid., 441, 443.

safety, is obliged to pray for the government and to support and assist it in the execution of its divine duties. For this reason, Hubmaier insists that Christians must pay taxes and serve the government as magistrates and soldiers if they are called or chosen for these positions. To support his position, Hubmaier appeals both to the Pauline principle in Romans 13 and, in Thomistic fashion,[9] to natural law:

> But Paul takes us further and says: "The authority is a servant of God," which uses its protecting power for the good of our neighbor and the preservation of the territorial peace. Where is it written, therefore, that a Christian may not be such a servant of God, who fulfills the command of God for the good of all people? Or that he may not undertake such a divine work, as Paul himself calls it, according to the ordinance of God? Well, then . . . do you see now, dear brothers, that your own conscience compels you to recognize that it is wise and helpful to punish the wicked and protect the good? That is called, in good German, the territorial peace. Thus, says Paul, to further and preserve this territorial peace we must pay taxes, customs, and tributes. . . . Therefore, even if there were no Scripture to make us obedient to the government, our own conscience and knowledge would tell us that we should help the government to protect, defend, discipline, oversee, perform statutory and compulsory labor, stand guard, and pay taxes so that we might remain in temporal peace with one another, for temporal peace is not contrary to the Christian life.[10]

---

9. Aquinas, *Summa Theologica*, 1:57.

10. "Aber Paulus feert für vnnd sagt: Der gwalt ist ein diener Gottes, der solhen schütz solle handhaben, vnnd das geschicht vnserem nechsten zů gůt, vnd zů vnderhaltung eins gmainen lanndßfriden. Wo steet es nun geschriben, das ein Christ nit müg ein solher diener Gottes sein, der da allen menschen zů gůt den beuelch Gottes volbringen müge. Oder das er ein solch Götlich werckh (wie es Paulus selbs nennet) nach der ordnung Gottes nit müge auß richten. Wol an . . . sichstu yetz, lieber Brůder, das dich dein aigen gewissen dar zů zwingt, das du rätlich vnd hilfflich seyest, darmit die bösen gstrafft vnnd die gůtten beschirmbt werdent. Das haist zů gůttem teütsch: Ein gmainer lanndßfriden. Eben disen landßfriden zů fürdern vnd zů vnderhalten, müessen wir, spricht Paulus, steůr, zoll vnd tribut geben. . . . Darumb ob khain schrifft were, die vns der Oberkhait vnderthenig machet, so sagts vns doch vnser aigen Conscientz vnd gwissen, das wir der Oberkait sollen helffen bschützen, bschirmen, straffen, hütten, fronen, robatten, wachen vnd steüren, auff das wir in einem zeitlichen friden bey ein ander bleyben mügen, denn zeytlichen frid haben ist nit wider ein Christenlichs leben." Hubmaier, *Von dem Schwert*, 457.

Entailed by this argument is the notion that Christians should wield the sword against anyone guilty of a capital crime or physically threatening the state. Hence, Hubmaier would make the case that for the Christian to use the sword under the guidance of the state in the performance of its divine obligations is not contrary to the will of Christ.

As previously noted, Hubmaier posits that God has given the sword to the state in order to fulfill its divinely ordained responsibilities. In order to forestall any concept of "holy violence," whereby the elect have the right to oppose unbelievers by force,[11] Hubmaier clarified that God has not bestowed the sword upon the church; rather, only magistrates and their soldiers are ordained by God to use the sword for his purposes. However, the best magistrates and soldiers in the reformer's estimation are Christians:

> You must, must, must all confess that a Christian government can perform and will do such much better and more earnestly than an unchristian one. . . . it is evident that the more pious they are, the better and more orderly they will bear the sword according to the will of God for the protection of the innocent and for a terror to evildoers.[12]

Hubmaier attempts to provide Scriptural backing for this claim through an exegesis of Matthew 26:52-54, in which Christ told Peter to put away the sword at Gethsemane. Hubmaier interprets this text not as an admonition to discard the sword but as a warning against wielding it on one's own authority:

> Moreover, you hear that Christ said to Peter, "Put your sword back into its sheath." He did not say, "Untie it and throw it away." For Christ rebukes him because he drew it and not because he had it hanging at his side. Otherwise he would have rebuked Peter long before if that were

---

11. Hubmaier knew the disastrous consequences of this principle all too well, as it comprised a pillar of Thomas Müntzer's rationale for the Peasants' War. This revolt, which Hubmaier opposed, proved catastrophic between 1524-25 for many of his parishioners in Waldshut, who were slain by the peasants. See Williams, *Radical Reformation*, 161-63.

12. "Jr müest, müest, müest ye bekhennen, das ein Christenliche Oberkhait solhs vil baß vnd ernstlicher verbringen müg vnd thon werde, denn ein vnchristenliche. . . . ist wissentlich, das ye frommer sy seind, ye baß vnnd ordenlicher sy das schwert nach dem willen Gotes zů beschützung der vnschuldigen vnd zů einer forcht." Hubmaier, *Von dem Schwert*, 437, 447.

wrong. . . . yet he wanted to stop [Christ's arrest] and drew the sword on his own authority.[13]

By allowing Peter to return the sword to its sheath, Christ, in Hubmaier's exegesis, delineates between the proper and improper use of the sword based on whether or not one has been given divine sanction to wield it. Hubmaier declares that, far from wishing to eliminate the sword, Christ implied in this command that the sword can be properly kept at the Christian's side and drawn on the divine authority exercised through the government: "Therefore, a Christian may also, according to the ordinance of God, bear the sword in the place of God against the evildoer and punish him. . . . Thus is Scripture true when it says, 'You judges, watch what you are doing. You have an office not of human beings but of God.'"[14] Such an interpretation corresponds with Hubmaier's conviction that the more knowledgeable a magistrate is of God's word and will, the more righteous that ruler will be and carry the sword according to God's will. Thus, the use of the sword by the Christian magistrate is for Hubmaier actually affirmed by Christ: "Do you realize here how Christ sanctions the sword, that one should punish those with it who use it for their own violence and wickedness?"[15] From this argument, Hubmaier proceeds to justify the existence of a Christian government while refuting the objections levied against it by the Anabaptists.

From the twin observations that godly judges ruled over Israel in the Old Testament and that Paul commands Christians to settle legal disputes before believing judges rather than unbelieving ones (1 Cor. 6), Hubmaier deduces that a Christian may in good conscience sit in court and council and serve as judges in temporal matters.[16] Combining this inference with the premise that Christ desires for believers in government to wield the sword properly, Hubmaier proclaims the validity of the entire governmental enterprise in both its judicial and executive functions:

---

13. "Dar zů hörstu hie, das Christus sagt zů Petro: Steck das schwert ein in die schaiden. Er spricht nit: Thůs ab, wirffs von dir. Denn darumb, das erß zuckht, strafft jn Christus, vnd nit darumb, das erß hett an der seytten hangen, er hett in sonnst vorlangst gestraffet, so es wer vnrecht gewesen. . . . noch wolt ers verhindern vnd zuckt das schwert auß aignem gwalt." Ibid., 437.

14. "Also mag auch einn Christ wol nach der ordnunng Gottes das schwert fierrn an der stat Gottes vber den vbelthatter vnnd jn straffenn. . . . Das will die Schrifft aigentlich, da sy sagt: Jr richter, lůgent was ir thůnd. Jr yebt nit ein ambt des menschens sonder Gottes." Ibid., 441.

15. "Merckest du wie Christus hye das schwert bestettigt, das man die mit straffen soll, die aigen gwalt vnnd freuel darmit treiben." Ibid., 437.

16. Windhorst, *Täuferisches Taufverständnis*, 207.

See, dear brothers, that councils, courts, and law are not wrong. Thus also the judge may and should be a Christian. . . . . If a Christian therefore may and should, in the power of the divine Word, be a judge with the mouth, he may also be a protector with the hand of the one who wins the suit and punish the unjust. For of what use would the law, court, and judge be if one were not allowed to execute and fulfill punishment against the malicious? Of what use would having a shoe be if one were not allowed to put it on?[17]

Hence the government is analogous to a shoe divinely given for the protection of the church in society which God expects each society to wear. In response to the Anabaptist reading of Luke 12:14 ("Friend, who set me to be a judge or arbitrator over you") that the court and council are rejected by Christ, Hubmaier believes Christ, who did not hold a governmental office, to be pointing out that people should not assume the position of judges unless they are called or, as in Waldshut and Nikolsburg, selected to serve in that capacity through the electoral process:

[Christ] was attempting to say, "I am neither chosen nor appointed to be judge. That is not my office; it belongs to another." Realize that Christ does not condemn the office of the judge, since it is not to be condemned, as will be shortly follow. Instead, he points out that no one should undertake to be a judge who has not been appointed or chosen for it. That is why we have the election of the burgomasters, mayors, and judges, all of whom Christ permits to remain, if with God and a good conscience they rule well over temporal and physical matters.[18]

---

17. "Sehent ir lieben Brüeder, das Ratt, gricht vnd recht nit vnrecht ist. Das auch der Richter mag vnd soll ein Christ sein. . . . Mag nun vnd soll ein Christ in krafft des Götlichen worts ein richter sein mit dem munnd, so mag er auch sein ein bschützer mit der hannd des, der recht gewinnt, vnd mag den vngerechten straffen. Denn was solte recht, gricht vnnd richter, so man die straff wider den boßhafftigen nit bedörffte, außfieren vnd volziehen. Was solt ein schůch, so man jn nit dörst anlegenn." Hubmaier, *Von dem Schwert*, 441.

18. "Also wolt er sagen: Jch bin nit erwölt noch gsetzt zum richter. Es ist mein ambt nit. Es gehört andern zů. Merckt da, das Christus das Richterambt nit verwifft, als es auch nit zů verweffen ist, wie bald wirdt hernach volgen. Sonder das zaigt er an, das kainer sich für einen Richter solle auffwerffenn, er sey denn darzů eruordert vnnd erwölet. Daher khummen die waalenn der Burgermayster, Schulthaissen vnd Richtern, die all laßt Christus beleyben, das sy mit Gott vnd gůtter gwissen wol zeytlich vnd in leiblichen hendlen regieren vnd richten mügent." Ibid., 439.

Hence Hubmaier concludes that only those who have been duly called or elected to civil service can use the sword appropriately. Moreover, Hubmaier counters the related Schleitheim-based criticism that Christians cannot use the sword, insofar as Christ came not to destroy souls but to save them (Luke 9:54-56), by calling attention to the difference between Christ's role as Savior and the governmental role as civil protector:

> Reflect, dear brothers, on why Christ came to earth and on what the authority and command given him by God was. . . . Christ came, as he himself said, not to judge, condemn, or punish people with fire, water, or sword. He did not become human for that. Instead, his command and authority was to save people by the Word. . . . On the contrary, the power and authority has been given by God to the magistrate to protect and guard the pious, and to punish and destroy the wicked.[19]

However, Hubmaier immediately qualifies this remark by reiterating that God has not ordained the use of the sword by the church under any circumstances, even to protect itself. Thus Hubmaier admonishes the church:

> It is not proper for you to carry [the sword]. You are not in authority; it is not your appointed place, nor are you called or elected for it. For, whoever takes the sword will perish by the sword. . . . No one shall take the sword himself, except one who has been elected and appointed for that purpose. For he does not take it up of himself, but it has been brought to him and given him.[20]

According to Hubmaier, then, the church and government are to remain separate due to the fact that their divinely ordained roles are fundamentally

---

19. "Sehent an, lieben Brüeder, warumb Christus khummen sey auff erden, was sein ambt vnd beuelh von Gott Jm geben gwesen sey. . . . Christus ist khummen wie er selbs redt, nit das er die menschen richten, vrtaylen oder straffenn solle mit feür, wasser oder schwert. Er ist nit darumb mensch worden. Aber sein beuelch vnd ambt was, mit dem wort die menschen selig zümachen. . . . Entgegen ist das ambt vnd ordenlicher beuelch von Gott der Oberkhait geben, das sy solle die frommen bschützen vnd bschirmen, auch die bösen straffen vnd vmb bringen." Ibid., 438.

20. "Es khert dir nit züfieren. Du bist nit im gwalt. Er ist dir nit beuolhen. Bist auch nit darzü berüefft noch erwölet. Dann wer das schwert nimbt, der soll durch dz schwert vmb khummen. . . . Aber nyemandt soll das schwert selbs nemen, sonder wo ainer erwölet vnd darzü eruordert wirdt, denn so nimbt erß nit auß jm selbs, sonnder man tregt jms dar vnnd gibt jmß." Ibid., 436-37.

distinct; nevertheless, both are servants of God and anointed by him for his purpose.

Elaborating on his concept that church and government are to be mutually supportive in the performance of their divinely appointed roles in the world, Hubmaier fleshes out the practical ramifications of putting such a model in place. While the government should serve as a buffer between the church and the evils of the kingdom of the world, the church is to render to the government gladly the type of support necessary to execute its duties according to the divine will. Hubmaier, in addition to revealing the antipathy between himself and the Anabaptists on this score, gives an account of his preaching in Waldshut concerning the government:

> Nonetheless, I proclaim before God and several thousand people that no pastor in the areas where I have lived has gone to more trouble and effort in writing and preaching than I to ensure that people are obedient to the government. Because the government is of God, who hung the sword at its side, one should without dissension render to it tolls, duties, tribute, honor, and respect. In both Latin and German I have written and preached on this topic so zealously that several people grew badly inclined toward me, walked out on my sermons, and, indeed, some even interrupted me openly in church on this topic, vilifying me as a blood-sucker whose sole purpose is to defend the governmental sword.[21]

Consequently, Hubmaier alleged that the church should not only pray for the government and support and cooperate with the government in the performance of its divinely ordained duties, but church members should also pay taxes, bear arms, and serve as judges and as other public officers.[22] Contrary to the practice of the Anabaptists, church members are not to isolate themselves from the government, but are rather to be active in civil affairs. This assures, in Hubmaier's thinking, that society will be ruled by Christians,

---

21. "Aber doch so bezeüg ich mit Gott vnd mit etlich tausent menschen, das kain Predicant der gegenden, da ich gewesen, mer müe vnd arbayt mit schreyben vnd predigen erlitten hat denn ich, darmit man der Obrigkayt gehorsam were. Wann sy seye von got, der hab ir dz schwert angehenckt, man solle jr on alle widerred zoll, maut, tribut, eer vnd forcht geben. Daruon hab ich in Latein vnd teutsch so ernstlich geschriben vnd predigt, das vill leütt mir abhold worden, mein predig geflohenn, ja, etlich in offenlicher kirchen mir in disen Artickel eingeredt vnd mich ein blůt sauffer, der da nichts thůe denn das schwert der Obrigkait beschirmen, außgeschryen." Hubmaier, *Entschuldigung*, 277.

22. Bergsten, *Hubmaier*, 407-08.

who will govern according to the divine will. Hence church members are to be good citizens of the government that rules under God.[23] Despite this close relationship between the church and government, Hubmaier repudiates the use of governmental force to procure doctrinal conformity. As pointed out in chapter four, Hubmaier maintained in *Von Ketzern und ihren Verbrennern* (1524) that the only sword that either church or state can use against heretics is the sword of the Word of God. In *Von dem Schwert* (1527), the reformer bolsters his thesis with a theological argument based on his distinction between the proper and improper use of the sword. For Hubmaier, God has entrusted the sword to the government for the sole and proper purpose of punishing the wicked who presumably are outside the church, or in the kingdom of the world. Therefore, when the government uses the sword to enforce right belief within the church, it violates God's purpose for the sword and thereby wields the sword improperly.[24]

Centrality of the Sacraments to Hubmaier's Ecclesiology

The existence of a free state church depended for Hubmaier upon believers' baptism and the Eucharist, since a person's willingness or unwillingness to participate in the sacraments determined whether or not the person wished to either be or remain under the disciplinary arm of the church. By submitting to believers' baptism and its corresponding baptismal vow (*Tauffglübde*), one enters the voluntary community of faith and its spiritual safety-net of fraternal discipline (*brüderliche Strafe*), in the protection of which the believer is guaranteed immediate entrance to Paradise at the moment of death so long as she or he heeds the threefold warning system against falling out of the net.[25] Such a system, in which the church looks out for the spiritual well-being of the faithful and assures their spiritual prosperity as long as they have turned from any misbehavior before the private, semi-private, and public admonition process has been exhausted, afforded Hubmaier's parishioners in Waldshut and Nikolsburg a great deal of spiritual security. However, Hubmaier hastens to point out, given the separation of powers between church and government, that protection from spiritual punishment does nothing to prevent church members from receiving the physical punishment that can be levied against criminals by the state. In his

---

23. Mabry, *Doctrine of the Church*, 194.
24. Ibid., 193.
25. Hubmaier, *Strafe*, 345-46.

novel exegesis of the quasi-Johannine story of the woman caught in adultery, Hubmaier attempts to substantiate his doctrine of the separation between spiritual and temporal powers biblically. According to the reformer, Christ did not object to the woman's being stoned by the Pharisaic judges, who had the authority to execute the Mosaic law, but rather declared that, since he did not hold the judicial office, he had no legal right to enforce the death penalty. But since Christ's office included unlocking the door to the kingdom of heaven, the key of which is now turned by the church through the ban, he administers his role by proclaiming the forgiveness of the adulteress's sins.

> This Christ teaches us very clearly when he asks the adulterous woman, "Woman, has no one condemned you?" She says, "No one, Lord." He says, "Neither will I condemn you. Go and sin no more," John 8. Note: Christ asks, "Woman, has no one condemned you?" It is as if he would have said: "If condemnation had fallen on you according to the law of God announced for adultery, I should not interfere with the judges, for it is the commandment of God my Father that they should stone adulterers. But since no one has condemned you, neither will I condemn you, for it is not my office. I have not been appointed a judge but a Savior. Therefore, go forth and sin no more. That is my office, to forgive sins and to command that people from this moment forth abstain from sins." Hear then, dear brothers, how Christ so properly exercises his own office and lets the judicial office stand in its own dignity. So must the church also do with its ban, and the government with its sword, and neither usurp the office of the other.[26]

---

26. "Solchs leert vnns Christus gar aigentlich, da er das eebrüchig weiblen fraget: Weib, hat dich nyemant verurtailt. Sy sagt: Nyemant, herr. Redet er: So will ich dich auch nit verurtailen. Gang hin, vnd für an soltu nit sünden. Joan. 8. Merckt. Christus fragt: Weib, hat dich nyemant verurtailt. Als wolt er sagen: So ein vrtail vber dich gefellt were nach dem gsatz Gottes von den eebrechern lauttende, wurd ich den Richtern nit darein reden, denn es ist der beuelch Gottes meins vaters, das man die Eebrecher verstainigen sol. Die weil dich aber ye niemandt verurtailt hat, so will ich dich auch nit verurtaylen, dann es ist nit mein ambt. Jch binn auch nit zů einem vrtailer gesetzt worden, sonnder zů einem Seligmacher. Darumb so gehe hin, vnnd sünnde fürbaß nimmer. Das ist mein ambt, die sünd zů verzeyhen, vnnd beuelhenn, das man sich füran vor den sünden hüette. Hört ir da, lieben Brüeder, wie Christus sein ambt so ordenlich braucht, vnd lasset dennocht das richterlich ambt in seinem werd beleiben. Also mügend sich auch die Kirch mit irem Bann, vnnd die Oberkhayt mit irem Schwert bey ein ander vergeen vnd khains dem andern in sein ambt greiffen." Hubmaier, *Von dem Schwert*, 444.

Hence the biblical model for cooperation between state and the free church within its midst differentiates between the mutually exclusive and respective rights of each body to punish temporally with the sword and to punish spiritually with the ban.

Encountering opposition to this model from South German radicals such as Hans Hut and Hans Denck upon their 1527 visit to Nikolsburg, Hubmaier quickly found himself forced to defend himself against the notion that the ban superseded the use of the sword among Christians.[27] One passage frequently quoted by Hut and Denck was Matthew 18:15-20, from which they argued that government among Christians would render church discipline redundant and unnecessary. Since Christ commanded believers to execute church discipline, they alleged, government among Christians is improper. Hubmaier furnishes firsthand testimony of such a charge: "Matt. 18:15ff.: From this passage the brothers again raise a grievous accusation against me and say: 'If government were to be allowed among Christians, then the Christian ban would come to nothing and be in vain. For where one punishes evildoers with the sword, the church does not need the ban."[28] By way of response, Hubmaier employs a two-pronged strategy. First, he calls attention to the distinctions both between the respective orders to enforce the ban and wield the sword and between the people to whom the orders were given, namely, the church in particular over against humanity in general:

The ban and punishment with the sword are two very different commands given by God. The first is promised and given to the church by Christ. . . . The second command relates to the external and temporal authority and government, which originally was given by God to Adam after his Fall. . . . Likewise God also entrusted the sword to other special and God-fearing people, including Abraham, Moses, Joshua, Gideon, and Samuel. Afterwards, however, the wickedness of humankind increased and became overflowing; indeed, the bulk of it became so rampant that the people at one time demanded a king from Samuel and abandoned God. Then Samuel gave them that very king at the command of God, but plainly indicated to them the consequent royal authority, obligations, and services to which they were bound to give the king from that point forward due to their sins, because they had de-

27. Bergsten, *Hubmaier*, 451-52.

28. "Mat. 18 [V. 15ff.]. Auß disem Text fierent die Brüeder aber einn schwere anklag wider mich vnnd sagent: So ein Oberkhait vnder den Christen sein solle, so würde doch der Christenlich Bann zünichtig vnd vergebenlich. Denn wo man mit dem Schwert strafft die vbelthätter, mag die Kirch den Bann nit brauchen." Hubmaier, *Von dem Schwert*, 442.

spised and abandoned God and had earnestly demanded from Samuel a king like the other nations and not from God.[29]

Here Hubmaier appeals to the monarchies of biblical Israel as well as their pagan neighbors in order to legitimate the necessity of magisterial government for both Christians and non-Christians. The reformer strengthens the point by turning to the Pauline principle in Romans 13, which specifically enjoins obedience to the government upon believers: "Such subjection and burden we must and should still today obediently and willingly bear and endure; also we must give and render tribute to whom tribute belongs, taxes to whom taxes belongs, respect to whom respect belongs, honor to whom honor belongs, Rom. 13."[30] The underlying subtext of Hubmaier's remark is the illegitimacy of the claim by Hut and Denck that submission of the faithful to government applied only in Old Testament times and displayed no continuity to believers living under the new covenant. As a result of Paul's rearticulation of the Old Testament decree, Hubmaier issues the following strong polemic against his anti-statist opponents: "Rom. 13: This passage, dear brothers, is alone strong enough to confirm the government against all the gates of hell, as Paul clearly declares that everyone should be subject to the government."[31] In the second horn of his argument, Hubmaier illustrates

---

29. "Bannen vnd mit dem Schwert straffen seind zween vnderschidlich beuelch von Got geben. Der erst ist verhaissn vnd geben der Kirchen von Christo. . . . Der annder Beuelch betrifft an den eüsserlichen vnd zeytlichen gwalt vnd regierung, wölher anfengklich von Gott ist geben worden dem Adam nach dem fall. . . . Also hat auch Gott nachmals andern sonderlichen vnnd gotsförchtigen menschen das Schwert angehenckt vnnd beuolhen, als namlich dem Abraham, Moisi, Josua, Gedeonj vnd Samuelj. Demnach aber die boßhait der menschen sich noch mer erreget vnd vberflüssiger worden, ja gar der massen vber hand genomen, das das volck danntzmal einem Künig von dem Samuele begeert hat vnd Gott verworffen. Den selben Künig hat jnen Samuel auß Götlichem beuelch auch geben, doch jnen darbey die khünigklichen gerechtigkaiten, bürden vnd dienstbarkaiten, die sy dem Khünig züthon füran schuldig werdent, von wegen irer sünden, darumb das sy Gott verachtet, verworffen vnnd einen Khünig, wie die andern Nationen, von dem Samuel vnd nit von Gott begeert haben, ernstlich anzaigen lassen." Ibid., 442-43.

30. "Solhe dienstbarkaiten vnd bschwerden müessen vnd sollen wir nun noch heüt bey tag gehorsamlich vnd willigklich leyden, gedulden vnd tragen. Roma. 13." Ibid., 443.

31. "Ro. 13. c. Diese Schrifft, Jr lieben Brüder, ist allain gnůg wider alle portten der hellen zů bestettigung der Oberkhait. Wann Paulus sagt ye haytter herauß, das yederman vnderthenig sein solle der Oberkait." Ibid., 455.

the divergent functions of but common divine authority underlying both physical and spiritual punishment. To reinforce the independence of these realms, Hubmaier highlights that not all sins are punishable by the state and therefore must be remedied by the church: "Indeed there is frequently good reason to employ the Christian ban, for instance, as with many secret sins where the sword can rarely be employed."[32] However, since both government and church cooperate to bring God's rule to the earth in the respective realms of common grace and special grace, Hubmaier declares: "See now, dear brothers, that these two offices and commands of the ban and external sword are not opposed to each other since they are both from God . . . out of love for the common good and territorial peace."[33] While the government dispenses common grace by punishing evildoers "for the sake of their souls' salvation," the church dispenses special grace through the spiritual safety-net of discipline "so that the pious remain at peace and unharmed."[34] Therefore, Hubmaier argues that any Anabaptist, who under the pretense of spirituality refuses to be subject to or assist the government, resists the mandate of God and will thereby suffer divine judgment.

While baptism enables one to enter the free state church, regular reception of the Eucharist permits one to voluntarily remain within the faith community and, consequently, under its spiritual supervision. Conversely, if one wishes to free oneself from the church's disciplinary arm, one need only stop receiving the Eucharist and choose not to listen to the resultant warnings which would be sure to follow (of course, this could also be done by committing some other sin and ignoring the warnings).[35] Just as failure to partake of the Lord's Supper was *prima facie* considered sacrilegious by Calvin, who rejected the physical presence of Christ in the sacrament,[36] even more so did Hubmaier regard the refusal to physically share in the real presence of Christ as a blasphemous neglect of God which bordered on an out-

---

32. "Dann der Christenlich Bann hat öfftermals stat vnd füeg, als namlich in vil haimlichen sünden, dar jnn das Schwert nit all weg mag gebraucht werden." Ibid., 444.

33. "Sehent ir nun, lieben Brüeder, das dise zway ämbter vnd beuelh des Banns vnd des eüsserlichen Schwerts nit wider ein ander seind, seydmal sy bayde von Gott seind . . . auß liebe des gmainen nutzs vnnd landßfridens." Ibid.

34. "die Oberkait straffen will die bösen, wie sy denn zúthon schuldig bey irer seelen säligkait. . . . auff das die frommen zú rüen vnd vnbeschedigt pleibend." Ibid., 455.

35. Sachsse, *Hubmaier als Theologe*, 207.

36. As abundantly evidenced by the Genevan Consistory Registers, in which Calvin berates those who neglect the Lord's Table without sufficient reason; see Kingdon, *Registers*, 28, 51-52, 72, 128, 158.

right rejection of him. As Hubmaier affirms in his 1526 catechism, every person rejecting the Eucharist "blasphemes [Christ], for he does not believe that Christ is the all-merciful and all-gracious one in heaven, our only intercessor, mediator, gracious one with the Father. That is a blasphemy against God opposed by all the Scriptures."[37] It should be noted that all who separate themselves from the spiritual discipline of the church in this or any other way cannot be compelled or in any way pressured to return to the church by the government; if such persons have not violated civil law, they are to be left alone. In his 1524 treatise on freedom of conscience Hubmaier proclaimed, "The authorities [must] judge the evildoers but not the godless," and that civil authorities who persecute the godless "are the greatest heretics of all, because in opposition to the teaching and example of Jesus they consign heretics to fire; and prior to the appointed time they root up the wheat with the tares."[38] Moreover, Hubmaier insisted that no restriction could exist which forbade a banned member of the church from holding political office. While the reformer believes that Christians make better rulers than non-Christians, he insists that God "will also let the infidels rule over us and if we try to escape Rehoboam we will run into the hands of Jeroboam" and that the faithful should "strive to live in peace under a heathen government."[39] Hubmaier thus commands his flock at Nikolsburg to obey the government regardless of the magistrates' faith or lack thereof: "Believing or unbelieving, we must be obedient and in subjection to it."[40] Endeavoring to render the ecclesial inclusion or exclusion of anyone a matter of that person's free choice, Hubmaier maintained that a miscreant could freely rejoin the church by being readmitted to the Eucharist. However, the return was more difficult than the departure because one had to take definite steps to prove to the bishop or priest that one was truly repentant. Through the respective proc-

---

37. "der lestert in. Denn er glaubt nit, das Christus der aller gnedigst vnd aller barmhertzigest sey in den himelen, vnser ainiger fürbitter, mitler vnnd gnediger gegen dem vatter, vnnd das ist ein gots lesterung wider all schrifften." Hubmaier, *Eine christliche Lehrtafel*, 319-20.

38. "Der gwalt richtett die boßhafften, aber nit die gotloßen. . . . die allergrösten ketzer sind, in dem das sy wider Christus leer vnd exempel die ketzer in das feür verurtailen vnd vor der zeyt der ärnd außrafuffend den waitzen zū samt dem vnkraut." Hubmaier, *Von Ketzern*, 98-99.

39. "Ja auch die weybischen vber vnns hörschen lassen, vnd wo wir schon den Roboam fliehen wöllen, werden wir dem Hieroboam in die hennd lauffen. . . . begeren wir jm friden zū leben vnder der Haidischen Oberkayt." Hubmaier, *Von dem Schwert*, 443, 457.

40. "Sy sey glaubig oder vnglaubig, solle man jr ye gehorsam sein vnd vnderthenig." Ibid., 455.

esses of return and departure, Hubmaier affirms that church discipline is effectively

> used according to [Christ's] will for the admission of the pious into her Holy Communion and the exclusion of the unworthy. So, the sins of whomever the Christian church forgives on earth, the same are surely forgiven also in heaven, and the sins of whomever she does not forgive here on earth, the same are also not remitted in heaven.[41]

In Hubmaier's balance between physical and spiritual discipline, therefore, the sacraments serve as the necessary means for implementation of a free state church, as they not only disclose the identity of the insiders and outsiders to the church, but they also enable the outsiders to freely become insiders and vice versa.

Practical Implementation of Hubmaier's Ecclesiology in Waldshut and Nikolsburg

Hubmaier's view of the relationship between church and government in the world was manifested by the way he carried out his own reformation in Waldshut (1523-25) and Nikolsburg (1526-28). Hubmaier had originally begun his reform movement in Waldshut by preaching a mixture of evangelical ideas with the need for believers' baptism, as exemplified by his *Achtzehn Schlußreden* (1523), and by passing out tracts to the general populace.[42] Following the magisterial approach to reform, among Hubmaier's initial aims was to persuade the Waldshut City Council of the validity of his theology, which met with success as the entire City Council was rebaptized no later than April 1523. Due to the reformer's spellbinding preaching, a growing evangelical sentiment quickly spread throughout the city and the surrounding regions, inciting the Bishop of Constance to brand Hubmaier as a Lutheran heretic (despite his divergence from Luther on free will and sac-

---

41. "den selben in einlassung der frommen in ir heilige gmainschafft vnd in außschliessung der vnndichtigen, nach seinem willen zûbrachen. Also, das wölhen menschen die Christenlich Kirch verzeyhet ire sünden auff erden, denselbigenn seinnd sy schon verzygen auch in den himeln, vnd wölhen sy ire sünden nit verzeihet hye auff erden, den selben seind sy nit nach gelassenn auch in den himelen." Ibid., 442.

42. Mabry, *Doctrine of the Church*, 194-95.

ramental theology) in May 1523.[43] Hubmaier supplies an account of the charges levied against him by his Catholic opponents:

> Hear this, O you dear pious Christians, what great things these witnesses speak against me. Yes, they shout with a loud voice that I am possessed and have seven devils in me who talk out of me. They maintain also that I am a Mammaluke (an infidel or apostate, in reference to the Mameluke military caste which dominated Egypt since the thirteenth century), that I have crosses branded on my heels and have goat's feet. . . . in sum, that I am the very worst Lutheran archheretic that one could find.[44]

Such testimony underlines the alarm of the Catholic hierarchy that Waldshut, a nominally Catholic city, was fast becoming a center of Hubmaier's new doctrines. By October 1523, the Catholic authorities of Austria were demanding that Hubmaier be divested of his bishopric and expelled from the city. However, since Hubmaier's reforms had the cooperation and support of the City Council along with the majority of the citizens, neither the government nor the populace would betray their bishop.[45] This noncompliance induced Archduke Ferdinand to send a royal delegation to Waldshut, which arrived on 5 December 1523 carrying two charges against Hubmaier: first, that he had violated the imperial mandate by which no one was to join the "Lutheran Sect"; and second, that he had falsely expounded the Holy Scriptures.[46] When the delegation insisted that Hubmaier be handed over to the Bishop of Constance, the Waldshut City Council, consisting of eight members in addition to the mayor, rejected the accusations of the Austrians together with their demand. Moreover, a large body of Waldshut citizens implored the Austrians that they be allowed to keep the "zealous guardian of their souls" on the basis of the *Nürnberger Mandat*.[47] Since this mandate,

---

43. Bergsten, *Hubmaier*, 122.

44. "Hörent zů, o jr lieben, frommen Christen, wie grosse ding dise zeügen wider mich sagen. Ja, sy reden auch überlaut, jch sey besessenn, hab syben teüfel bey mir, die selben reden auß mir. Jch sey ein Mammaluck. Jch hab brennte creütz vnden an den fersen vnd gayßfüeß. . . . in Summa, ich sey der aller böst Lutherisch ertzketzer, den man finden müge." Hubmaier, *Entschuldigung*, 273.

45. Sachsse, *Hubmaier als Theologe*, 132.

46. Karl Schib, *Die vier Waldstädte* (Vorderösterreich: Freiburg, 1959), 356.

47. August Kluckhohn, ed., *Deutsche Reichstagsakten: Jüngere Reihe* (Göttingen: Vandenhoeck & Ruprecht, 1962), 3:450.

which the Second Imperial Diet adopted on 6 March 1523, stipulated that the truth or falsity of doctrine should be determined by Catholic biblical scholars, of which Hubmaier, as an Ingolstadt *doctor theologiae*, was one, the people protested to the delegation, quoting verbatim the words of the *Mandat*, that Ferdinand was acting contrary to established law. Here it should be noted that a minority of Catholic citizens, who consented with the request of the delegation, were left unmolested by the City Council after the delegation left Waldshut emptyhanded.[48] Hence the City Council followed Hubmaier's requirement that the government could not persecute those it designated heretics even when its star preacher's career was at stake. At the close of 1523, then, Hubmaier remained safely in Waldshut, where he perpetuated his reforms both because of and with the full support of the civil government and most of its citizens.

Although 1524 brought mounting opposition from the Austrian imperial authorities against Hubmaier, he would be fully supported by the City Council during the remainder of his tenure in Waldshut. This vote of confidence from the Council was due in large part to the reformer's aforementioned view of the relationship between church and government, which the city officials found quite appealing.[49] Perceiving that the local government would continue to support their bishop, the Austrian authorities took matters into their own hands on Pentecost Day of 1524, as they attempted to capture Hubmaier by force. Their plan failed when both men and women of Waldshut, armed with weapons, marched on the town square to block the delegation and demand that Hubmaier remain in the city. According to the eyewitness testimony of Heinrich Küssenberg, moreover, Mayor Gutjahr not too subtly encouraged the populace to enjoin violence against the foreigners by detaching them from the protection of the law: "[He] neither would nor could promise them any protection, and [said he] did not know how to safeguard them in these days that were so charged with passion."[50] Consequently, the delegation retreated from the city on 17 May 1524. Hence all attempts by the Austrians to induce either the government or citizens of Waldshut to hand over their pastor and renounce his new teachings came to naught.[51] However, Hubmaier refused to exert military force to defend him-

---

48. Loserth, *Hubmaier*, 95-99.

49. Mabry, *Doctrine of the Church*, 195.

50. "[Er] kein Schirm versprechen wollte noch konnte, vnd [er sagt] mit Vermelden, er wüßte sie in dieser so hitzigen Verwirrung nicht zu beschützen." Heinrich Küssenberg, *Chronik der Reformation in der Grafschaft Baden, im Klettgau und auf dem Schwarzwalde*, ed. J. Huber (Solothurn, 1875), 10.

51. Bergsten, *Hubmaier*, 125-26.

self against the Austrians even when having the opportunity to do so. When asked on 31 July 1524, for example, by a band of 600 peasants from the territory of the Landgrave of Stühlingen, just northeast of Waldshut, whether he would join their cause, he vehemently refused to rebel against the Austrians.[52] Here we see that in times of crisis, Hubmaier did not abandon the theological commitments upon which his model of church-government relations were based.[53] While in Hubmaier's view both church and government are God's servants in the Kingdom of the World, with the responsibility of changing the world according to God's ordained will, neither the church nor the government is given the role of attacking or overthrowing evil institutions in the world.[54] Thus, the societal institutions that evildoers construct to carry out their wicked purposes in the world are not under attack in Hubmaier's system. Rather, both church and government are to focus solely upon evil individuals and their wicked acts. The church is to make its impact on the world by transforming the evil individuals within it into saints, not by waging a frontal attack on worldly institutions. These saints, then, indirectly transform their surroundings and gradually bring them into conformity with God's will.[55] To illustrate, the Christian magistrate judges and rules according to God's will, thereby implementing God's will in their domains and thus in the Kingdom of the World. The task of the church in government, however, is to lead other magistrates to regeneration and subsequently nurture them to lives of Christian righteousness.[56] Although Christians who hold civic offices will make their governments more godly in their actions and affairs, these benefits comprise incidental byproducts rather than primary goals of the ecclesiastical striving to conform each individual, not the government, to the likeness of Christ.

After Hubmaier and the City Council were forced out of Waldshut by the Austrian imperial forces in December 1525, the reformer addressed correspondence to the ruling Lichtenstein family of Nikolsburg, arguably the most tolerant city in Europe at the time.[57] As a result of reading Hubmaier's 1526 Eucharistic treatise, *Ein einfältiger Unterricht*, both Leonhard and Hans von Lichtenstein were converted to the reformer's ideals, whom they invited to their city as a replacement for the retiring bishop Martin Göschl.[58]

---

52. Sachsse, *Hubmaier als Theologe*, 136.
53. Hubmaier would not have died at the stake in 1528 otherwise.
54. Mabry, *Doctrine of the Church*, 196-97.
55. Sachsse, *Hubmaier als Theologe*, 138.
56. Windhorst, *Täuferisches Taufverständnis*, 84.
57. Estep, *Anabaptist Story*, 94.
58. Loserth, *Hubmaier*, 827.

Upon his arrival in June 1526, Hubmaier immediately baptized the two Lords von Lichtenstein, to whom he dedicated the first revision of his catechism, *Eine christliche Lehrtafel,* by casting Leonhard as the questioner and Hans as the respondent. Thus, Hubmaier's reformation in Nikolsburg was carried out with the cooperation of the civil authorities.[59] With the help of the members of the Lichtenstein family as well as the clergy of the town, Hubmaier rapidly transformed his Catholic parish into a free state church. Since Hubmaier had the opportunity to work for a year in Nikolsburg without interference, he was able to concentrate on his activities as a reformer and writer. As had transpired previously in Regensburg and Waldshut, his gifts as a popular religious leader soon became apparent.[60] Moreover, Hubmaier enjoyed the support of his publisher Simprecht Sorg, also known as Froschauer, one of Zwingli's former printers who embraced believers' baptism as a result of the Zurich debate between the two reformers in December 1525. When he was forced to leave Zurich because of his radical views, Sorg followed Hubmaier to Nikolsburg and set up his print shop there, from which press seventeen works of Hubmaier appeared in the course of the single year from June 1526 to June 1527.[61] There are several eyewitness accounts that a vigorous movement centered around Hubmaier's reforms sprang up in Nikolsburg; at least six thousand and at most twelve thousand freely chose to be baptized during that pivotal year.[62] Through Hubmaier, Nikolsburg became the center of a considerable religious movement, such that his Catholic opponents claimed not only that Nikolsburg had become a refuge for all kinds of heretics and apostates but also that Hubmaier had established such a reputation that almost everyone in Moravia and a good number from Austria flocked to him as to the oracle of Apollo in Delphi.[63] Hubmaier himself compared Nikolsburg with Emmaus and claimed that the city has also been dubbed Emmaus "by the cosmographers."[64] It was at Emmaus, Hubmaier argued, that Christ appeared after his resurrection to two of his disciples who asked him to stay with them, because the day was declining and night was coming on. Similarly, Christ had journeyed to Nikolsburg after the recent resurrection of his living Word, brought about in Saxony by Luther. There Christ's servants asked him to stay, for "the night

---

59. Vedder, *Hübmaier,* 151-52.
60. Estep, *Anabaptist Story,* 94-95.
61. Vedder, *Hübmaier,* 153-54.
62. These sources are discussed by Loserth, *Hubmaier,* 829; Vedder, *Hübmaier,* 152-53; and Estep, *Anabaptist Story,* 95.
63. Bergsten, *Hubmaier,* 410.
64. Hubmaier, *Ein einfältiger Unterricht,* 289.

is beginning and the last days have come."[65] This declaration, made by Hubmaier in the fall of 1526, serves as an indication of the atmosphere which prevailed at that time in the stirring religious life of Nikolsburg. In addition, it shows that in Nikolsburg, as previously in Waldshut, Hubmaier considered his work of reform as a part of the great evangelical movement that had begun with Luther, in spite of the former's anthropological and sacramentological divergence from the latter.

Notwithstanding the fact that Hubmaier worked in close accord with the government in Nikolsburg as in Waldshut, there is nothing in the source material to suggest that in either city baptism, from which church membership resulted, and participation in the Eucharist did not take place on the basis of the free decision of the individual.[66] Due to this state of affairs, Hubmaier's congregations in Waldshut and Nikolsburg can be described as both state churches and free churches. Hence, as Torsten Bergsten points out, the church-type "which bears Hubmaier's stamp is a unique historical occurrence of its kind. . . . It was the result of his consistent efforts to reformulate baptism and the Lord's Supper."[67] While Hubmaier's Waldshut and Nikolsburg parishes cannot be identified with the territorial churches of Luther and Zwingli, neither were they separatist conventicles like most of the churches founded by the Anabaptists. One pivotal event that reveals the differences between Hubmaier's church model and Anabaptist ecclesiology was the 1527 controversy surrounding the arrest of South German radical Hans Hut in Nikolsburg. In the spring of 1527, Hut's preaching tour of Moravia brought him to Nikolsburg, where he openly championed chiliastic ideas and insisted, despite his prohibition of those he perceived as authentic Christians punishing one another with the sword, on the use of the sword "by the godly against the ungodly" in setting up the kingdom of God.[68] For example, Hut sounded the following battle-cry during an open-air sermon on 15 March 1527:

> Then [shortly before the end of the age] all the godless will be destroyed, and that by true Christians; if their number [the true Christians]

---

65. "es fahe an nacht werden vnnd kummen die letsten tag." Ibid.

66. Bergsten, *Hubmaier*, 456; Windhorst, *Täuferisches Taufverständnis*, 154.

67. "Die von Hubmaier geprägte Täuferkirche ist eine in ihrer Art einmalige historische Erscheinung. . . . Sie ist das Ergebnis seiner konsequenten Bemühungen, die Taufe und das Abendmahl . . . neu zu gestalten." Bergsten, *Hubmaier*, 456.

68. Statement of Hans Hut, in Walter Klaassen, ed., *Anabaptism in Outline* (Scottdale, Pa.: Herald Press, 1981), 266.

shall be sufficient, they will go from Germany to Switzerland, and to Hungary, and have no regard to princes and lords. Then some thousands of them shall assemble, and everyone should sell his goods and take the money with him, so as to be sure, meantime, of food; then they shall wait until the Turk comes. If the Turk fails to strike down any of the princes, monks, priests, nobles, or knights, they will then be stricken and slain by the little company of true Christians.[69]

Against the convictions of Hut, Hubmaier immediately took a positive stand for his doctrine of the complementary but distinct roles of the government and church. Accordingly, Hubmaier upheld the legitimacy of the government and affirmed its exclusive right to wield the sword, and he ascribed sole authority in spiritual matters to the church. Thus, in rejecting the anarchistic principles of Hut, Hubmaier publicly departed from the nonresistant ethic of the *Schleitheim Confession*, but to a much less serious degree than had Hut.[70] By May 1527, a schism developed among the parishioners of Nikolsburg, as many of the common people and not a few of Hubmaier's most prominent disciples, such as Oswald Glaidt, were carried away by Hut's intoxicating ideology of holy violence.[71] Hubmaier quickly dubbed Hut and his followers as insurrectionists and called a theological disputation in an attempt to settle the matter through an examination of the biblical text. However, when the leaders met in Bergen on 21 September 1527, the discussion left them farther apart than before, as Hut not only refused to retract his militaristic views but proceeded to affirm, in a primitive unitarian fashion, that Christ was a great prophet, not God's Son, and that the angels had become men together with Christ.[72] On a positive note for Hubmaier, this disputation cost Hut the support of the Nikolsburg preachers, who were so outraged by his heterodox christology that they rejected his eschatology as well and realigned themselves with Hubmaier.[73] Moreover, Leonhard and Hans von Lichtenstein, fearing that Hut posed a serious threat to the public order, summoned the principals to their castle at Nikolsburg, where the whole subject was thoroughly analyzed in their presence on 5 October 1527.[74] When Hut persistently maintained that his teachings on the violent overthrow of the state by armed Christians constituted "the plain sense of the Scriptures," namely apocalyptic passages describing "the sword of the Lord" (Ezek. 21)

---

69. Sermon of Hans Hut, in Klaassen, *Anabaptism*, 320.

70. Estep, *Anabaptist Story*, 98-99.

71. Bergsten, *Hubmaier*, 452.

72. Vedder, *Hübmaier*, 167; Bergsten, *Hubmaier*, 459.

73. Bergsten, *Hubmaier*, 460.

74. Loserth, *Hubmaier*, 835.

and the battle of Armageddon (Rev. 19:11-20:10),[75] Leonhard von Lichten-stein arrested Hut and, with Hubmaier's approval, detained the Anabaptist leader as a prisoner in the castle.[76]

Not surprisingly in light of his great popularity as an evangelist, Hut's church-sanctioned imprisonment by the city magistrate immediately pro-voked the wrath of many Nikolsburg citizens as well as the Anabaptists in the surrounding Moravian districts. Both groups levied the charge of hypoc-risy against Hubmaier, as he allegedly revealed himself to be an inconsistent advocate of religious liberty who, in contradiction of his own treatises to the contrary and like the Catholics, Lutherans, and Zwinglians before him, per-secuted heretics when he had the opportunity.[77] In order to sustain peace among his parishioners, Hubmaier published the *Nikolsburg Articles* on 4 November 1527, which defended Hut's imprisonment on the basis of the separation of powers between church and government. Hubmaier argued that he never requested the imprisonment of Hut, and that the chiliastic preacher was not incarcerated on doctrinal grounds but as a result of his attempted subversion of the commonweal.[78] According to Vedder, Hubmaier's line of reasoning is corroborated by the historical evidence: "The action of the ruler, however, seems quite justified by the facts as we know them. Hut was plainly teaching sedition and murder . . . [including] murder as a duty in the near future. No principle of religious liberty requires that a government shall leave such a firebrand to go about in the community."[79] Hence the *Nikols-burg Articles*, borne out of a practical controversy that Hubmaier never an-ticipated, clarified the reformer's thinking on the following point: the only time that governmental authority may be exerted against a heretic is if that heretic also undermines the public order.[80] This elucidation seems to have been effectual among Hubmaier's flock in promoting a better understanding of his views on church and government, and controversy regarding the sword rapidly decreased in Nikolsburg.[81] While the *Articles* only heightened opposition to Hubmaier among Moravian Anabaptist leaders such as Jacob Wiedemann, who championed an extreme form of nonresistance (even to the point of refusing to pay taxes) and quickly branded Hubmaier as a *Schwert-*

---

75. Interrogation of Hans Hut, in Klaassen, *Anabaptism*, 273.
76. Vedder, *Hübmaier*, 167-68.
77. Bergsten, *Hubmaier*, 457-58.
78. Sachsse, *Hubmaier als Theologe*, 152.
79. Vedder, *Hübmaier*, 168.
80. Sachsse, *Hubmaier als Theologe*, 153-54.
81. Vedder, *Hübmaier*, 176.

ler (person of the sword) rather than a *Stäbler* (person of the staff),[82] these anti-statist opponents naturally lacked the political power needed to subvert Hubmaier's implementation of a free state church. By December 1527, the Nikolsburg church as a whole seems to have been satisfied that the proper course of action had been pursued against Hut; in the meantime, however, Hut escaped from the Nikolsburg castle, as some sympathetic hands let the preacher down with a rope over the walls by night, and fled to Augsburg.[83] With the departure of Hut, the apocalyptic fires in Nikolsburg were completely extinguished, and Hubmaier's ecclesiology emerged victorious from its only serious battle against the forces of internal collapse.

Synopsis of Hubmaier's Ecclesiology

The creation of Hubmaier's anomalous free state churches in Waldshut and Nikolsburg represents the first sixteenth-century attempt to forge a tenuous balance between the often encroaching realms of religious voluntarism and civil magistracy without resorting to the use of "holy violence." By endeavoring to place spiritual authority exclusively in the ecclesiastical sphere and to confine temporal authority within governmental borders, Hubmaier formulated a doctrine of church-state relations in which the two entities were distinct yet complementary agents appointed by God to usher human beings out of the kingdom of the world and into the kingdom of heaven. Reflecting yet modifying medieval Catholic ideas, Hubmaier posits that the church operates as a sort of "admissions office" to the heavenly kingdom, where the sacrament of believers' baptism (along with the corresponding baptismal vow) serves as the liminal door into the kingdom which anyone can freely enter.[84] Neglect of "the sacrament of the altar,"[85] either by directly refusing to receive coupled with a failure to heed the consequent threefold disciplinary warning or by indirectly refusing to receive (*i.e.* coming under the ban) through failure to heed the threefold warning for some other sin, conversely, serves as an exit door to the church of which anyone can freely avail oneself. Although it would require far more effort on the person's part, someone who had freely chosen to leave the church could freely reenter by taking the disciplinary steps for readmission to the Eucharist. For Hubmaier, because of the intrinsically voluntary essence of the Christian message, neither government nor church may use force or any other form of compulsion to bring

---

82. Estep, *Anabaptist Story*, 127-28.
83. Vedder, *Hübmaier*, 169.
84. Hubmaier, *Eine christliche Lehrtafel*, 314.
85. Hubmaier, *Ein einfältiger Unterricht*, 289.

persons into or keep persons within the kingdom of heaven; such compulsion would undermine the very substance of Christianity itself. On the ecclesiastical side, the Christian's sword is the Word of God and not a sword of steel against the so-called heretic. On the civil side, while the judgment and punishment of criminals is the jurisdiction of the "worldly power," the government has no right to harm an "enemy of God" who wishes to do nothing other than forsake the gospel.[86] According to Hubmaier, not only does faith or the lack thereof lie outside the civil jurisdiction, but to burn a "heretic" amounts to confessing Christ in appearance while denying him in reality. The theological subtext of Hubmaier's argument, therefore, is that persecution of a person for heresy is to deny the incarnation, for the God revealed in Christ is the God of the invitation, not of coercion.[87]

Due to Hubmaier's sacramental theology, in which believers' baptism guarantees a person eventual access into Paradise while freely remaining in the church at the moment of death guarantees that person immediate entrance into Paradise, the church is functionally equivalent to the kingdom of heaven. The church, under the rule of God, is in the world but not of it, while the worldly kingdom is under the control of Satan. Contrary to the Anabaptists, Hubmaier does not equate the kingdom of the world with the state; thus, although the kingdom of heaven and the kingdom of the world are mutually exclusive, the kingdom of heaven and the state experience points of conjunction. Like the church, the government is in the world but was never intended by God to be of it.[88] Since the church is pure and visible in Hubmaier's conception, however, the state is unlike the church in that only the state can defy God's plan by aligning itself with the world. Nevertheless, God has ordained both church and government as his servants in the world, and he has given both the authority and the means for executing their divinely appointed tasks. In harmonious fashion, the church is God's vehicle in the world whereby he reconciles the world to himself, and the government is the tangible guardian instituted by God to protect the church as it performs its duty in the world. Moreover, the church has been given the Word and the Spirit of God, and the government has been given the authority of God and the sword. In exchange for protecting the church from the evildoers of the world, the church is obliged to pray for the government and to cooperate with it in all matters wherein the government carries out its ordained tasks according to the divine will. These tasks include serving as magistrates and soldiers, both of which roles require wielding the sword according to Scrip-

86. Hubmaier, *Von Ketzern*, 98-99.
87. Estep, *Anabaptist Story*, 263.
88. Mabry, *Doctrine of the Church*, 202.

tural principles (aside from simply proof-texting Romans 13, however, Hubmaier never enumerates or explains precisely what these principles are), paying taxes, and taking oaths. The fact that wielding the sword at all, much less assuming civil authority, and taking oaths were anathema to Anabaptists both underlines the profound differences between Hubmaier and the Anabaptists and validates our identification of Hubmaier, according to George Huntston Williams' definition of these terms, as an atypical Magisterial Radical Reformer.[89] While Hubmaier's ecclesiology, as a component of his magisterial style of reform, is drastically removed from that of the Anabaptists, his doctrine of the church is in many respects distinct from that of Luther and Zwingli, especially relative to such concepts as baptism, the Lord's Supper, and freedom of conscience. It is these differences that render Hubmaier's ecclesiology distinctly his own. Moreover, his model of church-state relations appears to furnish a medium or common ground on which most of the ecclesiologies developed in the sixteenth century could meet, if the reformers were minded to do so. As Eddie Mabry rightly perceives on this score,

> [Hubmaier] obviously pulled significant elements from the prevailing theological positions of the period, and provided some similarities and commonalities by this. At the same time, however, he refused to move completely into any one theological camp, but walked a middle path. . . . His doctrine of the church, therefore, seems to be the kind of middle way that could have served as the basis for compromise for the whole protestant movement of the sixteenth century.[90]

Nonetheless, theological views were firmly entrenched during the early modern period, and compromise did not serve as the order of the day. As previously indicated, the life and works of Hubmaier came to an untimely end when he was burned at the stake in Vienna under the sentence of the Austrian King Ferdinand I on 10 March 1528; notably, the charge levied against him was not heresy but anarchy.[91] Such a charge is perhaps an indication of the impact of Hubmaier's ecclesiology, devised from the perspective of a highly trained systematic theologian and an essentially independent thinker, upon his contemporaries.

---

89. Fast, *Der linke Flügel*, xi-xxii.
90. Mabry, *Doctrine of the Church*, 203-04.
91. Bergsten, *Hubmaier*, 477-78.

Conclusion

A Magisterial Radical Sacramentalist

The sacramental theology of Balthasar Hubmaier may aptly be described as "radical" in the fullest sense of the term: not merely according to the nomenclature of George Huntston Williams as encompassing the baptism of believers, thereby returning to the theological root (radix) of early Christianity,[1] but also in the sense of carrying to logical extremes the most philosophically "realist" versions of baptismal and Eucharistic doctrine available in the sixteenth century. This realist emphasis echoes the exaltation of nature over grace in Bernard of Clairvaux, who recognized glimpses of the *imago Dei* throughout the created order and accordingly held that events in the tangible realm could participate in the divinity of the superior immaterial realm. For Bernard, moreover, such events are generated by the free decisions of human beings, a concept which Hubmaier firmly embraced as evidenced by his heavy literary dependence, both structurally and linguistically, on the former's *De gratia et libero arbitrio* for his two central treatises on free choice. As a result of his multifaceted theological pilgrimage leading up to his personal submission to believers' baptism, a journey predicated upon the notion that God grants salvation (at least in *potentia ordinata*) to persons who voluntarily avail themselves of his sacramental channels,[2] Hubmaier's discussion of human free will turned into the problem of baptism. Spawned by his reading of the early Luther, who declared that the sacraments could not be received without *fides*, through Bernardian lenses, Hubmaier instituted the practice of baptizing parishioners with *glaub*,[3] or those who had exercised their post-Fall natural capacity to believe (rather than, as for Luther, those to whom the Holy Spirit had granted the supernatu-

---

1. Fast, *Der linke Flügel*, xiii-xxii.
2. Hubmaier, *Das andere Büchlein*, 416-17.
3. Hubmaier, *Eine christliche Lehrtafel*, 313.

ral gift of *fides*, which may or may not immediately manifest itself in outward belief), at least two years before the reputed "first believers' baptism"
at the Zurich home of Felix Manz on 21 January 1525. No later than his second stint at Regensburg in 1522, Hubmaier introduced what I denominate as
"catechetical rebaptism," wherein children, who were baptized as infants and
acquired an adequate knowledge of the gospel through training in his catechism, received from the reformer the sacrament of believers' baptism in
place of the sacrament of confirmation. At some point between May 1521
and January 1523, Hubmaier successfully entreated his entire flock at Waldshut to be rebaptized, save the clergy whom he deemed, following Bernard's
doctrine of holy orders, as already "rebaptized" by virtue of their ordination.
When Wilhelm Reublin, a zealous preacher of anticlericalism, convinced
him of the spiritual impotence of holy orders, an anxious Hubmaier quickly
accepted believers' baptism from Reublin in front of his entire congregation
and proceeded to rebaptize personally his subordinate clergy on Easter Saturday of 1525.

Surpassing the Lutheran and medieval Catholic doctrine of baptismal
regeneration, Hubmaier argued that the baptizand is not only regenerated but
also inherits eternal security, or the assurance that she or he will eventually
be admitted to Paradise, *ex opere operato* at the moment the sacrament is
administered. In terms of his threefold anthropology, which he borrowed
textually from Bernard, Hubmaier defines regeneration as the divine restoration of the freedom of counsel, which enables the baptizand's spirit, like that
of the pre-Fall Adam, to generate good thoughts in and of itself. Hence the
act of baptism became, according to God's ordained will, the *ratio praedestinationis ex parte praedestini*, or the human basis upon which God elected
individuals in the possible world he chose to actualize. In contradistinction
to the Anabaptists, however, Hubmaier refused to anathematize the majority
of Christians since the decree of Pope Innocent I (407), rendering infant baptism the official practice of the church, but declared that God, in *potentia
absoluta*, saved all believers who lacked the combination of water and a baptizer through faith alone. Conversely, Hubmaier was quick to damn his sixteenth-century contemporaries who refused to submit to believers' baptism,
despite their possessing every opportunity to receive this sacrament, while
relying upon *sola fides* for their salvation.[4] Employing his detailed knowledge of church history gained as a doctoral student at Ingolstadt, Hubmaier
defended his reconceptualization of baptism, surprisingly not through an
appeal to Scripture, but by drawing together variegated doctrinal threads
from the pre-Augustinian Church Fathers. Thus Hubmaier, in magisterial

---

4. Hubmaier, *Von der christlichen Taufe*, 142-43.

fashion, sought a reformation that would bring the sixteenth-century church into continuity with its Patristic exemplar, rather than an Anabaptist restoration of the church along New Testament lines. Notwithstanding the desire to portray his doctrine of baptism as the logical outworking of Patristic concepts, Hubmaier did not hesitate to apply his theological creativity to the sixteenth-century baptismal debate in ways that departed from his ecclesiastical forebears. Perhaps most notable are his identification of baptism as the church's dominically bestowed key (Mt. 16:18) that unlocks the entrance door to the kingdom of heaven coupled with his understanding of this door as the baptismal vow which constitutes the first stage of church discipline.[5] While retaining the medieval Catholic view that the church held the authority to forgive sins, Hubmaier tempered this doctrine by transferring this "power of the keys" from the penitential realm to the sacramental realm; thus the visible church, identical for the reformer with the true church, exercised this power by transferring sinners from eternal bondage in the kingdom of the world to eternal citizenship in the kingdom of heaven through baptism. Even so, Hubmaier preserved the notion of divine accountability for persistent sin in the Christian life with his novel doctrine of purgatory, in which believers dying under the ban must serve a temporary sentence in hell, in which they are "purged" of serious sin, before their eventual entrance into heaven. In order to facilitate a predictable system of church discipline which serves as a spiritual safety-net for the faithful rather than a somewhat arbitrary system of shunning likely to provoke consternation, as typified by the Dutch Anabaptist communities of Menno Simons and Dirk Philips,[6] Hubmaier distinguished between fraternal discipline, consisting of the threefold Matthean warning in whose midst the accused remains eligible to receive the Eucharist, and excommunication, which disqualifies the miscreant from partaking of the sacred meal but does not cut him or her off from the life of the community.[7]

Unquestionably the doctrine proposed by Hubmaier which most "radically" diverges from all previous thought and best displays his independence and creativity as a systematic theologian is his concept of the Eucharist. Owing to his Alexandrian Christology, in which the doctrine of *communicatio idiomatum* enables Christ's ubiquity to transfer from his divine nature to his human nature, Hubmaier insisted upon the real presence of Christ in the Supper, as did the Catholic model of transubstantiation and Luther's model of consubstantiation. Unlike Catholicism and Lutheranism, however, Hub-

---

5. Hubmaier, *Form zu taufen*, 349.
6. Williams, *Radical Reformation*, 731-53.
7. Hubmaier, *Bann*, 367-68.

maier postulated that the bearers of the real presence were not the Eucharistic elements of bread and wine, but rather their human recipients in a literal sense. To formulate a coherent explanation of such an ontological change, Hubmaier drew upon the Anselmian distinction between various modes of God's presence, namely, the *praesentia definitiva* versus the *praesentia repletiva*, and included this distinction among the attributes which communicate over to the physical body of Christ.[8] Hence Christ's human nature is definitively present outside the space-time universe while repletively present within the universe. Central to this view of the real presence was Hubmaier's novel exegesis of both the Johannine parable of the vine and the branches, which the reformer contends was spoken by Jesus at the Last Supper, and the Pauline imagery of the church as one body with Christ as head. While the vine and the head comprise the respective sources of existence for the branches and body, the branches and body possess the same physical nature as the vine and head. For Hubmaier, the vine and head allude to the definitive presence of Christ's humanity at the right hand of God the Father, while the branches and body represent the sacramental mode of Christ's repletive presence on earth. It follows, likewise, that the individual grapes on John's branches symbolize the individual partakers of the Eucharist, for as each grape has its own "grapeness" distinct from the vine while simultaneously bearing the nature of the vine, each believer maintains his or her own "humanness" apart from Christ while simultaneously participating in the human nature of Christ. Appealing to the Pauline symbolic explication of the Eucharistic bread, furthermore, Hubmaier claims that when the church eats the one loaf, of which each member consumes a fragment, the church corporately and believers individually bear the repletive presence of Christ's physical body.[9] Since every believer at the Lord's Supper bears the human nature of Christ while simultaneously bearing his or her own human nature distinct from Christ, Hubmaier's Eucharistic theology is quite literally a "consubstantiation," *i.e.* the simultaneous possession of two distinct substances, of believers themselves rather than, as for Luther, the bread and the wine. In addition, as they partake of the elements, the Holy Spirit fills the faithful with a quasi-substantive actual grace which empowers them to do good and avoid evil and is necessary for progressing along the path to sanctification. Participation in such a sacred meal, then, gave new meaning to Paul's admonition against unworthily partaking of the sacrament, as those who so blaspheme are literally guilty of the body and blood of the Lord.

---

8. Hubmaier, *Ein einfältiger Unterricht*, 294-96; Anselm, *Proslogium*, 18, 24-26; Anselm, *Monologium*, 59.

9. Hubmaier, *Messe*, 103.

Concerned to forestall the unthinkable prospect of unrepentant sinners ontologically bearing and so defiling the humanity of Christ, Hubmaier placed the Eucharist and the final stage of church discipline in an antithetical relationship, quite similar to that devised later in the sixteenth century by Calvin in Geneva.

Just as Hubmaier identified baptism as the first of the two keys which opened the entrance door to heaven, so he recognized the Eucharist as the second key which, through its withholding, opened the exit door from heaven. Defining unworthiness to receive as having exhausted the triple disciplinary admonitions in *brüderliche Strafe* without repentance, Hubmaier conceived of the *Bann* as the prohibition of the unworthy from the Lord's Supper.[10] This implementation of the disciplinary climax announced publicly that each miscreant has been separated from the divine wellspring of the community, as denial of the Eucharistic channel of grace precluded the person from the spiritual replenishment indispensable for advancement in the sanctification process. Such a penalty bore immediate consequences for one's destiny during the afterlife: although a baptized believer was necessarily predestined to eternal life and thus could not be finally lost, a banned believer who died would endure a finite punishment in hell before entering heaven, which punishment was avoided entirely by those in good standing with the church. For this reason, *der Bann* amounted to the exit door from the heavenly kingdom.[11] Contrary to the Anabaptist practice of banishing the banned, whom they regarded as irredeemable, from all aspects of the community, Hubmaier declared that the only facet of church life in which the banned could not take part was the Eucharist. As illustrated by the Genevan Consistory registers, virtually the same practice was later established by Calvin, who never barred and often required those deemed as sacramentally unworthy to actively participate in the functions of the church, especially to attend additional sermon services.[12] Similar to Hubmaier's explicit declaration that the gathered body of believers in the Eucharistic meal represents the exact composition of the true church at any given moment, Calvin implicitly affirms that the partakers of the Lord's Supper constitutes the best visible approximation to the invisible church.[13] Although the breaking of bread and drinking of wine is therefore a reaffirmation and strengthening of the covenant between God and each of the elect for both reformers, Hub-

---

10. Hubmaier, *Entschuldigung*, 300-01.

11. Hubmaier, *Bann*, 368-69.

12. Kingdon, *Registers*, 26-27, 37, 75, 77, 95-96, 146.

13. Hubmaier, *Form des Nachtmals Christi*, 359-60; Calvin, *Commentary on Corinthians*, 1.11.25.

maier's covenant is synergistically established when believers freely undergo baptism, while Calvin's covenant is monergistically established by God before the foundation of the world in a manner independent of human freedom. To reaffirm and strengthen the rebaptismal covenant during the Supper services, Hubmaier developed a Eucharistic liturgy which featured the recitation of a *Liebespflicht* (vow of love) by the faithful prior to the clerical consecration of the elements.[14] In this pledge, believers affirm their intent to make good use of the grace to be transmitted through the vehicles of bread and wine, thereby making explicit the inseparability of receiving the love of Christ and offering it to others. Hubmaier's radically new conception of the Eucharist conveyed three profound ramifications directly applicable to the daily lives of the faithful. First, the Lord's Supper constitutes the sole means of grace wherein believers may access and appropriate the numinous power of Christ necessary to perpetuate the incarnation throughout history. Second, this divine empowerment helped beleaguered Christians, especially during the Austrian besiegement of Waldshut in December 1525 and the forcible suppression of Hubmaier's supporters in Nikolsburg after the reformer was burned at the stake in March 1528, to find meaning in their circumstances and prepared them to remain faithful even to the point of martyrdom.[15] Finally, reception of the Eucharist, like baptism, served as a visible mark of the saints whereby believers could recognize each other and find objective assurance that they were among the redeemed, whom God had guaranteed immediate access to Paradise at the moment of death.[16]

The linear progression of Hubmaier's theological system, in which his anthropological foundation of libertarian free will developed into an innovative sacramental theology, culminated in a free state ecclesiology emphasizing liberty of conscience, its preservation in the civil realm, and its actualization in the local church through individual decision-making as to the receipt of baptism and the Lord's Supper. In his 1524 *Von Ketzern und ihren Verbrennern*, the first early modern treatise championing religious freedom, Hubmaier contends that magistrates who sentence heretics to the fire are even more heretical than the godless individuals whom they burn, since they prematurely condemn people to hell who might later have repented of sin and become powerful witnesses of God's grace, which makes good out of evil, if they had lived out the full span of their years.[17] Moreover, by acting in diametric opposition to the dominical ethic of love for enemies articulated

---

14. Hubmaier, *Form des Nachtmals Christi*, 361-63.
15. Rempel, *Lord's Supper*, 88.
16. Armour, *Baptism*, 57.
17. Hubmaier, *Von Ketzern*, 98-99.

in the Sermon on the Mount, such magistrates deny Christ in reality while appearing externally to confess him, thereby rendering themselves more abominable than the infamous Judean king Jehoiakim who, although he incinerated the scroll of Jeremiah, never stooped to the level of incinerating human beings. Extending this admonition to the church, Hubmaier declares that anyone who attempts to engender religious conformity via compulsion implements zeal without Scriptural knowledge, which he regards as spiritually lethal. Although "faith is a work of God and not of the Heretics' Tower," Hubmaier hastens to remind his flock that this does not imply that the Christian has no obligation toward unbelievers.[18] On the contrary, he insists that the so-called "heretic" must be won by spiritual means, including the careful use of Scripture, prayer, patience, and a credible witness. An underlying theological motif which repeatedly manifests itself in Hubmaier's stance on religious freedom is the sovereign judgment of Christ over the souls of humanity, who alone possesses the authority to determine the time when the wheat should be separated from the tares. Therefore, Hubmaier alleges that magistrates and ecclesiastical officials alike usurp Christ's role as judge when they burn those perceived to be heretics, regardless of whether or not they are actually heretics in the sight of God.[19] To prevent humans from overstepping their bounds, God has, in Hubmaier's assessment, both set fixed boundaries upon the jurisdiction of civil government and clearly prescribed the appropriate methods of evangelism for the church. Nevertheless, it should be emphasized that in his theory of church-state relations, Hubmaier most perceptibly dissents from the standard Anabaptist position, as outlined in the *Schleitheim Confession* (1527), that the state is an instrument of Satan in which Christians can take no part.[20]

Far from the perspective of Michael Sattler and the signers of his *Schleitheim Confession*, according to which the most profound tragedy in church history proved to be the recognition of Christianity by the Roman Empire first as a tolerated religion under Constantine (313) and then as the official religion under Theodosius I (381),[21] Hubmaier esteemed as a divine blessing the civil-ecclesiastical Christendom amalgam, in which he believed that God ordained for government and church to play distinct yet complementary roles to advance his kingdom. Similar to Luther and Zwingli, Hubmaier propagated reform in both Waldshut (1523-25) and Nikolsburg (1526-28)

---

18. Hubmaier, *Entschuldigung*, 280; the German is quoted in footnote 134, page 208.
19. Hubmaier, *Von Ketzern*, 100.
20. Sattler, *Schleitheim Confession*, 36-37.
21. Michael Sattler, *Imprisonment: Letter to Horb*, in Yoder, *Legacy*, 60-62.

under the patronage of secular magistrates with whom he always remained on very good terms, as a result of which he dedicated twelve of his twenty-six treatises to nobles and employed their names as characters in his dialogues. In harmony with these magisterial tendencies, Hubmaier composed his rebuttal to the *Schleitheim Confession*, provocatively titled *Von dem Schwert* (On the Sword), just a few months after the Anabaptist doctrinal statement was formulated. While the Anabaptists made a total separation between the church and the government, Hubmaier first made a total separation between the church and the world and then differentiated between the government and the world. In Hubmaier's ecclesiology, the church amounts to the visible kingdom of Christ, the focus of which is on spiritual and eternal matters, which is essentially different from the kingdom of the world, one of sin, death, and hell under the control of Satan that exerts mastery over the earth. Since those of the kingdom of Christ are yet in (but not of) the kingdom of the world, God has established civil government as his servant on earth to protect the good and the defenseless from the evil of the world, thus furnishing the church with the security necessary to carry out the Great Commission. Moreover, God has both hung the sword at the side of the government and commanded the government to wield the sword for its ordained purpose.[22] In return for such protection, the church is obliged to pray for the state and to perform such duties of good citizenship as taking up the sword in defense of one's land, assuming governmental positions, and swearing civil oaths, all of which were anathema to the Anabaptists. In contradistinction to the *Schleitheim Confession*, which pronounces the government to be "the abomination," for Hubmaier the government is neither viewed as the enemy of the church nor even as a necessary evil, but as a friend of the church.[23] Consequently, the faithful must not isolate themselves from the government, as did the Anabaptists, but should remain active in civic affairs to ensure that the government will be run by Christians, which Hubmaier believes would translate into governance according to the divine will. For Hubmaier, therefore, the ideal relationship between church and state is one of mutual cooperation, wherein the state-protected church strives to reconcile fallen humanity to God while the Christian-led state rules under God by defending the rights of the innocent and peaceful. In this way, Hubmaier argues that church and government can forge a partnership aimed at the transformation of the kingdom of the world into the kingdom of Christ.

To prevent such an association from encroaching on the religious liberty of the citizens within the state, Hubmaier reasoned that a mechanism was

---

22. Mabry, *Doctrine of the Church*, 187.
23. Sattler, *Schleitheim Confession*, 38.

necessary which permits people to freely enter and exit the church. This mechanism was readily furnished by his sacramental theology, as baptism and the Eucharist constituted the respective keys in and out of the heavenly kingdom. Choosing to undergo believers' baptism spelled entrance into Hubmaier's free state churches in Waldshut and Nikolsburg, and regular reception of the Eucharist entailed the decision to remain under the spiritual supervision of the faithful. Alternatively, by neglecting "the sacrament of the altar" along with the resultant warnings for doing so, the individual could freely opt out of the faith community and its disciplinary system.[24] Attempting to forestall the potential use of "holy violence" by the church acting under the guise of the state or any conflict of interest between civil authority and the faithful, Hubmaier formulated his doctrine of the "separation of powers" between church and government. Accordingly, Hubmaier declared that by hanging the sword at the side of the government, God had forbidden the church from wielding the sword; hence, the only way a Christian could wield the sword is if she or he were duly appointed as a ruler or soldier of the state. In addition, Hubmaier creatively interpreted the quasi-Johannine account of the woman caught in adultery as a case study of the appropriate roles for government and church to play in the chastisement of criminals. Through his refusal to answer the Jewish legal authorities, Christ showed that he, and derivatively the church, had no legal right to either prevent or enforce the administration of capital punishment. However, Christ's response to the adulteress, "Go and sin no more" (Jn. 8:11), illustrated the ecclesiastical responsibility to forgive sin, thereby admitting people into the kingdom of God, and holding members of the fold spiritually accountable for their persistence in sin through church discipline.[25] Since the primary sources indicate that baptism, reception of the Eucharist, and thus church membership took place on the basis of the free decision of the individual in both Waldshut and Nikolsburg, in which Hubmaier's respective parishes were supported by the Waldshut City Council and the Lords von Lichtenstein, we can safely affirm that Hubmaier established free state churches in both cities. The only instance where the government punished a "heretic," *i.e.* the South German radical Hans Hut, during Hubmaier's career as a rebaptizer was due not to Hut's anti-trinitarian doctrines but to the fact that he was exhorting the Nikolsburg populace to take up arms and overthrow their lords, thereby undermining the public order. Such a church-state configuration, emphasizing a top-down program of reform through the magistrates as

---

24. Hubmaier, *Ein einfältiger Unterricht*, 290.
25. Hubmaier, *Von dem Schwert*, 444.

well as religious liberty, proved to be a unique historical modality in the sixteenth century.

We close this study by returning to the question of Hubmaier's status among the religious reformers of the early modern period. During the brief period of seven years (1521-28) in which Hubmaier formulated and implemented his reformation ideas, he made a tremendous impact on both Anabaptists and those who would come to be known as Protestant reformers. Such an influence, however, upon those with whom Hubmaier interacted was more a result of his theological independence than his adherence to any particular branch of the Reformation. Although his opponents labeled him an "Anabaptist" due to his rejection of infant baptism, a label which has persisted up to the present, Hubmaier was so different from the majority of those regarded as "Anabaptists" that he can scarcely be designated within the same category.[26] This dilemma can be solved by conjoining Williams' classification system with the prevalent definition of Anabaptism in contemporary literature on the Radical Reformation, thereby yielding the following definitions. The term "Magisterial" encompasses those who promote a top-down model of reformation through the magistrates, while term "Radical" denotes a practitioner of believers' baptism.[27] In addition, the term "Anabaptist" refers to one who regards baptism and the Lord's Supper as ordinances (which do not transmit grace) rather than sacraments in the classical sense (*i.e.* means of grace). As not only a practitioner but the originator of believers' baptism in the sixteenth century, Hubmaier must certainly be classed as a Radical Reformer. By the same token, however, Hubmaier cannot be regarded as an Anabaptist. Indirect evidence for this proposition is furnished by Hubmaier's dissent from six of the seven articles of the *Schleitheim Confession*. Notably, Hubmaier denounced the pacifist hallmark of the *Confession*, charging his "dear brothers" with undermining the Pauline admonitions for Christians to display a spirit of cooperative obedience toward the government through their misinterpretation of the Sermon on the Mount. Similarly, he opposed the perceived severity of the *Confession*'s model of the ban, which cut off all contact with the excommunicated and treated them as

---

26. Interestingly enough, this observation seems to have been implicitly made by at least one of Hubmaier's sixteenth-century contemporaries; in his list of religious groups that allegedly destroyed the unity of the church, Michael Hillebrant, the Catholic author of a 1536 polemical document, distinguished between the Lutherans, Zwinglians, Anabaptists, and the "Balthasarianer" (*Von der Einigen, wahrhafftigen, heyligen, Christlichen Kirchen* [Dresden, 1536], printed in Georg Veesenmeyer, *Über Balthasar Hubmör, einen der berühmtesten Wiedertäufer zur Zeit der Reformation* [Halle, 1826], 248).

27. Williams, *Radical Reformation*, xxviii-xxx.

dead, in favor of a "sacrament-powered" disciplinary model that permitted the banned to engage in all forms of ecclesiastical and community life except for the Lord's Supper. Direct evidence that Hubmaier was not an Anabaptist comes from his views on baptism and the Eucharist, as he formulated a genuinely "sacramental" theology wherein both sacred rites served as vehicles or channels of divine grace. In believers' baptism, Hubmaier argued, God imparts to the recipient the grace of regeneration, through which the Holy Spirit restores the recipient's spiritual freedom (freedom of counsel or freedom from sin) to derive good thoughts in and of itself. Due to Hubmaier's libertarian conception of free will, in which even the *initium fidei* was produced by human natural faculties, the fact that regenerating grace was given at believers' baptism rather than infant baptism rendered even the grace of baptism (along with all other forms of grace) cooperative rather than operative. Perhaps even more significantly, as a result of the believer's submission to baptism, God would seal one for the day of redemption by predestining that person to final salvation. Regardless of whatever sins the believer would henceforth commit, even if she or he died while banned from the Supper, a temporary period in hell before entering heaven comprised the worst possible fate that could befall that believer. In the Eucharist, the communicant receives the grace of physical union with Christ as she or he undergoes consubstantiation with Christ's human nature. Such an ontological participation in the human extension of God's being imparts to the believer a measure of "potential grace," necessary to living the Christian life and progressing along the path of sanctification, which the believer can "actualize" by freely choosing to cooperate with it. Recipients are thus motivated to hunger for the Eucharist, as partaking of the sacred meal constitutes the necessary condition for their personal replenishment of this empowering and numinous quasi-substance. Since Hubmaier developed a sacramental theology emphasizing the communication of grace, Hubmaier must be dismissed from the Anabaptist camp. In light of the fact that he carried out programs of reform with the full support of the Waldshut and Nikolsburg civil governments, Hubmaier also possesses the defining attributes of a Magisterial Reformer. This is especially evident in his demand for believers to serve God by seeking positions as Christian magistrates (a contradiction in terms for the Anabaptists) and to wield the sword in defense of their lands. Interpreted through the lenses of Williams and the "third wave" of Anabaptist scholarship, therefore, the evidence indicates that Hubmaier is most accurately understood as an atypical Magisterial Radical Reformer, who both borrowed concepts from highly diverse thinkers in the spectrum of church history, including the Church Fathers, Bernard of Clairvaux, Eck, and Luther, and blended these concepts with his doctrinal innovations to create a unique theological synthesis. Hubmaier's theology thus furnishes a corrective to the false dichotomy between Magisterial and Radical reform prevalent in the Reformation historical academy, as the Ingolstadt *doctor theologiae* did not share the perspective of contemporary scholars that one could not be pro-statist and a practitioner of believers' baptism at the same time. The resultant three-tiered system, progressing from a tripartite libertarian anthropology to a profoundly "realist" sacramental theology to a free church ecclesiology, forms a theological hybrid which reveals Hubmaier to be one of the sixteenth century's most sophisticated and creative thinkers.

Bibliography

Primary Sources

Anselm. *Proslogium, Monologium, An Appendix in behalf of the Fool by Gaunilon, and Cur Deus Homo.* Chicago: Open Court, 1926.

Aquinas, Thomas. *Summa Theologica.* 5 vols. Westminster, Md.: Christian Classics, 1981.

Augustine. *Ante Baptismum.* In *Corpus iuris canonici* [hereafter abbreviated *CIC*], ed. Aemilius Friedberg. Graz: Akademische Druck und Verlagsanstalt, 1959, 1:1383.

—. *City of God.* Trans. Henry Bettenson. New York: Penguin, 1984.

—. *De consecratione.* In *CIC*, 1:1362-1402.

—. *Enchiridion.* Trans. Albert C. Outler. Philadelphia: Westminster Press, 1955.

—. *Exposition of the Psalms.* In *Corpus christianorum, Series latina,* Vol. 38. Turnhout, Belgium: Brepols, 1953.

—. *On Nature and Grace.* Trans. John A. Mourant. Washington, D.C.: Catholic University of America Press, 1992.

Balthasar Hubmaier, Theologian of Anabaptism. Trans. H. Wayne Pipkin and John H. Yoder. Scottdale, Pa.: Herald Press, 1989.

Bernard de Clairvaux. *Ad milites Templi: De laude novae militae.* In *Sämtliche Werke lateinisch/deutsch* I [hereafter abbreviated *SW* I]. Innsbruck: Tyrolia-Verlag, 1990, 257-326.

—. *De consideratione ad Eugenium papam.* In *SW* I, 611-841.

————. *De diligendo Deo.* In *SW* I, 57-152.

————. *De gradibus humilitatis et superbiae.* In *Sämtliche Werke lateinisch/deutsch* II [hereafter abbreviated *SW* II]. Innsbruck: Tyrolia-Verlag, 1990, 29-136.

————. *De gratia et libero arbitrio.* In *SW* I, 153-256.

————. *De praecepto et dispensatione.* In *SW* I, 327-436.

————. "Fifth Sermon for the Feast of All Saints." In *Sermons for the Seasons and Principal Festivals* [hereafter abbreviated *SSPF*], trans. by a priest of Mount Melleray. Westminster, Md.: Carroll Press, 1950, 382-96.

————. "Fourth Sermon for the Feast of the Assumption." In *SSPF*, 246-57.

————. *On Grace and Free Choice.* Trans. Daniel O' Donovan. Kalamazoo, Mich.: Cistercian Publications, 1988.

————. *On Precept and Dispensation.* In *The Works of Bernard of Clairvaux.* Vol. 1, Treatises 1. Spencer, Mass.: Cistercian Publications, 1970, 73-152.

————. "On the Second Baptism." In *SSPF*, 421-25.

————. *Sermo LXXX super Cantica Canticorum.* In *Sämtliche Werke lateinisch/deutsch* VI. Innsbruck: Tyrolia-Verlag, 1995, 569-82.

————. "Sermon for the Feast of St. Clement." In *SSPF*, 25-32.

————. "Sermon for the Feast of the Nativity of the Blessed Virgin Mary." In *SSPF*, 281-305.

Bonaventure. *Breviloquium.* Trans. Erwin Esser Nemmers. St. Louis: Herder, 1946.

Bullinger, Heinrich. *Of the Holy Catholic Church.* Trans. G. W. Bromiley, *Zwingli and Bullinger* [hereafter abbreviated *ZB*]. Philadelphia: Westminster, 1953, 283-325.

Calvin, John. *Commentary on the Epistles of Paul the Apostle to the Corinthians.* Trans. John Pringle. Grand Rapids, Mich.: Baker, 1996.

———. *Institutes of the Christian Religion.* Trans. John T. McNeill and Ford L. Battles. Philadelphia: Westminster, 1960.

———. *Reply to Sadoleto.* In *Johannis Calvini opera selecta,* eds. Peter Barth and Wilhelm Niesel. 5 vols. Munich: C. Kaiser, 1926, 1:356-482.

Cyprian. *The Letters of St. Cyprian of Carthage.* New York: Newman Press, 1984.

Eck, Johann. *Denkschrift zu Papst.* In *Dr. Johann Ecks Denkschriften zur deutschen Kirchenreformation.* 2 vols. Gütersloh: C. Bertelsmann, 1895, 1:240-42.

Erasmus, Desiderius. *On the Freedom of the Will.* In *Luther and Erasmus: Free Will and Salvation,* eds. E. Gordon Rupp and A. N. Marlow. Philadelphia: Westminster, 1969, 35-100.

Fabri, Johann. *Reason Why Dr. Balthasar Hubmayr, Head and Founder of the Anabaptists, Was at Vienna.* Trans. William R. Estep, *Anabaptist Beginnings.* Nieuwkoop: de Graaf, 1976, 135-45.

Grebel, Conrad. *Letter to Thomas Müntzer.* Trans. George H. Williams and A. M. Mergal, *Spiritual and Anabaptist Writers.* Philadelphia: Westminster, 1957, 76-81.

Hillebrant, Michael. *Von der Einigen, wahrhafftigen, heyligen, Christlichen Kirchen.* In Georg Veesenmeyer, *Über Balthasar Hubmör, einen der berühmtesten Wiedertäufer zur Zeit der Reformation.* Halle, 1826, 247-49.

Hubmaier, Balthasar. *Achtzehn Schlußreden.* In *Balthasar Hubmaier Schriften* [hereafter abbreviated *HS*], eds. Gunnar Westin and Torsten Bergsten. Gütersloh: Gütersloher Verlagshaus Gerd Mohn, 1962, 69-74.

———. *Axiomata—Schlußreden gegen Eck.* In *HS,* 85-94.

————. *Brief an Rychard.* In Torsten Bergsten, *Balthasar Hubmaier, Seine Stellung zu Reformation und Täufertum.* Kassel: J. G. Oncken Press, 1961, 105-07.

————. *Das andere Büchlein von der Freiwilligkeit.* In *HS,* 398-431.

————. *Der uralten und gar neuen Lehrer Urteil, Ausgabe* I. In *HS,* 224-40.

————. *Der uralten und gar neuen Lehrer Urteil, Ausgabe* II. In *HS,* 241-55.

————. *Die zwölf Artikel des christlichen Glaubens.* In *HS,* 215-20.

————. *Ein einfältiger Unterricht.* In *HS,* 284-304.

————. *Ein Gespräch auf Zwinglis Taufbüchlein.* In *HS,* 164-214.

————. *Eine christliche Lehrtafel.* In *HS,* 305-26.

————. *Eine ernstliche christliche Erbietung.* In *HS,* 75-84.

————. *Eine Form des Nachtmals Christi.* In *HS,* 353-65.

————. *Eine Form zu taufen.* In *HS,* 347-52.

————. *Eine kurze Entschuldigung.* In *HS,* 270-83.

————. *Eine Rechenschaft des Glaubens.* In *HS,* 458-92.

————. *Eine Summe eines ganzen christlichen Lebens.* In *HS,* 108-15.

————. *Etliche Schlußreden vom Unterricht der Messe.* In *HS,* 101-04.

————. *Form.* In Geary Vessenmeyer, *Über Balthasar Hubmör, einen der berühmstesten Wiedertäufer zur Zeit der Reformation. Kirchenhist. Archiv* 4 [hereafter abbreviated *KA*]. Halle, 1826, 239-44.

————. *Grund und Ursache.* In *HS,* 327-36.

————. *Letter to a Friend in Ulm.* Trans. William R. Estep, *Anabaptist Beginnings.* Nieuwkoop: de Graaf, 1976, 87-88. (The original Latin document is preserved in the Stadt-und Universitätsbibliothek, Hamburg, Germany.)

————. *Letter to Beatus Rhenanus*. In *Briefweschel des Beatus Rhenanus*, eds. A. Horawitz and K. Hartfelder. Leipzig, 1886, 263.

————. *Letter to Johannes Adelphi*. In *KA*, 232-34.

————. *Letter to Johann Oecolampadius*. In *Briefe und Akten zum Leben Oekolampads*, 2 vols. Ed. Ernst Staehelin. New York: Johnson, 1971, 1:341-44.

————. *Letter to Johannes Sapidus*. In *Täuferakten Elsass* 1. Gütersloh: Gütersloher Verlagshaus Gerd Mohn, 1955, 40-42.

————. *Letter to Wolfgang Rychard*. In Johann Georg Schelhorn, Sr., *Acta Historico-Ecclesiastica Saeculi* XV & XVI. Ulm, 1738, 118-20.

————. *Öffentliche Erbietung*. In *HS*, 105-07.

————. *Predigt*. In *Die Stadt Waldshut und die vorderösterreichische Regierung 1523-26*, ed. Johann Loserth. Vienna: C. Gerold's Sohn, 1891, 108-11.

————. Untitled poem. In *HS*, 14.

————. *Von dem Ampt der Apostelen*. In *HS*, 134-46.

————. *Von dem christlichen Bann*. In *HS*, 366-78.

————. *Von dem Schwert*. In *HS*, 432-57.

————. *Von der brüderlichen Strafe*. In *HS*, 337-46.

————. *Von der christlichen Taufe der Gläubigen*. In *HS*, 116-33.

————. *Von der Freiheit des Willens*. In *HS*, 379-97.

————. *Von der Kindertaufe*. In *HS*, 256-69.

————. *Von der ordnung einer Christenlichen frombmachung.* In *HS,* 157-63.

————. *Von Ketzern und ihren Verbrennern.* In *HS,* 95-100.

————. *Waldshut an Straßburg.* In *Quellen zur Geschichte der Täufer.* Gütersloh: C. Bertelsmann, 1955, 4:391.

Huldrych Zwingli: Writings. Trans. H. Wayne Pipkin. Allison Park, Pa.: Pickwick Publications, 1984.

Hut, Hans. "The Mystery of Baptism." Trans. Rollin Stely Armour. *Anabaptist Baptism: A Representative Study.* Scottdale, Pa.: Herald Press, 1966, 83.

————. Statement. In *Anabaptism in Outline,* ed. Walter Klaassen. Scottdale, Pa.: Herald Press, 1981, 266-67.

Lombard, Peter. *Quattuor Libri Sententiarum.* Trans. Elizabeth F. Rogers. New York: S.U.I., 1917.

Luther, Martin. *Against the Antinomians.* In *Luther's Works, American Edition* [hereafter abbreviated *LW*], ed. Jaroslav Pelikan. St. Louis: Concordia Publishing House, 1955-86, 47:107-19.

————. *Avoiding the Doctrines of Men.* In *LW,* 35:127-53.

————. *The Babylonian Captivity of the Church.* In *LW,* 36:3-126.

————. *The Bondage of the Will.* In *Luther and Erasmus: Free Will and Salvation,* eds. E. Gordon Rupp and A. N. Marlow. Philadelphia: Westminster, 1969, 101-334.

————. *Commentary on Galatians.* In *LW,* 51:168-69.

————. *Disputatio de lege et fide.* In *D. Martin Luthers Werke* [hereafter abbreviated *WA*]. Weimar: Böhlau, 1888, 6:356-61.

————. "Ein Sermon von dem neuen Testament, das ist von der heiligen Messe." In *WA,* 6:362-70.

————. *House Postil.* In *WA*, 52:517-25.

————. *Lectures on Galatians. LW*, Vol. 26.

————. *Response to the Book of Master Ambrosius Catharinus.* In *WA*, 8:705-19.

————. *Scholia on the Epistle to the Romans.* In *WA*, 56:251-78.

————. *Sermon on Matthew 16.* In *LW*, 7:281-82.

————. *Sermons on the Gospel of John, 33.* In *LW*, 22:380-90.

————. *Sermons on the Catechism.* In *LW*, 51:162-93.

————. *Table Talk no. 584.* In *LW*, 54:105.

————. *To the Councilmen of Germany.* In *LW*, 45:349-420.

————. *A Treatise on the New Testament.* In *LW*, 35:77-124.

————. *Vom Anbeten des Sacraments des heiligen Leichnams Christi.* In *WA*, 7:682-96.

Molina, Luis de. *On Divine Foreknowledge.* Trans. Alfred J. Freddoso. Ithaca, N.Y.: Cornell University Press, 1988.

Pelagius. *Commentary on St. Paul's Epistle to the Romans.* Trans. Theodore de Bruyn. Oxford: Oxford University Press, 1995.

Philips, Dirk. *Enchiridion.* Trans. A. B. Kolb and Walter Klaassen. Aylmer, Ont.: Pathway Publishing, 1966.

Riedeman, Peter. *Account of Our Religion, Doctrine and Faith.* London: Hodder and Stoughton, 1950.

Ruckensperger, Sebastian. *Biechlen.* In J. C. Füsslin, *Beiträge zur Erläuterung der Kirchen-Reformationsgeschichte des Schweizerbundes.* 5 vols. Zürich, 1741, 1:252-53.

Sattler, Michael. *Imprisonment: Letter to Horb*. Trans. John H. Yoder, *The Legacy of Michael Sattler*. Scottdale, Pa.: Herald Press, 1973, 60-62.

————. *Letter to Bürgermeister and Council at Horb*. Trans. Myron Augsburger, in "Michael Sattler, d. 1527, Theologian of the Swiss Brethren Movement." Ph.D. dissertation, Union Theological Seminary, 1965, 89-91.

————. *Schleitheim Confession*. In Yoder, *Legacy*, 36-43.

Schaff, Philip and Henry Wace, eds. *Nicene and Post-Nicene Fathers*. 14 vols. New York: Scribner's, 1900.

Simons, Menno. *Admonition on Church Discipline*. Trans. J. C. Wenger, *The Complete Writings of Menno Simons* [hereafter abbreviated *CW*]. Scottdale, Pa.: Herald Press, 1956, 407-18.

————. *Brief and Clear Confession*. In *CW*, 419-54.

————. *Foundation of Christian Doctrine*. In *CW*, 103-226.

Special Resolution of the Regensburg City Council. In Johann Loserth, *D. Balthasar Hubmaier und die Anfänge der Wiedertaufe in Mähren*. Brünn: Verlag der historisch.-statist, 1893, 24.

Transcript of the Second Zurich Disputation. In Emil Egli and Georg Finsler, *Huldreich Zwingli Sämtliche Werke* [hereafter abbreviated *ZW*]. Leipzig: M. Heinius Nachfolger, 1908, 2:664-803.

Voltaire. *Treatise on Tolerance*. Trans. Simon Harvey. Cambridge: Cambridge University Press, 2000.

Waterworth, J., trans. and ed. *The Canons and Decrees of the Sacred and Oecumenical Council of Trent*. London: C. Dolman, 1848.

William of Occam. *Quaestiones et decisions in IV libros Sententiarum cum Centilogio theologico*. Lugduni, 1495.

Zwingli, Huldrych. *Antwort über Doktor Balthasars Taufbüchlein*. In *ZW*, 4:569-98.

————. *Explanation and Proof of the Conclusions or Articles.* In *ZW*, 2:1-457.

————. *An Exposition of the Faith.* In *ZB*, 239-82.

————. *On Baptism.* In *ZB*, 119-75.

————. *On the Lord's Supper.* In *ZB*, 176-238.

————. *Treatise on Providence.* In *Zwingli-Hauptschriften*, eds. Fritz Blanke, Oskar Farner, and Rudolf Pfister. Zürich: Zwingli-Verlag, 1940, XI: 260-94.

Secondary Sources

Adams, James Luther. *An Examined Faith: Social Context and Religious Commitment.* Boston: Beacon Press, 1991.

————. *Voluntary Associations: Socio-Cultural Analyses and Theological Interpretation.* Chicago: Exploration Press, 1986.

Armour, Rollin Stely. *Anabaptist Baptism: A Representative Study.* Scottdale, Pa.: Herald Press, 1966.

Arnold, Eberhard. *Early Anabaptists.* Rev. ed. Rifton, N.Y.: Plough, 1984.

Baylor, Michael G., ed. *The Radical Reformation.* Cambridge: Cambridge University Press, 1991.

Beachy, Alvin J. *The Concept of Grace in the Radical Reformation.* Nieuwkoop: B. D. Graaf, 1977.

Behr, Benita von, Jutta Bernard, and Kirsten Holzapfel, eds. *Metzler Lexikon Religion.* 4 vols. Stuttgart: Verlag J. B. Metzler, 2002.

Beilby, James K. and Paul R. Eddy. *Divine Foreknowledge.* Carlisle, U.K.: Paternoster, 2002.

Bender, Harold. *The Recovery of the Anabaptist Vision.* Scottdale, Pa.: Mennonite Publishing House, 1957.

Berger, Peter. *The Sacred Canopy*. New York: Anchor Books, 1967.

Bergsten, Torsten. *Balthasar Hubmaier, Seine Stellung zu Reformation und Täufertum*. Kassel, Germany: J. G. Oncken Press, 1961.

Brunotte, Heinz and Otto Weber, eds. *Evangelisches Kirchenlexikon*. 4 vols. Göttingen: Vandenhoeck and Ruprecht, 1961.

Bultmann, Rudolf. *Theology of the New Testament*. 2 vols. Trans. Kendrick Grobel. New York: Scribner's, 1951.

Cairns, Earle E. *Christianity through the Centuries*. 3rd rev. ed. Grand Rapids, Mich.: Zondervan, 1996.

Châtillon, Jean. "L'influence de S. Bernard sur la pensée scholastique au XIIᵉ siècle." *Analecta sacri ordinis cisterciensis* IX, 304 (1953): 268-88.

Clasen, Claus-Peter. *Anabaptism: A Social History, 1525-1618*. Ithaca, N.Y.: Cornell University Press, 1972.

Davis, Kenneth. "Anabaptism as a Charismatic Movement." *Mennonite Quarterly Review* [hereafter abbreviated *MQR*] 53 (July 1979): 219-34.

De Margerie, Bertrand. *Introduction à l'histoire de l'exégèse*. 3 vols. Paris: Les Éditions du Cerf, 1980.

Dinzelbacher, Peter. *Bernhard von Clairvaux*. Darmstadt: Primus Verlag, 1998.

Eliade, Mircea. *Rites and Symbols of Initiation: The Mysteries of Birth and Rebirth*. New York: Harper and Row, 1965.

Estep, William R. *The Anabaptist Story*. 3rd rev. ed. Grand Rapids, Mich.: Eerdmans, 1996.

Evans, Gillian Rosemary. *Bernard of Clairvaux*. Oxford: Oxford University Press, 2000.

———. *The Mind of St. Bernard of Clairvaux*. Oxford: Clarendon Press, 1983.

Fast, Heinold. *Der linke Flügel der Reformation.* Bremen: Carl Schünemann Verlag, 1962.

Fischer, John. "Freedom and Foreknowledge." *Philosophical Review* 95 (1986): 591-99.

Flint, Thomas P. *Divine Providence.* Ithaca, N.Y.: Cornell University Press, 1998.

Franks, Robert S. *A History of the Doctrine of the Work of Christ.* Reprint. Eugene, Ore.: Wipf and Stock, 2001.

Freddoso, Alfred J. "Accidental Necessity and Power over the Past." *Pacific Philosophical Quarterly* 63 (1982): 54-68.

———. *The Existence and Nature of God.* Notre Dame, Ind.: University of Notre Dame Press, 1983.

Friedmann, Robert. "Recent Literature in the Field of Anabaptism." *Church History* 32 (September 1963): 359-61.

———. *The Theology of Anabaptism.* Scottdale, Pa.: Herald Press, 1973.

Gerrish, Brian Albert. *Grace and Gratitude: The Eucharistic Theology of John Calvin.* Minneapolis: Fortress, 1993.

———. *Grace and Reason.* Oxford: Clarendon Press, 1962.

Gilson, Etienne. *History of Christian Philosophy in the Middle Ages.* London: Sheed and Ward, 1955.

Goertz, Hans-Jürgen. *The Anabaptists.* New York: Routledge, 1996.

———. "Geist und Leben: Überlegungen zur pneumatologischen Grundlegung der Theologie." *Kerygma und Dogma* 28 (October-December 1982): 284-86.

Gonzalez, Justo L. *A History of Christian Thought: From Augustine to the Eve of the Reformation.* Nashville: Abingdon, 1971.

Hall, Thor. "The Possibilities of Erasmian Influence on Denck and Hubmaier in their Views on the Freedom of the Will." *MQR* 35 (April 1961): 149-70.

Harrison, Wes. Review of *Anabaptist History and Theology*, by C. Arnold Snyder. *Sixteenth Century Journal* XXVII (Summer 1996): 586-87.

Hasker, William. "Foreknowledge and Necessity." *Faith and Philosophy* 2 (1985): 121-57.

Hiss, Wilhelm. *Die Anthropologie Bernhards von Clairvaux*. Berlin: Walter De Gruyter, 1964.

Jenson, Robert W. *Visible Words: The Interpretation and Practice of Christian Sacraments*. Philadelphia: Fortress Press, 1978.

Kelly, John N. D. *Early Christian Doctrines*. 2nd ed. New York: Harper, 1960.

Kingdon, Robert M. "The Control of Morals in Calvin's Geneva." In *The Social History of the Reformation*, eds. Lawrence P. Buck and Jonathan W. Zophy. Columbus: Ohio State University Press, 1972, 3-16.

————. "The First Calvinist Divorce." In *Sin and the Calvinists: Morals Control and the Consistory in the Reformed Tradition*, ed. Raymond A. Mentzer. Kirksville, Mo.: Sixteenth Century Journal Publishers, 1994, 1-13.

————. "The Genevan Revolution in Public Worship." *Princeton Seminary Bulletin* XX.3 (1999): 264-80.

————, gen. ed. *Registers of the Consistory of Geneva in the Time of Calvin, Volume 1: 1542-44*. Grand Rapids, Mich.: Eerdmans, 2000.

————. "Was the Protestant Reformation a Revolution? The Case of Geneva." In *Studies in Church History 12: Church, Society and Politics*, ed. Derek Baker. Oxford: Oxford University Press, 1975, 203-22.

Klaassen, Walter. *Anabaptism: Neither Catholic nor Protestant*. Waterloo: Conrad Press, 1973.

————. "Baptism of Adult Believers." *Mennonitische Geschichtsblätter* 46 (1989): 85-97.

Kluckhohn, August, ed. *Deutsche Reichstagsakten: Jüngere Reihe.* Göttingen: Vandenhoeck & Ruprecht, 1962.

Köhler, Walther. *Dogmengeschichte als Geschichte des christlichen Selbstbewusstseins,* Vol. II: *Zeitalter der Reformation.* Leipzig: M. Niehan, 1951.

Kremer, Christian Josef, ed. *Reallexikon für Antike und Christentum.* 15 vols. Stuttgart: Anton Hiersemann, 2000.

Küssenberg, Heinrich. *Chronik der Reformation in der Grafschaft Baden, im Klettgau und auf dem Schwarzwalde.* Solothurn, 1875.

Landgraf, Artur Michael. *Dogmengeschichte der Frühscholastik I, i: Die Gnadenlehre.* Regensburg: Friedrich Pustet, 1952.

Leclerq, Jean. *Bernard of Clairvaux and the Cistercian Spirit.* Trans. Claire Lavoie. Kalamazoo, Mich.: Cistercian Publications, 1976.

Lewis, David. *Counterfactuals.* Cambridge, Mass.: Harvard University Press, 1973.

Logan, F. Donald. *A History of the Church in the Middle Ages.* New York: Routledge, 2002.

Loserth, Johann. *D. Balthasar Hubmaier und die Anfänge der Wiedertaufe in Mähren.* Brünn: Verlag der histor.-statist., 1893.

Mabry, Eddie. *Balthasar Hubmaier's Doctrine of the Church.* Lanham, Md.: University Press of America, 1994.

————. *Balthasar Hubmaier's Understanding of Faith.* Lanham, Md.: University Press of America, 1988.

Mackoskey, Robert A. "The Life and Thought of Balthasar Hubmaier, 1485-1528." Ph.D. dissertation, University of Edinburgh, 1956.

Macy, Gary. *The Theologies of the Eucharist in the Early Scholastic Period.* Oxford: Clarendon Press, 1984.

Marlow, A. N. and B. Drewery. "The Lutheran Riposte." In *Luther and Erasmus: Free Will and Salvation*, eds. E. Gordon Rupp and A. N. Marlow. Philadelphia: Westminster, 1969, 12-15.

Marrou, Henry. *St. Augustine and His Influence Through the Ages.* Trans. Patrich Hepburne-Scott. New York: Harper Torchbooks, 1957.

McClendon, James William. "Balthasar Hubmaier, Catholic Anabaptist." *MQR* 65 (January 1991): 20-33.

McGinn, Bernard. Introduction to Bernard of Clairvaux. In *On Grace and Free Choice*, trans. Daniel O'Donovan. Kalamazoo, Mich.: Cistercian Publications, 1988, 3-52.

Moore, Walter L. "Catholic Teacher and Anabaptist Pupil: The Relationship between John Eck and Balthasar Hubmaier." *Archiv für Reformationsgeschichte* 72 (1981): 68-97.

Muralt, Leonhard von and Walter Schmid. *Quellen zur Geschichte der Täufer in der Schweiz.* Zurich: S. Hirzel, 1952.

Neufeld, Vernon. *The Earliest Christian Confessions.* Grand Rapids, Mich.: Eerdmans, 1964.

Oberman, Heiko. *The Harvest of Medieval Theology.* Cambridge, Mass.: Harvard University Press, 1963.

————. *Luther: Man Between God and the Devil.* New York: Doubleday, 1992.

Olson, Roger E. *The Story of Christian Theology.* Downers Grove, Ill.: InterVarsity Press, 1999.

Ozment, Steven E., ed. *Reformation Europe: A Guide to Research.* St. Louis: Center for Reformation Research, 1982.

Packull, Werner O. "Balthasar Hubmaier's Gift to John Eck, July 18, 1516." *MQR* 63 (October 1989): 428-32.

Padgett, Alan. *God, Eternity, and the Nature of Time.* New York: St. Martin's Press, 1990.

Pelikan, Jaroslav. *The Emergence of the Catholic Tradition (100-600).* Chicago: University of Chicago Press, 1971.

————. *Reformation of Church and Dogma (1300-1700).* Chicago: University of Chicago Press, 1984.

————. *Spirit of Medieval Theology.* Toronto: Pontifical Institute of Mediaeval Studies, 1985.

Pipkin, H. Wayne. "The Baptismal Theology of Balthasar Hubmaier." *MQR* 65 (January 1991): 34-53.

Posset, Franz. *Pater Bernhardus: Martin Luther and Bernard of Clairvaux.* Kalamazoo, Mich.: Cistercian Publications, 1999.

Raitt, Jill. "Calvin's Use of Bernard of Clairvaux." *Archiv für Reformationsgeschichte* 72 (1981): 98-121.

Rempel, John D. *The Lord's Supper in Anabaptism.* Scottdale, Pa.: Herald Press, 1993.

Rupp, E. Gordon. "Introduction: The Erasmian Enigma." In E. Gordon Rupp and A. N. Marlow, eds., *Luther and Erasmus: Free Will and Salvation.* Philadelphia: Westminster, 1969, 1-11.

Sachsse, Carl. *D. Balthasar Hubmaier als Theologe.* Berlin: Trowitsch und Sohn, 1914.

Schib, Karl. *Die vier Waldstädte.* Freiburg: Eugen Rentsch Verlag, 1959.

Seeberg, Reinhold. *Text-book of the History of Doctrine.* 4 vols. Trans. Charles E. Kay. Grand Rapids, Mich.: Baker, 1956.

Seewald, Gerd. "Text dieser Hubmaier-Schrift mit dem der Diatribe verglichen." Siegburg, Germany: n.p., 1961.

Skinner, Quentin. *The Foundations of Modern Political Thought.* 2 vols. Cambridge: Cambridge University Press, 1978.

Snyder, C. Arnold. *Anabaptist History and Theology*. Kitchener, Ont.: Pandora Press, 1995.

Sommerfeldt, John R. *The Spiritual Teachings of Bernard of Clairvaux*. Kalamazoo, Mich.: Cistercian Publications, 1991.

Spitz, Lewis W. *The Protestant Reformation*, 1517-1559. St. Louis: Concordia Publishing House, 1985.

Stayer, James M. "The Anabaptists." In Steven E. Ozment, ed., *Reformation Europe: A Guide to Research*. St. Louis: Center for Reformation Research, 1982, 135-39.

————. "Let a Hundred Flowers Bloom and Let a Hundred Schools of Thought Contend." *MQR* 53 (July 1979): 211-13.

————. Review essay of *Anabaptist History and Theology*, by C. Arnold Snyder. *MQR* 70 (October 1996): 473-82.

Stayer, James M., Werner O. Packull, and Klaus Deppermann. "From Monogenesis to Polygenesis: The Historical Discussion of Anabaptist Origins." *MQR* 49 (April 1975): 83-121.

Steinmetz, David C. *Reformers in the Wings*. Grand Rapids, Mich.: Baker, 1971.

————. "Scholasticism and Radical Reform: Nominalist Motifs in the Theology of Balthasar Hubmaier." *MQR* 45 (April 1971): 123-44.

Tambrello, Dennis. *Union with Christ: John Calvin and the Mysticism of St. Bernard*. Louisville: Westminster John Knox Press, 1994.

Tracy, James D. *Europe's Reformations: 1450-1650*. Lanham, Md.: Rowman and Littlefield, 1999.

Trigg, Joseph W. *Biblical Interpretation*. Wilmington, Del.: Michael Glazier, 1983.

Vasella, Oskar. "Zur Geschichte der Täuferbewegung in der Schweiz." *Zeitschrift für Schweizerische Kirchengeschichte*, XLVIII (1954): 172-95.

Vedder, Henry C. *Balthasar Hübmaier: The Leader of the Anabaptists.* New York: G. P. Putnam's Sons, 1905.

Walton, Robert. *Zwingli's Theocracy.* Toronto: University of Toronto Press, 1967.

Werblowsky, R. J. Zwi. Introduction. In *The Works of Bernard of Clairvaux,* Vol. 7. Kalamazoo, Mich.: Cistercian Publications, 1977, 115-24.

Williams, George Huntston. *The Radical Reformation.* 3rd ed. Kirksville, Mo.: Truman State University Press, 2000.

Windhorst, Christof. "Das Gedächtnis des Leidens Christi und Pflichtzeichen brüderlicher Liebe: zum Verständnis des Abendmahls bei Balthasar Hubmaier." In *Umstrittenes Täufertum 1525-1975,* ed. Hans-Jürgen Goertz. Göttingen: Vandenhoeck & Ruprecht, 1977, 111-37.

—————. *Täuferisches Taufverständnis, Balthasar Hubmaier Lehre zwischen traditioneller und reformatorischer Theologie.* Leiden: E. J. Brill, 1976.

Wood, Susan K. *Sacramental Orders.* Collegeville, Minn.: Liturgical Press, 2000.

Yoder, John H. "Enthusiastisches Christentum." *Ecumenical Review* 23 (January 1971): 74-76.

—————. *Täufertum und Reformation im Gespräch.* Zurich: EVZ-Verlag, 1968.

—————. "The Turning Point in the Zwinglian Reformation." *MQR* 32 (1958): 128-40.

Zagzebski, Linda T. *The Dilemma of Freedom and Foreknowledge.* Oxford: Oxford University Press, 1991.

Index of Scripture References

Subject Index

A

Abelard, 82

Abomination, 11, 108, 182, 227, 262

Absalom, 78

Absolute power of God, 14, 62-65

Achtzehn Schlußreden, 106, 113, 115, 243, 269

Actual world, 14, 67-71

Adam, 39, 41, 45, 47, 48, 50, 51, 52, 60, 77, 81, 115, 139, 141, 177, 207, 214, 239, 256

Adelphi, Johann, 27, 103, 104, 271

Affusion, 123, 168

Alexander of Hales, 22

Allegorical commentary, 43, 51

American Society of Church History, 5

Anabaptism, 4-9, 34, 107, 123, 129, 136, 264

  Evangelical, 9, 107

  Revolutionary, 5, 12

Anabaptist, 4-26, 33-35, 42, 62, 78, 81, 83, 85, 86, 88, 95, 107, 108, 114, 118, 120-24, 129, 132, 134-36, 140, 148, 151, 154, 158, 177, 180, 184-86, 190, 191, 195, 202, 211, 225, 227, 229, 230, 233, 234, 236, 241, 248, 250, 252, 253, 256, 257, 259, 261, 262, 264, 265

Analogy of sun, 73, 74

Anhypostatic, 81, 184, 185

Anima, 44

Anointing of God, 201, 208

Anselm, 22, 180, 188, 189, 194, 199, 223, 258, 267

Anthropology, 23, 35, 37, 38, 46, 48, 54, 61, 112, 117

  Tripartite libertarian, 16, 17, 19, 22, 35, 38, 39, 86, 88, 92, 114, 125, 128, 146, 180, 256, 266

Anthropomorphic, 67

Anticlericalism, 122, 256

Anti-statist, 2, 3, 144, 240, 251

Antithetical relationship, 34, 179, 212, 225, 259

Apologetics, 146

Apostles' Creed, 31, 61, 132, 155, 167, 171, 196, 220

Ark, 140, 176, 184

Armour, Rollin Stely, 15, 39, 76, 108, 274, 275

Ascension, 160, 185, 189, 211

Assensus, 113, 125, 131

Athanasius, 108, 138

Augustine, 8, 18, 32, 42, 46, 63, 67, 71, 100, 108, 131, 138-41, 148, 180, 192, 267, 277, 280

Augustinian, 15, 20, 32, 37, 42, 48, 50, 52, 57, 63, 87, 112, 139, 256

Auricular confession, 102

Austria, 5, 9, 11, 14, 36, 96, 109, 126, 144, 208, 244-47, 256, 260

Author of evil, 70

Ex puris naturalibus, 53

Excommunication, 126, 179, 211-23, 257

Executive, 233

Exegesis, 3, 13, 14, 29, 30, 43, 64, 67, 72, 73, 75, 150, 152, 162, 163, 189-91, 193, 196, 198, 199, 204, 218, 231, 236

Extra ecclesiam nulla salus, 33

F

Facere quod in se est, 14, 37, 43, 55

Faith, 6-8, 11, 13, 18, 26, 27, 29, 32, 34, 41, 42, 59, 76, 80, 85, 91, 92, 96-101, 105-15, 117-19, 125, 126, 128, 131-34, 136, 137, 140, 142, 148, 149, 152, 153, 155-58, 162-67, 171-72, 174, 175, 177, 178, 181, 195, 196, 199, 201-03, 206, 208-10, 212, 213, 215-18, 220, 222-24, 228, 237, 240-42, 252, 256, 261, 263, 273, 275

Fides, 92, 111-13, 125, 131, 255-56

Glaub, 111-13, 118, 125, 131, 162, 177, 255

Faithful reason, 27, 98

Fall, 15, 16, 18, 39, 45-51, 56, 57, 60, 61, 70, 76, 77, 87, 95, 108, 112, 114, 117, 161, 163, 167, 177, 239, 255, 256

Fast, Heinold, 3, 4, 8, 13, 255, 277

Fasting, 13

Ferdinand I, 15, 36, 79, 96, 207, 244

Fides caritate formata, 131

Filling, 31, 188, 216, 217

First Zurich Disputation on Baptism, 106, 119, 122, 127, 128

Foreknowledge, 15, 57, 61-75, 88, 156, 273, 275, 279

Conceptualist model, 67, 70

Perceptualist model, 66

Foreordination, 67

Four-dimensional space-time manifold, 66

Fourth Lateran Council, 225

Fourth Synod of Carthage, 133

Fouson, Besanson, 220

Frage und Antwort, 39

Fraternal admonition, 33, 164, 169-76, 237, 257

Free knowledge, 70

Free state church, 3, 7, 11, 145, 227, 237, 241, 251, 263

Free will, 14, 17-19, 23, 37, 38, 42, 43, 46, 49-51, 55, 57, 58, 62, 64, 71, 86, 87, 92, 110, 111, 131, 138, 146, 151, 177, 178, 200, 201, 243, 255, 260, 265, 269, 272, 280, 281

Libertarian, 15, 38, 44, 49, 68, 71, 76, 86-88, 92, 110-18, 125, 128, 132, 139, 145, 146, 151, 171, 180, 260, 265, 266

Compatibilist, 15, 16, 19, 35-36, 48, 71, 78, 142, 143

Freedom, 15, 16, 19, 36, 38, 39, 41-50, 52, 57, 58, 60-63, 68, 69, 73, 77, 83, 88, 95, 117, 145, 146, 152, 177, 200, 201, 242, 253, 256, 260, 261, 265, 269, 277, 278

From misery, 16, 19, 44

From necessity, 16, 19, 44, 45, 49, 50, 203

From sin, 16, 19, 44, 45, 52, 54, 178, 265

Of choice, 45, 46, 62

Of counsel, 45, 46, 48, 61, 73, 117, 177, 256, 265

Holy violence, 12, 84, 148, 232, 249, 251, 263
Homo diligit Deum propter ipsum, 59
Homo diligit Deum propter se, 53
Homo diligit se propter se, 48
Hoop before an inn, 26, 99, 108, 125, 126
Host, 103, 122, 126, 128, 129, 159, 187, 189, 196, 201
Hügline, Elizabeth, 83
Humanism, 20
Hungering and thirsting for right-eousness, 17, 87, 118
Husband, 170
Hut, Hans, 12, 136, 239, 240, 248-51, 262, 272
Hyperdulia, 83

I

Imago Dei, 4, 55
  Trinitarii, 16
In remissionem peccatorum, 95, 154
In sensu composito, 57, 69
In sensu diviso, 57, 69
Incarnationist, 30, 180
Infallibility, 165
Infant dedication, 24, 105, 106, 110, 136, 141, 143, 144
Ingolstadt, 9, 14, 20, 35, 37, 40, 91, 96, 97, 124, 125, 217, 245, 256, 266
Initium fidei, 17, 53, 87, 265
Inordinate love, 17, 53, 87, 265
Institutes of the Christian Religion, 7, 8, 17, 19, 33, 61, 80, 212-16, 218, 222, 269
Intercessory network, 83
Introspective, 40
Inwendigen christenlichen wesens, 152, 195, 203

J

Jehoiakim, 145, 261
Jeroboam, 242
Jerome, 108, 133, 138, 177
Jesuit, 14, 76
Jesus, 3, 19, 24, 29, 30, 32, 54, 80, 81, 97, 98, 101, 104, 135, 137, 145, 150, 152, 154, 157, 160, 161, 163, 170, 172, 174, 181, 184, 185, 189-92, 196, 201, 202, 204-06, 209-11, 217, 242, 258
Jews, 12, 25, 111, 149
Johannine, 145, 184, 190, 191, 196, 199, 203, 223, 238, 258
John the Baptist, 86, 97, 98, 160
Judicial, 104, 178, 233, 238
Justification, 114-18, 128, 133, 141, 146, 186

K

Kernel, 142
Keys, 25-35, 102, 136, 159-61, 164-78, 259, 263
Kingdom, 12, 22, 25-33, 56, 92, 93, 159-61, 180, 222, 242, 251, 261, 263
  of Christ, 92, 93, 159, 213, 214, 229, 262, 270, 271
  of God, 4, 11-13, 29, 84, 85, 96, 111, 128, 132, 143, 146, 178, 179, 210, 218, 224, 229, 238, 248, 251, 252, 259, 261-63
  of Satan, 4, 11, 227, 233
  of the World, 228, 236, 237, 246, 251, 252, 262
Kingdon, Robert M., 179, 202, 214, 215, 221, 222, 241, 259, 278
Knighthood, 84, 85
Knights Templars, 84

About the Author

Kirk R. MacGregor (Ph.D., University of Iowa) is a social and theological historian of Christianity specializing in Reformation studies and New Testament. Publications to which his writings have contributed include *The Sixteenth Century Journal*, *Review of Biblical Literature*, *Journal of the Evangelical Theological Society*, *Encyclopedia of World History*, and *World Empires: An Encyclopedia*. Among the scholarly societies in which he holds membership are the Sixteenth Century Society, Mennonite Historical Society, American Academy of Religion, American Society of Church History, Society of Biblical Literature, Evangelical Theological Society, and Evangelical Philosophical Society. Dr. MacGregor currently teaches religion at the University of Northern Iowa.

Made in the USA
Columbia, SC
02 September 2021

44743776R00172